ACCUMULATION AND SUBJECTIVITY

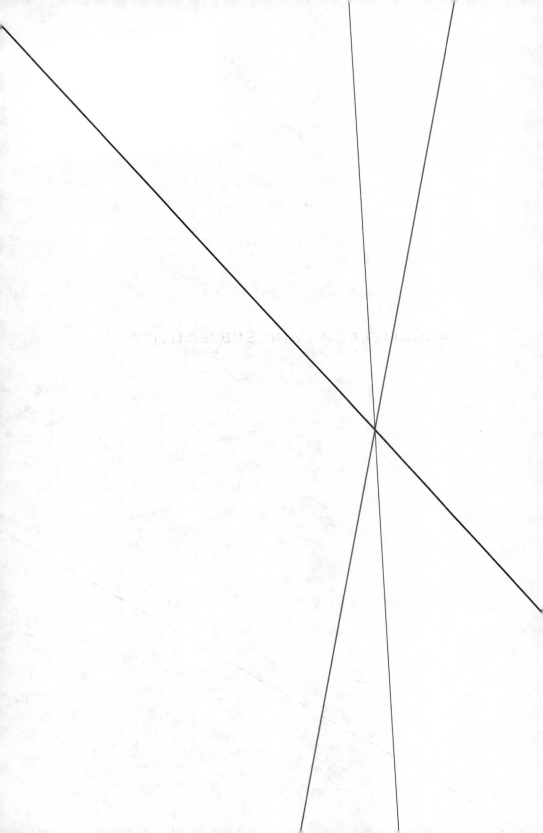

Accumulation
and   RETHINKING MARX IN LATIN AMERICA
Subjectivity

EDITED BY KAREN BENEZRA

SUNY PRESS

Cover: Joseph Renau, Photomontage diagram of Sindicato Mexicano de Electricistas mural's six ideal vantage points (1969). Valencia, Josep Renau Archive, IVAM. Courtesy of the Josep Renau Archive, IVAM, Valencia. (Code 15128 in the inex of the Renau Archive at the IVAM)

Published by State University of New York Press, Albany

For information, contact State University of New York Press, Albany, NY www.sunypress.edu

Library of Congress Cataloging-in-Publication Data

Names: Benezra, Karen, 1982- editor.
Title: Accumulation and subjectivity : rethinking Marx in Latin America / edited by Karen Benezra.
Description: Albany, NY : State University of New York Press, [2022] | Includes bibliographical references and index.
Identifiers: LCCN 2021054871 (print) | LCCN 2021054872 (ebook) | ISBN 9781438487571 (hardcover) | ISBN 9781438487588 (ebook) ISBN 9781438487564 (paperback)
Subjects: LCSH: Marxian economics—Latin America. | Saving and investment—Latin America. | Mass media—Latin America. | Subjectivity. | LCGFT: Essays.
Classification: LCC HB97.5 .A285 2022 (print) | LCC HB97.5 (ebook) | DDC 335.4098—dc23/eng/20211220
LC record available at https://lccn.loc.gov/2021054871
LC ebook record available at https://lccn.loc.gov/2021054872

10 9 8 7 6 5 4 3 2 1

Contents

List of Illustrations

Acknowledgments

An earlier version of chapter 1, "On Subsumption as Form and the Use of Asynchronies," by Massimiliano Tomba, was previously published in *Review (Fernand Braudel Center)* 38, no. 4 (2019).

An earlier version of chapter 4, "Accumulation as Total Conversion," by Karen Benezra, was previously published in *Revista de Estudios Hispánicos* 55, no. 2 (2021).

INTRODUCTION

Rethinking Marx in Latin America

KAREN BENEZRA

IN A LETTER FROM MARCH 1977, the Argentinean theorist, translator, and editor José Aricó discusses a series of upcoming projects with Ludolfo Paramio, then an editor at the publishing house Siglo XXI in Madrid. Among the projects under discussion, Aricó mentions one concerning "the issue of the existing nexus between the critique of political economy and the theory of class or politics or the state."[1] Citing several recent publications by Italian socialists and communists on the topic of hegemony, most notably Norberto Bobbio's *Quale socialismo?* (Which Socialism?, 1976), he asks whether it might not be useful to publish a collection on the topic.

The present volume does not pretend to offer a resolution to the relationship between accumulation and subjectivity, much less argue for something like the inherence or priority of the Latin American case. Instead, it conceives of itself as an intervention into the common sense and closed historical horizon that characterizes the reformist spirit of the late 1970s and that continues to structure much of the work of sociocultural interpretation in the field of Latin American studies today. Rather than recuperating a readymade historical or theoretical archive, the essays to follow explore the performative relationship between the collection's title terms in conceptual, historical-intellectual, and sociocultural terms. Contributions address the relationship between accumulation and subjectivity from within the colonial archive and with respect to the logic of history in Marx and in Latin American social

1

theory; by reconstructing key concepts for the critique of political economy specific to the intellectual history of the Latin American Left over the last forty years; as a problem or *problématique* manifest in its juridical and socio-cultural effects in the analysis of contemporary film, narrative, urban planning, and immigration policy; and by examining the topological place and historicity of the subject in poststructuralist theory and in Marx's economic writings. In doing so, *Accumulation and Subjectivity* attempts to question the turn away from the categories and problems of political economy that has defined post-Marxist political theory and critical approaches to the study of culture since the 1970s. It also aims to rediscover in Marx and Marxist theory from Latin America those concepts that might allow us to capture the dynamics of contemporary exploitation and expropriation specific to the region and, inversely, to explore the extent to which these theoretical and sociocultural case studies illuminate the historical logic of capital and the role of political, psychic, and ethical life within it.

In what sense, then, are we the addressee of Aricó's letter? Or, in slightly different terms, why impute the problem of accumulation and subjectivity to him? Though the present volume is not devoted principally or exclusively to Aricó, his intellectual and political trajectory speaks to its context and aims. His two major works from the 1980s testify to his ongoing research into nonteleological and nondeterministic theories of capitalist development and mass political organization and the relevance that he assigned to the analysis of political economy in a theoretical context that assumed the autonomy, if not directly the ontology, of politics. Aricó's question, in the letter cited above, regarding the relevance of a volume articulating political economy with politics or the state, could thus be said to fulfill a heuristic function for the purposes of introducing the present collection of essays. In his two major works from the period, Aricó's position is notable because it continued to assign an analytical function to political economy in a moment that tended to define politics in increasingly autonomous and ontological terms. Simultaneously, Aricó's gesture is also significant for the way that, in the author's own lexicon, it reveals a certain temporal missed encounter (*desencuentro*). If the turn away from political economy among political philosophers in the late 1970s and '80s was in many ways the product of a feeling of historical defeat, it was also indicative of the apparent inability of existing paradigms of Marxist political analysis either to account for the patterns of capitalist accumulation specific to the region historically, or to provide a window onto the nature of mass politics in an era increasingly defined by immaterial labor and the appropriation of wealth through financial speculation.

Several of the contributions to the present collection reconstruct and conceptualize the work of Latin American social theorists who aimed to advance a more nuanced and concrete picture of the unfolding of capitalism and to integrate the analysis of political economy into the interpretation of specific political conjunctures. In doing so, they both address parts of Aricó's project, as in the case of Marcelo Starcenbaum's analysis of the concept of socioeconomic formation, and extend it by interrogating overlooked theoretical works or conjunctural analyses whose nonmechanistic approach to the relationship between capitalism and class or politics mirrors and anticipates the approach of more recent interventions in the fields of postcolonial theory and political philosophy in the English-speaking world. At the same time, Aricó's letter speaks to the collection's even more ambitious aim of questioning the seemingly ubiquitous but unsatisfactory ways in which the dominant strains of post-Marxist theory since the 1970s have attempted to articulate the relationship between political economy and politics and, more broadly, capitalist accumulation and subjectivity. Contemporary theoretical discussions, concerned, alternately, with political subjectivation and the expropriation of wealth from increasingly intimate and informal realms of psychic and collective life, often take as their point of departure either a political ontology divorced from history or a social ontology that assumes the total or "real subsumption" of all forms of life and labor power under capital. By contrast, the present volume takes Aricó's untimely question as an occasion to reconsider its title terms in relation to theoretical problems and sociocultural processes specific to Latin America.

Aricó was one of the earliest translators of Gramsci into Spanish and a former militant of the Argentinean Communist Party who helped to articulate the broad theoretical interests of the country's intellectual New Left in the mid-1960s.[2] Despite this, his embrace of social democracy in the context of Argentina's democratic transition in the 1980s marked him, until very recently, as an influential but ambivalent figure for the Latin American Left. Aricó's political decisions were representative of those of many other leftist intellectuals of his generation. At the same time, his abiding historiographic and theoretical interests in political economy also stand out against the backdrop of Left defeatism that has defined discussions in Marxist and post-Marxist theory over the last forty years. Aricó conceived of the ongoing inquiry into the concrete social forms, popular modes of political organization, and theoretical vocabulary necessary to capture the specificity of class struggle in Latin America, as part of the groundwork for the rebirth of socialist internationalism. In this sense, it is worth pointing out that amidst the radicalization of the Peronist and socialist Left in Argentina in the 1960s and '70s, Aricó's interests diverted importantly from the dominant Guevarian *foquista* or Leninist vanguardist approaches to political organization and class consciousness. The reflections on populist political experiences and nondeterministic views of historical development that formed the nucleus of Aricó's editorial work thus remained at a critical remove from the common sense of the Latin American Left even or especially during the most acute years of struggle and military repression. The same could be said of his work with respect to the Eurocommunist horizon of the late 1970s and '80s. While Aricó embraced social democracy as the horizon of politics during the last decade of his life, his intellectual project remained irreducible to those of so-called experts in democratic transition or professional political philosophers, such as Chilean sociologist Norberto Lechner or philosopher Noberto Bobbio, cited above.[3] The reformist position that Aricó eventually adopted does not so much belie, as remain in tension, with his work to reestablish the bases of a historically nuanced socialist enlightenment.

Unlike many other interpreters of Gramsci's theory of the state and of hegemony in the era of democratic transition, Aricó wished to preserve the place that Gramsci assigned to the relations among property, the instances of civil society—importantly, the Church—and class in theorizing revolutionary politics in southern Italy's largely agrarian, Catholic society.[4] The tension between the theoretical and practical, political facets of Aricó's project, beginning in the late 1970s, is perhaps most clearly manifest in *La cola del diablo: itinerario de Gramsci en América Latina* (The Devil's Tail: The Itinerary of Gramsci in Latin America, 1988), a retrospective interpretation of Gramsci's reception in Latin America and of the political relevance of the theory of class hegemony for the present. In it, Aricó insisted on "the pretense of maintaining the unity of socialism and democracy."[5] However, rather than discarding or recoding the theory of hegemony or its relation to the state, as one finds in Ernesto Laclau's theory of radical democracy, Aricó attempted to preserve and reinterpret such concepts in relation to the experiences and theories of mass-based Latin American political movements. He maintained the historical materialist basis of Gramsci's concepts at the same time that he relegated the categories of property and class relations to an analytical level, thus suspending the Leninist horizon of their political application in Gramsci's own context.

For Aricó, the failure of the organized Left of the 1960s and '70s to articulate a mass-based form of class hegemony was indicative of a longer historical pattern in which, over the course of the late nineteenth and twentieth centuries in Latin America, worker and peasant movements often "remained alien and even opposed to one another."[6] The historical disidentification between workers' movements and other, more heterogeneous forms of popular political organization was the index, if not the outcome, of what, in *Marx and Latin America* (1980), he called the "missed encounter" between Marx and Latin America. With the notion of the missed encounter, Aricó referred to the failure of Marxist doctrine, as advanced by the region's nationally based communist parties, either to recognize or to formulate a revolutionary theory adequate to its national "realities." The actual articulation of capitalism—dependent, as it was, upon noncapitalist forms of labor and social organization, the military intervention of the United States, the duration and abolition of slavery, the scale and topology of agricultural production, the issue of national self-determination, and the position of the Church in political power and property relations, among many other noneconomic factors, such as the potentially revolutionary subjects—peasants, agrarian day-laborers, miners, urban factory workers, students, etc.—to emerge from it, remained hidden behind teleological assumptions about the development of class struggle and parochial ideas about the industrial working class as its protagonist. Simultaneously, Aricó's fortuitously named "missed encounter" also transcends the moment of self-critique motivating *Marx and Latin America*. By assuming the demand that there should have been a theoretical articulation of Marxist historiography and revolutionary theory worthy of the region's political experiences, the "missed encounter" can also be understood as the call for a radical new beginning for Marxist theory and cultural critique. The present collection is one possible response to that call.

Recent years have witnessed the authorship and translation into English of a number of historical, theoretical, and conjunctural analyses that articulate political economy with a theory or account of mass politics. Consider, for example, the English translations of Aricó's own *Marx and Latin America* (Brill, 2014); René Zavaleta Mercado's *Towards a History of the National Popular in Bolivia* (Seagull Books, 2016), a posthumously published study of the historical and political cycle of capitalism and national self-determination in Bolivia, between the War of the Pacific of the 1880s and the Chaco War of the 1930s, as well as a condensation of its author's highly original political theoretical framework; Álvaro García Linera's *Plebian Power: Collective Action and Indigenous, Working-Class and Popular Identities in Bolivia* (Brill,

2014), which, building upon Zavaleta's Gramscian framework, offers a series of historical and conjunctural analyses of leftist movements that emerged in opposition to Bolivia's neoliberal reforms of the 1980s and '90s; or Raquel Gutiérrez's *Rhythms of the Pachakuti: Indigenous Uprising and State Power in Bolivia* (Duke University Press, 2014), which analyzes the mass collective actions in the same country against the privatization of gas and water between 2000 and 2005. These recent translations speak to a growing interest in the hybrid Marxist theoretical paradigms of the 1970s and their adaptation for contemporary analysis.

Recent years have also produced a growing list of translations into English of the work of intellectual historians, explicators, and theorists dedicated to this same corpus of social thought. Take, for example, Martín Cortés's *José Aricó and the New Latin American Marxism* (Brill, 2019), whose conceptual reconstruction of Aricó's editorial and theoretical work aims, in part, to rescue its subject's legacy from the dominant social democratic appropriation of Gramsci; or Luis Tapia Mealla's *The Production of Local Knowledge: History and Politics in the Work of René Zavaleta Mercado* (Seagull Books, 2018), which explains and historicizes Zavaleta's corpus with respect to the historical cycle beginning with the popular democratic government of Bolivia's Revolutionary Nationalist Movement of 1952 and ending with the return to democracy in 1982.

Among recent publications we might also consider a number of analyses emerging from the social sciences concerned with the complex relation to the state sustained by populist and communal agrarian and urban social movements, both historically and in the recent Pink Tide governments of the early 2000s. Consider, for example, Donald V. Kingsbury's *Only the People Can Save the People: Constituent Power, Revolution, and Counterrevolution in Venezuela* (SUNY Press, 2018), which mobilizes the Negrian category of constituent power beginning with the 1989 Caracazo; and George Ciccariello-Maher's *We Created Chávez: A People's History of the Venezuelan Revolution* (Duke University Press, 2013), a history and political analysis of popular struggles beginning with the installation of Rómulo Bentancourt's formal democratic regime in 1958 and ending in the Caracazo, which examines the category of constituent power in order to reveal the mediation between the state and social movements. Jeffrey Webber's *Red October: Left Indigenous Struggles in Modern Bolivia* (Brill, 2011) details the concatenation of collective actors, sociopolitical circumstances, and historically rooted indigenous and working-class radicalism that contributed to Bolivia's Gas and Water Wars between 2000 and 2006 by privileging the analytical categories of class and class struggle in the analysis of social movements. To this necessarily partial list, we might also add the recent translation of Ruy Braga's *The Politics of the Precariat: From Populism to Lulista Hegemony* (2018), which offers a sociological study of the political practices and class politics of the precariat, or reserve army of precarious, largely unskilled labor, in the period spanning the populist Vargas regime in the 1930s and popular presidential administration of Luiz Inácio Lula da Silva in the early 2000s. Braga observes the relation of continuity and overcoming, rather than of rupture, in the dynamics structuring both the bureaucratic incorporation of syndical leadership into the state and of the capacity for self-organization of an expanded proletariat before and after the country's last military dictatorship.

In contrast to the macropolitical, or, in the language of Deleuze and Guattari, molar lens of such studies, a number of other analyses focus on the psychic, affective, and micropolitical dimensions of social and political struggles in the region. For the English-language reader, perhaps the most familiar illustrations of this approach is Brazilian analyst and art critic Suely Rolnik and Félix Guattari's *Micropolitics in Brazil*, a compendium of talks and interventions given during Guattari's month-long trip across Brazil in 1982 amid the incipient institutionalization of the Workers' Party and mobilizations against the authoritarian government. First published in 1986 in Portuguese and 2007 in English, the book documents and theorizes the place of desiring production in a social field characterized at once by the recodification of old class and racial hierarchies and the articulation of social movements beyond the union, party, or state. Spanish-language readers interested in the psychic effects of contemporary capitalism might consult Argentinean Spanish psychoanalyst Jorge Alemán's recent *Horizontes neoliberales en la subjetividad* (Neoliberal Horizons in Subjectivity, 2016). Alemán describes neoliberalism as social link defined by the withering of conventional forms of authority and the construction of subjects confronted with the seemingly insatiable demands and limitless power of capital. Alemán argues that the escape is not to be found in an individual cure, but rather in the finite discursive logic of Laclau's descriptive model of hegemony, which I discuss in further detail below.

Given the broad, speculative questions entertained by the present collection, it would be futile to argue that it completes or reveals the omissions of a given field of knowledge in any kind of positive sense. Rather, *Accumulation and Subjectivity* complements such recent studies and translations in social, political, and psychoanalytic theory in its attempt to articulate the relationship between its two title terms. In this sense, its purpose is neither to underscore the purported lack of attention to the ethical, psychic, or ideological mediation of political economy in sociological accounts of neoliberalism or the grassroots alternatives to it, nor, inversely, to demand that analyses of the symbolic, ethical, or psychic effects of contemporary capitalism incorporate a more detailed analysis of political economy. Rather, it aims to open a space for the reconstruction of conceptual genealogies and the analysis of theories and cultural phenomena that call into question the avowedly ontological or implicitly totalizing schemata that shape the approach to accumulation and subjectivity in the most ambitious and influential works of recent decades.

The present volume attempts to question two dominant theoretical frameworks structuring sociopolitical and cultural analysis over the last thirty years: the autonomy of politics in Ernesto Laclau and Chantal Mouffe's theories of populism and hegemony, and the immediately political nature of class struggle posited in Antonio Negri's analyses of the Keynesian state and its crisis beginning in the late 1960s. By alighting briefly on their proposals, alternately to sever and to identify the analysis of political economy and the subjective, political dimensions of class struggle, we can also appreciate the consequences of each at work in sociologist Verónica Gago's recent and widely read analysis of neoliberalism in the aftermath of Argentina's 2001 financial crisis.

Ernesto Laclau's theory of populism, first proposed in the final chapter of *Politics and Ideology in Marxist Theory* (1977), outlines a nondeterministic theory of political organization and subjectivity. Proposing a formal, structuralist approach to the experience of Peronism that extant uses of the term *populism* had overlooked, Laclau responded to the question of how to conceive of the class determination of ideology and politics. The chapter, titled "Towards a Theory of Populism," thus argues that "the class character of an ideology is given by its form and not by its content."[7] Irreducible to a given set of ideas or worldview, Laclau instead proposed a structuralist, discursive understanding of hegemony. In his view, class thus operates at the level of ideas and political organization by dictating the combination of class and national-popular elements. Together with Nicos Poulantzas, Laclau's earliest theory of populism participated in the reception and interpretation of structuralist Marxism as a way of accounting for the class or economic determination of mass-based politics in societies characterized by weak liberal institutions and heterogeneous historical temporalities and forms of property. Simultaneously, its attempt to outline a formal theory of populism marked its intervention into debates in modernization and dependency theory regarding the historical logic and political forms of capitalism specific to the region. "Towards a Theory of Populism" maintains a historical materialist understanding of universalism, such that, in Laclau's formulation, socialism would represent the highest form of populism.[8] At the same time, by casting the movement of Gramscian hegemony onto the structural plane of discourse, it also effectively weakened the analytic category of class by conflating it with the lonely "last instance" of economic determination. "Towards a Theory of Populism" thus lays the formal conceptual groundwork for Laclau and Mouffe's revisionist reading of class determination among thinkers of the II International in their highly influential *Hegemony and Socialist Strategy* (1985).

With respect to the present collection, it is less perhaps relevant to signal the evolution of the theoretical vocabulary in Laclau's employ—from structuralism to postfoundational political ontology to the metapsychology of identification in *On Populist Reason* (2005), than to note the ways in which the descriptive value of his framework occludes the specificity of the historical and theoretical contexts to which it responds. In his 1977 text, the mechanism of articulation of national-popular and class identities or elements addresses a question of causality or determination between subjectivity and accumulation, or the contingent and semantically singular realm of class politics and the objective position occupied by a given social group with respect to capital. By contrast, in *Hegemony and Socialist Strategy*, the articulation of class-based and non-class-based elements or demands appears as both the retroactive nucleus of Gramsci's theory of hegemony and as the necessary response to the fragmentation of the industrial working class in Western Europe and the United States. In Laclau and Mouffe's words, "It is impossible to talk today about the homogeneity of the working class, and a fortiori to trace it to a mechanism inscribed in the logic of capitalist accumulation."[9] If this conclusion reiterates the nondeterministic correlation between the objective and subjective dimensions of class politics, it also voices a more insidious and also more influential ahistorical vision of politics or political ontology. Laclau and Mouffe predicate their interpretation of hegemony— and the political ontology to which it gives rise—on the mimesis or mirroring among deindustrialized societies in which the wage no longer defines the dominant form of property and agrarian export countries where the wage could never be said to define the general form of labor. The descriptive efficiency of Laclau and Mouffe's theory of hegemony lies in the dehistoricizing nature of its attempt to codify the movement of class hegemony independent of the historical determination of class struggle.

Whereas Laclau and Mouffe sever any analytical tie between accumulation and subjectivity, Antonio Negri's writings from the 1970s and early '80s propose an immediate relationship between the two. Negri's theoretical and historical-political analyses from this period attempt to reformulate the principles of Italian workerism—for example, Mario Tronti's emphasis on the subjective capacity of living labor produced by the increasingly cooperative nature of industrial work—in order to account both for the new forms of control and exploitation produced by the crisis of industrial capitalism and for the new, expanded field of social antagonism taking shape beyond the setting of the factory or the sale and exploitation of wage labor. In Negri's view, Marx foresees the crisis of the social relation based on the exchange of wage labor in his development on the general intellect in the *Grundrisse*. According to Negri, Marx thus posits the development and imminent crisis of capitalism as one based on capital's decreasing reliance on the "theft of labor time" and increasing dependence on the general intellect, or scientific knowledge and technical know-how produced at a social level.[10] In Negri's view, the present crisis of industrial capitalism has similarly begun to incubate the communist society that will also subvert it. As Negri and other postautonomist Italian thinkers such as Maurizio Lazzarato and Paulo Virno have observed more recently, in this same passage Marx also affirms that capitalist development has brought about nothing short of an anthropological transformation or second nature. With this Marx refers to the inherently social techniques mediating the relationship that the individual sustains with his "inorganic body," or his means of existence. Setting this anthropological claim aside for the moment, Negri's key insight with respect to the periodization of capitalism lies in the way in which the radicalization of new social antagonisms in spheres traditionally assigned to the reproduction of class relations, also defines the expanded, social scope of the capital-labor relation.

In Negri's reading, the politicization of economic relations is more than an extreme response to increasingly molecular and violent forms of social control. Rather, he argues, it is the product of the "planner state," or a model of government aimed at containing and incorporating class struggle into the political sphere through state-centered economic planning.[11] Negri's point is not only that the subsumption of social labor power under capital has realized the social factory inadvertently posited by Keynes, but rather also that this new form of domination arises as a response to the uprisings of 1968–69 "within and against the system of the relative wage."[12] According to Negri, the restructuration of capital associated with the myriad dimensions of productive management and social control associated with postfordism is itself a response to the recomposition of the working class in both objective and subjective terms, as indexed by the expansive scope of struggles beginning in the late 1960s. With the concept of "class composition," Negri thus attempts to advance a political understanding of labor predicated on the incorporation of social labor into capital. Class composition can thus be understood an interpretation of class consciousness that refuses the separation between the objective function of labor power within capital and its enlightenment or process of self-consciousness in the realm of praxis or party organization. It proposes an immediate relationship between the incorporation of social labor into capital and the subjectivization of the collectivity produced as a result. In Negri's words, "[Class composition] is an historical process which combines material elements and becomes at the same time subjectivised; this in the sense that historical experience becomes transformed into irreversible qualities, into second nature."[13] Echoing Marx's description of the new social subject supposedly incubated within the technical processes of advanced industrial capital, Negri also describes the historical-political process of class composition in an anthropological, rather than gnoseological or practical, register. Negri's approach to the politicization of class struggle provides a convenient framework for describing social movements implicated in the dynamics of class struggle that nonetheless transcend struggles over the wage. However, despite its descriptive capacity in contexts, such as the Argentinean one, in which the regime of wage labor was never generalized nor was the politicization of labor ever confined to the space of the factory, the anthropological subject of class composition in Negri's framework assumes a historical tendency belied by ways in which capitalist development has proceeded by incorporating, rather than merely eliminating, heterogeneous temporalities and modes of production in the region. Stated slightly differently, if capitalism cannot be said to incubate the subject of a socialist society purportedly to come, then what conceptual vocabulary might allow us to apprehend the individual pscychic or collective political subjects produced by actual processes of accumulation beyond the wage relation?

Verónica Gago's *Neoliberalism from Below: Popular Pragmatics and Baroque Economies*, first published in Spanish in 2014, has been widely recognized for its account of neoliberal subjectivity. An experimental ethnography of La Salada flea market on the outskirts of Buenos Aires, it traces the historical-political process of class composition operative in the informal economies that emerged as a result of Argentina's economic crisis in 2001, and their subsequent incorporation into systems of private and state-sponsored finance under the center-left governments of Néstor Kirchner and Cristina Fernández. Gago's emphasis on the heterogeneity of these forms of sociability and mutual aid observed in La Salada serves to question the lasting center-left view of the Argentinean working class as one that is largely native-born, male, and industrial, and of the exploitation of wage labor as the principal source of capitalist accumulation. In slightly narrower terms, Gago's study also attempts to question Laclau's theory of populism as the one best suited to account for the subjectivization of the working class during the avowedly Peronist and populist administrations of Néstor Kirchner and Cristina Fernández. In Gago's view, the political ontology that Laclau ultimately derives from the experience of Peronism—including the "populist reason" that he borrows from the libidinal dynamics of identification with the charismatic leader or ideal in Freud's *Group Psychology*—ultimately proves inadequate to the collective forms generated, not only by the political rhetoric or redistributive policies of the state, but also by the material conditions of what she calls neoliberalism from below.

Gago documents the role of the state and of private banks in extracting wealth via debt through unemployment benefits packages, access to credit for consumption, and the microfinance of previously autonomous, informal networks of mutual aid and subsistence.[14] In her view, these marginalized segments of the population—poor women, immigrants, the unemployed or precariously employed, and the indebted lower middle class—constitute new forms of sociality that find themselves inevitably implicated in the extraction of value through rent. Gago argues that these collectivities should be understood, not merely as victims of neoliberal economic policy, but rather as the historical and anthropological face of an expanded working class. The new class composition that Gago describes emerges from the way that contemporary capital "puts to work" not only biopower but "ways of life."[15] In this sense, Gago shares with Negri a reading of Foucault filtered through the cataclysmic Marx of the *Grundrisse*. Indeed, it is around this point where Gago's study both locates and hides its most incisive insights about the relationship between accumulation and subjectivity in Latin America. Rather than questioning the historical teleology behind Negri's interpretation of the real subsumption of social labor under capital, Gago assumes it—tacitly, but also ambivalently. In other words, *Neoliberalism from Below* struggles to find the conceptual vocabulary adequate, not simply to the empirical heterogeneity of the subjects that it documents but rather to the multiplicity and layering of historical times and forms of sociability that neoliberalism brings under the command of financial capital without, for that reason, wholly subordinating them to it. What is at stake is more than a lexical problem or an assertion of the purported irreducibility of the Argentinean case. Rather, it is the ability to give a critical account of the historicity of capitalism as a social relation and of the forms of collective subjectivity produced and productive of it. Motley for the necessary plurality of methodological approaches and problems that it unfolds, the present volume participates in the search for a conceptual vocabulary adequate to the imbrication of accumulation and subjectivity in its varied historical forms.

Why insist on the relationship between accumulation and subjectivity? Why insist on the problematic nature of positing this relationship? Why Latin America? In theory, accumulation and subjectivity serve as the objects of wholly different fields of inquiry: historical materialism and philosophy, respectively. And yet, despite this, the two are also historically intertwined. To identify a collective subject of social transformation outside of determinate historical and political circumstances of struggle is to exit the realm of historical materialist analysis for that of metaphysics. Inversely, to speak of accumulation without subjectivity is to posit capital as some sort of autonomous, self-perpetuating entelechy and thus to participate in the ideological ruse that powers its own reproduction through the capture of labor power. In other words, there can be no account of the logic governing the extraction of wealth as such outside of a notion of the construction of the collective subjects implied in this operation at an institutional, juridical, moral, or psychic level. The collection's regional focus complicates matters further. Though social scientists in the English-speaking academy often call upon Latin America to provide the raw material for political thought, the present collection refuses the idea that its analyses offer any such ready-made models for life or products for academic consumption.

The collection instead aspires to present the reader with a set of critical-methodological tools or concepts. We might think of the latter in terms of what Aricó, glossing Gramsci, proposed as the labor of translation. Taking as his starting point an enigmatic remark by Lenin to the effect that the Russian Revolution had not yet been able to "translate" its language into Western European languages, Gramsci developed the notion of translation as a way of connoting a relationship of generality and particularity or conceptuality and instantiation that he then put to work in different theoretical discussions and registers.[16] As Martín Cortés has signaled, Aricó appropriated the term as a way of describing the simultaneously singular nature of Latin American socioeconomic formations and their circumscription within the necessarily universal reach of capitalism. From this perspective, Gramsi's notion of translation thus ponders the concepts necessary in order to render legible concrete national realities and seeks ways of transferring such concepts to the analysis of other historical-political contexts.[17] Neither a metaphor nor a method, in Aricó's approach to Gramsci, the work of translation is both interpretive and interventionist in nature. In this sense, positing the translatability of a given concept involves more than simply importing and applying an existing theory, but rather of extracting a way of reading or of performing theoretical work from within the singularity of a given national or regional situation.[18] Aricó deployed this notion of translation as a way of distinguishing between the singularity and purported irreducibility of different socioeconomic formations, thus anticipating the pitfalls of cultural particularism, and extending its objects of inquiry to texts and experiences that might or might not posit their object in terms of Marxist theory or class struggle. Just as the starting point for this critical maneuver was the ability to detect formal similarities in the sociopolitical morphology of distant regions—between Gramsci's Mezzogiorno and Aricó's Argentina, for example—the end result was a vision of Marxism as a constellation of debates traversed by both Marxist and non-Marxist thought from diverse regions.[19]

One of the collection's aims is to recuperate a series of problems and concepts, such as property, class, totality, and socioeconomic formation, first coined or treated at a problematic level in response to the discourses of development and dependency and intended to address both the social contradictions produced by industrialization and the political possibilities opened by the Cuban Revolution. A second aim of the collection is to localize and interpret the relationship between accumulation and subjectivity in specific sociocultural case studies: the cinematographic construction of political memory in Bolivia, the juridical category of the migrant, the moral dimension of debt, and the symbolic representation of femicide in the maquilas of Ciudad Juárez. The collection's third aim is to revisit concepts and logical operations central to Marx's own work and to interrogate their consequences for contemporary theoretical inquiry and political analysis.

One finds this third objective at work on the face of those essays that take leave of the social, cultural, and intellectual context of Latin America in order to examine the historicity of the individual subject as a construct of moral and juridical norms and their psychoanalytic subversion; to extend and return Alain Badiou's topology to the historical logic of capitalism; and to question the philosophical assumptions sustaining contemporary articulations of ecological Marxism. Simultaneously, the objective of revisiting and expanding Marx's categories cuts across virtually all of the essays, whether by addressing the category of hybrid subsumption in *Capital*; the metaphorical language of Marx's chapters on primitive accumulation in the context of contemporary migrancy at the U.S.-Mexican border; or the vicissitudes of the concept of property in colonial Mexican law and legal testimony.

The content and organization of the present volume thus attempt to demonstrate two broader critical-methodological points. The first speaks to the epistemological assumptions sustaining Gramsci's notion of translation. To the extent that the translation of a concept from one context to another supposes a creative and interpretive effort on the part of the theorist, inversely, it also supposes that the historical-political context or conjuncture, to use Althusser's term, poses these same problems objectively. Regardless of whether or not they place the history of Marxian concepts at the forefront of their inquiries, almost all of the essays to follow "think in the conjuncture."[20] That is, more than merely describe the objectively given elements of a given situation, they allow us to see how the logic of class struggle becomes visible only from within specific ideological and political determinations. Through their close attention to the history of policy, urban planning, film social movements, and intellectual debates, they not only give account of phenomena illustrative of the effects of capitalism on law, art, and literature but also pinpoint and mobilize the tensions and contradictions dynamizing each context in order to identify new theoretical and political problems. Rather than merely attending to the singular nature of the case in question, the studies included in the present volume illustrate concepts at once immanent to the processes that they describe and potentially extrapolatable from them. In so doing, they offer up instances of the kind of materialist political thought at stake in Althusser's formulation. Simultaneously, their sensitivity to the specificities of the conjuncture also speaks to the volume's second point.

For many of the authors anthologized, the technical language of Marxist political economy serves as the most precise vehicle for identifying the oftentimes obfuscated or tense relationship between capitalism and subjectivity. Despite this, the present volume does not pretend to offer an overview of Latin American Marxism, understood either as a positively given field of study or as a compendium of discrete national intellectual, social, or political traditions. To paraphrase Lacan, Latin American Marxism does not exist, or rather, it does not exist as a self-reflexively cogent or consistent set of theories, attitudes, or practices. The point is rather to interrogate two concepts whose relationship unsettles the implicit or professed assumptions about radical historical transformation that academic discourse wishes to capture when it invokes "Latin American Marxism." The book thus aims to question, rather than to reify, Marxism in its regional or national declinations. For this same reason, it also includes several essays that, though they do not focus on Latin American authors or contexts, do address the historical logic of capitalism and the potential place of the subject within it, thus allowing the reader a somewhat more formalized perspective on the historical case studies presented in previous sections.

The collection includes four sections, each of whose subheadings serves both a descriptive and heuristic function. The essays in the first section, titled "Property and History", represent different approaches to the definition of property—as a historical and ontological relation among individuals and between individuals and their means of existence—and as a set of economic and juridical relations straddling and blurring the border between the economic and political determinations of a given society. Each of the contributions to this section also examines how Marx, as well as Marxist and non-Marxist thinkers, attempted to define property or to conceive of the transformation of property relations under capitalism. In the first of these contributions, "On Subsumption as Form and the Use of Asynchronies," Massimiliano Tomba examines Marx's formulations of subsumption, or the incorporation of labor into capital, by asking what it might mean to consider formal and real subsumption, not as stages of historical development, but rather as ways of defining the social form of labor. To the extent that capitalism cannot create but rather must encounter its conditions of existence in "preexisting relationships of production, property and politics," Tomba's reading underscores the expedience, rather than the merely residual nature, of noncapitalist forms of labor for capital, thus asking us to view capitalism as a social relation defined by the violent encounter among different historical temporalities, and one open to nonbourgeois configurations of property and self-government. David Kazanjian's "'I am he': A History of Dispossession's Not-Yet-Present in Colonial Yucatán" questions assumptions about the juridical definition of property in the Spanish colonial archive. Kazanjian's case study of the late-seventeenth-century court case of the enslaved Afro-Yucatecan Juan Patricio, asks us to question the metaphysical foundations undergirding assumptions that challenge the notion of accumulation by dispossession on two counts: both as a narrow historical definition of Marx's formulation of primitive accumulation, and as a common trope among interpreters of the colonial period that tends to reinforce the purportedly metaphysical foundations of the individual's relation to others and to the land. My contribution, "Accumulation as Total Conversion," proposes a revisionist interpretation of the notion of transculturation at work in José María Argue-das's anthropological studies on the effects of capitalist expansion on the country's Southern Central highlands. Addressing the categories of property and subsumption in Kanzanjian and Tomba's contributions, the essay aims to show how, in Arguedas's account, the ethical and material life of the collective functions as a condition for and potential obstacle to capital. In close conversation with the other contributions in this section, Sergio Villalobos-Ruminott's "Latin American Marxism: History and Accumulation" traces how Latin American Marxist debates of the 1960s and '70s emerging as a reaction to the discourses and theories of development and dependency questioned lineal notions of progress. Villalobos-Ruminott argues that a reconsideration of these debates might help to articulate a Marxist analysis of the processes of *ongoing* primitive accumulation triggered by neoliberal globalization while questioning, at the same time, the limitations imposed by a naturalized understanding of historical temporality."

The essays grouped under the heading of "Class and Totality" examine how such terms sought to account for the concrete ways in which accumulation and subjectivity intersect in societies defined by neo-imperial economic relations and the articulation of heterogeneous modes of production. The essays in this section trace concepts and debates among Latin American social and political theorists of the 1960s and '70s whose worked alternately responded to and took advantage of the so-called crisis of Marxism by recasting the logic and ontology of history and the category of the subject charged with its transformation. Pablo Pérez Wilson provides a succinct interpretation of the purpose of the three essays in this section when he writes, "Rather than deriving a necessary outcome from a given conception, historically oriented research should pay attention to how the actual development of a specific social formation encapsulates the tensions and contradictions of capital itself." Pérez Wilson's "Class and Accumulation" is unique for the way that it traces how different theorizations of social class in Chile intersect with shifts in the pattern of global capitalist accumulation. Considering the work of Manuel Castells, Javier Martínez, Eugenio Tironi, Carlos Ruiz Encina, and Giorgio Boccardo, Pérez Wilson's essay questions the application of market-oriented research in recent critiques of neoliberalism by showing instead how we can understand social class and capitalist accumulation as part of the same historical process. Marcelo Starcenbaum's essay, "José Aricó and the Concept of Socioeconomic Formation," traces a genealogy of the concept of socioeconomic formation, which serves as an alternative way of naming the mode of production, in Marx and Lenin, and in the Cuadernos de Pasado y Presente in the context of debates about historical causality and transition in the mode of production in the 1960s and '70s. Starcenbaum underscores the importance of this nonmechanistic formulation of social and political determination in Aricó's work as a researcher and publisher, thus signaling the continuity between formal debates about the definition of mode of production and the kinds of concrete historical analyses of national self-determination and communalism that Aricó viewed as fundamental for the renewal of socialist internationalism and enlightenment. Jaime Ortega Reyna's contribution focuses on the tension between totality and contingency in the work of Bolivian sociologist René Zavaleta Mercado. Noting Zavaleta's newfound, posthumous recognition in the Anglophone world, "An Irresolvable Tension: The Part or the Whole? The Effects of the 'Crisis of Marxism' in the Work of René Zavaleta Mercado" argues that the central current animating Zavaleta's intellectual project and its place within the so-called crisis of Marxism can be defined by its insistence on the tension between the universal character of capitalism and the situated and contingent, or conjunctural, nature of politics. Ortega Reyna thus argues that Zavaleta's formulation of society's *abigarramiento* or becoming motley, should be read in the intellectual context of the thinker's mature work from the late 1970s and early 1980s in its attempt to address the question of historical determination, rather than describe a situation of cultural or linguistic heterogeneity, as championed by the Anglophone reception of his work in recent years. In addition to tracing the uses and reformulations of concepts pertinent to class and totality in Marxist theory, each of the essays in this section also emphasizes how such formulations emerged from and reflected upon the specificity of purportedly outlier cases, that is, socioeconomic formations and national political contexts—Bolivia, Chile, or Latin America, more broadly speaking—that prove central for questioning and reinventing the categories of Marxist analysis globally or universally. These chapters not only provide us with a nuanced glossary of new and familiar terms but also, and perhaps more importantly, ways of translating problems and formulations among the conceptual languages of specific historical-political conjunctures.

The essays collected in the section "Sovereignty and Debt" contemplate the relationship between contemporary forms of neoliberal governance and the legal, cultural, and psychic consequences of contemporary mechanisms of accumulation through rent with an emphasis on debt. In "Postmigrancy: Borders, Primitive Accumulation, and Labor at the U.S./Mexico Border," Abraham Acosta studies the role of jurisprudence in the dynamics of ongoing primitive accumulation through an analysis of the history of laws and policies governing Central American migration to the United States beginning in the 1980s. By taking as his point of departure the specific inflection of the "freedom" that Marx imputes to the English peasants dispossessed of their means of subsistence in the final chapters of *Capital*, Acosta coins the term *postmigrancy* in order to name a present defined by the implication and undecidability of freedom and rightlessness. Horacio Legrás's contribution, "Psychotic Violence: Crime and Consumption in the Apocalyptic Phase of Capitalism," underscores the extent to which the hermeneutic assumptions and shortcomings of journalistic and social scientific accounts of the femicide in Ciudad Juárez can be understood to be implicated in the "neoliberal redrawing" of both urban space and the function of the state with respect to the economy. Building upon Rita Segato's analysis of the Juárez murders, Legrás characterizes the social link sustaining neoliberal governance in the city as one best described by what analyst Jacques-Alain Miller terms "ordinary psychosis," such that that mutilation of the female body substitutes and supplements the symbolic deficiencies of a moral law reconfigured by capital. In "Debt, Violence, and Subjectivity" Alessandro Fornazzari reads the moral and economic logic of debt in the essays and chronicles of Ricardo Piglia and Pedro Lemebel, focused, respectively, on Witold Gombrowicz's time in Argentina (1939–1963) and with Pedro Lemebel's reflections on 1980s Chile. Mobilizing Giovanni Arrighi's and Maurizio Lazzarato's accounts of finance capital, Fornazzari skews the superficial thematic treatment of use and exchange value in Piglia's and Lemebel's writings, arguing instead that their texts reconfigure the subject's relationship to the future and to others beyond the purportedly totalizing culture produced by the creditor-debtor relationship and amplified by the rise of finance capital in the 1970s. In contrast to the literary and cultural analyses in the volume, Irina Feldman's "The 'Insurgent Subject' versus Accumulation by Dispossession in Álvaro García Linera and Jorge Sanjinés" focuses on the economic and political valences of accumulation in the progressive cultural agenda of Evo Morales's MAS (Movement Towards Socialism) government. Feldman examines the notion of accumulation as it pertains both to insurgent experience and to capital in Álvaro García Linera's extensive essay *Las tensiones creativas del Proceso de Cambio* (Creative Tensions of the Process of Change, 2012) and the film *Insurgentes* (Insurgents) produced the same year by Jorge Sanjinés and the Grupo Ukamau. By suggesting a continuity between the Katarista rebellions of the 1780s and the Bolivian Gas Wars of 2003, Feldman argues that *Insurgentes* performs García Linera's cultural program at the same time that it ponders the possible limitations of the MAS government's revolutionary aims.

The collection's final section, "The Subject and Nature," mirrors the first in its attempt to formalize the emergence of the subject in ontological and contingent historical-political terms. Bruno Bosteels's contribution asks whether it might be possible to conceive of a theory of the subject absent the Hegelian logic of presupposition, which Marx employs in order to describe the movement by which capital produces "the semblance that the conditions of its becoming are in reality the effects and attributes of its own being." Bosteels thus proposes "Marx's Theory of the Subject" as one that would allow us to historize the becoming ahistorical and transcendental of the subject in the theories proposed by Judith Butler, Alain Badiou, and Slavoj Žižek, among others. Gavin Walker's "'Non-Capital' and the Torsion of the Subject" looks to Badiou's *Theory of the Subject* (1982) in order to locate the emergence of a revolutionary subjectivity in the extimate place that labor power occupies with respect to capital. Walker thus relates Badiou's topological figure of torsion and Marx's passing reference to the notion of non-capital in order to formulate how a collective subject might emerge from within the critique of political economy. Orlando Bentancor's contribution, "The Impasses of Environmentalism: Subjectivity and Accumulation in the World-Ecology Project," examines the field of Marxist eco-criticism and, specifically, what theorist Jason Moore has proposed as the devaluation and transformation of the biosphere under capitalism. By reinterpreting the topological place of labor power, as discussed in Walker's essay, Bentancor proposes a critique of the ontology of nature at stake in Moore's project. Just as the volume begins with an elaboration on the Marx's scattered mentions of the subsumption of labor under capital, it ends with an attempt to locate and formalize a theory of the subject with respect to this same logical-historical movement.

As the reader may have already gleaned from the description of its individual contributions, the collection includes a variety of sociocultural, theoretical, and intellectual-historical objects and critical-methodological approaches, approaches that sometimes surface in productive tension with one another as part of the framework of a given essay. Literary scholars such as Legrás write about culture, not simply as a code word for nonliterary texts or phenomena, but as a way of underscoring the ethical structures and material practices constitutive of specific socioeconomic formations.[21] Intellectual histories and conceptual accounts relevant to the mode of production debates among Latin American social theorists of the 1960s and '70s, such as those of

Marcelo Starcenbaum, Jaime Ortega Reyna, Pablo Pérez Wilson, and Sergio Villalobos-Ruminott, illustrate the ways in which Marxist theory questioned teleological and mechanistic approaches to history. In doing so, they also revive the theoretical consequences of neologisms such as Zavaleta's *sociedad abigarrada* (motley society) and seemingly arcane concepts like *formación socioeconómica* (socioeconomic formation) and class, together with the possibility of thinking about the objective conditions for a transition away from capitalism. The colonial Mexican archive and the poetic ethnography of property relations in twentieth-century Peru do more than illustrate the ontological and philological problems of history and contingency at stake in the consideration of Marx, Moore, Badiou, and Žižek. They also consider these questions operatively and performatively through the singularity of their respective contexts. The diversity of these approaches speaks to the Aricosian aims of the collection: to define a vocabulary for considering the relationship between accumulation and subjectivity from theories, political experiences, and sociocultural texts whose material specificity also holds the key to their formalization and potential translation into other historical and contexts.

While opening a space for a wider and more sophisticated variety of theoretical approaches to the analysis of capitalism and subjectivity, the present collection also aims to underscore the structural fragility and contingency of capitalism as a social relation that depends upon something (labor power, as well as human and nonhuman nature) that it cannot itself produce. The theoretical interrogations, intellectual reconstructions, and sociocultural analyses anthologized here illustrate the expansiveness and complexity of the psychic, social, ethical, and biological relations that have functioned, historically, as both the source of and potential obstacle to the accumulation of wealth. And yet if they, like the present discussion, tend to privilege the concepts best suited to apprehend this operation, rather than, say, the histories of struggle produced by it, it is because the operation (of capital's own expansive self-reproduction) is itself simultaneously a historical and logical one. The point is not to deride the study of history, per se, but rather to question the assumption, common to non-Marxist and post-Marxist analyses, that it is either over or propelled, zombie-like, in the absence of one or more classes as its agent(s). The emphasis of many essays on the historical logic of capitalism's unfolding and thus on the specificity of the noncapitalist social forms that it must encounter for the sake of accumulation, offers neither utopian models nor immediate escape routes from capitalism. Rather, the reader should understand the insistence of such contributions on the specific historical-political conjunctures informing or reformulating Marxist concepts, as a call to, and not a retreat from, political struggle. So too, their interest in probing, questioning, and historicizing terms and concepts, from *primitive accumulation, class,* and *hybrid subsumption* to *mode of production, socioeconomic formation, abigarramiento, debt, psychosis, nature, postmigrancy,* and *torsion,* to name just a few, speaks to the generative, creative nature of the book's critical pursuits.

Notes

1. José Aricó, Letter to Ludolfo Paramio dated March 3, 1977. Correspondence: Box 3. Archivo de la Biblioteca José Aricó, Universidad Nacional de Córdoba.

2. Gaido and Bosch, "'A Strange Mixture,'" 218. As one of the founding editors of Cuadernos de Pasado y Presente (Past and Present Notebooks) and the collection titled Biblioteca del Pensamiento Socialista (Library of Socialist Thought), part of the publishing house Siglo XXI, Aricó published more than 150 translations and edited collections of Marx and Marxist theory.

3. For a representative work by Lechner, see *La conflictiva y nunca acabada construcción del orden deseado.*

4. It is indeed this critical gesture that distinguishes Aricó's position from that of other political theorists of the time, despite their shared practical support for a reformist view of democratic government. As Peter Thomas has perhaps demonstrated most extensively with respect to Gramsci's Italian and English-language reception in the 1970s, the uses or interpretations in question concerned the relationship between the state and civil society. With the notion of the integral state, Gramsci posited civil society as a moment or facet of the state and, inversely, proposed the state as the political form that emerged from the corporative struggle of the bourgeoisie within a specific set of property relations. Philosophers such as Bobbio confined the operation of Gramsci's notion of hegemony to the cultural and ideological instances of civil society, thus divorcing it from any notion of the institutional or ethical becoming of a revolutionary class. Thomas, *The Gramscian Moment,* 182.

5. Aricó, *La cola del diablo,* 151. In the author's words, this unity supposes "in political practice, the struggle to constitute a social and political order in which society's permanent conflictivity finds forms of resolution that favor its democratization without producing their own ungovernability."

6. Aricó, *La hipótesis de Justo,* 23.

7. Laclau, *Politics and Ideology,* 160.

8. Ibid., 196.

9. Laclau and Mouffe, *Hegemony and Socialist Strategy,* 82.

10. Negri, "Crisis of the Planner-State," 117.

11. Negri, "Keynes and the Capitalist Theory of the State," 18.

12. Negri, "Archaeology and Project," 208.

13. Ibid., 223.

14. Gago, "Financialization of Popular Life," 17.

15. Gago, *La razón neoliberal*, 17; Negri, "Marx after Foucault," 191.

16. Thomas, "Gramsci and the Political," 27–30. Gramsci uses the term in order to discuss the relationship sustained between dialects and national languages, philosophy and politics, and civil society and the state.

17. Cortés, *Un nuevo marxismo*, 27.

18. Ibid., 29.

19. Ibid., 43.

20. Althusser, "Machiavelli and Us," 18.

21. I borrow the latter formulation from Stuart Hall. See Hall, *Cultural Studies 1983*.

Works Cited

Althusser, Louis. *Machiavelli and Us*. Translated by Gregory Elliott. London: Verso, 1999.

Aricó, José. *La cola del diablo: Itinerario de Gramsci en América Latina*. Buenos Aires: Siglo Veintiuno Editores, 2005.

———. *Hipótesis de Justo: Escritos sobre el socialismo en América Latina*. Buenos Aires: Editorial Sudamericana, 2011.

Cortés, Martín. *Un nuevo marxismo para América Latina: José Aricó: traductor, editor, intelectual*. Buenos Aires: Siglo Veintiuno Editores, 2015.

Gaido, Daniel, and Costanza Bosch Alessio. "'A Strange Mixture of Guevara and Togliatti'": José María Aricó and the *Pasado Presente* Group in Argentina." *Historical Materialism* 22, no. 3–5 (2014): 217–50.

Gago, Verónica. "Financialization of Popular Life and the Extractive Operations of Capital." *South Atlantic Quarterly* 114, no. 1 (2015): 11–28.

———. *La razón neoliberal: Economías barrocas y pragmática popular*. Buenos Aires. Tinta Limón Ediciones, 2014.

Hall, Stuart. *Cultural Studies 1983: A Theoretical History*. Edited by Jennifer Daryl Slack and Lawrence Grossberg. Durham: Duke University Press, 2016.

Laclau, Ernesto. *Politics and Ideology in Marxist Theory: Capitalism, Fascism, Populism*. London: New Left Books, 1977.

———, and Chantal Mouffe. *Hegemony and Socialist Strategy: Towards a Radical Democracy*. London: Verso, 1985.

Lechner, Norbert. *La conflictiva y nunca acabada construcción del orden deseado*. Santiago: Facultad Latinoamericana de Ciencias Sociales, 1984.

Negri, Antonio. "Archaeology and Project: The Mass Worker and Social Worker." In *Revolution Retrieved: Writings on Marx, Keynes, Capitalist Crisis and New Social Subjects 1967–83*, 199–228. London: Red Notes, 1988.

———. "Crisis of the Planner State: Communism and Revolutionary Organization." In *Revolution Retrieved: Writings on Marx, Keynes, Capitalist Crisis, and New Social Subjects 1967–83*, 91–148. London: Red Notes, 1988.

———. "Keynes and the Capitalist Theory of the State Post-1929." In *Revolution Retrieved: Writings on Marx, Keynes, Capitalist Crisis, and New Social Subjects 1967–83*, 5–42. London: Red Notes, 1988.

———. "Marx after Foucault: The Subject Refound." In *Marx and Foucault: Essays*. Vol. 1, edited by Ed Emery, 188–198. Cambridge: Polity Books, 2017.

Thomas, Peter. *The Gramscian Moment*. Chicago: Haymarket Books, 2011.

———. "Gramsci and the Political: From the State as 'Metaphysical Event' to Hegemony as 'Philosophical Fact.'" *Radical Philosophy* no. 153 (2009): 27–36.

Archival Material

Aricó, José. Letter to Ludolfo Paramio. March 3, 1977. Correspondence: Box 3. Archivo de la Biblioteca José Aricó. Universidad Nacional de Córdoba.

PART ONE

Property
and
History

CHAPTER ONE

On Subsumption as Form and the Use of Asynchronies

MASSIMILIANO TOMBA

Formal Subsumption as Form

The concept of *subsumption as form* within the contemporary global capitalist framework refers to how different forms of exploitation merge with one another. In Marx, formal subsumption designates a process in which capital incorporates labor power and transforms the latter into capital. From this perspective and in the English history of originary accumulation, the labor incorporated in capital is wage-labor—the labor that constitutes the basis of the capitalist mode of production. In these pages I want to call into question the teleological view of the transition from the feudal mode of production to capitalism, a view that unfortunately has often been referred to as a kind of normative history for the rest of the world. Moreover, I want to free formal subsumption from a unilinear conception of time and stage theory of capitalism.

The historical condition of our present makes possible this redefinition of the concept of formal subsumption: the distinction between center and periphery, between the production of relative and absolute surplus value, vanishes to the extent that the periphery coexists temporally and spatially within the center, and vice versa. Similarly, as I have argued elsewhere,[1] the temporality of the production of absolute surplus value is intertwined with that of relative surplus value. This coexistence of different temporalities requires a new comprehension of the concept of formal subsumption. In order to distance ourselves from any Eurocentric approach, we must develop a non-historicist conception of formal subsumption that is relevant for the reciprocal implications of different forms of exploitations.

The capitalist mode of production does not create its own conditions of existence and reproduction ex nihilo, but meets preexisting relationships of production, property, and politics which are reconfigured differently. This encounter of different temporal trajectories gives rise to a "heterogeneous mix rather than the destruction of one made by another."[2] So, for example, the capitalist mode of production neither invents nor suppresses slavery, but encounters forms of slave labor that are reconfigured starting from new owner relationships and from the orientation of production, no longer aimed at the satisfaction of limited needs of the community but at the world market. Capitalistically subsumed into the world market, forms of slave labor become more brutal and intensive because it is no longer the will of the slave driver that beats the rhythm of labor, but the impersonal clocks of world stock markets.

Capital does not create differences and hierarchies from scratch, but inherits them from preexisting forms, which it reconfigures in a new way. The capitalist mode of production is neither ontologically racist nor inherently patriarchal. Rather, it has to be understood as a structure, which is abstract in the sense that it is based on an inversion (*Verkehrung*), according to which production is not primarily organized in order to satisfy human needs, but to valorize value. That inversion, pertaining to the objective of production, simultaneously changes social and political relationships and the entire configuration of property relations within the societal structure. However abstract in its structure, the capitalist mode of production requires concrete differentiations and hierarchies that are filled with historical, political, social and cultural content. For this reason, capitalism, even though it appears in historically and geographically different forms, expresses a common structure, as it is the skeleton in relation to the external appearance of an individual. The historical forms of domination that preexist the capitalist mode of production are reconfigured in the encounter with it and give rise to conflicts among different temporalities. When preexisting economic and political forms are formally subsumed into the capitalist mode of production, they change their own shape, even if they apparently maintain similarities with their preexisting semblance.

This intertwining between different forms is to be analyzed. On the one hand, there is a structural dimension: capital is articulated through hierarchies and forms of domination without identifying with any of them. On the other hand, these forms of domination have been produced and reproduced on the basis of existing traditional, cultural, and ideological relations. The relationship between these two dimensions is not definable in terms of structure and superstructure but, rather, of production and reproduction. It would be wrong to underestimate the weight of the reproduction of current hierarchical, racial, and gender relations within the capitalist division of labor. Similarly, it would be wrong not to consider the plasticity of the capitalist mode of production, which can use diverse hierarchical structures and any kind of preexisting differentiation. The relationship between capital and labor slavery is enlightening. The capitalist mode of production is not only compatible with slavery forms, but it has used and continues to use them in the process of the originary accumulation of capital. From the point of view of the structure of the capitalist mode of production, slavery is a form of domination that can be denoted in racial, gender, or religious terms. Each of them can perform a similar function in order to justify inferiority, discrimination, and enslavement. What I intend to assert is not only the compatibility between forms of slave labor and capitalism, but that capitalism is configured in different ways based on the political and economic forms that it encounters and on the resistance that it hits in its attempt to reshape the social fabric. This does not mean that there exist many diversified capitalisms based on the traditional, political, and economic elements met. The form of subsumption is given by the orientation of production toward the valorization of value and, therefore, toward the world market. In this way, socially necessary labor-time becomes normative for each individual capital that has to endure in the world market.

Before going on to analyze how historically the mode of production unfolds and produces a variety of asynchronies, I need to clarify the meaning of the notion of socially necessary labor. According to Marx, "the real value of a commodity . . . is not its *individual,* but its *social* value; that is to say, its value is not measured by the labor-time that the article costs the producer in each individual case, but by the labor-time socially required for its production."[3] The value of a commodity depends on the amount of socially necessary labor-time required for its manufacture; however, the amount of socially necessary labor-time objectified in the commodity is not the labor-time that is spent for its production. Socially necessary labor-time can be either greater or smaller than the individual time spent for the production of a use object. The generic human labor-time in the substance of value must be adjusted according to the time required by social labor to perform that same job. Thus, the value produced, which is an objectification of *socially necessary* labor, is not deductible from the labor actually expended in a single productive process, nor is surplus value a quantifiable amount within the accounting of a single firm or factory.

For example, an hour of high productivity work can correspond to two hours of socially necessary labor-time in places where technological innovation remains untouched by a society as a whole. The labor-time effectively exploited by the capitalist—who uses the new machine—is inferior to that which is socially necessary. Therefore, the capitalist, selling the commodity at its value, appropriates social surplus value and can exchange one hour of labor-time for two. As Marx explains, "The capitalist who applies the improved method of production appropriates and devotes to surplus labor a greater portion (*Extramehrwert*) of the working day than the other capitalists in the same business."[4] *Extramehrwert* corresponds to the quantity of social surplus value that the capitalist can withdraw from the society. Appropriating *Extramehrwert,* the capitalist extracts relative surplus value and exploits labor with a higher productivity level than the social average. In this way, a greater number of hours of work concretely performed pass through the hands of the capitalist who utilizes a greater productive power of work without violating the law of equivalence.

I reason, first, that the difference between capitalists who exploit work of diverse productivities is *therefore necessary* in order to extract relative surplus value from the benefits of technological innovation. According to Marx, the immediate repercussion of the absence of technological innovation is a *prolonging* of labor-time: "One of the first consequences of the introduction of new machinery, before it has become dominant in its branch of production, is the *prolongation* of the labor-time of the laborers who continue to work with the old and unimproved means of production."[5] The introduction of a new machine increases extra-relative surplus value only if the productivity of the necessary social labor remains lower. This becomes possible through the prevention of the general spread of new technological innovations and machines. In other words, automated production remains profitable while there are low-tech areas of production where the innovation has not been employed, and in which a proportional increase in the extraction of *absolute surplus value* occurs in order to compete within the capitalist market.

The relative surplus value is in fact *relative* because it must be placed *in relation* to absolute surplus value. This is emphasized when the capitalist who exploits a technological innovation concretizes at least a part of the relative surplus value that is potentially his own. This surplus value is then materialized through a social transfer of value from productive areas of high absolute surplus value to areas of high relative surplus value. The differential quota between a given productivity of labor and socially necessary labor makes possible a transfer of value from production spheres in which the productivity of labor is lower to areas in which capital exploits labor at a productivity that is higher than the social average.

As long as we want to think with Marx, we have to assume that machines neither create value nor produce surplus value: "As machinery comes into general use in a particular branch of production, the social value of the machine's product sinks down to its individual value, and the following law asserts itself: surplus value does not arise from the labor-power that has been replaced by the machinery, but from the labor-power actually employed in working with the machinery."[6] When a technological innovation becomes widespread, the growing productivity of labor obtained through its employment also becomes socially dominant, allowing few opportunities for extracting quotas of extra-surplus value. Secondly, I reason that capitalist development is necessarily differentiated. Absolute and relative forms of surplus value are interwoven and are implied in a reciprocal way within the global market. Therefore, no form of production can be considered backward or residual. Capital requires instead a vast differentiation of forms of exploitation, which are *synchronized* in the global market by socially necessary labor-time. In other words, different capitals directly competing with each other on the world market give rise to diverse geographical spaces with different labor powers and wages.[7] Colonial and neocolonial violence continuously create and recreate these differentiations (within and outside a country) and hinder the dissemination of technical innovation in the machinery. Borders, clearly in today's world, express their economic/political significance by directing flows of labor power, creating new ethnic divisions of labor, and defining wage areas that can only be reproduced by blocking a massive movement of migrants. Borders do not define only the perimeter of a state; rather, there are internal and external boundaries that define different zones of valorization. These differences are due to the relationship between two dimensions: cost of the labor force, and therefore control over the mobility of migrant workers;

and dissemination of machines and technology. The combination of these two dimensions defines the productivity of the process of value-production.

Technologies and machines are needed (1) to increase labor productivity, (2) to reduce its porosity, and (3) to create differentials of surplus value in the global market.[8] Indeed, the uneven distribution of knowledge is necessary to capital in order to differentiate the distribution of innovations and, therefore, of relative surplus value production in the global market. Stated differently, the reciprocal combination of absolute and relative surplus value pushes the global market toward an extreme differentiation of the forms of exploitation by stationing technologies and high organic composition of capital in some places, and in others, enormous concentrations of living labor, long hours, and high intensity of labor. The distribution of these spaces is no longer articulated according to the logic of center-periphery, but through their intertwining. Thus, these differentiations are to be understood not only in spatial terms, but also, and primarily, as temporalities. Moreover, these differentiations can be produced and reproduced only through the constant use of extra-economic violence, which intervenes by blocking development in some geographical areas or by obstructing the movement of the migrant labor force.

We need a concept of formal subsumption that is not based on the specific configuration of European history, but which is instead capable of understanding a multiplicity of forms of wage and nonwaged, free and forced labor. According to Marx, in order to define formal subsumption of labor under capital, "it is sufficient that handicraftsmen who previously worked on their own account, or as apprentices of a master, should become wage laborers under the direct control of a capitalist."[9] In other words, the capitalist mode of production has configured itself through the separation between laborers and the means of production. I would like to add two amendments. In capitalism, laborers do not have to be formally free wage laborers and laborers can own their means of production. However, this ownership does not necessary better their condition. On the contrary, workers who are de jure free entrepreneurs are de facto completely subjugated to the capital that assigns their work. In this way, the individual workers have to pay for their means of production, included housing and heating during the winter; they have to impose themselves the discipline required by capital; under the appearance of individual liberty, they must work according to the pace and productivity dictated by the socially necessary labor time; finally, they can be fired by interrupting the subcontract.

I think that it is the current proliferation of new hybrid forms of subsumption that allows us to analyze the many temporalities that constitute the whole career of the capitalist mode of production.

Forms of Subsumption and their Temporalities

I would like to raise the following question: What is the *form* in which many different modes of exploitation work together within the capitalist global market? As we have seen already, Marx's definition of capitalist production as an *inversion* can be useful to define the essence of capitalism. In this broader conception of the capitalist form of production, *formal subsumption* can be defined as the basis of capitalist production, that is to say, the production of surplus value in a process whose end is the production of commodities for the market; *real subsumption* incorporates previous social relations of production into the capitalist framework; it revolutionizes the technical processes of production and the configuration of social groups.[10] *Formal subsumption* and *real subsumption* coexist from the very beginning, since the subsumption of existing forms of production into the global market changes both the end of production and social and property relationships.

A rarely studied third form, the *hybrid* or "intermediate forms (*Zwitterformen*) of subsumption,*" can also be discussed in addition to *formal* and *real subsumption*.[11] It can help us to clarify the combination of different forms of exploitations. Marx speaks of the hybrid forms of subsumption for the first time in *Capital*. According to Marx, prima facie these types *of subsumption* are forms of transition to capitalism. He stressed that in these forms, surplus labor is not extorted by direct compulsion from the producer: "The producer has not yet become formally subordinate to capital," mentioning both usurer and merchant capital.[12] However, another, more interesting dimension of the hybrid forms is discussed in *Capital*: "As in the case of modern domestic industry, certain hybrid forms *are reproduced* here and there against the background of large-scale industry, though their physiognomy is totally changed."[13] Here, surplus labor is extracted from these forms by means of direct coercion.

Although the hybrid forms are not "formally" subsumed to capital and are not conditioned by wage labor, they fall under the command of capital. This allows us to comprehend the contemporaneity of seemingly anachronistic forms such as slavery and other hierarchical forms of domination, which are not mere residues of past epochs but forms that, though with an altered physiognomy, are produced and reproduced in the background of the *current* capitalist mode of production. Capitalism encounters preexisting forms of production and it "encounters them as antecedents, but not as antecedents established by itself, not as forms of its own life process."[14] Capital subsumes and reconfigures them in a new framework. The result, as Harry Harootunian points out, is a "heterogeneous mix" of temporalities and forms of life and production.[15] Capital comes into conflict with the preexisting forms of life because, by reconfiguring them, it tends to synchronize their different temporalities to the rhythm of socially necessary labor-time. This violence on the preexisting forms generates new friction and tension.

The productive power of socially necessary labor is enforced in the world market and imposes its own temporality, synchronizing the different forms of production; for instance, the patriarchal command and the whip of the slave driver intervene continually in order to synchronize that particular labor with the universal chronometer marked by the temporality of socially necessary labor. If "the place of the slave-driver's lash is taken by the over-looker's book of penalties," then these different forms of command also exist alongside each other and constitute a single time, in which the law of value is enforced in the work market.[16] As soon as seemingly anachronistic forms of labor such as slavery or the *corvè* "are drawn into the whirlpool of an international market dominated by the capitalistic mode of production . . . the civilized horrors of overwork are grafted on the barbaric horrors of slavery, serfdom, etc."[17] The subsumption of different social and productive forms within the capitalist *form* occurs when they begin to produce commodities for the world market instead of use-values for the needs of the community. In this same moment, they are incorporated into the global capitalist market. Although labor apparently remains within the same brutal form of subjection, command overpowers labor, changing its inherent nature. The law of valorization requires every single producer to employ either "social average labor" or labor of an intensity superior to that of socially necessary labor—where the resistance is hindered or the economic and extra-economic violence of the system enables it. As anything but a residual form of labor, slave labor is thus presented as a possibility for augmenting the intensity of labor and guaranteeing absolute surplus value to capital masses. Marx observed that, upon entering into the world market—that is, when the export of cotton was viable for the world market—the overworking of slave labor in the American plantation became a factor in a "calculated and calculating system."[18] Slavery became modern when the labor of slaves was directed to the production of commodities for the world market.[19] As Dale Tomich stated, the "world market and division of labor are not just the background for slavery in the Americas but the historical conditions of the existence of this particular form of production."[20] From the time that the productivity of labor had to be measured on the global stock market, labor-time was intensified and rendered as little porous as possible. What we are interested in pointing out is that slavery is formally subsumed to capital when it becomes "part of the organization of social labor on a world scale."[21] That is, when production becomes production of commodities for the world market and socially necessary labor-time asserts iteself as normative of productivity and the intensity of work done by non-waged slaves. Slavery was not abandoned because it was not sufficiently efficient and productive. Slavery was often more efficient than free labor. Indeed, slavery "transformed the southern states into the dominant force in the global cotton market, and cotton was the world's most widely traded commodity at the time, as it was the key raw material during the first century of the industrial revolution"[22] Abolitionists all over the world, as investors, could "share in revenues made by hands in the field. Thus, in effect, even as Britain was liberating the slaves of its empire, a British bank could now sell an investor a completely commodified slave."[23]

Slavery, subsumed in the capitalist mode of production inasmuch as it becomes labor destined for world commerce, takes on a new form in which the *rhythm* and *intensity* of labor are regulated by the pace of the socially necessary labor-time. Insofar as forms of slave labor enter the world market, they can no longer be considered as being remains of former times. The network of the world market supports various forms of exploitation by simultaneously combining them.

Asynchronisms and the Paths of Emancipation

The world market began in the seventeenth century with colonies and slavery. Its creation included new forms of wage, non-wage, and slave labor, giving rise, in the eighteenth century, to a new assortment of forms of waged and non-waged labor.[24] The preexisting forms of organization of labor were not destroyed, but were reshaped into a new constellation of political and economic powers. Understanding interwoven pluralities of temporal layers in the same historical dimension of modernity requires a historiography able to incorporate plural, spatial, and temporal relations within new causal models.

Historically, capital encounters a large spectrum of differences of gender, religion, and ethnicity, as well as differences generated by racism. Capital is able to use these differences for its own profit in order to differentiate wages and intensities of exploitation, thereby dividing the working class. These differences and hierarchies are understood to predate capitalism; however, as soon as capital subsumes them, they are reconfigured and reshaped. Capital uses these differences and hierarchies, but in order to subsume them they "must first be destroyed as independent forms and subordinated to industrial capital"[25] through economic and extra-economic violence. Those differences are neither historical invariants nor pure products of capitalism. Instead, already existing differences and practices are located in a different temporality and, even when they are reshaped and reorganized by capital, they can appear with the physiognomy of traditional hierarchical relationships. While subsuming these differences and converting them into dimensions of its own life-process, capital cannot prevent them from also appearing as nonsynchronisms that, when confronted with the dominant capitalist temporality, can disclose both emancipatory and reactionary possibilities. And sometimes these two sides are interwoven. The historical analysis that Marx made in *Capital* should be reinterpreted in light of a historiographical paradigm capable of contemplating a plurality of historical times that, like geological layers, are present at the same time and, in their movement, create friction and tension that can bring back to the surface that which is not otherwise visible.

Historically, if capitalists make use of formally free workers it is because they encounter them as a result of a different temporality: in Europe, as a result of the struggles against feudal subjugation. The freedom of the "new freedmen" was and is open to different possibilities: on the side of subjectivity, it is the result of the numerous struggles of the servants to free themselves from slavery and escape the dominion of corporations and guilds. On the side of the rising capitalist mode of production, in Europe, that freedom was formally subsumed into a new apparatus of domination and control: the "new freedman" was stripped of the means of production, even deprived of the guarantees offered by the feudal system, and finally forced to sell his labor power and ordered to do so through the "bloody legislation" against vagabonds who were trying to evade the new capitalist order of labor. Marx shows some of these measures aimed at realigning in spirit and body the new labor force: "whipping and imprisonment for sturdy vagabonds. They are to be tied to the cart-tail and whipped until the blood streams from their bodies, then to swear an oath to go back to their birthplace or to where they have lived the last three years and to 'put themselves to labour'.... For the second arrest for vagabondage the whipping is to be repeated and half the ear sliced off; but for the third relapse the offender is to be executed as a hardened criminal and enemy of the common weal."[26] The end of the English legislation during the sixteenth and seventeenth centuries was the discipline of the labor force, even through slavery, which was one essential component of capitalistic accumulation. Indeed, slavery was not an anomalous case in the colony but rather was a violent answer, to discipline and control the mobility of living labor on the market.[27] In the late 1590s the English parliament introduced a law to control the poor. "Tinkers, gypsies, begging scholars, palm readers, wandering musicians and actors were all defined as vagabonds. . . . Among the punishments was transportation."[28] The history of the emerging freedom of new formally free workers is intertwined with new forms of enslavement in the rising capitalist mode of production.

However, the freedom obtained by the new freedmen at the cost of hard struggles could have taken another trajectory. Indeed, besides the trajectory of private property and the modern state, on whose path there arise such names as Cromwell and the Le Chapelier law against corporations, other trajectories were possible. Along these alternative trajectories commons and associations are articulated. The transformation of feudal exploitation into capitalist exploitation is not a necessary historical outcome. The legal, political, and economic materials of the Middle Ages could have been configured in a way quite different from that formed by capitalist modernity. The Marxian chapter on accumulation shows the elements in play as if they were different temporalities combined and then synchronized into the capitalist mode of production.

The question of how to reconsider history, recounted in the chapter on accumulation, came to Marx from Russia. On February 16, 1881, Vera Zasulich posed Marx an important question, which probably gave him some troubles. She wrote: "Honored Citizen, you are not unaware that your *Capital* enjoys great popularity in Russia. . . . Nowadays, we often hear it said that the rural commune is an archaic form condemned to perish by history, scientific socialism and, in short, everything above debate. Those who preach such a view call themselves your disciples par excellence: 'Marksists'. . . . So you will understand, Citizen, how interested we are in Your opinion. You would be doing us a very great favor if you were to set forth your ideas on the possible fate of our rural commune, and on the theory that it is historically necessary for every country in the world to pass through all the phases of capitalist production."[29] Marx's agreement was with the populists instead of the "Marksists." Russia, he wrote, is not obliged to pass through the "fatal dissolution of the Russian peasants' commune," which can instead become "an element of collective production on a nationwide scale."[30] Displaying the persistence of noncapitalist communities that existed at the same time as capitalist production, Marx delineates the possibility of a new regime of combination of historical times. He urges a new historiographical paradigm: "The history of the decline of primitive communities (it would be a mistake to place them all on the same level; as in geological formations, these historical forms contain a whole series of primary, secondary, tertiary types, etc.) has still to be written."[31] The dissolution of common property and the spread of private property are not the necessary outcome of a historical development; different configurations of the secondary might and can arise from the primary. Different temporal layers coexist at the same time, combine and conflict with each other. There is no guaranteed outcome from this interweaving of temporalities. Just as, conversely, not even the outcome of capitalist modernity from the elements that formed its basis was guaranteed. From this perspective it is possible to reread the chapter on primitive accumulation.

The original constellation of so-called capitalist accumulation, read without the teleology of history, *does not* show a linear path from feudalism to capitalist modernity, but a mass of trajectories open to different outcomes. Various events intermixed, through the systematic use of extra-economic violence, in a war of private property against "communal property (*Gemeindeeigentum*)."[32] In his later years, Marx would become extremely interested in the changes in communal property in the Russian and extra-European contexts, which he learned from his dialogue with Maxim Kovalevsky.[33] In his comments to Kovalevsky, just as in his ethnological writings,[34] Marx presents history with many possible levels and trajectories.[35] The dissolution of community property gave different outcomes in different economic, political, and social contexts, so that European development ceases to be normative and, indeed, can be better understood from an extra-European perspective. In fact, Marx criticizes Kovalevsky for having found "European-western feudalism" in Indian community relations.[36] In this way, for Marx, and contrary to what he had supported, for example, in the *Grundrisse*, "feudalism" ceased to be a category applicable to all historical and geographical contexts.[37]

"Communal property" was not and is not destined for dissolution in the forms of modern European private property. It might and can be configured in forms different from those followed by the trajectory of dominant Western civilization. To cite one example of this, in the European context, in England, "common rights" and "common grazing" defended by the Diggers came into conflict with the *enclosures*.[38] The conflict between collective forms of property and its individualization could have had different outcomes. If Hobbes and Locke are celebrated in the official canon of political thought among theoreticians of the state and modern possessive individualism, Winstanley and the Diggers are the representatives of the alternative canon of countless practical and theoretical uprisings against private property.

Marx follows the long war against the commons through Kovalevsky's studies, which describe it in terms of the transition from common ownership by the community to its dissolution and "individualization" into individual private property.[39] The process of "individualization" is twofold: on the one hand, it concerns the transformation of common property from "inalienable" into privately owned and traded property, on the other hand, the transformation of relations between members of the community into relations between atomized individuals and competitors. This war against the collective required the constant intervention of extra-economic violence from the state, of countless "Acts for enclosures of Commons, in other words, decrees by which the landlords grant themselves the people's land as private property, decrees of expropriation of the people."[40] This war still continues today against collective forms of property and association. Marx describes how during the French Revolution this conflict passed through the Le Chapelier law, whose Article IV declared that if "citizens belonging to the same profession, craft or trade have joint discussions and make joint decisions with the intention of refusing together to perform their trade or insisting together on providing the services of their trade or their labours only at a particular price, then the said deliberations and agreements . . . shall be declared unconstitutional, derogatory to liberty and the declaration of the rights of man, etc."[41] The workers' associations were banned inasmuch as they were seen as an attempt to restore the old feudal corporations. This is why they were fought against in the name of human rights. But during the Revolution, associations and co-operatives did not represent a form of nostalgia for feudal privileges, but rather were reactivated by the radical exponents of the Sansculottes, who tried to reinvent the associations in a new form, the sovereign rights of the citizens' assemblies and the binding mandate, thereby undermining the concept, shared by both the Girondins and the Jacobins, of national unity and its representation. These associative and communal traditions were later reactivated during the Paris Commune and in the experiments of the workers' councils of the twentieth century.

The reactivation of seemingly secondary traditions, yet still vital in community life forms, triggers a conflict between temporalities providing energy to resist the violence of capitalist modernity and redirect its course. Social, political, and economic conflicts are also conflicts between times, and anachronisms are the fuse that is able to activate new configurations of common life. But if the friction between layers of time causes tension and conflicts, then the anachronisms point out possible directions and solutions. That is what Mariátegui gathers when he combines the socialist project in Latin America with the forms of archaic Inca communal organization, which can disclose a different, noncapitalist trajectory to the present.[42] Without having read Marx's letter to Zasulich, Mariátegui draws a parallel between the Russian and the Peruvian community and, like Marx, addresses the possibility of the political use of anachronisms. "I consider," writes Mariátegui, "that our agrarian problem has a special character due to an indisputable and concrete factor: the survival of the Indian 'community' and of elements of practical socialism in indigenous agriculture and life."[43] The archaic, being contemporary, is not condemned to die, but can be combined with the temporality of the working-class struggles, thus giving rise to a new social formation that is alternative to capitalist modernity. In other words, there is future that is still encapsulated in the past and can be freed from the contemporaneity of the archaic in constellation with other temporalities. Wherever and whenever existing forms come into contact and conflict with capitalist modernity, the result is a proliferation of temporalities and conflicting asynchronisms. In this clash of temporalities the archaic is no longer such, but rather it releases possibilities of emancipation and reorientation of the trajectories of modern civilization.

This idea escapes romanticist criticism only if one abandons the unilinear paradigm of historical time that reads everything in terms of before and after, backward, residual, and advanced. Instead, we must understand history as a vertical stratification of temporalities that can be reactivated in the present. Formal subsumption incorporates a heterogeneous mix of forms of life and temporalities that continue to conflict with each other. In these conflicts the archaic, like asynchronous time, can generate a reactionary configuration, as happened in Nazism,[44] or it can display a different trajectory for the present, the way Mariátegui tried, by combining socialism and Incan communism.

Notes

1. Tomba, "Pre-Capitalistic Forms of Production and Primitive Accumulation."
2. Harootunian, *Marx after Marx*, 206.
3. Marx, *Capital*, 434.

4. Ibid., 436.

5. Marx, *Ökonomisches Manuskripte 1861–1863*, 323.

6. Marx, *Capital*, 530.

7. Marini, *Dialéctica de la dependencia*, 8–10; Dussel and Yáñez, "Marx's Economic Manuscript of 1861–63 and the "Concept" of Dependency."

8. Tomba, "Differentials of Surplus-Value in the Contemporary Forms of Exploitation."

9. Marx, *Capital*, 511.

10. Ibid., 645.

11. Ibid., 511; Murray, "The Social and Material Transformation of Production by Capital: Formal and Real Subsumption in *Capital, Volume 1*."

12. Marx, *Capital*, 511.

13. Ibid., 511.

14. Karl Marx, *Theories of Surplus Value*, 468.

15. Harootunian, *Marx after Marx*, 27.

16. Marx, *Capital*, 427.

17. Ibid., 244.

18. Ibid., 244.

19. Benot, *La modernité de l'esclavage*, 123 and 162.

20. Tomich, *Slavery in the Circuit of Sugar*, 3–4.

21. Ibid., 5.

22. Baptist, *The Half Has Never Been Told*, 29.

23. Ibid., 422

24. Tomich, *Through the Prism of Slavery*, 97 and 118; Linden van der, "Plädoyer für eine historische Neubestimmung der Welt-Arbeiterklasse."

25. Marx, *Theories of Surplus Value*, 1496.

26. Marx, *Capital*, 723–24.

27. Boutang, *De l'esclavage au salariat*, 158.

28. Jordan and Walsh, *White Cargo*, 30.

29. Shanin, *Late Marxism and the Russian Road*, 98–99.

30. Marx, "Drafts of the Letter to Vera Zasulich," 349.

31. Marx, "Drafts of the Letter to Vera Zasulich," 358.

32. Marx, *Capital*, 714.

33. Harstick, Karl Marx über Formen vorkapitalistischer Produktion.

34. Krader, *The Ethnological Notebooks of Karl Marx*.

35. Anderson, *Marx at the Margins*.

36. Harstick, *Karl Marx über Formen vorkapitalistischer Produktion*, 76.

37. Tomba, "Pre-Capitalistic Forms of Production and Primitive Accumulation. Marx's Historiography from the *Grundrisse* to *Capital*."

38. Thirsk, "Enclosing and Engrossing," 200.

39. Harstick, *Karl Marx über Formen vorkapitalistischer Produktion*, 57–58.

40. Marx, *Capital*, 715.

41. Ibid., 730.
42. Mariátegui, "On the Indigenous Problem," 150.
43. Mariátegui, *Seven Interpretative Essays*, 33.
44. Bloch, "Nonsynchronism and the Obligation to Its Dialectics."

Works Cited

Anderson, Kevin. *Marx at the Margins: On Nationalism, Ethnicity, and Non-Western Societies*. Chicago and London: University of Chicago Press, 2010.

Baptist, Edward E. *The Half Has Never Been Told. Slavery and the Making of American Capitalism*. New York: Basic Books, 2014.

Benot, Yves. *La modernité de l'esclavage. Essai sur la servitude au coeur du capitalisme*. Paris: Éditions La Découverte, 2003.

Blick, Peter. *Die revolution von 1525*. München: Oldenbourg Verlag, 2004.

Bloch, Ernst. "Nonsynchronism and the Obligation to Its Dialectics." *New German Critique* no. 11 (1977): 22–38.

Boutang, Yann Moulier. *De l'esclavage au salariat. Economie historique du salariat bridé*. Paris: PUF, 1998.

Dussel, Enrique and Augustín Yáñez. "Marx's Economic Manuscript of 1861–63 and the 'Concept' of Dependency." *Latin American Perspectives* 17 (1990): 62–101.

Harootunian, Harry. *Marx after Marx. History and Time in the Expansion of Capitalism*. New York: Columbia University Press, 2015.

Harstick, Hans-Peter. *Karl Marx über Formen vorkapitalistischer Produktion. Vergleichende Studien zur Geschichte des Grundeigentums 1879–80. Aus dem handschriften Nachlaß*. Frankfurt-New York: Campus Verlag, 1977.

Jordan, Don, and Michael Walsh. *White Cargo. The Forgotten History of Britain's White Slaves in America*. New York: New York University Press, 2008.

Krader, Lawrence, ed. *The Ethnological Notebooks of Karl Marx: Studies of Morgan, Phear, Maine, Lubbock*. Assen: Van Gorcum, 1972.

Linden van der, Marcel. "Plädoyer für eine historische Neubestimmung der Welt-Arebeiterklasse." *Social Geschichte* no. 20 (2005): 7–28.

———. "Warum gab (und gibt) es Sklaverei im Kapitalismus? Eine einfache und dennoch schwer zu beantwortende Frage." In *Unfreie Arbeit. Ökonomische und kulturgeschichtliche Perspektiven*, edited by M. Erdem Kabadayi and Tobias Reichardt, 260–79. Hilesheim: Georg Olms Verlag, 2007.

Mariátegui, José Carlos. *Seven Interpretative Essays on Peruvian Reality*. Translated by Marjory Urquidi. Austin: University of Texas Press, 1971.

———. "On the Indigenous Problem." In *José Carlos Mari Mariátegui: An Anthology*, edited and translated by Harry E. Vanden and Marc Becker, 145–50. New York: Monthly Review Press, 2011.

Marini, Ruy Mauro. *Dialéctica de la dependencia*. México: Ediciones Era, 1991.

Marx, Karl. "Results of the Immediate Production Process." In *Capital*, Vol. I, 949–1084. Translated by Ben Fowkes. New York: Penguin, 1990.

———. *Capital*, volume 1, *Marx Engels Collected Works*, Vol. 35. London: Lawrence and Wishart, 1983.

———. "Drafts of the Letter to Vera Zasulich." In *Marx Engels Collected Works*, Vol. 24, 346–69. London: Lawrence and Wishart, 1989.

———. *Ökonomisches Manuskripte 1861–1863. Marx Engels Werke*, Vol. 43. Berlin: Dietz Verlag. 1990.

———. *Theories of Surplus Value*. Amherst, NY: Prometheus, 1990.

Murray, Patrick. "The Social and Material Transformation of Production by Capital: Formal and Real Subsumption in *Capital, Volume 1*." In *Capital, The Constitution of Capital: Essays on Volume I of Marx's "Capital*," edited by Riccardo Bellofiore and Nicola Taylor, 243–72. Basingstoke: Palgrave Macmillan, 2004.

Shanin, Teodor, ed. *Late Marxism and the Russian Road: Marx and "the Peripheries of Capitalism."* New York: Monthly Review Press, 1983.

Shaw, William H. "Marx and Morgan." *History and Theory* 23, no. 2 (1984): 215–28.

Thirsk, Joan. "Enclosing and Engrossing." In *The Agrarian History of England and Wales*, volume IV 1500–1640, edited by Joan Thirsk, 200–55. Cambridge: Cambridge University Press, 1967.

Tomba, Massimiliano. "Differentials of Surplus-Value in the Contemporary Forms of Exploitation." *The Commoner* no. 12 (2007): 23–37.

———. "Pre-Capitalistic Forms of Production and Primitive Accumulation. Marx's Historiography from the *Grundrisse* to *Capital*." In *In Marx's Laboratory: Critical Interpretations of the* Grundrisse, edited by Riccardo Bellofiore, Guido Starosta, and Peter D. Thomas, 393–411. Leiden and Boston: Brill, 2013.

———. *Marx's Temporalities*. Leiden: Brill, 2013.

Tomich, Dale. *Slavery in the Circuit of Sugar*. Baltimore and London: The Johns Hopkins University Press, 1990.

———. *Through the Prism of Slavery. Labor, Capital, and World Economy*. Lanham, MD: Rowman and Littlefield, 2004.

CHAPTER TWO

"I am he": A History of Dispossession's Not-Yet-Present in Colonial Yucatán

DAVID KAZANJIAN

AS "DISPOSSESSION" HAS BECOME an increasingly pervasive scholarly and activist concept in recent years, it has at times furthered a powerful, foundationalist presupposition: namely, that the dispossessed had prior possession over that which was taken from them by their dispossessors (their land, their labor, or their very bodies). When theories of dispossession claim or implicitly presume that the dispossessed previously owned that of which they were dispossessed, they certainly offer a strong moral basis for a critique of dispossession. Yet in studying cases of dispossession from what Marxists would call the era of so-called primitive or originary accumulation in the Americas, I have found that the dispossessed at times did not claim that they owned their land or their labor or their bodies prior to being dispossessed, and thus did not always respond to dispossession by seeking the return of their putatively prior possessions. In these instances, the dispossessed seem to have had quite different theories of dispossession, which is also to say they practiced different antidispossessive politics, than would follow from the presumption of prior possession—a politics set against possession as such.[1]

In this paper, I identify some of the conditions of possibility and impossibility for contemporary theories of dispossession that presume prior possession. I then examine a case of dispossession from late-seventeenth-century Yucatán in which an enslaved Afro-Yucatecan named Juan Patricio was accused of beating up a priest named don Ignacio de Esquivel to stop the priest from forcing a Maya girl named Fabiana Pech into service for his mother, doña Isabel de Solís. From the records of the case, both Juan Patricio and Fabiana Pech can be seen to proffer critiques of dispossession that do not presume prior possession. Consequently, Juan Patricio and Fabiana Pech help us to chart what I will call a history of the not-yet-present of our own antidispossessive politics.

From Originary Accumulation to Dispossession

The *locus classicus* for accounts of dispossession is Part 8 of Marx's *Capital*, vol. 1, entitled "So-Called Primitive Accumulation," or perhaps better translated "So-Called Originary Accumulation [*Die sogenannte ursprüngliche Akkumulation*]." This section of *Capital* sets out to explain how it came to be that a small class of people owned most of the world's wealth, leaving the rest of the people with nothing to do but work for that small class of wealth owners. Marx examines a period stretching from the fifteenth century through the eighteenth century during which land, labor, bodies, and lives were expropriated from rural, black, poor, and indigenous people throughout the globe by the agents of capitalism's rise, through the violence of colonization, slavery, and enclosure, as well as the legalization of that violence by way of the criminalization of the poverty it caused (vagabondage, petty theft, "idolness"). As many contemporary scholars of dispossession have insisted, that process did not end in the eighteenth century, but continues to this day in the form of an ongoing "accumulation by dispossession."[2] In this insistence, they renew earlier arguments about the ongoing character of so-called originary accumulation formulated by the likes of Peter Kropotkin, Rosa Luxemburg, and W. E. B. DuBois in the nineteenth and early twentieth centuries, and in schools of thought such as dependency theory, world-system theory, South Asian and Latin American subaltern studies, black radicalism, and Native American studies in the twentieth and twenty-first centuries.

Indeed, Marx himself implicitly gets at that ongoing character of accumulation by dispossession with the very title of *Capital*'s Part 8: the sarcastic "so-called," *sogenannte*. Like all of the terms Marx uses in *Capital*, "primitive" or "originary accumulation" is not his term, but is borrowed directly from the classical or bourgeois political economists whom he is critiquing. His critical method always involves taking up such terms, elaborating how they function in the discourse of the political economists, salvaging anything that might be useful in them, and debunking everything in them that is wrong or does not make sense—and he makes clear in Part 8 that there is very little to salvage from the particular term *originary accumulation*. Hence, the "so-called" of the title. As he famously writes:

> This originary accumulation . . . is supposed to be explained when it is told as an anecdote of the past. In times long gone by there were two sorts of people; one, the diligent, intelligent, and, above all, frugal elite; the other, lazy rascals, spending their substance, and more in riotous living. . . . Thus it came to pass that the former sort accumulated wealth, and the latter sort had nothing to sell except their own skins. . . . And from this original sin dates the poverty of the great majority that, despite all its labour, has up to now nothing to sell but itself, and the wealth of the few that increases constantly although they have long ceased to work. Such insipid childishness is everyday preached to us in defence of property. . . . As a matter of fact, the methods of originary accumulation are anything but idyllic.[3]

Marxists usually focus on his argument that so-called originary accumulation is not "idyllic" because it was originarily violent and brutal. But from this famous passage we can also see that another reason why so-called originary accumulation was not idyllic is that it was not, in fact, "of the past," that it did not happen "in times long gone by." The conditions of his own nineteenth-century present, he goes on to show, are thoroughly structured by a massive extraction of wealth from people and places that began in the fifteenth century. What the bourgeois political economists call "originary accumulation," then, is not over at all; it is part of Marx's present. We see him make this point even more directly in other places, such as his 1877 letter to Nikolay Mikhaylovsky, where he explains that "so-called originary accumulation" is also not a stage that every country has to pass through for capitalism to arise and, in turn, for socialism and communism to replace capitalism.[4] Just because England enclosed the commons between the sixteenth and nineteenth centuries in the ways he describes in Part 8, this does not mean that Russian peasant communes of the nineteenth century need to be destroyed and converted into private property so that they can eventually become truly communist entities. That is, peasants do not need to first become proletarians in Russia for capitalism to emerge and then be defeated; in fact, one ought to oppose the methods of so-called originary accumulation whenever they occur, as they indeed occur all the time.[5]

Still, despite this long history of critics—starting with Marx—understanding that dispossession was not a historically isolated event, but rather is an ongoing structure inherent to capitalism as such, some contemporary scholars and activists still build into their accounts of dispossession a trace of what Marx calls the "idyllic." Specifically, such accounts often contain a foundationalist presupposition: *that those who were dispossessed previously owned what was stolen from them and, for that reason, that they sought or should seek to get those prior possessions back.*[6] We find this presupposition in Pierre-Joseph Proudhon's slogan "property is theft," which he famously declared in 1840 in his text *What Is Property?*[7] Marx isolated the problem with this formulation in an 1865 letter to J. B. Schweizer, which was published in *Der Social-Demokrat*, and later as an appendix to *The Poverty of Philosophy* (whose title is itself a play on Proudhon's book *The System of Economic Contradictions, or The Philosophy of Poverty*): "The upshot is at best that the bourgeois legal conceptions of *'theft'* apply equally well to the *'honest'* gains of the bourgeois himself. On the other hand, since *'theft'* as a forcible violation of property *presupposes the existence of property*, Proudhon entangled himself in all sorts of fantasies, obscure even to himself, about *true bourgeois property*."[8] Marx here suggests that the notion of property theft entails a kind of tautology. How can property be considered "theft," if "theft" itself presupposes prior ownership over what was stolen, without then implying that all prior possessions were also once thefts? And if all prior possessions were once thefts, there would seem to be no precise way to differentiate one theft from another; theft itself would then appear to be as necessary or natural as property, and both would appear to be structurally "idyllic."

Despite this critique and his professed disdain for the "idyllic," Marx himself at times reproduced Proudhon's presupposition. He most often used the words *Enteignung*, typically translated as "expropriation," and *Aneignung*, typically translated as "usurpation" or "appropriation," to name what we now more often call "dispossession." However, Marx also used *Raub* [robbery] and *Diebstahl* [theft].[9] Indeed, even in the passage quoted above from Part 8 of *Capital*, Marx describes the dispossessed as having "nothing to sell except their own skins" and "nothing to sell but itself," with the words *own* and *itself* seemingly pointing to prior or foundational self-possession.[10] And still today critics often speak of dispossession as a kind of theft of the previously owned, with Peter Linebaugh's compelling book *Stop, Thief! The Commons, Enclosures, and Resistance* offering just one recent example.[11]

The foundationalist presupposition of theories of dispossession operates simultaneously on two levels: on the level of subjectivity, or a subject's relationship to themself, and on the level of a subject's relationship to land. In the first instance, subjects are presumed to own themselves, their bodies, or their labor before dispossession, and thus to seek the return of those stolen elements of their selves. In the second instance, land is presumably possessed by individuals or by collectivities, either by right or custom, as property or as commons, such that antidispossessive politics ought to seek the return of that land to the individuals or collectivities from which it was stolen. However, these presuppositions often do not specify in what sense subjects can be said to have previously owned themselves or their land, and thus fail to consider the political implications of imputing prior possession; as Marx put it in the passage on Proudhon above, "since '*theft*' as a forcible violation of property *presupposes the existence of property*."[12] So how might we understand dispossession as the taking of what was not always previously "possessed"?

Much scholarship amplifies these concerns. On the level of subjectivity, for instance, C. B. MacPherson argues that possessive individualism, or one's presumptive ownership of oneself as an autonomous and self-sufficient subject with a will capable of enacting its desires, was an effect of the rise of capitalism rather than a foundational precondition for the theft of labor and bodies from autonomous individuals.[13] For enslaved Afro-diasporans in the United States, Saidiya Hartman has shown us how the achievement of formal emancipation—or the presumptive ownership of one's self—did not alleviate the dispossessive forces of racial capitalism, and in fact entrenched crucial elements of that system by imputing liberal, racialized forms of freedom to the formally enslaved.[14] Relatedly, contemporary theories of the subject ask us to confront constitutive dispossessions that form the basis for subjectivity as such. For instance, as Athena Athanasiou has argued in her dialogue with Judith Butler, dispossession names not only "processes and ideologies by which persons are disowned and abjected by normative and normalizing powers that define cultural intelligibility and that regulate the distribution of vulnerability: loss of land and community; ownership of one's living body by another person, as in histories of slavery, subjection to military, imperial, and economic violence; poverty, securitarian regimes, biopolitical subjectivation, liberal possessive individualism, neoliberal governmentality, and precaritization."[15] The concept also names "a limit to the autonomous and impermeable self-sufficiency of the liberal subject through its injurious yet enabling fundamental dependency and relationality" such that "avowing the trace of primary passions and losses—as one's psychic and social attachment to the law that determines one's disposition to alterity—is a necessary condition of the subject's survival."[16] By both affirming the injustice of dispossession and insisting on the subject's formative relationship to alterity, or lack of absolute self-possession, Athanasiou and Butler question any presumption of a prior or foundational subjective propriety as a necessary condition for a critique of or challenge to dispossession.

On the level of land, it ought not surprise us that the vast diversity of indigenous communities across the Americas maintained diverse and changeable relationships to land, even as any contemporary understanding of those relationships is caught in the irreducible conflict between ongoing indigenous knowledges and European accounts saturated with colonizing interests. For instance, before European colonization the relatively strict social hierarchies of the Nahua people in what would become central Mexico seem to have generated geographies codified under the Aztec empire into rural and urban zones, in which elites and commoners were tied by relations of taxation, tribute, and exchange.[17] By contrast, the less imperial and urbanized Algonquian language communities in what would become New England seem to have maintained more flexible ties to their geographies.[18] There are countless other examples to consider in the vibrant range of the indigenous Americas. So while there were indigenous conceptions of ownership in parts of the Americas, even before the conquest, we can still say that some indigenous communities did not understand land as something that could be individually or privately owned, in the way colonizers understood such ownership. Indeed, a key tactic of colonial dispossession was the imputation of ownership on the colonizers' terms to colonized people, so as to facilitate the codification of dispossession through tactics such as treaties and land purchases. These tactics, as Glen Coulthard has shown, continue to structure even some indigenous efforts to redress dispossession.[19] Less often remarked but still important to any critique of such dispossession are the ways indigenous people at times appropriated land from other indigenous people, both before colonization and after, under pressure from settler colonials' appropriations.[20]

The relatively recent wave of celebrating the commons and so-called commoning as anticapitalist would seem to resolve the tautology of "property is theft" by claiming that, prior to colonization and/or the rise of capitalism proper, land was held "in common" by rural and indigenous people, until capitalists expropriated and enclosed the commons and converted them into private property. However, as Allan Greer has shown, in the Americas, European commons were imposed upon indigenous land, and so "commoning" functioned as an essential tactic of settler colonization rather than a prior practice of anti/non/pre-capitalism.[21] While some indigenous people certainly had their own common relationships to land prior to European colonization, currently existing systems of indigenous commoning blend precolonial and colonial social and economic relations. For instance, the *ejido* system in Mexico gives indigenous communities a certain measure of control over land, and has at times antagonized dispossession or even functioned as an active challenge to it. However, the very word *ejido* comes from a medieval and early modern Iberian practice of commoning, which should remind us that Spanish colonizers imposed their understandings of humans-in-space upon the Americas and its colonized people, leading those people to adapt and repurpose such understandings in their own interests rather than simply to defend some idyllic, prepossessive understanding of the land. Indigenous commons like the *ejido* are not simply precolonial remnants any more than they are merely imperial impositions. Rather, they represent ongoing efforts by indigenous people to repurpose social relationships to the land in the face of, and often within the very idiom of, capitalist dispossession.[22]

This rich range of subjective relationships to selves and social relationships to land troubles any presupposition that the colonized and enslaved owned their lands or their selves in strictly determinable or generalizable ways prior to dispossession. Consequently, theories of dispossession that implicitly or explicitly make such a presumption not only risk reproducing the tautology of "property is theft," they also fail to consider the dynamic forces of dispossession as well as the diverse and often dexterous responses to it by the dispossessed.

Juan Patricio

The archives of dispossession from North America during the late seventeenth and early eighteenth centuries—in the midst of the era of so-called originary accumulation—often do not square with the presumptions of prior propriety embedded in contemporary theories of dispossession that hue to the "property is theft" argument. Which is to say, one does not always find the dispossessed claiming prior possession or seeking the return of that which was stolen from them. Consequently, they prompt us to understand what theft without prior propriety might entail, as well as how challenges to dispossession might evade the entrenchment of propriety as such.

Consider one such case from Yucatán in the 1690s. The record of this case is contained in a *legajo* in the Archivo de Indias in Seville, and is entitled "Complusa de autos criminales seguidos por Doña Ysabel Solis, vecina de Yucatan, contra Juan Patricio esclavo, sobre haber apaleado à Don Ygnacio de Esquivel, clerigo: Año de 1696."[23] It involves a complicated cast of characters: at the center is an enslaved thirty-two-year-old black man named Juan Patricio, residing in Yucatán but previously from Santo Domingo, who was charged by a Creole woman named doña Isabel de Solís with beating her son, the priest don Ignacio de Esquivel, for taking a Maya girl named Fabiana Pech from the *encomienda* of Juan Patricio's master, don Pedro Enríquez de Noboa. It seems that in mid-August of 1690, the priest Esquivel sent at least two Maya "*tupiles*," or deputies, to the village of Tahmek in north-central Yucatán to take possession of Pech with the intention of bringing her to the city of Mérida to work as a domestic servant for his mother, Solís. However, Pech's Maya village was controlled by Enriquez de Noboa, who seems not to have known about the priest's plans for Pech. The Maya who were under the control of this *encomendero* in this region were not his slaves, like Juan Patricio was, in that by 1690 the Spanish Crown had long understood Indians throughout the Americas to be free humans and potential Christians with a host of rights and privileges. But these Maya were bound to follow their *encomendero*'s orders within certain well-defined limits. Although Juan Patricio *was* enslaved to Enriquez de Noboa, he was also an overseer of some of his masters' ventures, including his Maya laborers—a role that was common enough for Afro-Yucatecans that one historian has called them "the black middle" for the mediation they performed between Creoles and Maya.[24]

Indeed, according to Juan Patricio's testimony he was the one who first discovered Esquivel's deputies trying to take Pech away. He testifies that he ran into them by chance on the road from Tahmek to Mérida as he was going to check on the work some Maya masons were doing for his master.[25] He says he stopped the deputies from taking Pech by arguing with them and eventually striking them with a stick and driving them away. After this conflict, Juan Patricio told his master about Esquivel's effort to take Pech, while the deputies told Esquivel about Juan Patricio's efforts to thwart them. Esquivel was apparently angry that Juan Patricio intervened in his plan for Pech, and summoned Juan Patricio to speak with him. Juan Patricio did go to the priest, but not immediately; he testifies that he waited out a rainstorm first, which further angered the priest, who declared: "Come here, dog; I didn't send an Indian to bring you here for you to say that you didn't want to come [*Ven acá, perro, no te embié a llamar con un Indio, como me respondes que no querías venir*]."[26] When Juan Patricio respectfully but forcefully explained the reason for his delay—"I beg to tell you, Father, that you are misinformed. Because as I said when the rainstorm ceased, I would go [*suplico a usted mi Padre, que le an informado mal. Porque lo que dixe fue que encessando el agua iría*]"—he says the priest responded dismissively and rudely and then struck him with a stick, declaring: "The dog now understands that he is speaking as if with the shameless arrogance of his master [*entiende el perro que está hablando con el Baladrón deslenguado de su amo*]."[27] The priest here accuses Juan Patricio of stepping out of his station, of assuming airs, of being more than he is or ought to be.

Insulted and incensed, Juan Patricio began a concerted effort to obtain redress for his treatment at the hands of Esquivel. He first went to church officials in the city of Mérida to lodge a complaint against Esquivel and to demand an apology from the priest's superiors. With this, Juan Patricio seems to be disputing not just the priest's violation of his master's *encomienda*, nor just the priest's rude and violent treatment of him, but also the priest's presumption that Juan Patricio acted beyond himself, "as if" he were his own master. Not happy with the ecclesiastical response to his complaint, Juan Patricio eventually tracked down the priest on the road between the village of Tahmek and the village of Hoctún, got into a physical altercation, and broke the priest's arm. Juan Patricio then fled to Mérida to hide from the authorities, first in the black and indian barrio of Santiago, and later in some houses owned by his master in a Creole barrio. But he was soon apprehended by the *pardo* militia and held under *tormento* in a Mérida prison until trial—which is to say, he was tortured and forced to testify. Eventually, he was convicted of assault and deported to be imprisoned in Veracruz.

This case is in some general sense part of a larger system of dispossession, in which Spanish colonialism in Yucatán enslaved Africans and colonized Maya, reordering the Yucatán so as to more easily extract wealth from it and its people—which is to say, that in this larger system, bodies and labor and land were stolen from black and native people. Indeed, we can see the general outlines of the simmering agonisms and outright antagonisms among all the major, competing sectors of colonial Yucatecan society: first, the church, in the person of the priest don Ignacio de Esquivel; second, large landowners, in the person of the master Enríquez de Noboa; third, the state, in the militia that eventually apprehends Juan Patricio and in the judicial system that tries him; fourth, the Maya majority, in the person of Fabiana Pech as well as the priests' Maya deputies and the many other *indios* who testify; and finally the Afro-Yucatecans, many of whom were enslaved like Juan Patricio. To give a sense of scale, the ratio of Creoles to Afro-Yucatecans to Maya during this period was approximately 1:1:8; so there were equal numbers of Creoles and Afro-Yucatecans, and eight times as many Maya as either of those two groups.[28]

Yet when one delves into the more granular detail of the case, attending in particular to the language of the many statements made by the principals and other witnesses, one starts to see how contemporary theories of dispossession that rely on the presumption of prior possession do not really help us understand how those black and native people responded to this instance of dispossession. In his own testimony, Juan Patricio does not represent this scene in terms of the theft of something that was his or his master's. He does not decry his master's robbery of his freedom, he does not challenge his master's control over Maya or their lands, and he does not describe the priest's taking of Fabiana Pech as the theft of anyone's possession. What is more, he does not challenge this system of dispossession by seeking the return of anything he claims to have previously owned—such as his body, his freedom, or his land—or something his master previously owned, such as Fabiana Pech.

What he does do, however, is exercise a remarkably nimble mobility in his efforts to challenge the priest Esquivel's taking of Pech and to get redress for the priest's rude treatment of him. Juan Patricio moves with seeming ease between the rural pueblo of Tahmek and the city of Mérida. He knows the routes from his home to his master's fields to the Casas Reales in the village to the church's seat of authority in the city to the black and indian *barrio* in Mérida to his master's own dwellings there. He describes traveling to and from all these places in his account of how he first encountered the taking of Fabiana Pech, then challenged the priest's authority, and finally sought to evade punishment. Which is to say, he knows how to fight and flee, how to seek authority and how to hide from it, how to track down information and how to evade being informed upon. For him, fugitivity is like a skill set, a positive field of knowledge and potential power. He flees *to* at least as much as he flees *from*. Juan Patricio's response to so-called primitive accumulation is improvisational, but also apparently informed by a wealth of knowledge put to use in a world of dispossession.

We learn even more about this improvisational knowledge when we attend to the way Juan Patricio responded to the priest's declaration that "the dog now understands that he was speaking as if with the shameless arrogance of his master [*entiende el perro que está hablando con el Baladrón deslenguado de su amo*]." A *Baladrón* is a braggart, and *deslenguado* (literally to cut a tongue) can mean unkempt or a loss of composure, as well as shameless, foul-mouthed, or free-talking. So Esquivel says not only that Juan Patricio is taking on the airs of his master, but also that his doing so is a kind of wild, uncontrolled behavior. To this charge, Juan Patricio says in his testimony that he deliberately knelt in front of the priest and declared confidently: "I beg you my Father to understand, that I am the one talking with you and not my master, who is [away] in the city [of Mérida] [*Suplico a usted mi Padre se soportte, que yo soi el que habla con usted, y no mi amo que está en la ziudad*]." More literally translated, Juan Patricio here testifies to having said: "I am he who is talking with you." "I am he [*yo soi el que*]" is not the same as "I am me," and "I am he who is talking with you" is not the same as "I am talking to you." That is, Juan Patricio does not respond to the priest's reminder that Juan Patricio is owned by his master and cannot act like his master by simply claiming to be or to own himself. Rather, Juan Patricio performs a kind of momentary self-alienation in the interest of speaking otherwise than himself. This momentary self-alienation is complex: he kneels, showing his humility as well as his subservience to the priest, and he calls the priest by the formal "you" [*usted*], again recognizing the priest's authority. Yet by kneeling, Juan Patricio does so with a controlled and deliberate action, thereby undercutting the priest's *deslenguado* charge. What is more, he also claims the power to speak "with" the priest, as if the two were at that moment also equal. In contemporary terms, we might say that Juan Patricio here declares himself in some sense *igualado*: an excessive sense of equality that an inferior claims in the face of a superior. Crucially, then, Juan Patricio's performance consists in not being on the same footing *as well as* being on the same footing with elites like Esquivel. Phenomenologists would call this a moment of *compossibility*: two possibilities validly alongside each other but not consistent with one another.[29]

So to the priest's charge that Juan Patricio was trying to be more than he was, or trying to act like he owned himself when actually his master owned him, Juan Patricio did not assert prior possession by saying something like: "You are wrong, I own myself." Rather, Juan Patricio effectively replied: "You are right, I am not my own, but still, if only at this moment, I am he." "He" who? "He who is talking with you." This "he" thus offers a different theory of dispossession than Marx's formulation to which I referred at the beginning of this paper: "nothing to sell except their *own* skins," "nothing to sell but *itself*." "I am he" at once theorizes and puts into practice a powerful if fleeting self-dispossession, a stepping out of and beyond selfhood as such. We might say that Juan Patricio theorizes dispossession not so much as the theft of something he wants returned to him, but rather as the imputation to him of a fixed status. To use the idiom of Spanish colonialism, this fixing could be understood as an articulation of *reducción,* the complex Spanish system of organizing and ordering colonized people and places into communities and towns.[30] Recalling that the Latin root of the word *reducción* is *ducere*—to lead, draw, pull, think, consider, prolong, but also to mislead, cheat, incite, induce, even to charm—then we might consider *reducción* as a "fix" in two senses: imputing a controllable place to the colonized, to the point of inducing them to accept that place, as well as cheating them out of who, where, or how they might be otherwise. In turn, we might say that Juan Patricio's theory and practice of dispossession at once exposes this incitement to fixity and counters it with improvisational tactics aimed at unfixing the fix.[31]

What of Fabiana Pech? We can say less of her because she apparently did not give direct testimony in the case, and few others speak much of her. From what little is said about her, we can presume that she had some kind of relationship with Juan Patricio, given that he goes to such effort and risks so much to get her back from the priest's deputies, and to get redress for the injuries he suffered during that effort. Others who give testimony report that she did not want to serve the priest's mother, Solís, because she was known as a cruel mistress (although other indigenous witnesses testify to the contrary on Solís's behalf).[32] Given that Solís lived some distance away in the city of Mérida, it is notable that Pech knows about her and how she treats her workers. It is not clear whether Pech communicated her wariness of Solís to Juan Patricio prior to that day in mid-August of 1690, when the priest's deputies tried to take her. But Pech does seems to have had some sort of prior connection with Juan Patricio, since he intervened on her behalf in particular, rather than simply on behalf of his master's general claim over any and all Maya of the *encomienda.* This is suggested when Juan Patricio testifies that, in his initial encounter with the priest's deputies as they were leading Pech away, he tells them that she should not have to go with them because she is "*enferma,*" sick or perhaps even pregnant, and urges them to take another Maya girl instead: "*les dixo la dexassen, y que llevassen otra que estuviesse sana."*[33] When the deputies insist on taking Pech, declaring that Esquivel wants her in particular—*"aviéndoles replicado diciendo avía de ser aquella y no otra"*—Juan Patricio becomes even more concerned, striking them and driving them away—*"se enfuerció y les quitó la dicha India enferma dándoles a dichos tupiles algunos golpes."* Pech thus seems able to leverage her connections to Juan Patricio as well as her knowledge of the labor conditions that Maya faced in late-seventeenth-century Yucatán against the priest's attempted abduction of her, such that for some time at least she is able to remain in her village and rebuff the aims of two powerful figures who are agents of dispossession: a clergyman and his wealthy Creole mother.

There is much more to say about this case—for instance, about Juan Patricio's efforts to marry another enslaved woman in a seeming bid to be released from his master by ecclesiastical authorities, potentially linking him with a widespread Afro-diasporan tactic in New Spain well documented by Herman Bennett.[34] But at this point I would like to take stock of the implications of Juan Patricio's case for contemporary antidispossessive politics.

A History of the Not-Yet-Present

One of the most powerful aspects of what has come to be known as Michel Foucault's "history of the present" is the way it conceptualizes the questions it asks. By posing questions about pervasive understandings of the present, and then showing how their seemingly liberatory aspects are historically bound up with the very modes of power from which they seek to liberate us, such a history both unsettles the present and opens it to potentially different futures. So, for instance, rather than asking, "What are the origins of the prison reform movement?" in *Discipline and Punish* Foucault unsettles our understanding of "reform" by asking, "How might the supposedly more humane prisons of the present be said to be part of a centuries-old *dispositif* that determines what can be said about power as much as what can't be said about it?" By *dispositif,* Foucault means "a thoroughly heterogeneous ensemble consisting of discourses, institutions, architectural forms, regulatory decisions, laws, administrative measures, scientific statements, philosophical, moral, and philanthropic propositions—in short, the said as much as the unsaid."[35] Theories and practices of prison reform thus emerged from Foucault's history of the present as bound up with the very carceral brutalities they sought to overcome. A history of the present of dispossession, then, might reveal to us how antidispossessive politics that presume prior possession and that seek to restore such possessiveness are not as antidispossessive as they seem. For instance, rather than challenging regimes of private property or individual autonomy, such politics risk entrenching those regimes by seeking their supposedly more egalitarian restoration.

Perhaps more importantly, however, another implication of such a history of the present—albeit not central to Foucault's own work—is the way research into such a history might reveal archival traces of pasts that did *not* become "of the present," pasts that were exorbitant from the presents that would become our own. So I want to ask: How might one mobilize the critical, genealogical force of a history of the present to read archives of cases like Juan Patricio's for the impressions they offer not of outdated or antiquarian pasts, nor of hopelessly compromised presents, but rather of as-yet-unrealized futures? Such a history of the not-yet-present would no doubt be unverifiable, and thus fall outside the positivist idiom, even when rigorously responsible to the archive. But it might attend, speculatively, to the archival traces of how subalterns theorized in and through acting in the world in ways that have not yet become central aspects of contemporary thinking and acting. In turn, this speculative potential might challenge us to find other ways of realizing futures we desire, or even of imagining futures we never thought to want.

For instance, in my accounts of Juan Patricio and Fabiana Pech I am not trying to show how they were willful agents who pursued their own desires in resistance to those who would deprive them of that putative "right." A history of the present of dispossession would question whether the "recovery" of such individual agency from the past can offer an effective critique of dispossession, attending instead to the ways presumptions of such self-propriety actually facilitated dispossession.[36] Elsewhere I have argued that, while the recovery of the willful agency of historical subjects can at times be an important historiographic aim, its focus on the empirical evidence of subjective agency also tends to foreclose viewing our archives as scenes of speculative, subaltern theory.[37] Consequently, I am interested in reading archives of dispossession from the period of "so-called primitive accumulation" in the Americas for traces of how subalterns might have theorized the dispossessive forces they were facing; how that theorization emerges in and through mediated, archival traces of their actions; and how those traces urge us to rethink what theoretical practice itself might entail. Such readings can generate potent, if unverifiable, accounts of subaltern theoretical practices that do not conform to contemporary presumptions about theory or practice, in particular to presumptions about how theory and politics are grounded in a subject's willful pursuit of their own desire.[38]

My skepticism about acting as if we are freeing historical subjects from the neglected or oppressive past when we emplot their histories in the biographical mode of individual agency so pervasive since the rise of social history also has a presentist source. Like many of my friends and colleagues responding to the harsh policies President Barack Obama directed toward migrants, and the utterly vicious policies President Trump subsequently pursued, I have been working as a translator and advocate with migrants from Latin America who are seeking asylum in the United States. A crucial aspect of the asylum process is what is called the "credible fear interview," in which the migrant must give an account of how they cannot return to their country of origin because of—to quote the U.S. Citizenship and Immigration Services (USCIS)—"a well-founded fear of persecution on account of your race, religion, nationality, membership in a particular social group, or political opinion if returned to your country."[39] As the lawyers working pro bono on these cases often do not speak Spanish, translators like me mediate between the migrant and the lawyer to help the migrant prepare to tell their story of credible fear in front of an immigration judge. All this, thanks to amazing organizations that have responded to the urgency of the current conjuncture by linking lawyers and translators with migrants in detention centers across the country—organizations such as the Las Américas Immigrant Advocacy Center in El Paso, Texas; the CARA Family Detention Pro Bono project in Dilley, Texas; the North West Immigrant Rights Project; and the Immigrant Justice Campaign.

But the experience of working on these cases has also reminded me that storytelling should not be idealized as a way of revealing a subject's will, much less redressing their dispossession. Typically, when you first ask a migrant in detention why they must stay in the United States, they will either give you the sparest of details of generalized hardships they have suffered, or they will talk with much pathos about how they want to participate in the American Dream—none of which qualifies one for asylum under current U.S. law. After some back and forth, however, you eventually learn the real reasons they have come to the U.S., which is to say that you hear them speak of the very last things they want to speak of: their detailed stories of dispossession, violence, and fear in their homelands, often at the hands of gangs and local police. As many scholars have shown, those gangs and police were in large part created by and in the United States, and are part of a larger global system of racial capitalist and neoliberal dispossession.[40] Migrants give these accounts only after much dialogue, retracing of narrative steps, and intimate questioning. It is a kind of uneven pedagogy. It can often feel inappropriate, I might even say expropriative or dispossessive: a kind of extraction and exposure of trauma itself generated by dispossession in the first place. In other words, the process by which these migrants must learn to make their stories legible within the terms of U.S. asylum law is one fully within the terms of the *dispositif*, or apparatus of power-knowledge, that organizes the U.S. judicial system, including asylum law, the lawyers and translators and judges within that system, the experts who give testimony, the built environments of the migration route, the architectural form of the detention center, and the popular knowledge that circulates among migrants.

Juan Patricio and Fabiana Pech too were caught up in the power/knowledge structures of their time and place; anything we read about them or from them in archives is mediated through a *dispositif* designed to extract and mold their stories. For this reason, among others, I have been less and less inspired to read the archives of seventeenth- and eighteenth-century dispossession simply to reconstruct the stories of individuals' lives, as if those reconstructions gave them new life, freed them from the archive, or did justice to their dispossession. Instead, I look to what they are described as having done and said, listening for speculative echoes of how they might have theorized the dispossessive forces in which they were caught up and how they might have formulated an antidispossessive politics out of that subaltern theory—for echoes, that is, of how they beheld the spectacle of dispossession and, in turn, counterperformed in the face of that spectacle.

In sum, my argument is not that every instance of antidispossessive politics during the period of so-called originary accumulation in the Americas eschewed possessive individualism or claims to prior possession. Rather, I suggest that we learn how to read our archives for instances that do not conform to those foundationalist presuppositions: instances of an antidispossessive politics of self-dispossession and fugitivity like Juan Patrico's, or of quotidian knowledge-based improvisation like Fabiana Pech's, even if—or perhaps especially because—such cases do not fit comfortably within many contemporary critiques of dispossession that presume prior possession and seek its restoration. It is my hope that this speculative history of a not-yet-present of dispossession recalls a seemingly remote past that holds promise for our political futures; but not because that past is full of agential subjects whose willful lives and self-possessed subjectivities we can free from the archive. Rather, because the archive of this era of so-called original accumulation is full of fragmentary, subaltern efforts to theorize and to counter dispossession in terms that flee from possession as such, which is to say in terms that are yet to become, but may yet become, part of our present.

Notes

1. I have been inspired by recent work that troubles the presumption of prior possession in a range of dispossessive contexts: Banerjee-Guha, *Accumulation by Dispossession*; Belausteguigoitia Ruis and Saldaña-Portillo, *Des/posesión*; Butler and Athanasiou, *Dispossession*; Byrd, Goldstein, Melamed, and Reddy, eds., "Economies of Dispossession"; Coulthard, *Red Skin, White Masks*; Fortier, *Unsettling the Commons*; Fuentes, *Dispossessed Lives*; Greer, *Property and Dispossession*; Goldstein and Lubin, eds., "Settler Colonialism"; Murray Li, *Land's End*; Moten, *Black and Blur*, 85; Moten, *Stolen Life*; Nemser, "Primitive Spiritual Accumulation"; Roybal, *Archives of Dispossession*; Nichols, "Indigeneity"; Nichols, "Disaggregating Primitive Accumulation"; Simpson and Smith, eds., *Theorizing Native Studies*; Simpson, *Mohawk Interruptus*; Walker, "Primitive Accumulation"; Wang, *Carceral Capitalism*.

2. Harvey, *New Imperialism*.

3. Marx, *Capital*, 1:873–74.

4. Marx, "Letter on Russia."

5. For a thoughtful account of Marx's letter to Mikhaylovsky in relation to the questions I raise in this paper, see Nichols, "Indigeneity" as well as Nichols, "Disaggregating Primitive Accumulation."

6. For work that either implicitly or explicitly presumes such prior possession, see Bennholdt-Thomsen and Mies, *Subsistence Perspective*; Bollier and Helfrich, eds., *Wealth of the Commons*; Casarino and Negri, *In Praise*; Federici, "Women, Land Struggles"; Federici, "Witch-Hunting"; Federici, "Feminism"; Harvey, *New Imperialism*; Linebaugh, *Stop, Thief!*; and Linebaugh, *Magna Carta Manifesto*.

7. Proudhon, *What Is Property?* Proudhon may himself have drawn on earlier, eighteenth-century iterations of that claim, such as Brissot de Warville's *Philosophical Inquiries on the Right of Property* and Marquis de Sade's *Juliette*. See also de Luna, "Dean Street Style."

8. Marx, "On Proudhon" and Marx, *Poverty of Philosophy*.

9. See Nichols, "Disaggregating Primitive Accumulation," 20.

10. Marx, *Capital*, 1:873.

11. Linebaugh, *Stop, Thief!*

12. For an extensive history of this problematic, see Greer, *Property and Dispossession*.

13. MacPherson, *Political Theory*.

14. Hartman, *Scenes of Subjection*.

15. Butler and Athanasiou, *Dispossession*, 2.

16. Ibid.

17. See, for instance, Greer, *Property and Dispossession*, 27–64; Carrasco and Matos Moctezuma, eds., *Moctezuma's Mexico*; Cline, *Colonial Culhuacan*; Kellogg, *Law and the Transformation*; Lockhart, *Nahuas after the Conquest*; Ouweneel and Miller, eds., *Indian Community*.

18. Anderson, *Creatures of Empire*; Bragdon, *Native Peoples*.

19. Coulthard, *Red Skin, White Masks*.

20. Boone, "Glorious Imperium"; Greer, *Property and Dispossession*; Hämäläinen, *Comanche Empire*; Hassig, *Aztec Warfare*; Hicks, "Land and Succession."

21. Greer, *Property and Dispossession*. For accounts that celebrate contemporary commons, see Bollier and Helfrich, eds., *Wealth of the Commons*; Federici, "Women, Land Struggles" and "Feminism"; Linebaugh, *Stop, Thief!* and *Magna Carta Manifesto*.

22. This point was made vividly by one of the classic modern works on European commons, Thompson, *Customs in Common*.

23. "*Complusa de autos criminales seguidos por Doña Ysabel Solis, vecina de Yucatan, contra Juan Patricio esclavo, sobre haber apaleado à Don Ygnacio de Esquivel, clerigo: Año de 1696.*" AGI_MEX_0368, Archivo de Indias, Seville.

24. Restall, *Black Middle*.

25. "*Compulsa*," AGI_MEX_0368_0088-0101.

26. "*Compulsa*," AGI_MEX_0368_0092

27. Ibid.

28. Restall, *Black Middle*, 27.

29. Brown and Chiek, *Leibniz on Compossibility*.

30. Hanks, *Converting Words*.

31. See Katheryn Burns's wonderful essay "Unfixing Race," which has inspired me to think about racial fixing.

32. "*Compulsa*," AGI_MEX_0368.

33. "*Compulsa*," AGI_MEX_0368_0090.

34. Bennet, *Africans in Colonial Mexico*.

35. Foucault, *Power/Knowledge*, 194.

36. See Agamben, *Remnants of Auschwitz*; Hartman, *Scenes of Subjection*; Nichanian, *Historiographic Perversion*; Helton, Leroy, Mishler, Seeley, and Sweeney, eds., "The Question of Recovery: Slavery, Freedom, and the Archive"; Connolly and Fuentes, eds., "From the Archives of Slavery to Liberated Futures?"

37. Kazanjian, *Brink of Freedom*; Kazanjian, "Freedom's Surprise"; Kazanjian, "Scenes of Speculation."

38. See Hartman, "Venus"; Johnson, "On Agency"; Mahmood, *Politics of Piety*; Spivak, *Death of a Discipline*; Spivak, "Our Asias."

39. See https://www.uscis.gov/humanitarian/refugees-and-asylum/asylum/questions-and-answers-credible-fear-screening.

40. See Bruneau, Dammert, and Skinner, eds., *Maras*. Thanks to Josie Saldaña for conversations about her extensive work in progress on this front.

Works Cited

Anderson, Virginia DeJohn. *Creatures of Empire: How Domestic Animals Transformed Early America*. New York: Oxford University Press, 2004.

Agamben, Giorgio. *Remnants of Auschwitz: The Witness and the Archive*. New York: Zone Books, 1999.

Boone, Elizabeth. "Glorious Imperium: Understanding Land and Community in Moctezuma's Mexico." In *Moctezuma's Mexico: Visions of the Aztec World*, edited by David Carrasco and Eduardo Matos Moctezuma, 159-73. Boulder: University Press of Colorado, 1992.

Banerjee-Guha, Swapna. *Accumulation by Dispossession: Transformative Cities in the New Global Order*. New Delhi: SAGE, 2010.

Belausteguigoitia Rius, Marisa, and María Josefina Saldaña-Portillo. *Des/posesión: Género, territorio y luchas por la autodeterminación*. México: PUEG-UNAM, 2014.

Bennet, Herman. *Africans in Colonial Mexico: Absolutism, Christianity, and Afro-Creole Consciousness, 1570–1640*. Bloomington: Indiana University Press, 2005.

Bennholdt-Thomsen, Veronika, and Maria Mies. *The Subsistence Perspective: Beyond the Globalised Economy*. London: Zed, 1999.

Bollier, David, and Silke Helfrich, eds. *The Wealth of the Commons: A World Beyond Market and State*. Amherst: Levellers, 2012.

Bragdon, Kathleen. *Native Peoples of Southern New England, 1500–1650*. Norman: University of Oklahoma Press, 1996.

Brissot de Warville, Jacques Pierre. *Recherches philosophiques sur le droit de propriété . . . 1780*. Reprint of the first edition. Paris: Editions d'histoire sociale; Milan: Galli Thierry, 1966.

Brown, Gregory, and Yual Chiek. *Leibniz on Compossibility and Possible Worlds*. Cham, Switzerland: Springer, 2016.

Butler, Judith, and Athena Athanasiou. *Dispossession: The Performative in the Political*. Cambridge: Polity, 2013.

Bruneau, Thomas, Lucía Dammert, and Elizabeth Skinner, eds. *Maras: Gang Violence and Security in Central America*. Durham: Duke University Press, 2011.

Byrd, Jodi A., Alyosha Goldstein, Jodi Melamed, and Chandan Reddy, eds. "Economies of Dispossession." *Social Text* (135) 36, no. 2 (June 2018).

Burns, Katheryn. "Unfixing Race." In *Histories of Race and Racism: The Andes and Meso-America from Colonial Times to the Present*, edited by Laura Gotkowitz, 57–71. Durham: Duke University Press, 2011.

Carrasco, David, and Eduardo Matos Moctezuma, eds. *Moctezuma's Mexico: Visions of the Aztec World*. Revised Edition. Boulder: University Press of Colorado, 2003.

Casarino, Cesare, and Antonio Negri. *In Praise of the Common: A Conversation on Philosophy and Politics*. Minneapolis: University of Minnesota Press, 2008.

Cline, S. L. *Colonial Culhuacan, 1580–1600: A Social History of an Aztec Town*. Albuquerque: University of New Mexico Press, 1986.

Connolly, Brian, and Marisa Fuentes, eds. "From the Archives of Slavery to Liberated Futures?" Special issue, *Journal of the History of the Present* 6, no. 2 (2016).

Coulthard, Glen Sean. *Red Skin, White Masks: Rejecting the Colonial Politics of Dispossession*. Minneapolis: University of Minnesota Press, 2014.

de Luna, Frederick A. "The Dean Street Style of Revolution: J.-P. Brissot, Jeune Philosophe." *French Historical Studies* 17, no. 1 (Spring 1991): 159–90.

de Sade, Marquis. *Juliette*. Translated by Austryn Wainhouse. New York: Grove Press, 1968.

Federici, Silvia. "Feminism and the Politics of the Commons." http://wealthofthecommons.org/essay/feminism-and-politics-commons.

———. "Witch-Hunting, Globalization, and Feminist Solidarity in Africa Today." *Journal of International Women's Studies* 10, no. 1 (October 2008): 29–35.

———. "Women, Land Struggles, and the Reconstruction of the Commons." *WorkingUSA: The Journal of Labor and Society* (WUSA) 14, no. 61 (March 2011): 41–56.

Fortier, Craig. *Unsettling the Commons: Social Movements Within, Against, and Beyond Settler Colonialism*. Winnipeg: ARP Books, 2017.

Foucault, Michel. *Power/Knowledge*. New York: Vintage, 1980.

Fuentes, Marisa J. *Dispossessed Lives: Enslaved Women, Violence, and the Archive*. Philadelphia: University of Pennsylvania Press, 2016.

Greer, Allan. *Property and Dispossession: Native Empires and Land in Early Modern North America*. Cambridge: Cambridge University Press, 2018.

Goldstein, Alyosha, and Alex Lubin, eds. "Settler Colonialism." Special issue, *The South Atlantic Quarterly* 107, no. 4 (Fall 2008).

Hämäläinen, Pekka. *The Comanche Empire*. New Haven: Yale University Press, 2008.

Hanks, William F. *Converting Words: Maya in the Age of the Cross*. Berkeley: University of California Press, 2010.

Hartman, Saidiya. *Scenes of Subjection: Terror, Slavery, and Self-Making in Nineteenth-Century America*. New York: Oxford University Press, 1997.

———. "Venus in Two Acts." *Small Axe* (26) 12, no. 2 (June 2008): 1–14.

Harvey, David. *The New Imperialism*. Oxford: Oxford University Press, 2003.

Hassig, Ross. *Aztec Warfare: Imperial Expansion and Political Control*. Norman: University of Oklahoma Press, 1995.

Helton, Laura, Justin Leroy, Max A. Mishler, Samantha Seeley, and Shauna Sweeney, eds. "The Question of Recovery: Slavery, Freedom, and the Archive." Special issue, *Social Text* (125) 33, no. 4 (December 2015).

Hicks, Frederic. "Land and Succession in the Indigenous Noble Houses of Sixteenth-Century Tlaxcala," *Ethnohistory* 56, no. 4 (2009): 569–88.

Johnson, Walter. "On Agency." *Journal of Social History* 37, no. 1 (Fall 2003): 113–24.

Kazanjian, David. *The Brink of Freedom: Improvising Life in the Nineteenth-Century Atlantic World*. Durham: Duke University Press, 2016.

———. "Freedom's Surprise: Two Paths through Slavery's Archives." *History of the Present: A Journal of Critical History* 6, no. 2 (Fall 2016): 133–45.

———. "Scenes of Speculation." *Social Text* 12 no. 33, issue 4 (December 2015): 77–83.

Kellogg, Susan. *Law and the Transformation of Aztec Culture, 1500–1700*. Norman: University of Oklahoma Press, 1995.

Lévi-Strauss, Claude. *The Savage Mind*. Chicago: University of Chicago Press, 1966.

Li, Tania Murray. *Land's End: Capitalist Relations on an Indigenous Frontier*. Durham: Duke University Press, 2014.

Linebaugh, Peter. *Magna Carta Manifesto: Liberties and Commons for All*. Berkeley: University of California Press, 2008.

———. *Stop, Thief! The Commons, Enclosures, and Resistance*. Oakland: PM Press, 2014.

Lockhart, James. *The Nahuas after the Conquest: A Social and Cultural History of the Indians of Central Mexico*. Stanford: Stanford University Press, 1992.

MacPherson, C. B. *The Political Theory of Possessive Individualism: Hobbes to Locke*. Oxford: Oxford University Press, 2011.

Mahmood, Saba. *The Politics of Piety: The Islamic Revival and the Feminist Subject*. Princeton: Princeton University Press, 2005.

Marx, Karl. *Capital: A Critique of Political Economy*. Vol. 1. New York: Penguin, 1992.

———. "A Letter on Russia." *The New International* 1, no. 4 (November 1934). Transcribed at https://www.marxists.org/history/etol/newspape/ni/vol01/no04/marx.htm.

———. *The Poverty of Philosophy*. New York: Prometheus Books, 1995.

———. "On Proudhon," Letter to J. B. Schweizer. *Der Social-Demokrat* 16 (Feb. 1, 1865). Reprinted in https://www.marxists.org/archive/marx/works/1865/letters/65_01_24.htm

Moten, Fred. *Black and Blur: Consent Not To Be a Single Being.* Durham: Duke University Press, 2017.

——. *Stolen Life: Consent Not To Be a Single Being.* Durham: Duke University Press, 2017.

Nemser, Daniel. "Primitive Spiritual Accumulation and the Colonial Extraction Economy." *Política Común,* vol. 5 (2014): 1–21.

Nichanian, Marc. *The Historiographic Perversion.* Translated by Gil Anidjar. New York: Columbia University Press, 2009.

Nichols, Robert. "Disaggregating Primitive Accumulation." *Radical Philosophy,* no. 194 (Nov.-Dec., 2015): 18–28.

——. "Indigeneity and the Settler Contract Today." *Philosophy and Social Criticism* 39, no. 2 (2013): 165–86.

Ouweneel, Arij, and Simon Miller, eds. *The Indian Community of Colonial Mexico: Fifteen Essays on Land Tenure, Corporate Organizations, Ideology, and Village Politics.* Amsterdam: CEDLA, 1990.

Proudhon, Pierre-Joseph. *What Is Property?* Cambridge: Cambridge University Press, 1994.

Restall, Matthew. *The Black Middle: Africans, Mayas, and Spaniards in Colonial Yucatán.* Stanford: Stanford University Press, 2009.

Roybal, Karen R. *Archives of Dispossession: Recovering the Testimonios of Mexican American Herederas.* Chapel Hill: University of North Carolina Press, 2017.

Simpson, Audra. *Mohawk Interruptus: Political Life Across the Borders of Settler States.* Durham: Duke University Press, 2014.

——, and Andrea Smith, eds. *Theorizing Native Studies.* Durham: Duke University Press, 2014.

Spivak, Gayatri Chakravorty. *Death of a Discipline.* New York: Columbia University Press, 2003.

——. "Our Asias—2001: How to Be a Continentalist." In *Other Asias,* 209–38. Malden, MA: Blackwell, 2008.

Thompson, E. P. *Customs in Common: Studies in Traditional Popular Culture.* New York: New Press, 1993.

Walker, Gavin. "Primitive Accumulation and the Formation of Difference: On Marx and Schmitt." *Rethinking Marxism* 23, no. 3 (2011): 384–404.

Wang, Jackie. *Carceral Capitalism.* South Pasadena, CA: Semiotext(e), 2018.

CHAPTER THREE

Latin American Marxism: History and Accumulation

SERGIO VILLALOBOS-RUMINOTT

Introduction

Latin American Marxism has always been both a political theory, that is, a practice of organization and empowerment, and a theory of historical development. (I use the notion of theory in a way that is not restricted to its academic use). It is in relation to this second dimension, that of historical development, that Marxism, in general, might be considered as an alternative to capitalism's philosophy of history, a philosophy of history that structures a normative narrative about the region according to a schematic and lineal notion of progress and fulfillment. With this in mind, I will revisit some formulations of the problems of historical development and so-called structural underdevelopment in Dependency Theory, and of the question of transition in the mode of production in debates among Latin American Marxist theorists in the 1970s. I contend that a new consideration of such problems might prove both useful for rearticulating a Marxian analysis of the processes of ongoing primitive accumulation triggered by so-called neoliberal globalization while also questioning the limitations imposed by naturalized understandings of historical temporality.

Let me begin with a disclaimer: whether we think of it as a tradition, a field, or a horizon of thinking, Latin American Marxism is complex, heterogeneous, and almost impossible to represent. Speaking about it demands multiple mediations and specifications. However, what I wish to do here is to survey this field's theoretical potential, particularly in relation to the questions of history and accumulation. This is already a controvertible decision, as one can always demand a different reconstruction, that is to say, one can always punctuate the history of Latin American Marxism according to different criteria. The goal of my disclaimer, therefore, is to prevent any reading of the present text as a conclusive and categorical statement about Marxism in Latin America that would consider it as a closed tradition; in fact, anything one might say regarding this field is and should always be tentative and preliminary, precisely because of its complexity, but more radically, because of its open-ended condition. I would even suggest that regarding Latin American Marxism as a problematic field is different from approaching it as a tradition, and it is on this difference that the following pages wish to dwell.

In what follows, I will consider Latin American Marxism as an ongoing elaboration of the relationship between historical development and processes of accumulation. To deal with such a complex topic, I will organize my narrative by emphasizing how the relationship between accumulation and history manifests itself as a theory of historical development and, at the same time, as the basis for a precise conception of the political. In other words, I will argue that Latin American Marxism has never been a mechanical extrapolation of what I refer to above as capitalism's philosophy of history. Of course, I will not be able to consider the long list of Latin American thinkers (intellectuals and/ or militants) identified with this horizon.[1] Instead, I will limit my comments to some key authors and debates that have shaped Latin American Marxism as a mode of historical thinking.

My last premise is that the distinctive problematic of Latin American Marxism, considered from the viewpoint of the relationship between historical development and processes of accumulation, is today as important as ever, and this, despite the so-called crisis, bankruptcy, or exhaustion of Marxism, which is related to the disaster of its historically limited political instantiation, reinforced, in the context opened with the end of the Cold War period, by the globalization of the American way of life. This is a difficult claim because it implies not only an assertion regarding the actuality of Marxism, but also its centrality for an active understanding of the ongoing process of neoliberal globalization and its flexible accumulation processes. Marxism might not be sufficient, but it is certainly necessary to elaborate a critique of accumulation capable of addressing its metaphysical and historicist dimensions. In other words, the problems defining Latin American Marxism have not been resolved; rather, they have been postponed or replaced by other problems framed by an anti-Marxist as well as post-Marxist perspective, a perspective concerned with the processes of democratic transition, pacification, and global integration. It is my aim in the following pages to reactivate some of the problems that define the relevance of Latin American Marxism for the present.

Capitalism's Philosophy of History

With capitalism's philosophy of history I refer to a conventional, pervasive, and hegemonic narrative about Latin American historical processes that has at least three dimensions: (1) a performative dimension related to the archeo-teleological organization of Latin American history; (2) an ideological dimension related to the imaginary representation of history's real processes as an evolving and progressive development; and (3) a political dimension that informs the agenda of different political sectors and defines the goals of politics at large in Latin American history. In this sense, capitalism's philosophy of history is not just another philosophy of history; it is, on the contrary, a complex narrative with analytical and normative consequences that has organized the region's historical processes and defined the scope of its political imagination.[2] Whether we refer to the Discovery and Conquest or the Revolutions of Independence as the decisive events triggering the region's modern history (already immersed within the expansive logic of financial capitalism), what matters here is the archeo-teleological logic of this narrative, which purports to determine the end of history from its beginning. In this sense, the incorporation of Latin America into capitalism's own process of universalization is, at the same time, the determination of Latin American history according to capitalism's historical development, from evangelization to pacification, urbanization, modernization, and industrialization, all the way to global integration. In short, the subsumption of Latin American history to the evolving logic of capitalism implies the reduction of its historical processes, by nature heterogeneous and multiple, to the logic of fulfillment through which any new historical period is already determined by the whole archeo-teleological disposition of historical time inherent to capitalism and its spatialization of temporality. The spatialization of temporality subsumes the heterogeneous condition of history, and its multiple temporalities, to the time of commodity production, circulation, and exchange, that is, to the time of capital, which works as an imperative that defines political agendas, class identities, and historical expectations. In this sense, the disclosing of the commodity's secret is at the same time the critique of capitalism's philosophy of historical time.

It is against this determination that Marxism in Latin America can be understood as an ongoing problematization of history and as an alternative elaboration of historical development.[3] In other words, Marxism has been, from the beginning, a problematic field whose real concern is the production of a counternarrative to the one that I have just referred to as capitalism's philosophy of history. This is, for example, the main problem confronted by José Carlos Mariátegui, the Peruvian writer who is unanimously recognized as one of the first and most prominent Marxist intellectuals and whose interventions coincided with the influence of the Russian Revolution and the subsequent internationalization of Marx's critique of capitalism. But Mariátegui was not alone; the political influence of Luis Emilio Recabarren, the Chilean founder of the Communist Party and an activist and journalist who played a decisive role in organizing the Chilean working class at the beginning of the twentieth century, is equally worthy of note. So too, the influence of the Afro-Caribbean psychiatrist Franz Fanon, whose intervention played a fundamental role in articulating the problem of race and violence within the class-oriented politics of Latin American Marxism, thus initiating a necessary reconsideration of race as more than a merely secondary or superstructural variable with regard to the practices of exploitation and accumulation.[4]

Mariátegui occupies a central position in this complex and heterogeneous set of Marxist thinkers in Latin America, not only because he was among the first to conceive of Marxism as a theoretical framework and as a sociopolitical movement, but also because he was a critical and creative thinker who was able to adapt Marx's analysis of European capitalism to the singularity of the Andean region. His famous *Seven Interpretative Essays on Peruvian Reality* (1928) was already an exemplary study of the problems that indigenous people confronted in modern Peru. It did not appeal, as was customary at the time, to social Darwinism to explain those problems, but instead mobilized a materialist analysis of the structure of property and the role of landowners in that country, in tandem with the brutal abrogation of indigenous communitarian economic practices. He understood, in other words, that the class-centered analysis articulated by Western Marxism needed be adapted in order to incorporate the ethnic, communitarian, and agricultural variables of the Andean region. For Mariátegui, in short, the *ayllu* (the Incan system of collective production and social organization) was not a remainder of the past that the proper implementation of capitalism would suppress; it was, on the contrary, a form of life that complicated the most rigid version of capitalism's philosophy of history and the *criollo* version of the nation as an indivisible identitarian whole. As José Aricó indicates in his study of Mariátegui,[5] even though the Peruvian thinker was a contemporary of Antonio Gramsci, it would be simplistic to say that Gramsci was a dominant influence on him, since the kind of problems and formulations that Mariátegui articulated were specific to Andean reality. However, the proximity between the Peruvian and the Italian thinkers lay in the fact that both had to confront the historical conditions of societies that did not fit within the purportedly ideal model of social and political modernity found in northern Europe. In other words, both Mariátegui and Gramsci had to deal with the so-called *Southern Question*. They not only adapted Marxism to the specificities of their respective realities, but also became important intellectuals and political organizers.

The Marxist debates of the 1960s and '70s attempting to define the mode or modes or production in Latin American and the nature of the transition between feudalism, capitalism, and socialism assumed and expanded upon Mariátegui's gesture and insights. The central hypotheses and positions of these debates highlight the singular creativity with which Latin American Marxist thought has approached issues concerning ethnic heterogeneity, plural temporalities, and the question of the nation.

Anti-imperialism and Dependency

During the 1960s and 1970s, an intense debate took place in Latin America, centered on how to organize a historical narrative linking social evolution with the superposition of the modes of production in the region. Developmentalists, *Cepalianos, Dependentistas,* and Marxists attempted to characterize the historical past of Latin American societies, and in doing so, to determine whether the mode of production in the region could be classified as a feudalist or capitalist one.[6] Simultaneously, they also aimed to define both the potential and the limitations of a continent radically impacted by the Cuban Revolution and the anti-imperialist rhetoric of the national liberation movements of that period. The main problem they confronted, once again, was that in Latin America, capitalism appeared differently than in Northern Europe. Both mechanical Marxist accounts of historical development and what I refer to as capitalism's philosophy of history reinforced the latter as a model of social and political development.[7] Of course, Latin America was considered by many as an imperfectly developed society, full of remnants from a historically overcome precapitalist system, that needed to be dealt with in order to reach a properly capitalist stage that might make possible a purportedly subsequent socialist revolution.

According to this mechanical view of history, if Latin America was not (fully) capitalist, that is, if slavery and feudal-like forms of property defined its past and determined its present—a present dominated by the relevance of agricultural and semi-feudal practices—then a bourgeois-democratic revolution was in order. The political consequences derived from these premises were oriented towards a policy of alliances invested in the national development and full deployment of capitalism. On the contrary, however, if Latin America was a capitalist society, marked from the outset by its exceptional colonial condition and its specific modes of accumulation, despite slavery and the massive presence of peasants, the political consequences were, therefore, radically different since they dictated that Marxists should aspire, not to a bourgeois-democratic revolution, but to a socialist one. However, one of the misunderstandings plaguing several of the participants in this debate was the conceptualization of peasants as an archaic remnant that belonged to a precapitalist social formation, and thus a sector that was destined to disappear as soon as the process of proletarianization began, thanks to the full articulation of the capitalist mode of production. In this sense, the very existence of traditional agricultural workers appeared as a symptom of the failed implementation of capitalism in the region, and thus an error that needed to be corrected before one could even consider social justice, equality, or democracy, let alone socialism.[8]

To this "stageist" conception of historical development we should add the representatives of national-developmentalism, who prioritized industrialization (via the import substitution model) as the only path to achieve the standards of a modern society. In the end, the ruling imperative of that time was to free the processes of accumulation in order to favor capitalization, an operation, they thought, that would trigger social development and proletarianization as much as it would favor the necessary process of agrarian modernization. However, as was evident then and still is today, traditional agricultural workers not only made up a large part of the general population, but also performed a fundamental economic function, both which troubled the narrative and project of imposing a properly capitalist mode of production. This undeniable presence of rural (and indigenous) populations was essential, in other words, not only for understanding the limits of this rigid and schematic version of historical development but also for characterizing the mode of production in Latin America. In political terms, the classical discussion regarding the role of peasants in revolutionary processes; the feasibility of an alliance between peasants and industrial workers; and the lack of strategic directionality associated with rural insurrections, among others, already figured as important topics in Marxist debates. Now, however, the point was very specific: if Latin America was already capitalist, no matter how uneven its actual development was (to recall the Leninist "weakest link" hypothesis), then the conditions for a socialist revolution were already ripe, even when the political subject of this revolution was a small urban avantgarde pretending to represent massive rural populations.

Many Marxist thinkers intervened in the political and conceptual dimensions of this debate. However, what matters for the present discussion is the elaboration of a series of specifications at the analytical and conceptual levels, as these specifications remain relevant for understanding capitalism today. In fact, these discussions about the status of Latin American societies were instrumental for developing new historical, sociological, and political perspectives. In the first case, the task was to determine the characteristics of the processes of conquest and colonization in order to decide whether Latin American history was feudal or capitalist, since that characterization hinged on the "maturity" of the capitalist relations of production in the present. The issue of the historical status of Latin American societies bore on politics insofar as the purported "maturity" of capitalism in the region might, in time, make the project of a socialist revolution more feasible, which many thinkers considered to be a regional process, despite social differences and disparities among different national realities. However, as Ernesto Laclau observed:

> Despite their mutual opposition, both theses [Latin America as feudalist or capitalist] coincide in a fundamental aspect: since they designate as "capitalism" and "feudalism" phenomena related to the sphere of commodity exchange and not to the sphere of production, then the presence or absence of a link to the market becomes the decisive criterion to distinguish between both kinds of society. And such a conception is clearly opposed to the Marxist theory according to which capitalism and feudalism are, above all, *modes of production*.[9]

With this comment, Laclau, among many others, tried to link such historiographical discussions with the Marxist analysis of the mode of production, defined by the actual processes of commodity production and exchange. In other words, Laclau aimed to substantiate a political position based on the materialist analysis of Latin America's actual situation. Among antiimperialist critics, the Leninist hypothesis of the "weakest link," sometimes complemented by the Trotskyist "law of uneven and combined development," yielded an understanding of Latin American underdevelopment as part of a global model emphasizing the articulation of the international market, the general circulation of commodities, the uneven rules of exchange, the hyperexploitation of labor, and the subordination of the third world's national bourgeoisies to the imperatives of metropolitan elites. Despite its emphases on the uneven terms of exchange and circulation of commodities (circulationism), this anti-imperialist narrative was the dominant one at that time, thanks to *Guevarismo* and other forms of radical politics, such as urban guerilla movements and popular power, etc.). As such, it was instrumental in justifying revolutionary practices against the more reformist strategies of "collaborationism," a set of policies characteristic of Latin American communist parties which, following the Seventh Congress of the Comintern (1935), were oriented toward a policy of cooperation and fortification of popular fronts against fascism.

In this context, it bears mentioning how U.S. foreign policy, framed by the anticommunist strategy of containment, intervened in Latin America with a series of focused policies preventing the propagation of the Cuban example, from the so-called Embargo and the subsequent international isolation of Cuba, to the Alliance for Progress. U.S. foreign policy also included official and unofficial practices of collaboration between the security apparatuses of the United States and Latin America, a collaboration that would play a crucial (and bloody) role in enabling the region's military dictatorships and repressive policies of counterinsurgency. At the ideological level, this is the context in which national developmentalism and theories of modernization, which still framed Latin American history according to the American narrative of progress, favored state-led processes of industrialization.[10] Developmentalist policies supposed that industrialization would expand consumption, dissuade rebellions, and adapt the Keynesian model of the welfare state to Latin American societies.[11] As a reaction to this series of policies, a diverse group of intellectuals, including Andre Gunder Frank, Enzo Faletto, Fernando Henrique Cardoso, and Ruy Mauro Marini, among others, questioned the intrinsic evolutive assumptions regarding the path of industrialization by disclosing the structural character of Latin American underdevelopment, which they framed within the geopolitics of global capital. Dependency theory, which was influenced by the Cuban Revolution and the struggles of different third world popular liberation movements, thus appeared as a solid and articulated response to the limits of developmentalism and modernization, and, at times, to the reality of imperialism.[12]

Dependency theory's main claim rested on its explanation of Latin America's sociopolitical condition in terms of a conventional geopolitics of commodity circulation and markets, or circulationism. From this perspective, no bourgeois democratic revolution could reverse the delayed development of productive forces and the obvious underdevelopment of national economies characterizing the region. Dependency theory sustained this position even as it applied to bourgeois democratic revolutions defined by a strong national component and program of industrialization oriented toward the full deployment of capitalism and the transformation of society as a whole. Following from this, insofar as capitalism was a global system, the solution to underdevelopment was a socialist revolution with a strong regional character oriented toward overcoming the capitalist stage of the current relations of appropriation and exchange. Dependency theory was not, properly speaking, however, a purely Marxist theory, aside from the influence of Marxism on many of its exponents. Rather, it constituted an alternative understanding of the economy as an international and interrelated phenomenon. It was so, in part, thanks to the way it integrated into its own formulationscontributions from different scholars dealing with the world-system character of capitalism.

Dependency theory explained the economic underdevelopment of third world countries in ways that foregrounded the imperfection of the circulation of commodities and the inequality of the exchange processes. Dependency theory did not, however, understand dependency, underdevelopment, or colonialism, as phenomena inherent to the "combination" of diverse socioeconomic formations within the capitalist mode of production. In this sense, dependency theory's inability to formulate the "articulation" of the capitalist mode of production with different precapitalist socioeconomic formations limits its analysis to questions related to the hyperexploitation of the local labor force as well as the hyperexploitation of natural resources, the uneven condition of circulation and exchange of commodities, and the inherent inequalities of the global market, understood according to a bipolar geopolitical representation of global power (the center and the periphery). In this sense, dependency theory failed to interrogate the complex articulation of the capitalist mode of production with different social formations, or, alternatively, to understand the historical (aleatory) nature of the actual processes of capitalist accumulation, then or now. As Roger Bartra asserts:

> The trap in which this kind of arguments falls consists in analyzing the relations between developed and undeveloped countries as relations of circulation and markets that define both the wealth of the first and the

misery of the second ... the big mistake of these theories consists in studying the circulation and the market as if they were not expressions of relations of production. Especially within the conditions imposed by the originary accumulation of capital, the mercantile peculiarities of the relations between the capitalist mode of production and the precapitalist mode of production in Latin America (before the mid-nineteenth century), express a relation of production and exploitation of the kind that Marx named the "formal subsumption of labor to capital."[13]

By paying attention to Marx's analysis of the difference between the formal and real subsumption of labor to capital, Bartra and other Marxist thinkers were able to understand the dynamic condition of Latin American capitalism, not only as the effect of discrete contingencies and superstructural dependency, but in relation to the historical characteristics of accumulation processes that tended to develop more elaborated forms of surplus-value extraction, that is to say, which tended to transition from the extraction of absolute to relative surplus-value.

It is important to emphasize how Bartra's analysis considered as a given the aleatory condition of primitive accumulation. In Bartra's account, primitive accumulation appears as an ever-present, virtual possibility to be actualized within specific historical combinations of the capitalist mode of production and not, as more conventional accounts would have it, as a phenomenon of the past long since overcome by the development of productive forces. As John Kraniauskas would put it, primitive accumulation is not a discrete phenomenon of the past but another name for an "ongoing process" that is more complex than we used to believe.[14] Taking Bartra's and Kraniauskas's insights a step farther, not only do the processes of primitive accumulation become aleatory; the mode of production itself now appears as a complex combinatory rather than a singular path. For Marxist theorists such as Bartra, then, the problem was to determine the characteristics of the predominant pattern of accumulation in Latin America, precisely there, where peasants and the agricultural economy, together with the massive presence of indigenous communities and their collective organizations of labor and life, had been considered to be residual formations of the past delaying the proper deployment of capitalism. Against this archeo-teleological and normative conception of historical development, Latin American Marxists' theories of history struggled to understand the passage from the formal to real subsumption of labor under capital without any predilection regarding the dominant or tendential process of surplus-value extraction.

In theory, the capitalist mode of production tends to articulate itself through the operation of real subsumption (which is what Marx called the "properly" capitalist mode of production) in combination with formal subsumption. However, Marx did not determine the historically specific process of surplus-value extraction (relative or absolute) that might correspond to the combination and articulation of modes of production characteristic of Latin American societies. According to Bartra:

> The capitalist mode of production expresses, in its own singularity, relations with other modes of production, under the form of absolute surplus-value extraction. This demonstrates the concrete character of the mode of production as a concept that is able to express its articulation with previous and different modes of production without, in doing this, altering its own specificity, since this articulation is possible thanks to a category that is only meaningful for capitalism: absolute surplus-value extraction.[15]

One detects in this "aleatory" formulation, both a resonance with the law of uneven and combined development, and what Bolivian sociologist René Zavaleta Mercado termed the "motley" nature of Bolivian society (*sociedad abigarrada*), a phrase he coined in order to express the flexible patterns of capitalist accumulation and the complex cultural consequences stemming from them.[16] Bartra's elaborations question both lineal and normative theories of historical development and Stalinist accounts of the necessary concatenation of modes of production. In this way, they present a relevant set of theoretical tools for examining contemporary problems in political economy, for example, as they pertain to the role of the state in relation both to noncapitalist communitarian social forms and contemporary processes of accumulation.[17]

Accumulation and History

Thinkers such as Bartra thus posited the problem of primitive or originary accumulation in relation to the flexible combination of relative and absolute surplus-value extraction, and, more importantly, to a nuanced and historically informed understanding of the transition from a noncapitalist to a capitalist mode of production.[18] Already in the introductory study to *Formaciones económicas precapitalistas* (which was published as an independent book but belongs to the first volume of the *Grundrisse*, 1857–58), Eric Hobsbawm observed the ambiguities surrounding the transition from feudalism to capitalism in Marx's published works, introducing questions about the status of primitive accumulation as it pertains to capitalism's own origin story; the transition to capitalism from an "other than feudal" society; and the status of communitarian and collective work in precapitalist socioeconomic formations. Thanks to these interrogations, primitive accumulation can no longer be reduced to a temporary historical phenomenon, purportedly destined to be overcome and dissolved by the expansive logic of capitalism. Rather, it reappears, randomly, articulated with the flexibility that defines the actual accumulation processes at play in concrete historical moments.[19]

Marxist critiques of dependency and circulationism showed that it was possible to question the rigid model of evolution implicit in the Stalinist theory of modes of production and their concatenation. It is no wonder, then, that contemporaneous publication of the section of Marx's *Grundrisse* dedicated to precapitalist economic formations acquired a certain centrality in theoretical discussions, since it allowed for a more complex formulation of the transition from precapitalist to capitalist society.[20] These discussions proposed viewing the question of transition and of the logic of capitalist development from three different and interrelated perspectives: (1) From the point of view of the transition from a precapitalist to a capitalist mode of production, which also implies the characterization of precapitalist socioeconomic formations, the characterization of feudalism, and the very possibility of transitioning toward capitalism from an other than feudalist society, along with the question about the status of so-called primitive or originary accumulation; (2) the combination between the capitalist mode of production and noncapitalist socioeconomic formations, which, in turn, implies the status of other modes of production such as the Asiatic, the hydraulic, and the Incan or Andean mode of production, and opens onto a question about the coexistence and cohabitation of different social temporalities within the same mode of production (the question of a nonreactionary anachronism); and (3) the determination of the nature of capitalism (its level of maturity) from the nature of the extraction of surplus-value, keeping in mind the difference between absolute and relative surplus-value and their aleatory combination with the formal and real subsumption of labor to capital.[21]

The Marxist elaboration of the problem of history suggests a more nuanced and complex notion of mode of production than its conventional, almost normative, version. In contrast to Marx's so-called method in *A Contribution to the Critique of Political Economy* (1859), thinkers such as Bartra offer a nuanced notion of mode of production that is neither reducible to an analytical category nor merely an aggregation of empirical facts. The 1971 translation into Spanish of Marx's *Grundrisse* made it possible to understand mode of production in terms of the articulation of interrelated processes connected to the historical conditions of the production, circulation, distribution, and exchange of commodities. In other words, this complex notion of mode of production as a "concrete totality" makes it possible, not just to distinguish between different socioeconomic formations, but also to understand their particular historical articulation in a given moment. In this sense, Latin American Marxists confronted problems similar to those of important European thinkers who, around that same time, were already questioning the schematism of Soviet Marxism (with regard to the Chinese question, for example), and for whom the work done by Althusser and his group proved relevant.[22]

Let us dwell briefly on this point: if we take the classical narrative upheld by the Marxist tradition, the mode of production appears as a totality that is structured around the tension produced by the development of the productive forces and the social relations of production, and whose superstructure corresponds to the juridical, political, and ideological dimensions of a society's given moment. Hence Marx's classic formulation:

> In the social production of their existence, men enter into definite, necessary relations, which are independent of their will, namely, relations of production corresponding to a determinate stage of development of their material forces of production. The totality of these relations of production constitutes the economic structure of society, the real foundation on which there arises a legal and political superstructure and to which there correspond definite forms of social consciousness. The mode of production of material life conditions the social, political and intellectual life-process in general. It is not the consciousness of men that determines their being, but on the contrary it is their social being that determines their consciousness. At a certain stage of their development, the material productive forces of society come into conflict with the existing relations of production or— what is merely a legal expression for the same thing—with the property relations within the framework of which they have hitherto operated. From forms of development of the productive forces these relations turn into their fetters. At that point an era of social revolution begins.[23]

This classical formulation is at the root of numerous misunderstandings, namely, a deterministic view of history and a tendency to negate the question of political agency, insofar as the passage presents revolution as the result of a logical contradiction between objective productive forces and not as the product of subjective actions or wills.[24] In other words, for many detractors, the relationship between the so-called base and superstructure, no matter how dialectical, still represents a deterministic concept of history, if not a blunt economicism. In this context, Althusser's notions of *overdetermination* (which Freud used to explain the complex nature of psychic phenomena), and that Althusser subsequently borrowed to improve the Hegelian notion of determination, and *relative autonomy* (limited immediately by the notion of "determination in the last instance"), worked as corrections meant to improve upon the Marxists' theory of history and its relationship to politics.[25] In fact, one might argue that the history of contemporary Marxist theory, including Nicos Poulantzas's analysis of the class structure of the bureaucratic state and his debate with Ralph Miliband, as well as the continuation of Poulantzas's analyses in the work of Bob Jessop; the further development of Althusser's aleatory materialism; and even the contributions of neo-Gramscian approaches of scholars such as Osvaldo Fernández Diaz, José Aricó, and Ernesto Laclau, could be read as supplements to Marx's theory of history, and as parallel and complementary contributions to those elaborated among Latin American Marxist thinkers of the 1960s and 1970s. In other words, one might even venture to say that the problem addressed by Latin American Marxists during the 1960s and 1970s was (and still is) the following: To what extend does the Marxist theory of the mode of production, including its possible correction and improvement, still represent a relevant contribution for the critique of contemporary capitalism?

In order to begin answering this question, it is important to distinguish conventional, schematic notions of mode of production from other, more complex ones. Much as one finds in the metaphysical notion of *epoch*, the conventional understanding of mode of production confuses the concept's descriptive and normative dimensions, thus producing, as an effect, a rigid conception of historical development and fulfillment. The second understanding, which contemplates the aleatory condition of primitive accumulation, the complex and contingent relationship among socioeconomic formations and modes of production, and the notion of overdetermination, enables a more sophisticated view of the mode of production, such that the concept no longer functions to designate a series of dogmatic or normative "stages," but rather to help reflect the multiple elements present in a particular historical moment. In order to sustain this complex notion, however, it is not sufficient to consider the conventional view of the mode of production in relation to the logics of articulation and combination. Rather, we must also emphasize the very logic of Marx's analysis of capitalism in order to avoid treating it as if it were the foundational discourse of political economy. As Óscar del Barco stated clearly in the early 1980s, Marx's critique of political economy was not part of political economy; it was not more of the same. Rather, reaching beyond the conventional operations and conceptualizations of such a discipline, it required the radical interrogation of the temporal and individualistic premises informing its narrative. Del Barco's estimation continues to be relevant today, especially when confronting the vulgar criticism of the so-called failure of Marx's analysis. The point is not to defend it, but rather to understand that such an analysis cannot and should not be reduced to the restrictive criteria of conventional disciplines. In other words, Marx's analysis of capitalism is incompatible with any historicist criteria determining the valid condition of a theory and cannot be reduced to what has been called *historical materialism*, understood as a general theory of historical evolution.[26]

The redefinition of the mode of production and of primitive accumulation that emerged from the mode of production debates of the 1960s and 1970s bear on a number of other, more contemporary concerns: (1) the Asiatic and hydraulic modes of production and their usefulness for understanding indigenous economies and cultures; (2) colonialism, neocolonialism, and what Pablo González Casanova termed "internal colonialism";[27] (3) the nature of Latin American revolutions, in general; (4) agrarian economy and the indigenous collective organization of work and life in the present; (5) the process of proletarianization process and subsequent debate regarding the informal sector and the industrial reserve army in the context of accelerated industrialization and urbanization; (6) the transformation of labor and the notion of marginality, full employment, and the informal economy; (7) social identities, social classes, and class struggle in relation to political conflicts and political strategies; (8) the character, nature, and form of the Latin American state, and its mutation within the process of globalization; (9) the autonomy of the political; and/or its transformation or exhaustion within the ongoing metamorphosis of modern institutions; (10) the ongoing debate about neostructuralism or neo-extractivism and its relationship with the kind of developmentalism that still haunts Latin American politics; and (11) the historical modes of subjectivation, beyond proletarianization, produced within contemporary capitalism.

This, in other words, is the context in which we should approach Marxism in Latin America: not only a problem for the intellectual history of the Left, but also as a series of concepts directly relevant for current theoretical and political debates. The formulations that emerged from the mode of production debates produced nuanced readings of important sections of Marx's then recently translated corpus. Simultaneously, these debates and theoretical elaborations serve as a kind of material testimony to the problematic character and potential inherent in Latin American Marxism. Thanks to these formulations, the field, far from being exhausted, remains as an open alternative to neoliberal devastation and the current, axiomatic version of capital's philosophy of history. Marxism in Latin America has always been oriented toward the production of radical politics, and today, as before, the link between its analytical and political dimensions continues to be a problematic zone, despite wishful attempts to close this gap. The risk one runs in closing the gap between the analytical and political dimensions of Marxist theory in any definitive way not only amounts to a kind of opportunism; it also threatens to overlook the singular character of historical processes in the name of a political commitment and an "ethical" imperative that ultimately suppresses the eventful, aleatory, condition of history.

Notes

1. In fact, the number of studies dedicated to these thinkers is also steadily rising. Let me refer here to just three different examples: The classical volume of Michael Löwy, *Marxism in Latin America from 1909 to the Present*, published in 1992; the more contemporary and focused monograph by Stefan Gandler, *Critical Marxism in Mexico*, first published in German in 1999; and Martín Cortés's *Translating Marx: José Aricó and the New Latin American Marxism*, first published in Spanish 2015.

2. Capitalism has, however, been able to overcome its own philosophy of history through the contingent articulation of its processes beyond any normative criterion. This is what Deleuze and Guattari term "axiomatic" (1987) in the second volume of *Capitalism and Schizophrenia*. Until recently, interpretations of Latin American historical processes have nevertheless disregarded their own implication in the philosophy of history, by refusing to question this normative and evolutive schema. Revisiting such a normative framework is crucial for coming to terms with the Bourbon reforms of the late eighteenth century, the pacification and nation-formation processes of the nineteenth century, the modernization theories of the mid-twentieth century, and the current neoliberal orientation of Latin America toward the global market. Antecedents for a critique of this philosophy of history are everywhere present in the work of Latin American Marxist thinkers, from José Carlos Mariátegui to José Aricó and Bolívar Echeverría, among others.

3. Of course, this is something one might relate to Bolívar Echeverría's reception of the Frankfurt School and, particularly, Walter Benjamin's *Theses on the Concept of History* (see his translation of the *Theses*, 2008; and his edited volume, *La mirada del ángel*, 2005). However, my claim is that within the discussions about the modes of production in Latin America, during the 1970s, this critique of capitalism's philosophy of history was already at stake.

4. See the aforementioned volume by Martín Cortés and Raúl Burgos, *Los gramscianos argentinos* (2004). Something of the sort might be said of the Argentine José Aricó, director of Cuadernos de Pasado y Presente, an editorial collection that published ninety-nine important volumes of Marxist thought and helped shape Latin American debates during the second half of the twentieth century; the Argentine philosopher Óscar del Barco, author of some of the most appealing critiques of Leninism and the shortcomings of the Russian Revolution (*Esbozo de una crítica de la teoría y práctica leninistas* [1980] and *El otro Marx* [1983]); the Ecuadorian philosopher Bolívar Echeverría, author of a rather complex cultural theory of capitalist accumulation and modernity; Argentine philosopher Enrique Dussel, whose thinking not only influenced the philosophy of liberation of the 1960s, but also attempted a controversial reading of Marx's *Grundrisse* of 1857–58 and the rarely known Manuscripts of 1861–63 *La producción teórica de Marx* (1985); *Hacia un Marx desconocido* (1988); *El último Marx* (1990); and his most recent *Las metáforas teológicas de Marx* (2014); Bolivian theorist Álvaro García Linera, who has produced a nuanced integration of Marxism and Indigenism in the line of José Carlos Mariátegui; Roger Bartra, who was one of the first Marxists to question the schematic version of history based upon the lineal concatenation of modes of production that was inherited from the Stalinist official model; and Ernesto Laclau, who not only participated actively in the debates about the modes of production in the 1970, but also produced a well-known post-Marxist appropriation of Gramsci's notion of hegemony in which he updated it in order to describe contemporary social movements (*Politics and Ideology in Marxist Theory* [1977]; his coauthored volume [with Chantal Mouffe], *Hegemony and Socialist Strategy* [1985]; and his early and influential text "Modos de producción en América Latina [Modes of Production in Latin America]," [1973]).

5. *Mariátegui y los orígenes del marxismo latinoamericano* (1978).

6. Along with the foundation of the United Nations Economic Commission for Latin America and the Caribbean, the influence of European Keynesianism allowed for the development of modernization and development theory in Latin America. In turn, these theories bore the imprint of the sociological theory developed by Talcott Parsons at Harvard University. Argentinean economist Raúl Prebisch was one of the first to lay the groundwork for what would later become Dependecy Theory, together with Andre Gunder Frank, Fernando Henrique Cardoso and Enzo Faletto. W.W. Rostow's

general theory of development and Irma Adelman and Cynthia Morris's analysis of the conditions for development in developing countries contributed to modernization theory.

7. Stalin, *Dialectical and Historical Materialism* (originally published in 1938).

8. The historiographic aspect of this debate is monumental, and we should mention that its participants included, among others, Sergio Bagú, Luis Vitale, and Hernán Ramírez Necochea. Vitale was the author of a multivolume study, *Interpretación marxista de la historia de Chile*. See also, Agustín Cueva, *El desarrollo del capitalismo en América Latina*, with a polemical *Afterword* included in the 1990 edition. To this we might add the multiauthored volume, *Modos de producción en América Latina* (with texts by Laclau, Sempat Assadourian, Ciro Cardoso, Horacio Ciafardini, and Juan Carlos Caravaglia), as well as the alternative volume, published by Delva Editores in Peru and edited by Roger Bartra: *Modos de producción en América Latina*, with the texts presented at the *Congreso Internacional de Americanistas*, which took place in Mexico in 1974, as well as another anthology of texts compiled by Roger Bartra, *El modo de producción asiático*.

9. Laclau, "Modos de producción en América Latina," 23–24.

10. Modernization theory was based in the social sciences, particularly structural and functionalist anthropology and sociology.

11. The United Nations Economic Commission for Latin America and the Caribbean, also known in English as UNECLAC or ECLAC, and CEPAL in Spanish, was founded in Santiago de Chile in 1948, and was instrumental in propagating those developmentalist policies. The theory of dependency emerged precisely as a critical alternative to the CEPAL's vision. See Tomás Amadeo Vasconi, *Las ciencias sociales en América del Sur y en Chile 1960–1990*, which is a commemorative volume edited by Universidad ARCIS. See also Jaime Osorio's *Las dos caras del espejo*.

12. The work of Walt Whitman Rostow, Karl Polanyi, Karl A. Wittfogel, Hans Singer, Raúl Prebisch, Celso Furtado and Aníbal Pinto influenced Dependecy Theory. Dependency Theory also echoed debates about imperialism initiated by Lenin and continued in Paul A. Baran and Paul Sweezy's work on political economy.

13. Bartra, "Sobre la articulación de modos de producción en América Latina," 11. The shortcomings of dependency theory resound in the shortcomings of contemporary decolonial theory. Just as dependency theory remained trapped in a circulationist approached to the unequal terms of exchange and participation in the global market in accounting for the region's situation, one might add that decolonial approaches remain trapped, in an analogous sense, at the epistemological level insofar as they understand the abrogation of indigenous communities as the effect of the correspondence between modernity,

capitalism, and colonialism, thus proposing these distinct historical processes as homologous.

14. Kraniauskas, "Difference against Development." In this sense, the series of debates about the so-called Asiatic mode of production, as well as the Hydraulic and the Incan variations, should not be read either as secondary formations or as detours from the official model of five stages. See the already mentioned volume by Roger Bartra, *El modo de producción asiático*, and in that volume, Bartra's critical observations against Karl Wittfogel who, in order to elaborate a political critique of the Soviet Union, coined the term *Hydraulic civilization* to characterized what he called oriental despotism, making use of Marx's term in a rather loose form. See Wittfogel's *Oriental Despotism*.

15. Bartra, "Sobre la articulación," 9.

16. Zavaleta Mercado, *Lo nacional-popular en Bolivia*.

17. This is, indeed, the context in which we should read Álvaro García Linera's crucial book *Forma valor y forma comunidad*, as his approach intersects with Mariátegui's classical "adaptation" of Marxism to the Andean region and the ongoing debate (fleshed out in the interventions of Cornejo Polar, Zavaleta Mercado, Aníbal Quijano, Luis Tapia, etc.) regarding the (im)possible fulfillment of the (*criollo*) nation (as in the already mentioned volume by Zavaleta Mercado, or, in Cornejo Polar's *Escribir en el aire*, originally published in 1994). The important work of García Linera continues the attempt to articulate a Marxist analysis of the Andean social formation. Although this effort is valuable in itself, one runs the risk of universalizing these regional conditions and, in doing so, obliterating the concrete characteristics of other places in Latin America. This is one of the main consequences one can infer from Jean Tible's *Marx Selvagem*, a recent study that, by combining Marxism with the political anthropology of Pierre Clastres, attempts to understand the singular condition of Amazon's nomadic indigenous people without reducing them to the "Incan hypothesis," and assimilating their them to the monumental model of the pre-Colombian empire.

18. Once again, Roger Bartra's problematization of the rigid concatenation of modes of production remains an important reference for questioning the consequences of an undertheorized conception of primitive or originary accumulation. The same is true for Bolívar Echeverría, who developed a Marxist cultural theory for Latin American societies with the notion of "symbolic" primitive accumulation. Rather than restrict primitive accumulation to the moment of Latin American encounter with capitalism, Bolívar Echeverría views it as an ongoing process that follows the mutation of modernity's historical *ethos*.

19. We can thus understand the supposedly ambiguous status of primitive accumulation in Marx. The fact that it seems to be a historical category, and, at the same time, an analytical notion, becomes crucial, as contemporary

scholars have demonstrated. To mention just a few examples, see Glassman, "Primitive Accumulation"; Mezzadra "Topicality of Prehistory"; and Hall, "Primitive Accumulation." Each of these contributions discusses the notion of "accumulation by dispossession," coined by David Harvey and first introduced in his 2003 book *The New Imperialism*. To these, one might add so-called narco-accumulation, financial accumulation or accumulation through debt, war-accumulation, and flexible accumulation, among others. For a rigorous and pertinent problematization of the aleatory condition of primitive accumulation, see Read, *The Micro-Politics of Capital* (2003). Consider, as well, other formulations of this problem within the Italian school (from Mario Tronti and Toni Negri to Sandro Mezzadra and others), as well as the seminal contributions of Rosa Luxemburg.

20. The following translations played an important role in theoretical discussions regarding the question of transition in the mode of production (I refer to the Spanish editions given their relevance for the present argument): Marx's *Formaciones económicas precapitalistas* and *El Capital, Libro I, Capítulo VI (Inédito): Resultados del proceso inmediato de producción*, in 1971; the controversial volume 30 of Cuadernos de Pasado y Presente; Marx and Engels, *Materiales para la historia de América Latina* (1972); volume 30 of Cuadernos de Pasado y Presente; Marx and Engels, *Escritos sobre Rusia* (1980); Volume 93 of Cuadernos de Pasado y Presente: Marx, *Progreso técnico y desarrollo capitalista* (1982); and Lawrence Krader's edition of *Los apuntes etnológicos de Marx* (1988). All of these reverberate in other important volumes such as Teodor Shanin's, *El Marx tardío y la vía rusa*, originally published in English in 1983 and then in Spanish in 1990; Kevin Anderson's *Marx at the Margins*, first published in 2010 and then reprinted in an expanded edition in 2016; Álvaro García Linera's *Forma valor y forma comunidad*; and the recent edition, by Silvia de Alarcón and Vicente Prieto, of Karl Marx's, *Escritos sobre la Comunidad Ancestral*, in 2015. To this list one must also add the fundamental work done by Pedro Scaron, Miguel Murmis, and José Aricó with the translation and edition of the *Grundrisse* (1971–72) and by Pedro Scaron for the Siglo XXI edition of *El Capital* (1975–1981).

21. See the already mentioned *Capítulo VI (Inédito)*.

22. This is one of the links between the problems I have described in the context of Latin American mode of production debates, the present-day work of important Italian Marxists such as Massimiliano Tomba and Vittorio Morfino, among many others, and the seminal contribution of Althusser and his "students." See Althusser et al., *Reading Capital*; Morfino, *Plural Temporality*; and Tomba, *Marx's Temporalities*.

23. Marx, *A Contribution to the Critique of Political Economy*, 4–5.

24. This, for example, is the main argument that Ernesto Laclau and Chantal Mouffe make in their critique of Marx's lack of a political theory, since, for them, the political in Marxism is strictly the reflection of objective forces

onto the "subjective" social realm. See their *Hegemony and Socialist Strategy*. My problem, however, is not only that Laclau and Mouffe adopt an approach that allows them to differentiate between contradiction and antagonism, for example. Rather, the issue that concerns me is how to problematize Laclau and Mouffe's claim about the political as an autonomous, discursive, and "ontological" realm almost independent from the material forces "conditioning" social processes and practices without reducing Marx to the authors' scarecrow version of the Hegelian dialectic. One should remember here that the difference between base and superstructure is not equivalent to the difference between objective and subjective forces, as the latter is a pre-Marxist and mechanical assumption.

25. See Althusser, *La revolución teórica de Marx*. In fact, Althusser's influence in Latin America, from Marta Harnecker to Fernanda Navarro, Roger Bartra, and many others, to the recently published volume *Lecturas de Althusser en América Latina*, compiled by Marcelo Rodríguez Arriagada and Marcelo Starcenbaum, requires a different and complementary work that is being carried out by many scholars today. My point, however, is not archivist or historiographic but conceptual (which does not imply a criticism of these scholars on my part).

26. del Barco, *El otro Marx*. See "Sobre el problema del 'método' marxista," 27–51, and "Notas sobre el marxismo y la 'ciencia,'" 145–53. In an alternative but convergent development, see Felipe Martínez Marzoa's radical critique of historical materialism as the schematic Marxist version of what we have called capitalism's philosophy of history, in *La filosofía de "El Capital" de Marx*. Despite their many differences, both coincide in detaching Marx's analysis of capitalism (which Marzoa thinks of as an ontology of capital) from the evolving narrative related to historical materialism.

27. See "Colonialismo interno," published in 1969, and collected in the volume *De la sociología del poder a la sociología de la explotación* (129–56).

Works Cited

Althusser, Louis. *La revolución teórica de Marx*. México: Siglo XXI Editores, 1967.

——, et al., *Reading Capital. The Complete Edition*. New York: Verso, 2016.

Anderson, Kevin B. *Marx at the Margins: On Nationalism, Ethnicity, and Non-Western Societies*. Chicago: University of Chicago Press, 2016.

Aricó, José. *Mariátegui y los orígenes del marxismo latinoamericano*. México: Siglo XXI Editores, 1978.

——. *Marx y América Latina*. México: Alianza, 1982.

Bartra, Roger. *El modo de producción asiático. Antología de textos sobre problemas de la historia de los países coloniales*. México: Ediciones ERA, 1969.

————, ed. *Modos de producción en América Latina*. Perú: Ediciones Delva, 1976.

Benjamin, Walter. *Tesis sobre la historia y otros fragmentos*. Translated by Bolívar Echeverría. México: Itaca-UACM, 2008.

Burgos, Raúl. *Los gramscianos argentinos. Cultura y política en la experiencia de 'Pasado y Presente.'* Buenos Aires: Siglo XXI Editores, 2004.

Ciccariello-Maher, George. *Decolonizing Dialectics*. Durham: Duke University Press, 2017.

Cortés, Martín. *Un nuevo marxismo para América Latina. José Aricó: traductor, editor, intelectual*. Buenos Aires: Siglo XXI Editores, 2015.

Cueva, Agustín. *El desarrollo del capitalismo en América Latina*. México: Siglo XXI Editores, 1990.

del Barco, Óscar. *Esbozo de una crítica de la teoría y práctica leninistas*. México: Universidad Autónoma de Puebla, 1980.

————. *El otro Marx*. México: Universidad Autónoma de Sinaloa, 1983.

Deleuze, Gilles, and Félix Guattari. *A Thousand Plateaus: Capitalism and Schizophrenia*. Translated by Brian Massumi. Minneapolis: University of Minnesota Press, 1987.

Dussel, Enrique. *La producción teórica de Marx. Un comentario a los Grundrisse*. México: Siglo XXI Editores, 1985.

————. *Hacia un Marx desconocido. Un comentario de los manuscritos del 61–63* México: Siglo XXI Editores, 1988.

————. *El último Marx (1863–1882) y la liberación latinoamericana*. México: Siglo XXI Editores, 1990.

————. *Las metáforas teológicas de Marx*. México: Siglo XXI Editores, 2014.

Echeverría, Bolívar. *La modernidad de lo barroco*. México: Ediciones ERA, 2000.

————. *La mirada del ángel. En torno a las* Tesis sobre la historia *de Walter Benjamin*. México: Ediciones ERA, 2005.

Gandler, Stefan. *Peripherer Marxismus: Kritische Theorie in Mexiko*. Hamburg: Argument Verlag, 1999.

García Linera, Álvaro. *Forma valor y forma comunidad. Aproximación teórica-abstracta a los fundamentos civilizatorios que preceden al Ayllu universal*. La Paz: Ediciones La muela del diablo, 2009.

Glassman, Jim. "Primitive Accumulation, Accumulation by Dispossession, Accumulation by 'Extra-Economic Means.'" *Progress in Human Geography* 30, no. 5 (2006): 608–25.

González Casanova, Pablo. *De la sociología del poder a la sociología de la explotación. Pensar América latina en el siglo XXI*. Colombia: CLACSO, 2009.

Hall, Derek. "Primitive Accumulation, Accumulation by Dispossession, and the Global Land Grab." *Third World Quarterly* 34, no. 9 (2013): 1582–1604.

Harvey, David. *The New Imperialism*. New York: Oxford University Press, 2003.

Krader, Lawrence, ed. *Los apuntes etnológicos de Marx*. México: Siglo XXI Editores, 1988.

Kraniauskas, John. "Difference against Development: Spiritual Accumulation and the Politics of Freedom." *boundary 2* 32, no. 2 (2005): 53–80.

Laclau, Ernesto, Sempat Assadourian, Ciro Cardoso, Horacio Ciafardini, and Juan Carlos Caravaglia. *Modos de producción en América Latina*. México: Siglo XXI Editores, 1973.

Laclau, Ernesto. *Política e ideología en la teoría marxista: capitalismo, fascismo, populismo*. México: Siglo XXI Editores, 1978.

Laclau, Ernesto, and Chantal Mouffe. *Hegemony and Socialist Strategy. Towards a Radical Democratic Politics*. London: Verso, 1985.

Löwy, Michael, ed. *Marxism in Latin America from 1909 to the Present: An Anthology*. Translated by Michael Pearlman. New York: Humanity Books, 1992.

Mariátegui, José Carlos. *Siete ensayos de interpretación de la realidad peruana*. Lima: Minerva, 1928.

Marx, Karl. *Formaciones económicas precapitalistas*. México: Siglo XXI Editores, 1971.

——. *El Capital, Libro I, Capítulo VI (Inédito). Resultados del proceso inmediato de producción*. México: Siglo XXI Editores, 1971.

——. *Elementos fundamentales para la crítica de la economía política (borrador) 1857–1858*. 2 volumes. Santiago: Siglo XXI Editores-Editorial Universitaria de Chile, 1971–1972.

——. *El Capital*. 8 volumes. México: Siglo XXI Editores, 1975–1981.

——. *A Contribution to the Critique of Political Economy*. New York: International Publishers, 1979.

——. *Progreso técnico y desarrollo capitalista (manuscritos de 1861–1863)*. México: Ediciones Pasado y Presente, 1982.

——. *Escritos sobre la Comunidad Ancestral*. Edited by Silvia de Alarcón and Vicente Prieto. La Paz: Ediciones de la Vicepresidencia del Estado, 2015.

——, and Friedrich Engels. *Materiales para la historia de América Latina*. México: Ediciones Pasado y Presente, 1972.

——. *Escritos sobre Rusia. II. El porvenir de la comuna rural rusa*. México: Ediciones Pasado y Presente, 1980.

Marzoa, Felipe Martínez. *La filosofía de "El Capital" de Marx*. Madrid: Taurus Ediciones, 1982.

Mezzadra, Sandro. "The Topicality of Prehistory: A New Reading of Marx's Analysis of 'So-called Primitive Accumulation.'" *Rethinking Marxism* 23, no. 3 (2011): 302–21.

Morfino, Vittorio. *Plural Temporalities. Transindividuality and the Aleatory between Spinoza and Althusser*. London: Haymarket Books, 2015.

Osorio, Jaime. *Las dos caras del espejo. Ruptura y continuidad en la sociología Latinoamericana*. México: Editorial Triana, 1995.

Read, Jason. *The Micro-Politics of Capital*. Albany: State University of New York Press, 2003.

Rodríguez Arriagada, Marcelo, and Marcelo Starcenbaum, eds. *Lecturas de Althusser en América Latina*. Santiago: Editorial Doble Ciencia, 2017.

Shanin, Teodor. *El Marx tardío y la vía rusa*. Madrid: Editorial Revolución, 1990.

Stalin, Joseph. *Dialectical and Historical Materialism*. New York: International Publishers, 1975.

Tible, Jean. *Marx Selvagem*. São Paulo: Annablume, 2013.

Tomba, Massimiliano. *Marx's Temporalities*. London: Haymarket Books, 2014.

Vasconi, Tomás Amadeo. *Las ciencias sociales en América del Sur y en Chile 1960–1990*. Santiago: Universidad ARCIS, 1996.

Vitale, Luis. *Interpretación marxista de la historia de Chile*. 7 volumes. Santiago: LOM Edicones, 1967–2000.

Wittfogel, Karl. *Oriental Despotism. A Comparative Study of Total Power*. New Haven: Yale University Press, 1957.

Zavaleta Mercado, René. *Lo nacional-popular en Bolivia*. México: Siglo XXI Editores, 1986.

CHAPTER FOUR

Accumulation as Total Conversion

KAREN BENEZRA

JOSÉ MARÍA ARGUEDAS'S anthropological studies of the Mantaro River Valley and the town of Puquio to its south focus on the sociosymbolic effects of dispossession and social stratification that resulted from the liberal economic modernization of the 1950s and '60s. In so doing, they paint a vibrant picture of both the experience and mechanism of capitalist accumulation in a social setting defined by the juxtaposition of capitalist and noncapitalist forms of labor and property.

As Arguedas's interpreters have observed, the issue of transculturation serves as both the motor and horizon of his anthropological studies.[1] Arguedas adopted the term from Cuban anthropologist Fernando Ortiz in order to refer to the paradoxical way in which, in order to preserve itself or the essence of its worldview, Andean culture needed to continually transform itself by integrating foreign elements of Hispanic Catholic practice and representation. In a particularly striking passage, Arguedas explains the operation that permits the simultaneous conservation and transformation of Indigenous communities as one that requires the "total conversion" of indigenous highlanders into bourgeois individuals.[2] With the phrase "total conversion" Arguedas likely intended to name an experience of ethical transformation whose effects he often noted in the kinds of social disintegration and material dispossession that resulted from the processes of capitalist expansion during this period. Moreover, as an instance of what literary critic Ángel Rama referred to as the author's "mestizo" period, total conversion might also have represented an ideal for Arguedas insofar as it promised to allow indigenous society to coexist with the nationalist ideology and developmentalist goals of the state.[3] Simultaneously, however, Arguedas's recourse to the motif of Pauline transformation speaks to the complexity of his view of culture. More than merely reflecting the supposedly destructive, lineal force of capitalist development, Arguedas instead viewed Andean social practices and forms of symbolization as intertwined, historically, with the ethical and material life of the community.

Arguedas's anthropological studies are marked by the lament for the inevitable loss of the Andean lifeworld and a faith in the capacity of culture to repair the material and spiritual fragmentation wrought by capitalism. And yet it is perhaps for this reason that his ethnological writings provide a compelling picture of the symbolic effects of capitalist expansion in the Peruvian highlands. By observing how changes in the morphology of Andean myths and social practices were intertwined with historical changes in the regimes of labor and property, Arguedas's writings also reveal a more and less explicit understanding of transculturation as a process that was irreducible to the cultural phenomena that it named. If Arguedas's work as a folklorist addressed the ways in which Andeans signified the fragmentation and transfiguration of existing forms of material and symbolic property, his ethnography of the Mantaro River Valley treats transculturation at once as a social logic synonymous with capitalism and as a practical stopgap measure to contain it.

Literary critic William Rowe has observed the ambivalent attitude toward modernization displayed in Arguedas's studies of the Mantaro River Valley and the town of Puquio in the 1950s. According to Rowe, Arguedas endorses the capacity of transculturation and of culture, in general, to repair the cosmic damage inflicted by capitalism—Arguedas's "naïve utopianism," in Rowe's words—while also criticizing the new individualist ethos emerging together with the transformation of property relations in the highlands.[4] In some passages, Arguedas elevates the cases of Puquio and the Mantaro River Valley as counterexamples to the symbolic and material impoverishment suffered, for example, among the former peons of the Vicos hacienda. At other times, however, he displays a more circumspect attitude toward the purported ethical good of private property and the overall effects of capitalist expansion despite the relative prosperity it produced for towns such as Puquio. Rowe underscores this ambivalence in order to argue that it is only in Arguedas's fictional works—and, specifically, the novel *Todas las sangres* (1964)—where the author is able to imagine the symbolic life that might correspond to a noncapitalist form of property beyond either feudalism or bourgeois individualism. The present essay recognizes this same ambivalence in Arguedas's anthropological writing, and thus also in the cosmological consequences the author assigns, alternately to the maintenance and privatization of the *allyus* in one region or another of the country's highlands. However, in contrast to Rowe, I am interested in the symptomatic relationship sustained between culture and property or, in other words, transculturation and capitalism, in the text of Arguedas's anthropological studies. Beyond Arguedas's own, albeit circumspect, liberal attitude toward modernization and faith in the restorative power of culture in the 1950s, I take as my point of departure the idea that Arguedas's studies from this period register the collective, cultural effects of capitalist subsumption in a sociohistoric context that belies lineal or mechanistic understandings of capitalist development. In doing so, Arguedas's studies allow us an insight into the profound ways that capitalism transforms culture or consciousness. Moreover, they do so without, for that reason, subscribing to the historical narrative of capitalism's imminent demise underpinning considerations of the purportedly anthropological effects of accumulation among Italian post-Autonomist thinkers such as Antonio Negri, Maurizio Lazzarato, or Fraco Berardi.

One of Peru's best-known novelists, Arguedas was also among the first generation to receive formal training as an anthropologist at the recently established Instituto de Etnología y Arqueología within the Facultad de Letras of the Universidad Nacional Mayor de San Marcos (UNMSM) in Lima.[5] Drawing upon a broad range of historical and oral sources, he studied the changing use and hybridization of Quechua and Spanish, Andean myths and religious rituals, the production, sale, and consumption of indigenous artisan crafts and syncretic devotional objects, the constitution and growth of urban commercial centers, the use and organization of communal property, and the historical organization of modes of exchange. Arguedas's anthropological work was both representative and singular within the context of the discipline's institutionalization and the broader social dynamics of modernization in1950s and '60s. Their focus on indigenous cultural integration and on the social stratification of the high lands aligned Arguedas's studies with the interests and influence of U.S.-based development anthropology in Peru at the time. Simultaneously, his approach was unique for the ways in which it resisted the objective, scientific pretenses and economism of applied anthropology, whether oriented toward popular struggle or capitalist development in line with the goals of the state.[6] His writings tended to emphasize the cultural and linguistic specificity of the region, a fact facilitated by his knowledge of Quechua, and to privilege the oral tradition of mythology as a way of registering the collective, subjective effects of socioeconomic change.[7]

Similarly, their attempt to portray the whole of highland society brought into view the implication of Andean cosmology in the historical transformation of property relations. As he would note in his comparative study of the "Myth of Inkarrí," Arguedas viewed the preservation of indigenous symbolic life as tied to the mutual implication between the individual's relation to other members of the community and to the means of his existence. For Arguedas, the "culture" at stake in the process of transculturation comprehends a form of sociosymbolic life supposed and effected by different, historically specific modes of appropriating and distributing the land and its products. In other words, for Arguedas, the anthropological subject of "total conversion," or of institutional and spiritual transformation, is this very nexus of collective material and symbolic life. The issue that Arguedas's use of transculturation attempts to address does not concern the conservation-through-change of a given practice or myth, but of this historical subject of property. In this light, the moment of "total conversion" both presents and suppresses the messy, historical struggle to capture and subordinate this subject to capital.

My aim in what follows is neither to defend Arguedas's notion of transculturation nor to reinitiate critical discussions about the role of culture in the nation-state projects of the past century. Rather, by attempting to read transculturation against the grain of Arguedas's intentions, I hope to reveal the extent to which these writings illustrate, alternately, the experience of capital's encounter with noncapitalist social forms, and the mechanism of accumulation. Read against the grain of its author's intentions, Arguedas's liberal utopian view of modernization also reveals transculturation as a way of coding the historical-logical operation by which capital must incorporate the modes of production and sociality that it finds at hand and, at the same time, stage the semblance of its own autonomy, such that the capture of labor power necessary for capital's reproduction appears to be the product of its own economic logic. As I will try to show, to the extent that Arguedas's use of transculturation helps to illuminate the logical operation by which capital subordinates and sublates existing social relations, it also points to the collective ethical and material subjects of Arguedas's research as the condition for and potential obstacle to capital.

Subsumption

The short-lived but influential readings of the Latin American Subaltern Studies Group often pointed to Arguedas and, more specifically, the notion of transculturation in his work, as an illustration of the purportedly totalizing and homogeneous horizon of nationhood and its potential subversion. Their critiques of the contradictions of Latin American modernity took aim at the outsized role that the lettered tradition—both the institutional role of intellectuals and the symbolic weight of literature—had played in the region's national state projects, and the ideology of *mestizaje* or transculturation that defined the state's claims on universality. Citing Arguedas's undergraduate thesis on the effects of capitalist expansion in the Mantaro River Valley in the 1950s, Gareth Williams notes that in these texts, "Arguedas indicates the intimate relationship between transculturation, geographic and social integration, and capitalist production."[8] As Williams goes on to argue, "Within this narrative [of nation-state formation] the term transculturation could also go by the name of acculturation or even subsumption, for the ground from which Indian transculturation is negotiated at all times reflects the Creole/mestizo understanding of the relation between the land and the capitalist mode of production."[9]

While "transculturation" indeed functions as a central concept in Arguedas's studies from the 1950s, it does not necessarily serve to establish the identity among culture, social integration, and capitalist production, as Williams and others argued. The equivalence that Williams suggests among "acculturation," "transculturation," and "subsumption" confuses the logic by which capital renders different types of labor abstract for the sake of its own valorization, and the concrete heterogeneity of modes of production that it requires in order to generate surplus value, historically, on a global scale.[10] One might argue, instead, that it is precisely the logic of capital's expansive reproduction that subalternist interpretations, such as Williams's, tended to obfuscate by collapsing the telos, or closed historical horizon of the twentieth century's modernizing state projects, with the logic of capital's expansive reproduction.[11] While the state may have seen the promotion of a national mestizo identity as a necessary tool for capitalist modernization, capital's subordination of labor and its concomitant social relations does not itself demand the homogenization of historical times or forms of ethical or political collectivity.

Against Williams's position, we might say that the reproduction of both the nation and capital is indebted to the presuppositional logic or appearance that each produces its own conditions of possibility. To the extent that both present themselves as autonomous and self-positing, to suggest the identity between the two, as Williams does, is also to hide from view the necessary obfuscation of the contingent, historical moment (of the capture of linguistic and cultural heterogeneity and labor power) that serves as the condition of their reproduction. As Marx identified in his discussion of "so-called primitive accumulation and its secret," the expropriation of labor power, capital must find or create the conditions for its own reproduction outside of itself, most often through extra-economic—political, ideological, or military—means.[12] The logical-historical problem of "so-called primitive accumulation" is thus also a way of describing the operation of capitalist accumulation.[13]

The notions of formal and real subsumption, which Marx developed at greatest length in the originally unpublished chapter of *Capital*, Volume 1, known as "The Immediate Results of the Labor Process," serve to describe the operation by which capital incorporates labor power. Marx associates the formal and real subsumption of labor with two historical/technical stages or ways of expropriating surplus value: first through the extension of the working day (absolute surplus value), and then through the intensification and relative efficiency of this process facilitated by the technological advances of the second industrial revolution (relative surplus value).[14] As some more recent approaches have signaled, however, the tendency to collapse formal subsumption with a given historical mode of exploitation tends both to occlude the historical specificity of capital as a social form of wealth and to posit a teleological account of its development that supposes its technological development and eventual demise, an assumption that Marx himself made in the notebooks for *Capital*, Volume 1.

Discussing formal subsumption as a way of organizing the social relations of production rather than a stage in the historical development of capitalism, philosopher Patrick Murray thus observes that while "the *social* transformations involved in formal subsumption are epochal, the *material* transformations are slight."[15] With this "epochal change," Murray refers to the ways in which the subordination of existing labor processes to the ends of generating surplus value imply profound structural changes to the organization of social life at all levels, including the inverted perception of the source of social wealth that Marx associated with the problem of commodity fetishism. Murray thus insists on appreciating the ways that capitalist social relations transform collective relations among producers, as much as they do interpersonal forms of authority and individual perceptions independent of the technical transformation of the labor process. As a folklorist, Arguedas documented precisely these kinds of ethical transformations and their symbolic expression in the oral transmission of myth among Andean populations affected in different ways by the articulation of capitalism. However, the social processes unfolding in the Peruvian highlands during the middle decades of the twentieth century were both empirically and structurally different from the generalization of the wage or the historical articulation of the commodity form of labor that Marx and Murray have in mind.

In attempting to conceive of the historical coexistence of wage labor with noncapitalist forms of exploitation, such as slavery or tenant farming, Massimiliano Tomba expands upon Marx's more limited discussion of "hybrid subsumption." More than accounting for their empirical co-juxtaposition, the notion of hybrid subsumption would allow us to conceptualize the logic by which these different modes of exploitation function for the purposes of generating surplus value on a global scale. Following Tomba's argument, while the bartered peonage of highland peasants, like the unpaid labor of slaves, had not been "formally subsumed" under capital, it nonetheless produced commodities for the world market and can thus be considered to fall under the command of capital.[16] In a tangible, historical sense, this means that direct and purportedly precapitalist forms of violence and domination serve to control the rhythm and intensity of labor for the market and that previously unrecognized forms of social struggle often emerge where they do.[17] In a more formal register, the reproduction of earlier modes of production (the technology used in the production process and the techniques of controlling labor and its social reproduction) speaks to the necessity of such purported anachronisms for the accumulation of capital.[18] Furthermore, according to Tomba, if we accept that the contingent historical conditions for the accumulation of capital—in the English case, the enclosure of the commons, the alienation of peasants from the land, the criminalization of the poor through vagrancy laws, etc. that Marx referred to as "primitive accumulation"—take different forms in different contexts, then we must also accept the other historical paths that capital has taken (for example, in the preservation and transfiguration of non-waged familial and communal production in the Andean highlands) and indeed might have taken in its confrontation with noncapitalist forms of labor and property. The accelerated socioeconomic processes in the back-ground of Arguedas's anthropological works illustrate the determinant role of noncapitalist forms of labor within the country's export economy.

The Possession of the Land

Arguedas's most productive decades coincided with the period of "liberal modernization" beginning with the conservative military coup led by Manuel Odría in 1948 and ending with the "populist" military coup led by Juan Velasco Alvarado in 1968.[19] To offer just one example of the effects of these changes, in 1940 some 65 percent of the population lived in the high-lands, whereas in 1981, 65 percent lived on the coast.[20] The massive internal migration and growth of urban coastal cities was an effect of the growth and diversification of the country's agricultural and extractive economy and precarious industrialization via import substitution.[21] The same twenty-year period also witnessed successive, failed attempts at land reform and the increasing syndical organization and mobilization of highland communities from north to south, surpassing both the regional extension and reformist, juridical claims of a similar wave of protests in the 1940s.[22]

The period's increasingly intense confrontations over land and centuries-old forms of social and political marginalization, together with the growing contradiction among more and less productive sectors of agricultural and industrial capital, produced a rapid and important change in the organization of rural property. That organization was one defined by largely noncapitalist forms of labor and domination, nonetheless oriented toward a capitalist export economy.[23] The modernization of the country's agricultural economy that took place over the first half of the twentieth century depended upon a highly uneven distribution of land, among large and mid-sized *haciendas* and mid-sized *fundos,* on one hand, and private family farms and communally owned property, on the other, and a hierarchy of different kinds of non-wage labor.[24] Peru's export economy depended upon the reproduction of a combination of heterogeneous forms of rent and exploitation: in addition to the exploitation of wage labor, capitalist haciendas with better land and more sophisticated technology profited thanks to their relative superiority over less advanced haciendas with poorer natural resources, by renting marginal lands to tenant farmers, and through the exchange of goods and services with less-developed "satellite" haciendas, generally in the highlands, which formed part of noncapitalist and sometimes nonmonetary peasant economies.[25]

The 1950s and '60s brought the fragile relations of dependence within the country's agricultural sector to a breaking point. Successive land reform laws, the growing threat of indigenous peasant rebellions and occupations, and the increasing disparity between the country's industrial and most advanced agricultural sectors, on one hand, and the productive organization of semicapitalist and traditional haciendas, on the other, brought about the decapitalization of large haciendas, the increasing fragmentation of small, individual farms (as a perverse effect of land reform laws), and the accelerated proletarianization and stratification of landless tenant farmers and seasonal workers with varying ties to the *allyus* or communally owned lands surviving at the margins of the hacienda economy.

Arguedas's "La posesión de la tierra. Los mitos posthispánicos y la visión del universo en la población monolingüe quechua [The Possession of the Land. Posthispanic Myths and the Vision of the Universe in the Monolingual Quecha Population]" (1967), illustrates the simultaneously materialist and liberal utopian currents in his work. The essay compares different versions of the origin myth of the god Inkarrí circulating among the residents of the prosperous southern town of Puquio, where Arguedas had done part of the fieldwork for his undergraduate thesis, and the ex-peons of the Vicos hacienda, a publicly owned parcel of land known for its especially exploitative working conditions and the subject of a well-known experiment in applied anthropology.[26] It begins with a commentary on the connotation of the Quechua word *wakcha* or *orphan*: "Among the Indians of southern and central Peru, *wakcha* is not the orphan who has lost his mother or father; rather, it refers to the man who doesn't have land, or who has been left without land. One's social security is not based on one's kinship ties, rather those ties are established in function of the possession of land."[27] Arguedas concludes that the variations, between one region and another, of the creation tale of the first god, Inkarrí, attest to the capacity of each group to reconcile its respective position in the colonial (and republican) social order. He observes that whereas the landed peasants of Puquio narrate a tale of resurrection that allows them to prosper economically and preserve traditional customs and kinship ties, the former peons of Vicos view their suffering as part of a providential tale of destruction and rebirth effectively justifying their condition.

Arguedas structures his comparison around a paradoxical distinction between the essence and appearance of Andean culture that remains consistent throughout his ethnological writings. While both versions integrate elements of Christian providence, according to Arguedas, the Indians of

Puquio do so to a lesser degree, conserving more non-Christian structures and incorporating Christian ideas only superficially. This, Arguedas argues, allows them to imagine their current situation as transitory and to place their faith in the restoration of a precolonial order at the hands of the god Inkarrí. By contrast, the version of the story found in Vicos represents the current social order as inevitable—the *mistis* or white people will only be punished in a transitory paradise—and, in so doing, reproduces the punishment and destruction of the "idolatrous" Incan order typical of colonial catechism. Despite the denunciatory tone of Arguedas's analysis, its point is ultimately a socially and culturally conservative one. In Arguedas's view, possessing land allows the residents of Puquio to preserve the essence of a worldview that further endows them with a sense of dignity within an unjust socioeconomic regime. At the same time, this brief text, like his more extensive work on the Mantaro Valley, paints a picture of historical consciousness that takes as its premise the mutual supposition between the collective subject and the material conditions of its existence. These earlier studies, which were even more closely aligned with the ideals of *mestizaje* nationalism, illustrate the changes to historical consciousness wrought by the economic transformation of the region, at the same time that they pose a question about the structural necessity of the subject for capital.

Total Conversion

Up until the very last years of his life, Arguedas advanced a paradoxical understanding of transculturation as an operation of cultural conservation through change. In his view, an autochthonous culture that failed to renew its collective forms of expression because of isolation, subjugation, or fragmentation was one that risked dying away. In the 1950s, Arguedas thus viewed a moderate dose of economic prosperity and sociocultural integration as the key to a felicitous process of transculturation. In this sense, the relationship that Arguedas posited between capitalist development and the conservation of traditional Andean culture is representative of what critic Alberto Flores Galindo has referred to as Andean utopianism, which he describes as the collective desire for a just and peaceful preconquest world as an alternative to the present. While Arguedas remained convinced that the transformation of Indians into capitalist mestizos was inevitable, he also wished to see an indigenous Andean hegemony re-established.[28]

In his ethnographic writings, transculturation does more than describe the synthesis of cultural practices or beliefs. It also traces the contours of

Peru's sociopolitical organization over time and space. Let us note, for example, the contrast that he draws between the finite character of the process of cultural fusion that purportedly characterized the link between peoples of the Incan empire, and the seemingly infinite nature of that same process as stimulated by the foreign capital investment in railroads and highways that linked the central highlands with the coast, beginning in the early 1920s:

> The difference [between the pre-Hispanic moment and the current one] resides in the fact that the current moment will not be interrupted. In antiquity these moments of cultural fusion were the result of historical facts that we could call internal and finite, circumscribed within a closed geographical and cultural area. Now, the determinate force of the exchange is not only national, but comprehends the entire universe: it [the internal migration from highlands to coast] comprehends the profound effort to join a higher social rank, towards which the many nations of all continents are marching. In Peru, the coast is the region that has advanced the most towards this higher status, and thus its attraction.[29]

If transculturation began by moving from east to west, "past to present," thanks to the increased commercial traffic between highlands and coast, Arguedas adds that before long the direction of the movement (of commodities and of cultural influence) will reverse itself because of the growth of highland urban centers: "Before long, the direction of movement [of culture and people] will have become circular ... and then Peru will no longer proceed like a head dragging the long, fiery tail that encumbers it."[30] Only progress, the march to "a higher social rank" worldwide, will be able to articulate the national state as a unity defined by the egalitarian inclusion and exchange among different ethnic groups and regions. Arguedas describes the conditions for this articulation in his studies of Huancayo and Puquio, two exceptional cases of modernization and cultural renewal.

As Arguedas recounts in "La evolución de las comunidades indígenas," the published version of his undergraduate thesis, the fact that Spanish conquistadors quickly abandoned the Mantaro River Valley as a potential commercial or administrative center allowed the region's indigenous communities to maintain both a precolonial administrative structure and the possession of their lands under what he refers to as the merely nominal dominion of the encomenderos or commanders over colonial land grants. Within the exceptional colonial experience of the valley as a whole, Arguedas similarly underlines the singular ability of the city of Huancayo to capitalize upon the arrival of the railroad and the industrialization of the mining industry and thus to determine the course of the social and economic changes that would follow from it. In his account, Hauncayo, like Puquio, to the south, produced a class of small property owners capable of overcoming the caste divisions among ethnic indigenous and mestizos that persisted in other parts of the country, just as the vision of Puquio as a town of small farmers or parceleros allowed its indigenous residents to reap the benefits of the highway built to connect Lima and Cuzco in 1926. The purportedly unique forms of property distinguishing Puquio and the Mantaro Valley from other regions of Peru made possible, in Arguedas's words, "a process of transculturation en masse."[31]

Despite their exceptional status in Arguedas's accounts, at a material level, both cities were implicated in the increasingly complex division of labor and class stratification that accompanied and conditioned the preservation of the *allyu* as a municipal subdivision and as a social and political unit. The commonplace vision of Puquio as a town of parceleros, or small farmers, distorts the historical concentration of land in the hands of relatively few haciendas, with something like 8 percent of landowners possessing 65 percent of the terrain. It similarly obfuscates the extent to which the communities of small farmers depended upon the seasonal labor of other landless peasants.[32] While Puquio had been spared the most destructive forms property—dispossession and servitude—capitalist modernization had nonetheless exacerbated class contradiction within indigenous communities, at the same time that the subsistence of collectively farmed small parcelas could be seen as the historical side effect of ineffective land reform and the decapitalization of the sierra among large landowners in the years leading up to the land reform of 1969. Over and against the loss of indigenous culture and the emergence of what he refers to as a "skeptical individualism," Arguedas would thus seem to propose a static vision of communal life at the margins of the highland *fundo* or mid-sized plantation. It is an idealized vision of property relations, in which the microdivision of parcels impedes the productivization of the land and yet protects community members from the perverse effects of dispossession engendered by state's attempts at land reform during the 1960s.

Arguedas's ambivalence toward the effects of modernization is most notable in the contrast he establishes between these processes in the cities of Puquio and Huancayo, which, he suggests, represented parallel and exceptional cases of transculturation. In both cities, the relative sociocultural autonomy from both Hispanic Catholic culture and the most exploitative forms of servitude spared indigenous communities from the most profound spiritual and material effects of dispossession. For this same reason, both were able to reap the benefits of the construction of highways and railroads as part of the state's modest efforts at modernization in the 1920s. However, while Arguedas perceives the ways in which relative commercial prosperity and movement allowed the indigenous communities of both cities to incorporate aspects of mestizo culture in merely superficial ways, he perceives the potentially destructive effects of this adaptation only in Puquio. He observes in Puquio, for example that "Catholic devotion is practiced ostentatiously, however it appears to obey norms that are not related in any substantial way with primary religious needs but that are rather more clearly linked to those of recreation and socialization."[33] Despite this, he also notes that the tendency to supplement the familial subsistence economy through commerce with Lima had already tended to transform, in his words, "the dominant ideal," or the ethical ideals and form of communality prevalent among Puquio's residents:

> Individuals' lives are directed towards the kind of training (*adiestramiento*) that will allow them to better achieve this goal. This movement, which comprehends an alliance with the entrepreneurial class of mestizo merchants, is turning the entire religious edifice upside down. The weakening of traditional beliefs and forms of devotion . . . is removing the fundaments of communal life, which remains solid but which is fiercely embattled among the agents of this change.[34]

In contrast to the capacity for dynamic cultural preservation that Arguedas observes in Huancayo, the process of social and economic modernization in Puquio implies a gradual disintegration of the existent social and spiritual order: "Residents now seem to follow the path opened towards a skeptical individualism, since their links to the gods, who regulated their social conduct and harmoniously inspired their arts, which we contemplate and in which we find a perfect and vigorous beauty, have been weakened."[35]

Aruguedas's description of the parallel process of commerce and sociocultural change in Huancayo adds an additional level of complexity to this account. In "La sierra en el proceso de la cultura peruana [The Highlands in the Peruvian Cultural Process]," he suggests that it is in fact by transforming the very organizing principle of society that Huancayo has remained the same. Noting Indians' seemingly "absurd" and "incongruous" relationship to money as the barrier preventing them from achieving a more complete and definitive form of *mestizaje*, he then describes the "special circumstances" by which an Indian comes to form part of modern Peruvian society:

Their entire cultural structure has achieved a complete readjustment around a single axis or base. Not by changing "one of the superficial elements of its culture" but rather its very fundament, the disconcert that we observe in their culture appears to us as ordered, clear and logical: in other words, that their behavior is identical to our own. And this, by having become an individual who really participates in our culture! A total conversion in which, naturally, some of the elements will continue to exercise an influence as simple terms specific to his or her personality, but which will nonetheless have been moved most substantively by incentives and ideals similar to our own. This is the case of the ex-Indians of the Mantaro River Valley . . . the first case of transculturation en masse.[36]

He argues, paradoxically, that in order to conserve the essence of Andean culture, the indigenous subjects of his case study had to transform themselves into mestizos and into bourgeois individuals, in the author's words, with "ideals similar to our own."[37] With the phrase "total conversion," Arguedas describes the kind of ethical rebirth that had served as the condition for the simultaneous conservation and dynamic change of Andean culture. One could make the case that "total conversion" describes the experience of a collective subject incorporating the national symbolism and ethical ideals of liberal *mestizaje*. However, as we have seen in the comparison of Huancayo and Puquio, and in the analysis of the myth of Inkarrí, the moment of conversion also fulfills a structural function in transculturation's paradoxical operation of conservation through change. In both cases, Andean cosmovision and kinship ties constitute the supposedly essential elements of culture that transculturation helps to conserve. However, it is only in this later text on the possession of the myth of Inkarrí that Arguedas announces more clearly the historical determination of transculturation: kinship ties are maintained in function of the possession of land; however, the changing historical forms of property represent the greatest threat to their conservation. History is the condition of and impediment to the preservation of indigenous culture.

While it is unclear whether total conversion describes a collective, lived experience, one might argue that it nonetheless fulfills a logical function in Arguedas's utopian vision of transculturation. Indians become spiritually bourgeois while the social and ethical relations of highland society remain materially the same. If the recourse to "total conversion" is what allows Arguedas to make the case for the profound transformation of the social relations of production and their conservation, for the same reason, it also designates a moment of logical impossibility. The scene of conversion for

Arguedas's anthropological subjects is also the scene of the historical capture and erasure of labor power for capital. Total conversion is the condition of capital's reproduction and also the obstacle to laying bare this moment from within its view.

Taking a step back from Arguedas's formulations, there is also a more compelling reason to consider the moment of "total conversion." Arguedas's passage brings to mind the often-cited, formally and historically analogous example of flax in the section on primitive accumulation in *Capital*, Volume 1. The material continuity between the world before and after total conversion recalls Marx's description of flax, whose body remained the same, even as the self-sustaining Westhphalen farmers who cultivated it found themselves proletarianized, turned into day laborers or entirely displaced from the countryside: "The flax looks exactly as before. Not a fiber has changed, but a new social soul has popped into its body."[38] Marx's phrasing is jarring for the metonymical relation that the becoming capital of flax sustains with the becoming capital of the labor power of the peasants who spin it. Regardless, the social soul in question refers to the relation of property—the relation of the individual to other individuals and to the material conditions of his existence—in Puquio, as in Westphalen. In Marx's example, that relation is governed by the exchange of wage labor and the valorization of value for its own sake. Its soul is a society of individualized wage laborers.

Marx alludes to a similar scene of transformation in a passage from the *Grundrisse* in which he describes the creation of new needs and new industries presupposed by the extraction of relative surplus value, or value expropriated through the technical efficiency of labor relative to the value expropriated from extensive forms of labor:

> Hence the exploration of all of nature in order to discover new, useful qualities in things; universal exchange of the products of alien climates and lands; new (artificial) preparation of natural objects, by which they are given new use values. The exploration of the earth in all directions . . . likewise the discovery, creation and satisfaction of new needs arising from society itself; the cultivation of all the qualities of a social human being, product of the same in a form as rich as possible in needs, because rich in qualities and relations—production of this being as the most total and universal possible social product, for, in order to make gratification in a many-sided way, he must be capable of many pleasures [*genussfäig*], hence cultured to a high degree—is likewise a condition of production founded on capital.[39]

As Tomba observes with regard to this passage, Marx describes capitalism as a social relation that implies, in his words, "an anthropological modification . . . a new kind of human being: the cultivating of all of the qualities of 'social man.'"[40] The passage rehearses the dialectic of nature in which the relation to the conditions of one's biological and social being have been destroyed and rearticulated. Nature is no longer man's "inorganic laboratory," as Marx describes it in the section on "pre-capitalist social formations," but rather an object for use. Tomba's point in signaling this passage is to show how, through it, Marx constructs a narrative of genesis, development, and crisis. The new social man of capitalism anticipates the development of capital's forces of production and their limit, located in their decreasing dependency on labor power as part of this historical course. In Tomba's reading, the operation of anthropological transformation described in this passage likewise anticipates the capabilities of the socialized worker of industrial production described in the "Fragment on Machines."[41]

By revealing Marx's passing assumptions about the imminent crisis of capital, Tomba's textual and conceptual reconstructions point instead to the asynchronies and expedient heterogeneity of the social forms of labor necessary for its survival. This social form, illustrated in the dependency on noncapitalist forms of labor sustaining Peru's export economy, also allows us a more nuanced understanding of the relation between the kind of sameness or identity advanced, politically, by the ideal of mestizaje, and the historical-logical dynamics by which capital subordinates and reconfigures different forms of labor and sociality. Once again, though, just as we saw through the textual example of "total conversion," anthropology, or the documentation of a collective experience, both hides and reveals its own relation to accumulation. Arguedas's ethnological writings portray the symbolic effects of the historical processes of dispossession and proletarianization—and the resistance to them—that Marx described as the primitive accumulation of capital in the English case. Read at face value, even in its most felicitous cases, the far-reaching effects of economic modernization suppose both a drastic reconfiguration of collective life and a profound spiritual and ethical transformation. At the same time, the more or less apparent contradictions of his treatment of transculturation also make manifest the mechanism of accumulation in a way that is not limited to the particular phenomenon of dispossession.

What, then, should we make of the anthropological transformations or total conversions that Marx and Arguedas describe? For each, this transformation implies something more than a new sensibility or set of practices.

And this is not simply because the conversion (subjective for Arguedas, objective and subjective for Marx) implies the supra-sensible social determination of sensible things. Or rather, to the extent that for both Marx and Arguedas, this human transformation implies the imposition of a new social being or soul, it also implies a radical transformation in the historical form of the mutual determination of ethical and material life. It is perhaps at this point that Arguedas's anthropology offers something to Marx's in thinking about the relation between accumulation and subjectivity. It is not in the experience of total conversion that we find this answer, but rather in the logical operation that it announces, where the symbolic and practical effects of capital, the historical consciousness of hybrid subsumption, become a new terrain of struggle.

Notes

1. Ortiz, *Contrapunteo cubano*, 92. Beverley, *Subalternity and Representation*, 43. de la Cadena, "La producción," 110. Arguedas's use of the term derives from that of Cuban anthropologist Fernando Ortiz, who coined the term *transculturation* as a way of defining a notion of cultural evolution that assumed the dynamism and agency of subaltern cultures in colonial or postcolonial contexts over and against the passivity implied by the notion of acculturation. Historical anthropologist John Murra served as a link between Oritz and Arguedas and as a node in an intergenerational network of Afro-Caribbeanist and Indigenist intellectuals invested in the issue of cultural assimilation in the broader context of national self-determination in the early 1950s. The treatment and recodification of the issue of cultural assimilation had longer roots in the region and in the relationship with the U.S. academy. Born of the work an earlier generation of Mexican and Peruvian Indigenist intellectuals beginning in the late nineteenth century, the term *acculturation* was recognized by the American Anthropological Association in 1936, placing an academic and imperial stamp on the alternately liberal and popular notions of *mestizo* nationalism at stake in these earlier discussions.

2. Arguedas, "La sierra en el proceso de la cultura peruana," 26.

3. Rama, Introducción, xvii. In his introduction to the collection *Formación de una cultura nacional indoamericana*, Rama distinguishes the earlier, dualistic view of society present in the narrative that predated his field work in the Mantaro River Valley from his later, implicitly felicitous "discovery" of *mestizos* as a social group and as a protagonist of indigenous sociopolitical integration: "[C]orresponderá a Arguedas descrubir la positividad del estrato social mestizo, será quien cuente con delicadeza su oscura y zigzagueante gesta histórica y mostrará cómo reelabora las tradiciones artísticas que en un

nivel de fijeza folklórica custodiaban los indios, introduciéndolas ahora en la demanda nacional."

4. Rowe, *Mito e ideología*, 139.

5. Landa Vásquez, "José María Arguedas nos engañó," 130; Pozo-Bujele, "Arguedas o la antropología como institución," 57. Arguedas's literary career began with the publication of his first book of stories, *Agua* (Water), in 1935, and ended with the posthumous publication of the novel, *El zorro de arriba y el zorro de abajo* (The Fox from Up Above and the Fox from Down Below), following the author's suicide, in 1969. After earning an undergraduate degree in literature in 1937, he went on to earn a second one in anthropology in 1957. He undertook field research in the Mantaro River Valley and the prosperous town of Puquio in the Southern Central Highlands between 1952 and 1956 and, in 1958, went on to conduct doctoral research on the surviving institutions of communal property in the province of Zamora in Castilla y León in northwestern Spain, thanks to a grant from UNESCO.

6. Montoya, "Antropología y política," 26.

7. Benítez Leiva, "La novela de arriba," 129–41. Rivera Andía, "El saber artístico," 151–52. Since the 1990s, a number of anthropologists have underlined the extent to which the poetic qualities of his prose and use of first-person narrative "anticipates" the more contemporary forms of experimental ethnography.

8. Williams, *The Other Side of the Popular*, 27.

9. Ibid.

10. Tomba, "Subsumption as Form," 28.

11. Walker, "The Postcolonial and the Politics of the Outside," 4. Gavin Walker expresses the logic of presupposition and the moment of ideological erasure common to the structure of the nation-state and capital: "Just as labor's expropriation, the violence of its capture, is erased by plugging up the ontological gap in capital's smooth circuit-process through the semblance of labor-power, so too the nation-state's postcolonial condition always attempts to erase the traces and continuities of colonial violence by means of its own refined violence (a violence which was itself perfected in the colony)."

12. Walker, *The Sublime Perversion of Capital*, 81; Tomba, "On Subsumption as Form and the Use of Asynchronies," unpublished manuscript.

13. Ibid.

14. Marx, *Capital*, 645–66.

15. Murray, "The Transformation of Production by Capital," 252–53.

16. Tomba, "Subsumption as Form," 33–34. Marx, *Capital*, 645. Tomba cites and elaborates on a brief reference by Marx to transitional modes of exploitation and hybrid forms of subsumption in the chapter on "Absolute and Relative Surplus Value" in *Capital*, Vol. 1. As we can see from the following quotation, Tomba does not intend to remain faithful to Marx's definition,

insofar as, for Tomba, the comingling of noncapitalist and capitalist forms of exploitation represents more than a passing historical moment or categorical omission, but rather a structural necessity for the extraction of surplus through the differentiation among the temporal efficiency of different modes of production under capital's command. We can contrast Tomba's elaboration with Marx's comments: "It will be sufficient if we merely refer to certain hybrid forms, in which although surplus labor is not extorted by direct compulsion from the producer, the producer has not yet become formally subordinate to capital." Noting the predominance of usury as a noncapitalist form of exploitation that could be considered transitional in the movement between feudalism and capitalism, Marx concludes these remarks with the following observation: "Finally, as in the case of modern 'domestic industry,' certain hybrid forms are reproduced here and there against the background of large-scale industry, though their physiognomy is totally changed."

17. Ibid.

18. Ibid. Just as capital assumes and transfigures the forms of exploitation and sociality that it finds at hand, the highland commune or *allyu* should not be considered the residue of an earlier mode of production, but rather the historical product of class and property relations articulated under the effects of monopoly capital beginning in the last third of the nineteenth century in Peru. Among Marxist thinkers in Latin America, José Carlos Mariátegui was the first to diagnose the material and ideological unevenness of capitalism. In his *Seven Essays on Peruvian Reality* (1927), Mariátegui argued that indigenous poverty and social marginalization were the products of a hybrid and historically dynamic organization of social relations and an equally dynamic intra-class conflict among landowning and mercantile sectors of the bourgeoisie.

19. Yepes, *La modernización en el Perú*, 58–59.

20. Ibid.

21. Ibid., 60–69.

22. Flores Galindo, *Buscando un inca*, 358–66.

23. Matos Mar and Mejía, *La reforma agraria en el Perú*, 28.

24. Ibid., 34. Anthropologists José Matos Mar and José Manuel Mejía summarize the heterogeneity and economic dependence that characterized the social organization of production in Peru in the 1950s: "Small agricultural units and peasant communities, subordinate to traditional and modern haciendas [large tracts of land, generally not operated by their owners, but rented to tenant farmers]; traditional haciendas and fundos [medium-sized farms, usually operated by owners] dominated by modern haciendas; microregions and depressed provincial areas dependent upon developed microregions and provincial areas; and backwards regions subordinated completely or partially to more modern ones, constituted the great mosaic of disparities through which the profit and biopower that became concentrated in a few privileged

spaces to the benefit of a reduced sectors of the economy." (Translations and bracketed phrases are mine unless otherwise noted.)

25. Ibid., 35. This same hierarchal integration of capitalist and noncapitalist relations of production became the obstacle to the integration of agriculture with the new industrial sectors emerging in the same period. For the most technologically advanced sectors of the agricultural economy, reproducing the exploitation or superexploitation of noncapitalist labor eventually proved more profitable than confronting the high costs of investing in more efficient, inevitably foreign technology. In addition to impeding the creation of an internal market for domestic goods, the dependence on noncapitalist forms of production also meant that accumulation in the agrarian sector usually ended in luxury consumption or investment in urban financial speculation.

26. After three years of research, beginning in 1949, The Cornell-Peru program leased the expansive, publicly owned Vicos hacienda, home to some 1,700 Quechua-speaking Indians in the Callejón de Huaylas in the northern central highlands, with the goal of liberating its inhabitants from traditional forms of subjugation, providing them with basic healthcare and education, and leaving them economically self-sufficient and able to buy the land themselves by the end of the project in 1966. Allan Holmberg, a professor of anthropology at Cornell and the head of the program, described it as an experiment in modernization and an attempt to "help this community to change from a position of relative dependence and submission in a highly restricted and provincial world to a position of relative independence and freedom in the framework of Peruvian national life." Holmberg, cited in Osterling and Martínez, "Notes for a History of Peruvian Social Anthropology," 345.

27. Arguedas, "La posesión de la tierra," 201. [Entre los indios del sur y del centro de Perú, *wakcha* no es el huérfano que ha perdido a su madre o a su padre; denomina al hombre que no tiene tierras, que ha quedado sin tierras. La seguridad social no está basada en los vínculos de parentesco sino que tales vínculos se establecen en función de la propiedad de la tierra.] Translations from Spanish are mine.

28. Lienhard, "La antropología" 55.

29. Arguedas, "La sierra en el proceso de la cultura peruana," 10. [La diferencia reside en que el actual movimiento no será interrumpido; porque en la antigüedad, estos periodos de fusión fueron el resultado de hechos históricos que podríamos denominar *internos* y finitos, circunscriptos a un área y cultura cerradas. Esta vez la fuerza determinante del intercambio no es sólo nacional, viene de todo el universo humano; se trata del esfuerzo profundo por ingresar a un estatus social superior, al que se encaminan por múltiples pueblos de todos los continentes. La costa es, en el Perú, la región que más ha avanzado hacia ese status superior; por eso atrae.]

30. Ibid., 11. [No pasará mucho tiempo, y la dirección del movimiento se habrá convertido en circular, y comprenderá las tres regiones; entonces el Perú avanzará no ya como una cabeza de fuego que arrastra una larga cauda pesada y lastrosa.]

31. Ibid., 11–12.

32. Montoya, *Capitalismo y no-capitalismo en el Perú*, 53, 54.

33. Arguedas, "Puquio, una cultura en proceso de cambio," 76. [El culto católico se practica ostentosamente, sin embargo muestra apariencias de obedecer a normas no sustancialmente relacionadas con las necesidades religiosas primarias sino a funciones más claramente vinculadas a otras necesidades como la recreación y la promoción social.]

34. Ibid., 77–78. [La vida de los individuos es orientada hacia el adiestramiento para alcanzar mejor este objetivo. Todo el complejo religioso está siendo sacudido por este movimiento que cuenta con la alianza de la clase de los mestizos comerciantes con espíritu de empresa. El debilitamiento de las antiguas creencias y culto (oficial y local) remueve las bases de la vida comunal, que se muestra aún firme, pero duramente combatida por los agentes que hemos señalado.]

35. Ibid., 79. [Siguen ahora, aparentemente, un camino abierto hacia el individualismo escéptico, debilitados sus vínculos con los dioses que regularon su conducta social e inspiraron, armoniosamente, sus artes, en las que contemplamos y sentimos una belleza tan perfecta como vigorosa.]

36. Arguedas, "La sierra en el proceso de la cultura peruana," 26. [Toda su estructura cultural logra un reajuste completo sobre una base, un 'eje'. Al cambiar no 'uno de los elementos superficiales de su cultura' sino el fundamento mismo, el desconcierto que observamos en su cultura se nos presenta como ordenado, claro y lógico: es decir, que su conducta se identifica con la nuestra. ¡Por haberse convertido en un individuo que realmente participa de nuestra cultura! Una conversión total en la cual, naturalmente, algunos de los elementos seguirán influyendo como simples términos especificativos de su personalidad que en lo sustancial será movido por incentivos, por ideales, semejantes a los nuestros. Tal es el caso de los ex indios del valle de Mantaro . . . primer caso de transculturación en masa.]

37. Arguedas, "La sierra en el proceso," 26.

38. Marx, *Capital*, 909.

39. Marx, *Grundrisse*, 409.

40. Tomba, "Pre-Capitalist Forms of Production," 394.

41. Ibid., 395.

Works Cited

Arguedas, José María. "La posesión de la tierra. Los mitos posthispánicos y la visión del universo en la población monolingüe quechua." In *Obra antropológica* 7, 201–12.

——. "La sierra en el proceso de la cultura peruana." In *Formación de una cultura nacional indoamericana*, edited and introduction by Ángel Rama, 9–27. México: Siglo Veintiuno Editores, 2006.

——. "Puquio, una cultura en proceso de cambio. La religión local," In *Formación de una cultura nacional indoamericana*, edited and introduction by Ángel Rama, 34-79. México: Siglo Veintiuno Editores, 2006.

Benítez Leiva, Luciano. "La novela de arriba y la antropología de abajo. ¿Los zorros de Arguedas como etnografía experimental?" *Anthropologica* 29, no. 29 (2011): 129–41.

Beverley, John. *Subalternity and Representation: Arguments in Cultural Theory.* Durham: Duke University Press, 1999.

Cotler, Julio. *Clases, estado y nación en el Perú.* México: Universidad Nacional Autónoma de México, 1982.

de la Cadena, Marisol. "La producción de otros conocimientos y sus tensiones: ¿de la antropología andinista a la interculturalidad?" In *Saberes periféricos: ensayos sobre la antropología en América Latina*, edited by Carlos Iván Degregori and Pablo Sandoval, 107–52. Lima: Instituto Francés de Estudios Andinos and Instituto de Estudios Peruanos, 2008.

Flores Galindo, Alberto. *Buscando un inca: Identidad y utopía en los Andes.* México: Consejo Nacional para la Cultura y las Artes and Grijalbo, 1993.

Gonzales, Osmar. "The Instituto Indigenista Peruano: A New Place in the State for the Indigenous Debate." *Latin American Perspectives* 39, no. 5 (September 2012): 33–44.

Landa Vásquez, Ladislao. "José María Arguedas nos engañó: Las ficciones de la etnografía." *Revista de crítica literaria latinoamericana* 36, no. 72 (2010): 129–54.

Marx, Karl. *Capital: A Critique of Political Economy*, Vol. 1. Translated by Ben Fowkes. New York: Penguin, 1990.

——. *Grundrisse: Foundations of the Critique of Political Economy (Rough Draft).* Translated by Martin Nicolaus. New York: Penguin, 1993.

Matos Mar, José, and José Manuel Mejía. *La reforma agraria en el Perú.* Lima: Instituto deEstudios Peruanos, 1980.

Montoya, Rodrigo. *Capitalismo y no-capitalismo en el Perú: Un estudio histórico de su articulación en un eje regional. Lima*: Mosca Azul Editores, 1980.

——. "Antropología y política." In *José María Arguedas, veinte años después: huellas y horizonte, 1969–1989*, edited by Rodrigo Montoya, 17–30. Lima: Escuela de Antropología de la Universidad Mayor de San Marcos, 1991.

Ortiz, Fernando. *Contrapunteo cubano del tabaco y del azúcar*. Caracas: Biblioteca Ayacucho, 1978.

Osterling, Jorge P., and Héctor Martínez. "Notes for a History of Peruvian Social Anthropology, 1940–80." *Current Anthropology* 24 (1983): 327–41.

Pozo-Bujele, Erik. "Arguedas o la antropología como intuición: Apuntes para una propuesta de articulación." In *Arguedas: el Perú y las ciencias sociales: nuevas lecturas*, edited by Ricardo Cuenca and Ramón Pajuelo, 263–87. Lima: Instituto de Estudios Peruanos, 2014.

Rama, Ángel. *Transculturación narrativa en América Latina*. México: Siglo Veintiuno Editores, 1982.

Rivera Andía, Juan Javier. "El "saber artístico" de un antropólogo y el estudio de la cultura en el Perú. A propósito de una obra olvidada de José María Arguedas." *Anthropologica* 29, no. 29 (2011):143–54.

Rowe, William. *Mito e ideología en la obra de José María Arguedas*. Lima, Instituto Nacional de Cultura, 1979.

Tomba, Massimiliano. "Pre-Capitalistic Forms of Production and Primitive Accumulation. Marx's Historiography from the *Grundrisse* to *Capital*." In *In Marx's Laboratory: Critical Interpretations of the* Grundrisse, edited by Riccardo Bellofiore, Guido Starosta, and Peter D. Thomas, 393–411. Leiden and Boston: Brill, 2013.

———. "On Subsumption as Form and the Use of Asynchronies." In *Accumulation and Subjectivity: Rethinking Marx in Latin America*, edited by Karen Benezra, 27–43. Albany: State University of New York Press, 2022

Walker, Gavin. *The Sublime Perversion of Capital: Marxist Theory and the Politics of History in Modern Japan*. Durham: Duke University Press, 2016.

———. "The Postcolonial and the Politics of the Outside: Return(s) of the National Question in Marxist Theory." *Viewpoint Magazine* 6 (2018). Accessed April 22, 2019. https://www.viewpointmag.com/2018/02/01/postcolonial-politics-outside-returns-national-question-marxist-theory/.

Williams, Gareth. *The Other Side of the Popular: Neoliberalism and Subalternity in Latin America*. Durham: Duke University Press, 2002.

Yépes, Ernesto. *Economía y política: La modernización en el Perú del siglo XX: ilusión y realidad*. Lima: Mosca Azul, 1992.

PART TWO

Class
and
Totality

CHAPTER FIVE

José Aricó and the Concept of Socioeconomic Formation

MARCELO STARCENBAUM

Introduction

Socioeconomic formation is one of the most productive and talked-about notions in the history of Marxism. Its origins date back to Marx's writings, where socioeconomic formation (*ökonomische Gesellschaftsformation*) was used as an alternative to "mode of production" to designate the totality of social relations that define a historically given society. Against mechanistic and economistic temptations, this concept allowed Marx to present an analysis of social configurations that were determined on the basis of their structural and superstructural dimensions. However, as we shall see, the fact that this concept was in some instances presented in a way that did not differentiate it from that of mode of production, or which placed socioeconomic formations in successive order, inaugurated a set of quarrels regarding its place within Marx's work.

Lenin frequently addressed the concept of socioeconomic formation during his dispute with the Russian populists. In *What the "Friends of the People" Are and How They Fight the Social-Democrats*, the notion of socioeconomic formation appears as a refutation of subjective sociology, which tended to think of social configurations in terms of generality. Furthermore, Lenin presented it as a concept that allowed for the scientific analysis of society based on the defining character of relations of production, which led to thinking of social configuration in terms both of singularity and of repetition and regularity. Lenin's reading of *Capital* was mediated by the importance of the concept of socioeconomic formation such that the analysis of relations of production appeared as a *skeleton* that had to be covered with the flesh and blood of the superstructure. Lenin treated capitalist socioeconomic formation as a *living organism* that he analyzed alongside facets of everyday life, as well as the real manifestation of class antagonism, its political institutional expressions, and its ideological dimension.[1]

The present text analyzes the place occupied by the concept of socioeconomic formation in the context of the Marxist renewal undertaken by Argentinian intellectual José Aricó in the 1960s and '70s. As is well known, his work as an editor, translator, and intellectual found the light of day mainly through the journal *Pasado y Presente*, which had an initial publishing phase between 1963–65 and a second phase in 1973, as well as in Cuadernos de Pasado y Presente, a publishing initiative between 1968–83 that managed to print almost one hundred volumes during its existence. In the context of the crisis of the Communist International movement, the development of third world revolutionary processes, and the revision of national-popular experiences within the region, the rereading of the Marxist corpus undertaken by Aricó sought to furnish interpretive blueprints that would allow the Argentinian Left to account for the specificities of Argentinian society and the requirements of an effectively transformative political practice. This theoretical and political operation attempted to overcome the rigid frameworks provided by orthodox Marxism and upheld by the Argentine Communist Party, whose leaders and intellectuals had confined Argentine reality within predetermined historical interpretations and political strategies.[2]

The present essay proposes that the concept of socioeconomic formation played a fundamental role in the renewal of Marxism. Faced with the limitations of social and historical analyses mediated by the concept of mode of production, that of socioeconomic formation made it possible to approach a totality composed of elements that belonged to different modes of production. Furthermore, against economistic interpretations, this concept allowed for a nonreductionist understanding of superstructural circumstances. In opposition to political strategies posed on a global scale, the concept of socioeconomic formation helped to prioritize the social and historical singularity of the society in which political action was intended. Likewise, in the face of evolutionist approaches, this concept enabled a thinking of politics as a practice whose development and outcome were not guaranteed by the general laws of history.

We will attempt to gauge these effects by analyzing the process of translation and dissemination of Marxism that Cuadernos de Pasado y Presente carried out. As the scholarship on Aricó and the Cuadernos has pointed out, this experience represents a *publishing* initiative with clear *political* objectives. In this sense, while each of the Cuadernos contains a brief introduction by Aricó, the most significant aspect of this experience lies in the consequences of the translations that were undertaken, as well as the texts, authors, and theoretical debates that the series helped to disseminate. Therefore, rather than attending to Aricó's theoretical production, I will attempt to make the Cuadernos speak. In other words, the present essay asks: What components of the theoretical and political conundrums addressed within the pages of the Cuadernos were important to Aricó's interest in theoretical and political renewal of the Argentinian Left? By privileging the concept of socioeconomic formation, I will focus on two extensive sets of the Cuadernos. The first set intervenes into Marx's own corpus. This first set includes texts where Marx outlines the concept of socioeconomic formation along with other other materials that provide analytical variables for its interpretation. The second set salvages contemporary debates revolving around the concept of socioeconomic formation. This second set of Cuadernos published texts that reactivated the concept of socioeconomic formation in Italian and French Marxism during the 1960s and 1970s.

Each of these sets of the Cuadernos contributed specific elements to the concept of socioeconomic formation. The first group helped to disseminate Marx's texts along with contemporary analyses that counteracted the effects of evolutionist and teleological Marxist frameworks. On the one hand, novel readings of Marx permitted the rebuttal of a linear understanding of the succession of socioeconomic formations. On the other, the recovery of a Marx that was attentive to the problems of capitalism's periphery contributed to a critique of the notion of progress and foregrounded the national question. The second group of Cuadernos presented a combination of different interventions sparking a debate about the concept of socioeconomic formation. While the published texts catered to the diverse traditions that propitiated this debate—Italian historicism on the one hand, French structuralism on the other—on the whole they buttressed a conception of societies as complex structured totalities.

Their peculiarities not withstsanding, the texts propagated by these two sets of the Cuadernos situate the concept of socioeconomic formation as a primary tool for a Marxist interpretation capable of accounting for the specificity of Argentinian society and thus able to provide the knowledge necessary for its transformation. As we will see in what follows, the relevance of the concept of socioeconomomic formation also extends beyond these volumes. When Aricó systematized his theoretical positions in the latter part of the 1970s, the concept of socioeconomic formation assumed a dominant role within contemporary Marxist debates. Analyzing these two different instances of Aricó's work will allow us to appreciate the extent to which the concept of socioeconomic formation constituted one of the pillars of Aricó's revision of Marx and Marxism in the 1960s and '70s.

Rereading Marx

The introduction of the concept of socioeconomic formation within the Cuadernos can be approached from the same angle as Aricó, who viewed this publishing project as a reappropriation of the Marxist corpus. The volumes that deal with the problems pertaining to this concept are part of a set of texts that give account of an effort to transform the ways in which Marx's work had been interpreted during the first half of the twentieth century. In this regard, Horacio Crespo has referred to the existence of a series of Cuadernos that exhort philological readings of Marx.[3] In a similar vein, Martín Cortés has underscored Aricó's tendency to work on texts that allowed for the dismantling of ossified narratives and for rethinking the deployment of Marx's own thought.[4]

Approaching these Cuadernos from the perspective of the concept of socioeconomic formation requires, at the same time, limiting ourselves to two subsets. On the one hand, this allows us to focus on a group of publications that introduced the concept and provided the necessary interpretive tools for understanding it. The first Cuaderno, which published a translation of Marx's *A Contribution to the Critique of Political Economy* in 1968, can be situated here, as can Cuaderno 20, from 1971, which published the section of the *Grundrisse* titled *Pre-Capitalist Economic Formations*. Following the terms outlined above, while the first of the Cuadernos facilitated an approach to the Marxist conception of socioeconomic formation, the second Cuaderno accounted for a set of problems pertaining to its conceptualization.

The notion of socioeconomic formation occupies a central place in the principles that Marx outlined in the Preface to *A Contribution to the Critique of Political Economy*. After highlighting the guiding thread of Marx's analyses—which was the decisive character that relations of production have on the juridico-political realm and the treatment of the problem of development pertaining to the contradiction between forces of production and social relations of production—socioeconomic formations appeared to represent the various stages of human history. Therein appears the famous phrase that characterized the Marxist conception of the problem while at the same time laying the foundations of the debate: "Asiatic, ancient, feudal and modern bourgeois modes of production can be designated as progressive epochs in the economic formation of society."[5] Marx's assertion consisted of a list of societal forms and the attribution of a progressive character to their succession throughout the course of human history. These same lines also propose the conditions for historical transformation. A social formation cannot disappear until the forces of production that satisfy it have been fully developed. Likewise, new relations of production must be engendered within the contradictions of the society that preceded them.

In this sense, the publication of Marx's *Pre-Capitalist Economic Formations* enabled the appropriation of both a set of analytical variables concerning the development and succession of social formations and a series of arguments to counteract earlier, ossified interpretations of Marx's work. In this respect, we should emphasize that while the *Formen* played a fundamental role in these activities, it was Eric Hobsbawm's introduction, above all, that provided the space for a novel approach to the Marxist corpus. This was due both to the difficulties inherent in reading the *Formen*, a text comprised of at times impenetrable annotations, as well as to the fact that Hobsbawm's analysis, which occupied the same space as Marx's text, was fundamentally aimed at clarifying the problem of the development and succession of socioeconomic formations. On the one hand, Hobsbawm's introduction could be said to reorder Marx's corpus. In this sense, he described the *Formen* as the most systematic attempt to address the problem of historical evolution. Hobsbawm's introduction thus exercised a corrective effect on historical interpretations buttressed by theoretical frameworks to be found in other parts Marx's work as well. In Hobsbawm's own words, "[A]ny Marxist historical discussion which does not take into account the present work—that is to say virtually all such discussion before 1941, and (unfortunately) much of it since—must be reconsidered in its light."[6]

On the other hand, we can also consider the importance of the publication of the *Formen* and of Hobsbawm's introduction, in interpretive or conceptual terms. In this regard, Hobsbawm treated the theoretical outlines offered by the *Formen* and the Preface to *A Contribution to the Critique of Political Economy* in extremely abstract terms. His reading understood Marx's formulations as proposing the general mechanisms of all social change. In other words, for Hobsbawm, the analysis of the contradictory relation between the forces and relations of production was not limited to the description of specific historical periods. He thus characterized Marx's famous declaration in the Preface to *A Contriubtion to the Critique of Political Economy*, cited above, as a "brief, unsupported, and unexplained list of epochs in the progress of the economic formation."[7] Hobsbawm thus addressed the question of the succession of socioeconomic formations from two converging lines of reasoning. He argued, on the one hand, that Marx's list of historical epochs, like his analysis of specific historical moments, was the product of observation and not a theoretical derivation. According to Hobsbawm, the general theory of historical materialism requires a succession of modes of production, "though not necessarily any particular modes, and perhaps not in any particular predetermined order."[8] On the other hand, Hobsbawm argued that the evolutionary nature of the succession of historical stages pertained to a much more general level of analysis. In other words, as Hobsbawm explains, Marx's *Formen* present neither a chronological succession nor the evolution of a system from its predecessor. From Hobsbawm's perspective, Marx's assertion that socioeconomic formations are progressive refers to humans' separation from their originary state, and "does not therefore imply any simple unilineal view of history, not a simple view that all history is progress."[9]

A Contribution to the Critique of Political Economy and *Pre-Capitalist Economic Formations* can be understood within the context of a series of Cuadernos introducing and treating the concept of socioeconomic formation in theoretical terms. In parallel fashion, another set of Cuadernos mobilized and investigated the concept with respect to a set of determinate historical and political situations. A significant portion of Aricó's editorial work toward the end of the 1970s was devoted to disseminating those texts in which Marx distills a heterodox vision of the capitalist world's periphery. Part of the reconfiguration of Marx's corpus, the writings on Ireland and Russia allowed for the appropriation of a materialist perspective that departed from evolutionist and fatalist interpretive models. As Cortés has insisted, it is in the exercise of recovering the *late Marx* or the *Marx at the margins* where we find one of the main wellsprings of Aricó's renewal of Marxism, insofar as these texts allowed for a more nuanced approach to the Marxist theoretical tradition in the sense that they offered "a critique of progress [and] the outline of a theory of capitalism's unequal development" while also "attending to national specificities as the core of concrete analysis."[10]

A significant portion of this work of recovery took place in 1979 with Cuaderno 72, which was devoted to the Irish question. Titled *Imperio y colonia. Escritos sobre Irlanda* (Empire and Colony: Writings on Ireland), this volume gathered the correspondence between Marx and Engels, as well as the letters they each exchanged with other pillars of the international socialist movement, revolving around the Irish revolutionary process of the 1860s. Of particular importance was Marx's 1867 letter to Engels, in which Marx discusses the specific traits of the political program that was to be deployed in Ireland. Marx here declared that, "what the Irish need is: 1. Self-government and independence from England. 2. Agrarian revolution [and] 3. Protective tariffs against England."[11] Marx's creation of such a program entailed the correction of previous positions in relation to the needs of the Irish revolutionary movement. He replaced his earlier view regarding the subordinate character of the overthrow of the Irish regime as it concerned the the English working class with one that assumed the necessity of Ireland's national liberation. As he communicated to Sigfrid Meyer and August Vogt in 1870, having engaged the Irish question for years, Marx reached the conclusion "that the decisive blow against the English ruling classes (and it will be decisive for the workers' movement all over the world) [could] not be delivered *in England* but *only in Ireland*."[12]

The Cuaderno dedicated to Ireland bears witness to the transformation of Marx's own views and, simultaneously, wagers on the potential theoretical and political consequences of this change. Take, for example, Italian Renato Levrero's text on the national question in Marx and Engels. Levrero, who specialized in the Marxist analysis of colonialism and imperialism, situated the writings focused on Ireland in the context of a decisive shift in Marx and Engels's thinking. According to Levrero, these texts, deemed as minor or marginal during the first half of the twentieth century, revealed the way that the two thinkers had distanced themselves from a conception of revolution that rested on the purported priority or predominance of capitalist relations of production in Western Europe, the existence of a homogeneous international proletariat, or the total reduction of national factors to the interests of class. Aricó's introductory note similarly illustrates the ambitions of the Cuaderno on Ireland. Strongly influenced by Levrero's hypothesis, Aricó focused on the change in perspective in Marx's positions on Ireland. While Marx and Engels had reached the conclusion that Irish national emancipation was the primary condition for achieving the social emancipation of English workers in general, the Irish situation became a component that allowed for a novel approach to the problem of the relation between class and national struggle. In Aricó's words, "the Europe-centered Marx who privileges the objectively progressive effects of capitalism gives way to an hitherto unknown Marx, one that is nuanced, profoundly dialectic and, we could even say, 'of the Third-World,' and for whom social revolution is no longer what solves the national question. Rather, for this Marx, it is the liberation of the oppressed nation that constitutes the social emancipation of the working class."[13]

The other Cuadernos that aided in the recovery of the forgotten Marx addressed the Russian question. In 1980, two volumes, whose combined title was *Escritos sobre Rusia* (Writings on Russia), were published. The first volume, *Revelaciones sobre la historia secreta del siglo XVIII* (Revelations of the Secret History of the 18th Century), was a collection of writings dedicated to the relationship that British international policy sustained with czarist Russia. The second volume, *El porvenir de la comuna rural rusa* (The Future of Russia's Rural Commune), brought together texts by Marx and Engels on the issue of Russia's development and the traits that the revolutionary movement of that region was determined to acquire. It is worth paying particular attention to the texts gathered in the second volume. One of these texts is the response provided by Marx to Vera Zasulich on the fate of Russia's rural commune. As interpreters of the letter have noted, the most salient aspect of Marx's response was to be found in his assertion that the fate of capitalism was "expressly restricted to the countries of Western Europe and that the rural commune could constitute the fulcrum for social regeneration in Russia." Another text included in the volume was the letter that Marx sent to the magazine *Notes of the Fatherland* concerning the way that his work had been read in Russia. As has been pointed out, the power of this text resides in its critique of the transformation of its historical sketch of the genesis of capitalism in Western Europe "into a historico-philosophical theory of the general course fatally imposed on all peoples, whatever the historical circumstances in which they find themselves placed, in order to arrive ultimately at this economic formation which assures the greatest expansion of the productive forces of social labour, as we as the most complete development of man."[14]

Besides these two Cuadernos, we should mention another publishing enterprise that paid just as much attention to Marx's approach to the Russian context. In 1981, the Biblioteca del Pensamiento Socialista, which Aricó directed for the publishing house Siglo XXI, published the correspondence that Marx and Engels had exchanged with populist Nikolai Danielson. Based on Aricó's introduction to this volume, we can surmise that, in his estimation, two particular aspects from the published texts deserved special attention. The first aspect had to do with the suitability of the fundamental principles of Marxism for the analysis of concrete situations. In this regard,

Aricó lamented the scant interest generated by these texts, given the fact that they embodied "a prolonged dialogue in which the fundamental hypotheses tried to measure themselves productively against a situation so supremely singular as that of turn-of-the-century Russia."[15] The second aspect arose from the context of Marx's own changing perspective, and had to do with the importance of the Russian question at the outset of a line of innovative problems. According to Aricó, in the exchanges with Danielson Marx questions the transformation of his own earlier analyses into a reifed doctrine or ideology concerning the development of the forces of production, outlines "a critique of the notion of capitalist 'progress' and a precise delimitation of the historico-geographic area that validates his analysis; and questions the ineluctability of the process of expropriation of direct producers, [which implies] an acute perception of the possibility of a non-capitalist model for development in underdeveloped countries, and an explicit acknowledgment of the revolutionary potentiality held by their rural masses."[16]

Like his insights on Ireland, Marx's approach to the Russian situation signified a change of perspective. While the Irish question entailed prioritizing the struggle for national liberation and thus shifting attention away from the central analytic position of the metropolitan working class, Marx's analyses of the Russian situation displaced the stereotypical backwardness of the region and instead underscored how the singularity of the Russian context might offer conditions conducive to a revolutionary process. As Teodor Shanin has argued, at the core of Marx's novel approximations to the Russian question we find a prioritization of the problems of capitalism's combined and uneven development and of the multiple avenues for social transformation within the global framework of mutual and differential impact.[17] Over the last few years, much has been said about the traits that define Marx's late writings. Scholars have examined the true scope of the evolutionist perspective of Marx's earlier texts, which has also led them to reconsider the significance and context of his subsequent departure from this position. Marx's Orientalist framework has also been the subject of discussion, which has led scholars of his work to consider the theoretical potential in the re-orientation of his later writings toward the peripheries of capitalism.[18] Nonetheless, beyond these discussions, it is possible to verify in these texts a series of issues that Aricó deemed relevant for his rereading of Marx's corpus. As Kevin Anderson has pointed out, Marx's turn toward the capitalist periphery foregrounds the idea that all these societies "possessed social structures markedly different from those of Western Europe" and that oppressed nationalities and ethnic groups should deploy a politics distinct from that of revolutionary subjects in nonperipheral countries.[19]

Echoes of a Contemporary Debate

1973 was a decisive date in the reception of the issues related to the concept of socioeconomic formation. Cuaderno 39, titled *El concepto de formación económico-social* (The Concept of Socio-Economic Formation), was published in that year and brought together articles by Italian and French Marxist intellectuals. Aricó thus combined in a single volume two conversations that had been taking place simultaneously in Italy and France. The first one was the counterpoint between Emilio Sereni and Cesare Luporini in the Italian magazine *Critica marxista* occasioned by Sereni's publication of "Da marx a Lenin: la categoria di 'formazione economico-sociale.'" The second one was the special issue of the French magazine *La Pensée*, which included writings by Christine Glucksmann, René Gallisot, Guy Dhoquois, Jacques Texier, Pierre Herzog, Pierre Gruet, and Georges Labica on this topic.

This Cuaderno was part of the revival of the debate on the concept of socioeconomic formation, which had developed in the context of European Marxism between the late 1960s and early '70s. The publication of the two sets of debates together, in a single volume, revealed theoretical sources that led to the renewed interest in the concept of socioeconomic formation. We find the first of the two in the theoretical and historiographic work of Sereni, who, since the 1950s, had begun recuperating the concept of socioeconomic formation on behalf of a rigorous intellectual practice that was committed to the needs of the Italian Left.[20] According to one interpreter of his work, the concept of socioeconomic formation allowed Sereni to undertake a historical and political interpretation of the Italian context while honing in on the specificities of Italy's democratic, socialist revolution.[21] We find the second of these sources in the rereading of Marx undertaken by Althusser and his collaborators, who argued that socioeconomic formation was an abstract concept that replaced the ideological notion of society and that allowed them to conceive of the object of the science of history as a totality composed of articulated instances with respect to a particular mode of production.[22]

In this respect, the Cuaderno's inclusion of Luporini's article, "Dialéctica marxista e historicismo," published originally in *Crítica Marxista*, is relevant. Luporini's theoretical production from the late 1960s to the early '70s can be regarded as a vector between the two aforementioned sources. Molded in the Marxist historicist tradition, in those years Luporini had become one of the most insightful readers of Althusser and a foremost promoter of his work within the Italian Left.[23] As André Tosel has pointed out, the specificity of Luporini's work must be thought of within the context of the decomposition of the philosophy of praxis and the return to Marx that comprehended the core of Italian Marxism.[24] Buttressed by Althusser's reading of Marx, Luporini developed a critique of historicism on the basis of its inability to analyze different social formations and its tendency to subsume that difference under a set of tactical options. In contrast to this historicism, Luporini proposed studying the various ways of transitioning to a different type of society within a context in which the relations of production and superstructural circumstances follow an unequal mode of development.

As part of this research program, Luporini proposed a scientific notion of socioeconomic formation. From a theoretical space that was intended to overcome the limitations of historicism but that was still cautious of structuralist formalism, Luporini insisted on the need for an interpretive model of socioeconomic formations that would be both universal in character and flexible in terms of its potential applicability. An inquiry into this insistence allows us to see that behind the efforts to construct a model with such characteristics was a critical evaluation of the dogmatic Marxism of the Second International. Luporini understood the consequences of this experience in historiographic and political terms. In the foreground he signaled the imposition of the Western feudalistic structure on the history of Eastern peoples and the demotion of problems related to the Asiatic mode of production. Meanwhile, in the background he underlined the notion that all peoples should puportedly experience the same stages of development as those of Western countries and that the latter should fulfill a decisive role in the historical evolution of dependent regions.

In this sense, Luporini's task entailed the recuperation of a set of interpretive variables that can be found in Marx's work but that had been obscured "by an interpretation of Marxism that is at once exaggeratedly *evolutionist* and laudatory of *necessity* with respect to the historical phases traversed by human societies."[25] Against this interpretation, Luporini underscored the necessity of socioeconomic formation as an interpretative framework capable of accounting for heterogeneous modes of historical experience, the same experiences that would serve as a basis for constructing the model. Luporini's recuperation of the concept would prove consequential historiographically and politically for the dogmatic views inherited from the Second International. It activated a historical understanding of capitalism's insertion into non-Western societies and stripped away the apparent demand that such societies pass through a bourgeois-democratic phase of politics in order to achieve socialism.

The problems that Luporini attributed to the concept of socioeconomic formation differed in important ways from those of Sereni, whose work represented one of the sources of the renewed interest in the term during the period. Sereni recuperated the term within a historicist framework that attempted to respond directly to Althusser. Sereni described Althusser's approach to socioeconomic formation as just another instance of the sociological and idealist attack on the Marxist tradition. Sereni wished to detach the concept from the static view of history inherent in mechanical models and instead to bring such models closer to the concrete and real dynamics of historical processes. In this sense, Luporini's approach in fact represented a departure from the sense that Marx would have given to the concept of socioeconomic formation and thus an attempt to reformulate it in light of a dynamic conception of social unfolding. This explains the dense philological undertaking that was the trademark of Sereni's work, and which consisted mainly in showing Marx's transition from using a static term (*Form*) to a dynamic one (*Formation*).

Nonetheless, beyond these differences, it is possible to single out a set of problems where we see the readings of both Italian Marxists converge. Just as Luporini emphasized the antiteleological nature of socioeconomic formation as a concept, Sereni harked back to Zasulich's response in order to insist that the progressive character that Marx granted to the succession of social formations should not be understood in the sense of "a *value judgement* nor [in the sense of] a *single, mandatory line of succession* of diverse social formations or historical epochs."[26] And just as Luporini highlighted the antimechanistic effects of the concept, Sereni turned to Lenin to verify that the notion of socioeconomic formation refers to the totality and unity of all spheres of social life. In this sense, Sereni's inclusion of superstructural circumstances in the reality to which the concept refers tended to prioritize the "*global* historical and not merely economic incidence of the notion of socio-economic [*sic*] formation."[27] This convergence testifies to the potential usefulness embodied by this notion for a new approach to Italian historical and political reality. As noted by Paolo Favilli, the analyses mediated by the concept of socioeconomic formation carried both a rejection of any and all philosophies of history and a refusal to of think the structural and superstructural spheres separately.[28]

The terms under which Aricó justified the publication of the Cuaderno dedicated to the concept of socioeconomic formation suggest that his reading gravitated toward the two previously analyzed issues. On the one hand, the reproduction of the debate was mediated by a valorization of the two sources involved in the concept's renewal. In this regard, we can infer that Aricó found Luporini's innovative reading more productive than Sereni's findings. While shaped, like Sereni, in Marxism's historicist mold, Aricó's openness to dialogue with the nascent Althusserian tradition guaranteed his convergence with Luporini.[29] In this sense, the fact that Aricó laments that the problems related to the concept of socioeconomic formation should be raised in conflicting terms during "the controversy between historical and structuralist interpretations of Marxism, which has influenced much of the research and debates of the past few years," is indicative of his sympathies.[30] In other words, in Aricó's view, a proposal such as Luporini's might allow us to find a way of circumventing the separate treatment, on the one hand, of economic determination and the objective structural causality that governs the movement of capitalist society and, on the other, the specific effectiveness of political struggle and the role played by subjectivity and political action.

In this sense, too, we can appreciate the importance of approaches attempting to comprehend the totality and unity of different spheres of life for the analysis of contexts like the Argentinian one. In this regard, Aricó's statement about how significant it was to publish these texts deserves attention. For him, at stake was not only the fate of a theoretical debate. Rather, these writings also announced a demand generated at the core of revolutionary struggle, which was the demand to overcome the mechanicism proper to the Marxism of the Second International. In other words, economistic interpretations and the reformist politics to which they give rise could no longer provide an understanding of how historical movements arise and develop in relation to economic sturcture. In short, the discussion taking place in Europe provided the means to think about "the problems revolving around the construction of a proletarian hegemony in social and national liberation movements in dependent, colonized and semi-colonized countries, and the issues surrounding the formation of the dictatorship of the proletariat in the transition to a classless society."[31]

Lastly, let us highlight an important point in the reception of the European debate for the concept of socioeconomic formation. The Cuaderno that came after the one in which the Italian and French texts appeared was devoted to the issue of modes of production in Latin America. Including texts by Ernesto

Laclau, Carlos Sempat Assadourian, Ciro Cardoso, Horacio Ciafardini, and Juan Carlos Garavaglia, *Modos de producción en América Latina* [Modes of Production in Latin America] (1973) elucidated the various positions taken up by Latin American historians on modes of production, circulation, and exchange during the colonial period. In this regard, the fact that the concept of mode of production was clearly displaced by that of socioeconomic formation in the Cuaderno itself is extremely telling. With references to *A Contribution to the Critique of Political Economy* and to Sereni's and Luporini's texts, the introduction penned by Juan Carlos Garavaglia argued that while the concept of mode of production designates an explanatory model through which the components shared by a series of societies are contemplated, that of socioeconomic formation always refers to the concrete and accountable reality of a historical and temporal location. Consequently, Garavaglia tried to prove the usefulness of looking at the spaces of colonial Latin America not so much through the concept that gave the Cuaderno its title as through the notion that had been foregrounded in the previous Cuaderno. As Cortés has remarked, both Cuadernos—*El concepto de formación económico-social* and *Modos de producción en América Latina*—can be understood together as part of "a concern for the structure specific to Latin American societies, and what this would mean in political terms (the problem of the revolutionary subject and of transition)."[32]

Conclusion

Much as one finds in the handful of texts in which Aricó provides us with a systematic presentation of his reading of Marx, Aricó's *Nueve lecciones sobre economía y política en el marxismo* [Nine Lessons on Economy and Politics in Marxism] (2011) also sheds light on the concept of socioeconomic formation and its place within the author's larger intellectual and political project. In this text—the outcome of a course taught at El Colegio de México between 1976 and 1977—the concept of socioeconomic formation assumes a privileged role in the author's approach to the foremost problems faced by contemporary Marxism. The approach to this concept sought to demonstrate the difference that Lenin's formulations had activated with respect to the postulates of the Second International. According to Aricó, the way Lenin used the concept was fundamental from a theoretical standpoint, "given that its essential trait is to conceive of all phenomena related to material production as mediations of human social relations."[33] In this way, Aricó returned to the *skeleton* metaphor to emphasize that thanks to the concept of socioeconomic formation, Marxism had become a theory dedicated to analyzing not so much economic life, but the totality of social life. Likewise, in addressing Lenin's work, he emphasized the fact that it had touched on problems related to the concept of socioeconomic formation not through previous methodological readings, but through a reasoning determined by the requirements of political practice in Russia.

In *Nueve Lecciones*, Aricó examined the uses of the concept of socioeconomic formation in Lenin's work in order to show the effects that would come about from breaking with a dogmatic brand of Marxism. In his view, this distancing could be thought of in the context of three theoretical and political conundrums. One of them was the need for development. According to Aricó, it was possible to surmise in Lenin a refusal to transform the analysis of primitive accumulation into a philosophy of history with an evolutionist bent. In this way, he addressed the problem of historical necessity thorough analyses of the present juncture instead of a future utopia. The other conundrum has to do with the link between science and revolution. With respect to this issue, the distancing of evolutionism and the prioritization of the current moment pushed the problem of science toward an analysis of socioeconomic formations. Aricó thus displaced questions about the scientific mediation of reality toward the analysis of the antagonistic relations unfolding in historically determinate societies. Finally, Aricó examined the implications of the concept of socioeconomic formation insofar as they pertain to the relationship between theory and social transformation. In this regard, he singled out the Leninist conception of class consciousness as one that emphasized the knowledge and scientific determination of class relations in a given socioeconomic formation.

The reading of Lenin that Aricó undertook in *Nueve lecciones sobre economía y política en el marxismo* is the culmination of a long process of following and disseminating issues related to the concept of socioeconomic formation. He assumed this task in the context of an immense and meaningful rereading of Marx's oeuvre and of contemporary Marxist methods. As part of this process, he presented the concept of socioeconomic formation as a privileged means to support a Marxist interpretive structure capable of giving account of the specificity of Argentinian society and of furnishing the knowledge necessary for a truly revolutionary political practice. The recovery of this concept and the calculation of its effects was channeled, in one sense, by reappropriating Marx's corpus. While the most innovative readings of

Marx's work facilitated the appropriation of a heterodox explanation of the problem of the succession of socioeconomic formations, an inquiry into the Marx that dealt with the periphery enabled the incorporation of a Marxist schema that was critical of the notion of progress—a schema, too, that was cognizant of the unequal nature of capitalist development and attentive to the national question. The Cuadernos developed this work, in turn, through a close examination of contemporary debates revolving around the concept of socioeconomic formation. In this case, the development of Italian and French Marxism during the 1960s and '70s promoted the importance of exploring this concept in the name of a Marxism that would be capable of giving account of social configurations as complex structured totalities.

Notes

1. For a comprehensive presentation of the concept within the Marxist tradition, and distinct analyses of the Marxist and Leninist moments, see Gallino, "Formazione"; see also Godelier, "Formation."
2. For a retelling of Aricó's theoretical and political itinerary, see Cortés, *Un nuevo marxismo*. To read about the journal and the Aricó-led group that spearheaded it, see Burgos, *Los gramscianos*. On the experience of Cuadernos, see Crespo, "En torno."
3. Crespo, "En torno," 192.
4. Cortés, *Un nuevo marxismo*, 20.
5. Marx, "Preface," 426.
6. Hobsbawm, "Introduction," 10.
7. Ibid., 11.
8. Ibid., 19–20.
9. Ibid., 38.
10. Cortés, *Un nuevo marxismo*, 126. Unless otherwise indicated in the References, English translations from Spanish sources are by the translator.
11. Marx, "Marx to Engels, November 30," 236.
12. Marx, "Marx to Sigfrid Meyer," 473. For a comprehensive reconstruction of the Irish question in Marx and Engels, see Hazelkorn, "*Capital*," and "Reconsidering."
13. Aricó, "Advertencia," in Marx, *Imperio*, 11.
14. Marx, "A Letter to the Editorial," 136.
15. Aricó, "Presentación," xii.
16. Ibid., xxii.
17. Shanin, "Late Marx," 17–18.
18. For a systematic look at these debates, see Musto, *L'ultimo Marx*.

19. Anderson, *Marx at the Margins*, 2–3.

20. See Sereni, *Il capitalismo* and "Annalisi."

21. Riva, "La nozione," 119–20.

22. See in particular Balibar, "On the Basic." For a comprehensive retelling of the concept's reactivation as well as the debate it subsequently ignited, see Simoni, *Tra Marx*.

23. See his introduction to the Italian edition of *For Marx*, "Notta introduttiva," as well as his *Dialettica e materialismo*. For an overview of Althusser's reception in Italy, see Iacono, *Althusser in Italia* and Izzo, "Althusser and Italy."

24. Tosel, "The Development."

25. Luporini, "Dialéctica marxista," 30.

26. Sereni, "La categoría," 61.

27. Ibid., 74.

28. Favilli, *Marxismo*, 236–37.

29. The fact that Luporini's article was printed only in book form in the eleventh Cuaderno seems to confirm this hypothesis.

30. Aricó, "Advertencia" in Luporini, *El concepto*, 8. This articulation is expressed, to a great extent, in Cuaderno 19, titled *Gramsci y las ciencias sociales*. I have fleshed out the Gramsci-Althusser connection in Aricó and the experience of *Pasado y Presente* in Starcenbaum, "Más allá."

31. Aricó, "Advertencia." In Luporini, *El concepto*, 7.

32. Cortés, *Un nuevo marxismo*, 74.

33. Aricó, *Nueve lecciones*, 146.

Works Cited

Anderson, Kevin. *Marx at the Margins. On Nationalism, Ethnicity, and Non-Western Societies.* Chicago: University of Chicago Press, 2010.

Aricó, José. "Advertencia." In Karl Marx and Friedrich Engels, *Imperio y colonia. Escritos sobre Irlanda*, 11–12. México D.F.: Pasado y Presente, 1979.

———. "Advertencia." In Cesare Luporini et al., *El concepto de "formación económico-social,"* 7–8. Buenos Aires: Pasado y Presente, 1973.

———. *Nueve lecciones sobre economía y política en el marxismo.* México D.F.: El Colegio de México, 2011.

———. "Presentación." In Karl Marx, Nikolái Danielsón, and Friedrich Engels, *Correspondencia (1865–1895)*, xiii–xxiii. México D.F.: Siglo XXI, 1981.

Balibar, Étienne. "On the Basic Concepts of Historical Materialism." In Louis Althusser and Étienne Balibar, *Reading Capital*, 199–308. London: New Left Books, 1970.

Burgos, Raúl. *Los gramscianos argentinos. Cultura y política en la experiencia de Pasado y Presente.* Buenos Aires: Siglo XXI, 2004.

Cortés, Martín. *Un nuevo marxismo para América Latina. José Aricó: traductor, editor, intelectual.* Buenos Aires: Siglo XXI, 2015.

Crespo, Horacio. "En torno a Cuadernos *de Pasado y Presente, 1968–1983.*" In *El político y el científico. Ensayos en homenaje a Juan Carlos Portantiero,* edited by Claudia Hilb, 168–95. Buenos Aires: Siglo XXI, 2009.

Favilli, Paolo. *Marxismo e storia. Saggio sull'innovazione storiografica in Italia (1945–1970)* Milan: Franco Angeli, 2006.

Gallino, Luciano. "Formazione economico-sociale." In *Dizionario di Sociologia,* 320–23. Turin: Unione Tipografico-Editrice Torinese, 1978.

Godelier, Maurice. "Formation économique et sociale." In *Dictionnaire critique du marxisme,* edited by Gérard Bensussan and Georges Labica, 473–76. Paris: Presses Universitaires de France, 1982.

Hazelkorn, Ellen. "*Capital* and the Irish Question." *Science & Society* 44, no. 3 (1980): 326–56.

———. "Reconsidering Marx and Engels on Ireland." *Saothar* 9 (1983): 79–88.

Hobsbawm, Eric. "Introduction." In Karl Marx, *Pre-Capitalist Economic Formations,* edited by Eric Hobsbawm, 9–65. New York: International Publishers, 2007.

Iacono, Cristian Lo. *Althusser in Italia. Saggio bibliografico (1959–2009).* Milan: Mimesis, 2011.

Izzo, Francesca. "Althusser and Italy: A Two-Fold Challenge to Gramsci and Della Volpe." *International Critical Thought* 5, no. 2 (2015): 200–10.

Luporini, Cesare. *Dialettica e materialismo.* Rome: Riuniti, 1974.

———. "Dialéctica marxista e historicismo." In Cesare Luporini et al., *El concepto de "formación económico-social,"* 9–54. Buenos Aires: Pasado y Presente, 1973.

———. "Nota introduttiva." In Louis Althusser, *Per Marx,* vii–xxvii. Rome: Riuniti, 1967.

Marx, Karl. "A Letter to the Editorial Board of Otechestvennye Zapiski." In *Late Marx and the Russian Road: Marx and the "Peripheries of Capitalism,"* edited by Teodor Shanin, 134–37. New York: Monthly Review Press, 1983.

———. "Preface to A Critique of Political Economy." In *Karl Marx: Selected Writings,* edited by David McLellan, 424–27. Oxford: Oxford University Press, 2000.

———. "Marx to Engels, November 30, 1867." In Karl Marx and Frederick Engels. *Selected Correspondance,* 234–37. Moscow: Foreign Languages Publishing House, 1956.

———. "Marx to Sigfried Meyer and August Vogt in New York, April 9, 1870." In Karl Marx and Frederick Engels. *Collected Works, Marx and Engels 1868–1870, Volume 43,* 471–76. London: Lawrence and Wishart, 1975.

Musto, Marcello. *L'ultimo Marx (1881–1883). Saggio di biografia intellettuale.* Rome: Donzelle, 2016.

Riva, Tomasso Redolfi. "La nozione di formazione economico-sociale nel marxismo di Emilio Sereni," *Il pensiero economico italiano* XVII, no. 1 (2009): 119–20.

Sereni, Emilio. "Analisi strutturale e metodologia storica," *Critica Marxista* 5–6 (1966): 1–37.

———. *Il capitalismo nelle campagne (1860–1900)*. Turin: Einaudi, 1947.

———. "La categoría de 'formación económico-social.'" In Cesare Luporini et al., *El concepto de "formación económico-social,"* 55–95. Buenos Aires: Pasado y Presente, 1973.

Shanin, Teodor. "Late Marx: Gods and Craftsmen." In *Late Marx and the Russian Road: Marx and the Peripheries of Capitalism*, 17–18. New York: Monthly Review Press, 1983.

Simoni, Nicola. *Tra Marx e Lenin. La discussione sul concetto di formazione economico-sociale*. Naples: La Città del Sole 2006.

Starcenbaum, Marcelo. "Más allá del principio de exclusión: Gramsci y Althusser en *Pasado y Presente.*" *Prismas. Revista de historia intelectual* 18 (2014): 199–203.

Tosel, André. "The Development of Marxism: From the End of Marxism-Leninism to a Thousand Marxisms—France-Italy, 1975–2005." In *Critical Companion to Contemporary Marxism*, edited by Jacques Bidet and Stathis Kouvelakis, 52–60. Leiden and Boston: Brill, 2008.

CHAPTER SIX

An Irresolvable Tension: The Part or the Whole?

THE EFFECTS OF THE "CRISIS OF MARXISM" IN THE WORK OF RENÉ ZAVALETA MERCADO

JAIME ORTEGA REYNA

THE WORK OF BOLIVIAN SOCIOLOGIST René Zavaleta Mercado has become an obligatory reference in recent years. After a period of relative obscurity in the nineties, the twenty-first century has witnessed a renewed interest in his work.[1] Like Peruvian Aníbal Quijano, Mexican Pablo González Casanova, Ecuadorian Agustín Cueva, and Brazilian Ruy Mauro Marini, Zavaleta is today an obligatory reference for students of Latin American social and political theory. This is due in large part to the easily accessible electronic anthologies published by the Consejo Latinoamericano de Ciencias Sociales. The growing interest in Zavaleta's work is likewise the effect of a number of recent translations, editions, and critical analyses of his oeuvre. Zavaleta's posthumous work *Lo nacional-popular en Bolivia* [Toward a History of the National-Popular in Bolivia] (1986) has been translated into English and, at long last, his collected works have been fully edited, allowing us access to early texts, newspaper articles, and, of course, the works that made him a reference point for so-called Latin American sociology, a somewhat problematic term that encompasses a large swath of the theoretical production of the seventies and eighties.[2]

The present essay will analyze the insertion of Zavaleta's work within the wider context of those theorists, such as Cueva and Marini, who questioned Dependency Theory and, through this questioning, reached broader conclusions regarding the status of Marxism as a "finite theory," to use Louis Althusser's term.[3] Zavaleta's proposal privileged the categories of mode of production, social formation and, in general, articulation. These terms—and their problematic terrain—expressed both the possibility for the renewal of Marxist discourse in the seventies and its subsequent stagnation in the late eighties. Both moments signal the limits of Marxism as a "finite theory" and thus encourage us to consider so-called crisis of Marxism from a different vantage point.

Recent explicators of Zavaleta's work have located in this seemingly arcane set of debates one of his most radical theoretical proposals. Indeed, one finds in these apparently niche discussions about the mode of production a set of propositions on historicity, as well as a distinct (and tense) conception of time irreducible to history. Zavaleta's use of the term *abigarramiento* (becoming motley) thus does more than merely name social diversity or heterogeneity, a recurring theme (almost to the point of saturation) in contemporary analyses of his work. Rather, it alludes to something more radical and fundamental, prefiguring a "post-Marxism" that is different from the one that was eventually canonized.

The present text maintains that Zavaleta's mature work is permeated by a tension between a Marxist notion of totality, understood as a set of relations and processes that, comprising the whole, subsume each part or segment and re-purpose it according to a *telos* or project; and an understanding of temporality implied by the emphasis, in Lenin and Gramsci, on the analysis of concrete situations. Zavaleta understood this tension as one relating the universalist theory of capital and the autonomy of the political, thus leading us to question whether any Marxist political theory can exist without a consideration of the plural temporalities of capitalist development.

"Western Marxism"

This same tension is one of the causes of the so-called crisis of Marxism. The "crisis of Marxism" refers to an ensemble of discussions concerned with the loss of a sense of certainty once guaranteed by Marxism's function as a philosophy of history. These discussions questioned the purportedly revolutionary role of the industrial working class and the category of historical progress, at the same time that they entertained the idea of multiple paths toward socialism not restricted to the development and crisis of the forces of production. Such critiques and alternative theories of socialist transition addressed assumptions central to so-called Western Marxism, whose contours I shall now discuss.

Those who owe a direct debt to Marx, such as Georg Lukács, proposed the first step in this analysis: that of the epistemological privilege of the expressive form of the totality and the consideration of a transcendental subject that brings it to life. In their efforts to incorporate nineteenth-century Hegelianism into Marxist theory, they managed to implant a predilection for the global analysis of processes over specific moments, underpinning as the engine of it all the existence of a sovereign subject capable of generating his or her self-consciousness. Perhaps inadvertently or unwittingly, amid the radical transformation of the productive matrix (accumulation model) and conflict management (welfare state), they rehabilitated for the twentieth century the various philosophies of history proposed by the previous century, with important consequences and long-lasting effects.

According to critics of so-called Western Marxism, Lukács and all those who came after him—including the Frankfurt School, Eastern European Marxism, and the philosophy of praxis—dismissed the problems that did not fit within this Hegelian perspective. One such problem was the popular conformation of the nation and, with it, the dynamics of mediation between capitalism and its concrete forms of emergence.[4] According to its critics, Western Marxism supposed a homogeneous process, in which capitalist totality imposes itself indistinctly and the global process of capitalist valorization serves as the yardstick for specific instances of class struggle. Critics of so-called Western Marxism thus argued that it resisted attempts at theoretical renewal that appealed to the concrete or relational traits of any specific moment. From this Euro-centered perspective, capital imposed itself as a single, dominating logic, stripping those who faced different dynamics in the fields of production or circulation of the conceptual tools necessary to apprehend them.

An effect of this conception was the imposition of a certain way of understanding historical time, one that was marked by an idealistic conception of continuity and simultaneity. From the point of view of its critics, Western Marxism thus failed to account for instances of historical rupture, noncorrespondence, or crisis. As is well known, Gramsci questioned these assumptions in his famous text about the Russian Revolution against *Capital*, but also, and much more significantly, when he put forth an alternative by bringing the issue of the national-popular into Marxist debates. In political terms, the Lukácsian-Hegelian horizon located this tension in the central role attained by the proletariat and the certainty of an unfolding of history as the simultaneity of a single, homogenous time. The so-called crisis of Marxism advanced this perspective by questioning long-standing certainties regarding the historical face of the class subject of revolution together with the idea that historical progress could be pursued through a single path. The political translation of such discussions resounded in Latin American debates in which the question of national self-determination often superimposed itself onto that of class and in which the peasantry often displayed a much greater revolutionary will than the urban proletariat. As Zavaleta observed in his mature work, the time of national-popular politics proved more heterogeneous and complex than the idyllic image advanced by Lukács's Hegelianism. On a theoretical plane, it wasn't until the mid-sixties that Althusser managed to propose an alternative to the epistemological dimension, when he insisted on discarding all speculative forms while criticizing the conception of historical time as a homogeneous form. This perspective opened up the space for a "Marxist anthropology,"[5] that is, for the ability to understand diverse forms of production and consumption, something that was impossible within the framework of a philosophy of history.

Zavaleta's work maintains a permanent tension between these two frameworks. On the one hand, it accepts the centrality of the notion of totality and, with it, of social class, in the vein inaugurated by Lukács's *History and Class Consciousness*. We see this problem play out recurrently in Zavaleta's work insofar as it conceives of Marxism as the intellectual development of class in its political action, a position that he attributes to the experience of the Bolivian mining proletariat. The Althusserian influence in Zavaleta's work is similarly fraught with tension. Beyond rejecting the concept of "Ideological State Apparatuses,"[6] his work is besieged by the problem of the articulation of different modes of production. But the way that Zavaleta works through this is not as others have suggested (that is, via an exploration of the "feudal" traces found within the dominant capitalist form,[7] or by looking at traditional forms nestled within the modern, nor by appealing for a discussion of the "Asiatic mode of production").[8]

The way in which Zavaleta tackles this problem departs radically from the aforementioned approaches and mobilizes a set of different registers. In what follows, I will attempt to locate some of those theoretical and political articulations that belong, alternately to the epistemological and sociopolitical registers of his analyses. In so doing, I will try to show how his work constructs a viewpoint for which Marx's work serves as the horizon of visibility of an era rather than as the index of some ideal type to which all societies in their particular versions should be subjected. Zavaleta's diverse influences illuminate problems and perspectives that are often ignored in discussions concerning the relationship sustained among accumulation, subjectivation, and state formation. His work thus opens up a space to rethink the so-called crisis of Marxism alongside its origins and effects.

One tends to associate the crisis of Marxism with the crisis of socialism. The origins of this false association can be located in a certain discontentment in the 1970s with the conventional ways in which Marxist theory envisioned the transit to socialism, and what many critics perceived as the absence of sufficient mechanisms for political participation in really existing socialist societies. In this sense, the origins of the so-called crisis of Marxism emerged in the realm of politics before migrating to the theoretical sphere. To use Lenin's terminology, Zavaleta's work allows us to question those weakest links in the very origins of the supposed crisis of Marxism, in order to consider both radical democracy and the transition to socialism.

Marxist political theory of the 1970s attempted to circumscribe a field of inquiry defined by the failure of Marxist theory to address problems in political economy and, more specifically, the theory of the state in light of the ways that changes in the pattern of capitalist accumulation had molded the social relations of production over the course of the twentieth century. For Marxists, the State is one of the principal organizers of social relations and a space where relations of force are concentrated. In Zavaleta's estimation, though the State was neither an autonomous nor autonomized entity, one nonetheless had to account for its specificity. At stake in his approach is the distinction betweem the notion of "social formation," or the articulation of different configurations of production; mode of production, or the instance overdetermining the form assumed by the social relations of production; and "superstructural effects," or the specific institutions of legal, political, and bureaucratic domination in a given society. Each of these three categories presumes a totalizing vision of society.

Another topic relevant to the so-called crisis of Marxism—less influential despite its importance—focuses on the discussion of the role of the forces of production. This topic has been less explored, although it constitutes, to a large extent, the heart of a version presented from the point of view of philosophy of history (where forces of production, in fact, are seen as the demiurges of history) as well as from the point of view of articulation, as they express the regulation of social formations. However, the most relevant aspect of the latter concept is the unity-distinction it illuminates between the State and the global market in societies like those of Latin America. Zavaleta, like others in Mexico during his last exile (including Armando Bartra and Bolívar Echeverría),[9] takes up in original ways the problem of the forces of production from a nontechnicist perspective. Scholars and researchers have paid scarce attention to this issue or its treatment among Marxist theorists in the 1970s, yet it serves as a gateway for outlining a vision of Marxism anchored in relations of power and tensions sustained among agents, subjects, and groups.

Finally, another path offered by Zavaleta, and which in fact criss-crosses both discussions, is the one that openly engages with the problem of temporality. Zavaleta found himself confronted by the same dilemma that other Marxists have encountered: on the one hand, a concept of history full of riches, in the center of which is the evidence that this history is the result of human beings' actions insofar as they organize their lives socially or communally, and, simultaneously, a poor conception of the historical time inhabiting that same notion of history. Though standard Marxism holds a materialistic concept of history, it also imposes an idealistic notion of historical time in which a demiurge or transcendental element (beyond effective practices) functions as its "engine." Zavaleta attacks this notion, arguing that while an understanding of history must confront the juxtaposition of different modes of production, it must also dismantle its idealist vestiges, that is to say, break with any ultimate guarantees. Addressing the issue of the forces of production thus allows Zavaleta the necessary element in order to entertain a notion of totality (and thus of history), without for that reason subordinating the specificity of historical time (that is, the conjuncture). Zavaleta thus wishes to reestablish an adequate temporality of the whole from which to be able to think of the time of political intervention—that is to say, the time of the conjuncture. The criticism of the technical centrality of forces of production is what allows him to consider history, or the whole, insofar as it is implicated in with the part, or conjuncture.

The Forces of Production Are the Relations of Production

As is well known, traditional, or Fordist, Marxism emphasized the forces of production as a device capable of explaining history's *telos*. Within a narrative of this type—i.e., a teleological one—human beings conquer nature in ever more profound ways, generating in this manner the possibility of freeing up time for work in favor of time for life.

Marx developed this familiar perspective in his prologue to *A Contribution to the Critique of Political Economy*. The forces of production, understood in their technical dimension, allowed human beings to seize nature in order to increase productivity. As time passed, these forces of production would contradict or cease to correspond to social relations. Marx predicted that, in their narrow capitalist limitations, social relations would soon be halted by the development of technical forces of production: humans would conquer "true history" when they finally rid themselves of those social relations and developed technical forces of production in infinite fashion.

It was not easy to cut the intricate knot of this narrative. The prevailing notion within the Marxist tradition adhered to a certain automatism of history, where the deployment of technical forces would provide the social conditions of possibility for a society of abundance, which in turn would be characterized by transparent social relations and the elimination of all forms of submission, violence, and exploitation. This historical automatism can only be associated with a technicist and progressive formula of history. Simultaneously, juxtaposed with the Marx who yields to the regime of technical forces of production, we find the Marx that thinks of conjunctures, events, and the dynamics of force and contingency in general within a framework of necessity. It certainly presents an ambiguous scenario where the bourgeoisie is as much praised for its creations as it is denounced for the power it unleashes yet cannot control.

Zavaleta himself referred to Marxism's mechanicist assumptions about historical development as "the constraints of his time," and criticized the way these notions operate at the very core of critical discourse: "We could say that the myth of indefinite progress enveloped everything then, including, of course, at least in certain moments, Marx himself."[10] To be sure, other readings of Marx have brought this perspective into tension in a much better way. Zavaleta's approach, however, neither discards the existence of the forces of production in their technical dimension nor underestimates their importance. On the contrary, it situates them as an expression or form dependent on relations of production. As an early note by Zavaleta indicates: "[T]he forces of production of a given society are defined by the relations of production." His most fundamental thesis is this: the forces of production are always already social relations of production.

The status or evaluation of the social form that contains various modes of production cannot be undertaken outside of this consideration. In other words, the problem to be considered at the heart of the Marxist problematic is not the technical status of society determining its level of articulation, but rather the balance of its [productive] relations. Zavaleta states this point succinctly:

> The so-called real forces of production (methods, means, instruments, base materials) are nothing but consequences: in the end, steel is the result of the separation between producer and means of production. The key to all forces of production is always a human being in relation to another human being to produce life.[11]

Taken on its own, this statement could be considered both limited and biased. Nonetheless, we must consider the weight—both then and today—of what Althusser described as the idealist position, where a final guarantee exists (in this case, the forces of production or the proletariat) to assure the unfolding of history. Zavaleta undertakes a critical operation that resonates with what Althusser does in his later works: to situate the primacy of the relation above any other level of social life, particularly the one that converges with forces of production.

The primacy of relations above forces of production (that is, the capacity for agency that diverse subjects have on the objects they build) is a lesson cemented by Marx in the *Grundrisse* that encourages seizing power from objects and returning it to humans: "Each individual possesses social power in the form of a thing. Rob the thing of this social power and you must give it to persons to exercise over persons."[12]

This situation reanimates the need to think that among human beings there exists no possibility of a totally transparent relation, since relations are mediated by power and dispute, that is, by the irresolvability of conflict. The same thing occurs at the core of Zavaleta's work, where the problem of the primacy of relation gives us back the notion of a constitutive confrontation: there is no possibility of restoring a beautiful totality without conflict, violence, or contradictions. In retrospect, one finds these contradictions simultaneously open and enshrouded by the power of financial automatism.

It is thus with good reason that Zavaleta highlights this portion of Marx's *Grundrisse*, for it presents both the potential for and limitation of any discourse regarding the forces of production. In these important manuscripts, as Enrique Dussel calls the first drafts of *Capital*,[13] Marx addresses both the harrowing dimension of capital as well as the process of automatization. The work of Antonio Negri highlights this dimension of Marx's manuscripts. Yet Zavaleta's interest is mobilized by a different facet of the *Grundrisse*.

That other facet is the one that must be situated within the issue of the existence and destruction of the ancestral community as the premise for the

existence of relations of capital. In fact, this topic traverses all the 1857 manuscripts, yet barely resurfaces in the 1861–63 manuscripts or in later editions of
Capital.[14] This is the problem of community at the moment of its destruction
by the new, abstract logic of value that imposes money as the only form of
relationality.[15] What was the perspective from which Zavaleta understood
the problem of the common, the communal, and community as such? Our
opinion is that he understood these issues from the perspective of the forces
of production and their consequences as a specific form of social relations.

In other words, with Zavaleta, we witness the birth of a way of thinking
not about the automatism of a new reason of history, but about the material
scaffold of the forces of production understood as the deployment of social
relations, and thereby subject to their unrest: "When Marx said that one must
consider the community 'as itself the first force of production,' what could
he have been saying other than that we should consider the State as one of
society's forces of production?"[16] Thus, Zavaleta again refers to the thesis
that Marx expounded in the *Grundrisse*: "The community itself appears as
the first great force of production; particular kinds of production conditions
(e.g. stock-breeding, agriculture), develop particular modes of production
and particular forces of production, subjective, appearing as qualities of
individuals, as well as objective [ones]."[17]

In these lines Zavaleta highlights a hypothesis that has yet to be explored
to its full extent, the analytical possibilities of which only become evident
when seen from multiple perspectives. This hypothesis would rest on the idea
that the modern world is the result of the way that different forces of production become articulated. In the first place, the articulation of technical forces
(industry, machinery), which can only exist when they subjugate, represses,
or mediates other dimensions: mainly, nontechnical forces of production.
Among those forces not taken into consideration by this technical dimension
we find: community, cooperation, nation, and the State. Zavaleta considers
the State, along with the nation, as a nontechnical force of production.[18]

Throughout his work, Zavaleta strives to define these concepts as a way
of countering their fetishization by capital. Capital displaces and tears apart
the community and, in its place, configures a society composed of atomized
property owners, which manage to reverse the disintegration process only
when capital mobilizes them into cooperation (just as described in the fourth
section of *Capital*). When it lacks a "popular" sense, the nation is nothing
but a weak mediation between various capitals and the global market.
Finally, once it manages to produce its autonomy, the State becomes a force
of production. What, Zavaleta wonders, does the State produce? The answer

is: hegemony. Thus, we should not be surprised when Zavaleta states that "in certain instances, the State becomes the only form of popular unity."[19] This problem allows us to pinpoint the difficulty of conceiving of a society defined by multiple temporalities and the articulation of diverse social forms.

Temporality and Articulation

Zavaleta theorizes the nature of the relationship between technical and nontechnical forces of production (the State, the nation, etc.) through the concept of socioeconomic formation. In Zavaleta's work, the term describes the way that technical and nontechnical forces of production overlap and are overdetermined. In the author's words, "What remains is to speak of socio-economic formations, of the survival of different modes of production that are articulated with respect to each other under a concrete hegemony or, in fact, only articulated at their most formal point."[20] Who generates that hegemony? What makes the articulation only formal and not real in the sense that Marx's *Capital* understands these terms? This is precisely what leads Zavaleta to question the real possibility of utilizing the Marxist "toolbox" for understanding Bolivia, which he characterized as "a socio-economic formation that is only hegemonically capitalist, and that sometimes only has the capitalist mode of production as an enclave, and runs into various obstacles."[21] At the same time, Zavaleta must recognize that this is not an anomaly or a consequence of the lack or absence of capital, but rather a result of its presence: "Uneven development is intrinsic to this mode of production."[22]

Zavaleta coined the term *abigarramiento* in order to describe the motley nature of Bolivian society, not only in linguistic and racial terms, but, equally as importantly, in sociopolitical ones. With the notion of *abigarramiento* Zavaleta defines a social space that is formally shared by different modes of production—with their specific forms of articulation and temporalities—and, in so doing, aims to question progressive or teleological understandings of history in Marxist theory. Zavaleta thus reads Marx with the help of Lenin's recognition of the juxtaposition of multiple social formations as a central problem or issue for the theory of hegemony and of Gramsci's insights regarding the unity and distinction between structure and superstructure. This is what allows the concept of *abigarramiento* to function both as a way of describing the Bolivian socioeconomic formation and theorizing its revolutionary potential.

Zavaleta describes the sociopolitical present in terms of "the late resolution of the national question and the early appearance of finance capital."[23]

His diagnostic contains a clue as to how we might translate the concept of *abigarramiento* into the political sphere. How is this late resolution of the national question translated? Though not totally resolved by him, the solution begins with Marx. The reason it wasn't resolved is because Marx himself did little to theorize the nation in the historical horizon of nineteenth-century Europe. Additionally, Marx was unable to predict the form that the exportation of capital would take in the era of "imperialism," as formulated by Lenin. The reason we need to think with, but also beyond, Marx thus becomes clear.

With this, we enter the labyrinthine path of the concept of *abigarramiento*. Initially, we are faced with two conundrums. The first refers to the state of political translation, in other words: What is the fate of concepts such as "the State"? The second is related to the temporality implied by the specific form of capitalism's reproduction, whose characteristic is the incompleteness of the national question and the dominance of imperialism (or of the global market, which I use indistinctly from this point on).

This is where the tension foreshadowed by the title begins: between Marx, who is compelled to understand the form in which value is valorized through the colonization of the domains of life, and Lenin (and subsequently also Gramsci), who allows for a relatively autonomous thinking of the problems of the relations of force that play out in the State relation. With utmost clarity, Zavaleta poses the following question:

> What, indeed, is the degree to which the superstructural sector that we call the State is part of the stability of the capitalist mode of production, meaning that part of society that is subject to laws (almost in the same sense as the natural sciences) and to which, for the purposes of knowledge, one can apply the principle of reiteration?[24]

This extremely important question already prefigures the *insoluble tension*: capital is in fact a mode of regularity that can be grasped from the point of view of its expanded reproduction. But the State and the political realm are not part of this model of regularity, since they summon the mobilization of elements that are not reiterative, that cannot be grasped by any supposed law (even if one can point to certain tendencies), and are therefore difficult to apprehend methodologically. Zavaleta returns to the ensuing theoretical problem, yet connects it, as we have seen, to the problem of historical epoch: "[W]e argued that the totalization of society is one of the traits of this mode of production. The possibility of speaking about a single part as independent, but also exclusively about superstructure, etc., reflects the fact that capitalism has not achieved the task of totalization."[25]

These comments signal two crucial elements for underscoring the tension between totality and political conjuncture in Zavaleta's framework: On the one hand, the problem of the historical epoch, that is, the state of imperialism (or that of the global market in its process of incessant expansion), which prevents the constitution of the nation-state in the peripheries of capitalism; on the other hand, the fact that the totality of capital's social relations are not fully expressed—in other words, that there are loopholes and spaces of autonomy that can be constructed or preserved. Both elements generate a new problem: the problem of temporality.

When referring to temporality—in conjunction with the budding issue of totality and of the historical epoch where the national question does not unfold as the main motive of capitalist development—Zavaleta signals the following:

> We had seen that, via this concept, the model of regularity or mode of production reveals the unity of the history of the world, its present homogeneity, insofar as the superstructures show its conspicuousness, diversity and incomparability. The behavior of these social phases is, nonetheless, opposite when each formation is regarded in its autonomous movement or internalness.[26]

From the perspective of totality, the mode of production appears as a law that imposes itself unrelentingly, as opposed to the contingency and nonlinearity that characterizes politics. This temporality coexists with another one: the temporality that emerges when what is considered as a unit of analysis is not the totality (capital in general), but an "economic-social formation," where the development of the capitalist form of social labor shows its nontotalization and the structure of the state expresses the order of legality and uniformity.

The problem of temporality also concerns the object under analysis. As Zavaleta's work illustrates, Marxist theory has made a clear contribution to the analysis of capitalist temporality, however little has been made of the temporality of spaces only formally subsumed under capital. Thus, the issue is not that Marx fails to properly account for his object of study (and its corresponding temporality), but that what Zavaleta foregrounds requires different approaches (with Lenin and Gramsci as the most important referents). We could say that Zavaleta understood the dilemma faced by "Western Marxism," which can be summed up thus: between totality and conjuncture, it is the latter where intervention is possible. The time of politics is the time of transformation.

Zavaleta foregrounds the relationship between totality and conjuncture, such that the former refers to the extension of the domain of value form (structure) and the latter refers to those moments pertaining to politics and the State (the superstructure): "the superstructure's autonomy, the moments in which superstructural aggregations are independently self-determined. It is in this sense that we can say that the superstructure expresses the movement and diversity of history. Reduced now to a repetitive nucleus, the economic base, meanwhile, refers to the constants as well as the unity of capitalism as such."[27]

Once again, we gradually see how the problem of temporality shapes the problem of understanding and distinction within Marxism and its crisis. If "Western Marxism" was configured on the basis of the category of totality, and therefore on the axis of a temporality proper to the "mode of regularity," the version that Zavaleta nurtures thinks from the privilege of the conjuncture, where the important thing is neither *continuum* nor repetition, but rather the movement and diversity that unfold within various histories. Like few others, Zavaleta brings about an epistemological and political rupture within the ranks of Western Marxism.

The problem of articulation can finally be situated on a different terrain, one where the forces of production do not constitute the main axis. We find the core of Zavaleta's gesture in the rupture with the continuum of the model of regularity, whose only space is that of intervention in the conjuncture. We call it epistemological rupture because that is how it is presented: "We argue that superstructural forms have their own manner of causal aggregation and, consequently, to speak of laws here in the same sense as when we are dealing with the model of regularity is to transport an analytic program from one area to another without it being appropriate."[28] He goes on to say:

> Put otherwise, superstructural forms, within the terms not belonging to capitalism's model of regularity, are part of the spatial accumulation (we could say phenotypic: because this corresponds . . . to the field of chance, at least in relative terms, and not those of necessity or repetition) of each socio-economic formation, and it is in this sense that we affirm that, in the epoch of world history, the model of regularity that we call mode of production is what expresses the unity of the history of the world (that is comparable) insofar as superstructures signal (except within the part of that model to which they belong) their structural heterogeneity. Diverse superstructures, with ideological recurrences that are distant from each other, with very different juridico-political results, can nonetheless all

serve in the same way to guarantee (which is not the same as to say they themselves reproduce, which is an action proper to the base) the reproduction of the same and sole mode of production. In this sense, what Lenin referred to as the state type must correspond to the economic base, while the state form corresponds to the superstructural course that brings that formation from the past, that is, the way that human freedom has a way of inserting itself in the shaping of history.[29]

This long quote accurately expresses the set of theoretical and political guidelines that Zavaleta arrives at. Furthermore, it shows the way in which the tension that is produced out of the "crisis of Marxism" (the absence of political theory and the need to overcome teleology) opens up two superimposed problems whose thought is nonetheless autonomous. We find, on the one hand, Marxism's highest moment of development: the moment of the "critique of political economy" as the understanding of the deployment of capital's dominion in the conformation of the global market. On the other hand, we encounter the need to think beyond this space, beginning with the intervention into the conjuncture, and the time of politics as such, which is the space of freedom, creativity, force, and open possibility.

Zavaleta's position clearly shows the tension between "the part" and "the whole," the immediate effect of which is the formulation of the concept of *abigarramiento*. Beyond its quotidian use among Latin Americanists, it is worth insisting on the profound implications of this notion. It does not merely refer to a society characterized by various overlapping modes of production, nor is it an allegory for social diversity, but something much more significant. Zavaleta's solution is grounded in a turn to Lenin and Gramsci, without of course forgetting Marx. He assumes and reassembles the notion of forces of production (technical and nontechnical), inserts them into the discussion of "economic-social formations," and extends them into his considerations of the State and politics.

The tension generated by each of these moments results from the consequences of accepting one of these moments as the central one, or limiting or subordinating the others. Zavaleta thus adopts a perspective in which the temporality of the conjuncture appears as the most important moment. And this is because, in the spirit of overcoming the so-called crisis of Marxism he assumes that the historicity outlined by the global market nullifies those temporalities in which an intervention is possible. What we might call "Zavaleta's lesson" is that Marxism cannot nullify, hide, or suppress those other temporalities under the banner of diversity or as part of the drama proper to a nontotalized society, but should instead consider them as possibilities for political intervention.

Notes

1. Commentators such as Mauricio Gil and Luis Tapia have divided Zavaleta's work into three "periods": (1) a youthful period linked to revolutionary nationalism following the 1952 revolution; (2) a robust and orthodox "Leninist" period in the late seventies that was in open confrontation with Bolivian Trotskyism and which had a strong labor presence; and (3) a so-called critical Marxist period where the works of Gramsci and Lukács, as well as that of Max Weber, acquired a central role. These divisions serve to frame long periods of time, but we must remember that they are neither rigid nor necessarily clear-cut.

2. Within the Latin Americanist tradition developed in Mexico, it is common to pinpoint periods of theoretical expansion which, in certain instances, erase disciplinary frontiers. Dependency theory, as well as theories emerging out of liberation philosophy and liberation theology, represent some of the most well-known perspectives. "Latin American sociology" (or "social theory") typically assumes a broad swath of intellectual production, including marginality theory, modernization studies, and the social impact of dependency, among others. The category of social theory circulated during the heyday of the Congreso Latinoamericano de Sociología (Latin American Congress of Sociology), which hosted debates on various issues pertaining to the consequences of dependency theories, including the 1979 Costa Rica congress. One speaks of "dependency theories" in the plural in order to connote Marxist and structuralist theories, as well as those theories focused on the dynamics of unequal exchange that most often grouped under this rubric. Despite their differences, all of these theories ultimately draw on Marx's work. The centrality of Marxism and the attempt to break free from "intellectual colonialism" are the hallmarks of this trend.

3. Althusser, "Marxism." With the term *finite theory* Althusser proposes a theory that questions or opposes its own capacity to "encompass" the totality of history philosophically. In other words, for Althusser, a finite theory would be one that limits itself to the horizon of capitalist society. According to Althusser, a finite theory is also one that is open to new problems arising within the explicative horizon defined by capitalism. In his view, Marxism would thus not attempt to restore a teleological understanding of history capable of justifying the current state of things, but would rather open itself to discussing contingent processes emerging every day in the heart of capitalist society.

4. Losurdo, *Antonio Gramsci*, 298–312.

5. Graeber, *Towards an Anthropological Theory*, 85.

6. The rejection of this concept is shared by figures like Carlos Pereyra. Perhaps this is because, taken out of the context in which it was produced, the text on "Ideological State Apparatuses" comes across as reductionist. We know today that this text was part of a broader discussion regarding the "primacy" of relations over forces of production. Althusser, *On the Reproduction*, 209.

7. The category of "feudalism" was important during the first half of the twentieth century. José Carlos Mariátegui referred to Peru in the same fashion, employing its equivalent term, *gamonalismo*. As the century progressed, Marxists increasingly abandoned this category. It was only for party intellectuals or within partisan documents that feudalism remained a category that mobilized political strategies, doing so in one of two ways. The first way—and this was exhibited mainly by the communist parties of the region—was as a category that allowed for thinking the articulation of national demands with sectors of the bourgeoisie; thus, eliminating the trace of feudalism was as beneficial for the nation's bourgeoisie as it was for strengthening the proletariat. Feudalism, in this sense, is a conspicuously political category. The second way refers principally to Trotskyist organizational experiences, which concentrated their efforts on distancing themselves from the region's communist parties by criticizing the latter's alliance with sectors of the national bourgeoisie. Nonetheless, feudalism as a category allowed Trotskyist to point to the "backward" or "prepolitical" state of the peasant contingent, thereby focusing on the creation of a "vanguard" centered on the working class.

8. Asiatic mode of production is a category that enacted a certain rupture in the historical linearity of Marxist discourse; its impact is yet to be evaluated to its full extent. See the compilation edited by Roger Bartra, *El modo de producción asiático*. Also by Bartra, *Marxismo y sociedades antiguas*. Other—less explored—authors belonging to the genealogies traced by this issue have also made important contributions. See Plá, *Modo de producción asiático y las formaciones económico-sociales inca y azteca*; and Castaingts, *Articulación de modos de producción*.

9. Bartra, *Hacia un marxismo*, 137. Echeverría, *El discurso*, 19.

10. Zavaleta, *Towards*, 119.

11. Zavaleta, "Las formaciones," 435.

12. Marx, *Grundrisse*, 157–58.

13. Dussel, *La producción*, 329.

14. He writes in the final version: "The exchange of commodities begins where communities have their boundaries, at their points of contact with other communities, or with members of the latter." Marx, *Capital*, 182.

15. Marx indicates: "Where money itself is not the community [*Gemeinwesen*], it must dissolve the community," *Grundrisse*, 224.

16. Zavaleta, "Las Formaciones," 435.

17. Marx, *Grundrisse*, 495.

18. Following the recent publication of an old text by Tronti, it is worth adding that, from Zavaleta's perspective, technical forces of production are, in effect, the "reason of history." This reason is linked to submission, dominance, and exploitation. On the contrary, non-histories are made up of those other nontechnical forces of production: community, nation, and the State. It is no coincidence that, moved by a desire to break with the *continuum* of history—which would be that of the technical forces of production—Tronti demands that we look at the State as a microcosm for the organization of labor.

19. Zavaleta, "El Estado," 621.

20. Zavaleta, "Clase," 383.

21. Ibid., 388.

22. Zavaleta, "Las luchas," 395.

23. Zavaleta, "Notas," 460.

24. Zavaleta, "Las formaciones," 428.

25. Ibid., 429.

26. Ibid., 437.

27. Zavaleta, "Notas," 459.

28. Zavaleta, "Las formaciones," 429.

29. Ibid., 430.

Works Cited

Althusser, Louis. "Marxism as a Finite Theory." Translated by Asad Haider. *Viewpoint Magazine* (December 2017). https://www.viewpointmag.com/2017/12/14/marxism-finite-theory-1978/.

———. *On the Reproduction of Capitalism*. Translated by G. M. Goshgarian. London: Verso, 2014.

Bartra, Armando. *Hacia un marxismo mundano: La clave está en los márgenes*. México: UAM-Xochimilco, 2016.

Bartra, Roger. *El modo de producción asiático: Antología de textos sobre el problema de la historia de los países coloniales*. México: Era, 1969.

———. *Marxismo y sociedades antiguas: El modo de producción asiático y el México preshispánico*. Grijalbo: México, 1975.

Castaingts Teillery, Juan. *Articulación de modos de producción*. México: El Caballito, 1979.

Dussel, Enrique. *La producción teórica de Marx: Un comentario a los Grundrisse*. México: Siglo XXI, 1985.

Graeber, David. *Towards an Anthropological Theory of Value: The False Coin of our own Dreams*. New York: Palgrave, 2001.

Echeverría, Bolívar. *El discurso crítico de Marx*. México: Fondo de Cultura Económica, 2017.

Losurdo, Domenico. *Antonio Gramsci: Del liberalismo al comunismo crítico*. Madrid: Oriente y Mediterráneo, 2015.

Marx, Karl. *Capital: A Critique of Political Economy*, Vol. 1. Translated by Ben Fowkes. New York: Penguin, 1990.

———. *Grundisse: Foundations of the Critique of Political Economy*. Translated by Martin Nicolaus. London and New York: Penguin Books, 1993.

Plá, Alberto J. *Modo de producción asiático y las formaciones económico-sociales inca y azteca*. México, D.F.: El Caballito, 1979.

Tronti, Mario. *La autonomía de lo político*. Translated by Martín Cortés. Buenos Aires: Prometeo, 2018.

Zavaleta Mercado, René. "Clase y conocimiento." In *Obra completa II*, 383–90. La Paz: Plural, 2013.

Zavaleta Mercado, René. "El Estado en América Latina." In *Obra completa II*, 611–36. La Paz: Plural, 2013.

———. "Las formaciones aparentes en Marx." In *Obra completa II*, 425–58. La Paz: Plural, 2013.

———. "Las luchas antiimperialistas en América Latina." In *Obra completa II*, 391–412. La Paz: Plural, 2013.

———. "Notas sobre fascismo, dictadura y coyuntura de disolución." In *Obra completa II*, 459–70. La Paz: Plural, 2013.

———. *Towards a History of the National Popular in Bolivia, 1879–1980*. Translated by Anne Freeland. London and Calcutta: Seagull Books, 2018.

CHAPTER SEVEN

Class and Accumulation

PABLO PÉREZ WILSON

OVER THE LAST FORTY YEARS a new common sense or orthodoxy rejecting the category of class has been imposed. The core of this position has to do with the weakening of political economy and the displacement of social class as a central category for social and political analysis. One finds this displacement in two forms, one moderate and another one more radical.

The moderate form of this position proposes the equivalence of race, gender, and class such that the first two terms function as correctives of Marxism's blind spots. While maintaining class as part of a categorial expansion, this moderate position has progressively erased class from the original triad in order either to further diminish the realm of political economy or to assume it from a nonclass perspective, as in the emphasis on governmentality, sovereignty, and financialization in recent critiques of neoliberalism; or the disentanglement of race and class and the turn away from the problem of social reproduction in feminist critiques.[1]

In its radical form, however, this weakening of class has not been conceived as a corrective to Marxism but rather as a full departure from political economy, which it understands as a form of teleological eschatology associated with the identification of the working class with the privileged subject of revolutionary practice. One finds two concatenated operations at the core of this position. The first operation examines Marxism's main concepts as a way of maintaining a critical connection to them while also emphasizing a series of political rather than economic texts from Marx to the Third International.

The second operation seeks a categorial weakening or debilitation of any ground, foundation, or metaphysical residue of political philosophy as such, including the very notion of the subject and correlatively of class.[2]

Parallel to this new common sense or orthodoxy on the issue of class are the multiple accounts of deindustrialization in Western Europe and the United States since the 1980s. The exhaustion of the Fordist model that dominated the industrial twentieth century, paired with the collapse of the Soviet Union, which was fundamentally the crisis of a federalist planned economy, created the conditions for a growing consensus about the end of class, as it pertained alternately to a historical period, a form of collective consciousness or organization, and a mode of social analysis. Unfortunately, what most of these accounts overlooked was that the deindustrialization relative to the parameters of Fordism in Western Europe and the United States did not imply the disappearance of the working class but rather a planetary redistribution of industrial production sites. China, South Asia, and Latin America have been the not-so-silent recipients of these tectonic shifts, which have also created a new global configuration of class and class struggle. Closely related to this new configuration of class are the deep transformations of work itself fueled by the technological revolutions defining production beginning in the nineteen seventies.[3]

There is another consensus that functions as a counterbalance to the progressive erasure of class as analytical category. The combined economic growth and moderate or limited redistribution reforms over the last forty years have significantly expanded the so-called middle class in the global periphery. The vaguely defined term *middle class* entails a positive upward movement out of poverty but usually a difficult path toward stability, a path associated with the increasing precarity of labor regimes and a reduced or minimal social welfare system. Hundreds of millions have been effectively lifted out of poverty and even propelled upward, creating a complex social stratification thanks to the uneven regimes of accumulation that govern the global economy. Certainly, the flip side of the middle-class consensus is that an even greater number of people have been completely excluded from the monetized economy, that is, from the realms of production or even consumption. This sector constitutes an increasing proportion of the world's population and the most vulnerable sector in regions affected by war and climate disasters.[4]

How is it, then, that class has practically disappeared from consideration in social, political, and cultural theories but at the same time remains both a significant social fact and almost common parlance term? A possible answer to this problem can be found in the historically grounded nature of the intersection between class and accumulation. That is to say, in the determinate way in which the unfolding of class relations over time has given rise to different forms of accumulation and, as part of the same movement, how, in the interaction between regimes of property, different forms of appropriation and expropriation emerge. Rather than deriving a necessary outcome from a given conception, historically oriented research should pay attention to how the actual development of a specific social formation encapsulates the tensions and contradictions of capital itself. Following this mode of inquiry and contrary to the double orthodoxy and consensus surrounding the end of class, complete with its middle-class paradox, one can point to the rise of the service sector and the rapid growth of state bureaucracy as two intertwined factors that help to counterbalance the end of class as an end of history thesis. Considering these complex factors highlights the need to pay attention to the ways in which class continues to be a relevant analytical tool.

The overall point that I wish to sustain is that, strictly speaking, shifts in capitalist accumulation cannot be separated from changes in class structure and composition. This proposition implies a class-subject of accumulation produced in the interplay between appropriation and expropriation. What constitutes a social class, in this understanding, requires a historical consideration of accumulation. Within that framework a social class is a set of positions relative to the appropriation and expropriation of the social product whose historical instantiation is constituted by the constant transformation of a given social formation. Accumulation happens under the universal expansion of capital but is determined by the singular qualities of a given social formation, marking the latter as a privileged object of historical analysis. The logical consequence of the inextricable nature of the relationship between class and accumulation is that there is no such thing as accumulation without the appropriation and expropriation of labor power. That is to say, in order to understand the relationship between class and accumulation it is necessary to consider both its functional logic and historical, situated nature. The Marxist tradition, in turn, has designated this situated nature in terms of the complex set of relationships that fall under the national parameters of a given social formation. The intersection between class and accumulation, in this regard, is of vital importance to the national question, not only in relation to the ideological constitution of the nation state, but also in the localized unfolding of capitalism itself.

In order to focus my analysis, I will examine a limited set of hypotheses about the Chilean context. Interrogating the relationship between class and accumulation is particularly important within the context of Chilean neoliberalism and, more specifically, its critique in recent years. As I will examine in more detail below, the last three cycles of significant social unrest led by student protests, the movement for the elimination of the private pension system, and the most recent wave of revolts demanding a dignified life have contributed to a sort of return of class as an analytical tool in academic circles.

The present contribution can be considered a response to the achievements and limitations of Carlos Ruiz Encina and Giorgio Boccardo's *Los chilenos bajo el neoliberalismo: Clases y conflicto social* [Chileans Under Neoliberalism: Classes and Social Conflict]. First published in 2014, the book critically reconstructs the impact of the Christian and Social Democratic administration of neoliberalism between 1990 and 2010, placing particular emphasis on the way in which both state policies and social mobilizations have shaped class composition in Chile. In my view, the key element of the book is that it deploys an understanding of class that tends to rely on a characterization of the social structure defined more by income and consumption patterns and less by changes in labor itself. Perhaps against its own intentions, this reading of class supposes a categorial definition of class structure derived from market-oriented research in the field of social inquiry. While the authors' objectives clearly differ from conservative sociology, they refrain, at least in this study, from offering an alternative characterization of class to those derived from a Parsonian sociological model.[5]

The problem that one finds in *Los chilenos bajo el neoliberalismo* can be traced to its methodological predecessor, the influential *Las clases sociales en Chile: Cambio y estratificación, 1970–1980* [Social Classes in Chile: Change and Stratification, 1970–1980] co-authored by sociologists Javier Martínez and Eugenio Tironi. Published in 1985 by the independent think tank SUR, *Las clases sociales en Chile* brings together a perspective on class analysis and a conception of social change removed from a revolutionary or advanced democratic horizon. For these sociologists, objective or scientific research should not contain what is now conceived of as a specific prognosis or judgment on the actuality or prospects of society. While the previous generation of researchers tended to privilege militant investigation as a part of their political commitment, Martínez and Tironi's conception of social change falls under a reformist, limited democratic horizon. The key to this book, however, is its capacity to reframe class analysis as stratification. Their objective was to remove the conflictive nature of class and instead to treat it as a tabulated distribution of income and consumption. The importance of *Las clases sociales en Chile* is that it in essence serves as a hinge between a form of class analysis somehow identified with Marxism and partisan political commitment and a more strictly disciplinary one associated with the late reception of sociological structural functionalism. In short, Martínez and Tironi kept the notion of class but emptied its association with class struggle.[6]

A prime example of the type of work displaced by Martínez and Tironi's *Las clases sociales en Chile* is Manuel Castells's *La lucha de clases en Chile* [Class Struggle in Chile], first published in 1974. As indicated in its title, Castells privileges class struggle to in order to carry out a form of in-depth conjunctural analysis at the intersection of class and politics. For Castells, social conflict and antagonism are synonymous with class struggle. Politics and social structure are related thanks to the mediation of what the book calls internal hierarchies, which, in turn, it understands to be derived from objective social laws. Castells's book combines a theoretical understanding of class and class struggle in line with Marxist structuralism but with an acute sense of historical development in terms of alignment of political forces. For Castells, class struggle functions as the key to identifying not the one-to-one relation between socioeconomic position and political adscriptions but rather the actual instances of struggle that point to the distribution of politico-economic forces at a given time.

The three perspectives on class represented by Castells, Martínez and Tironi, and Ruiz Encina and Boccardo share a relative consensus on the objective definition of the Chilean social formation. The most important elements of this common ground have to do with how to periodize the cycles of Chilean capitalism and the decisive role of the state. Between 1932 and 1973 the state was the key engine of Chilean economic development thanks to a more or less articulated set of policies that combined medium range industrialization via import substitutions and agrarian reform. The relative consensus regarding the gradualism of the implementation of these reforms was broken with the 1973 military coup backed by the oligarchy, bourgeoisie, and middle sectors representing both national and international capitalist interest. The transitional period, understood as an adjustment to a different form of accumulation, was undertaken between 1975 and 1982. During those years the military junta radically transformed the legal basis of the state and its role in the national economy. Contrary to assumed notions about neoliberalism, the main characteristic of the state's relationship to the economy was not a reduction in size or a withdrawal from its public role but rather a redirecting of the imported substitution industrial model with its focus on internal consumption and protectionism toward a different form of accumulation.[7]

Broadly speaking, this new accumulation pattern was based on the reorganization of property and class relations. Industrialization by import substitution was abandoned to favor imported manufactured goods. Agrarian reform was redesigned to consolidate land property and increase productivity. New regulations allowed the dynamization of the financial sector at the same time that the banking system associated with the old land property system collapsed. The direct consequence of these policies, on the side of capital, was the literal destruction of the older land-based oligarchy, the drastic reduction of the national industrial bourgeoisie, and the complete reorganization of the banking system. A new labor law facilitated the transition to flexibilization and precarization and heavily restricted collective bargaining and unionization. The policies now commonly associated with neoliberalism in the form of privatization of social rights such as pensions, health care, education, and housing not only served to disentangle the state from its prior public mandate but also to helped structure accumulation in such a way that further accentuated class restructuration. The absence of a true welfare system, like the ones developed in most Western European countries, the United States, Canada, and the corresponding socialization of resources in the Soviet Union and the Eastern bloc, helped to facilitate the transition. Stripped of entitlements and protections, labor was fully reconstituted as a new societal structure emerging from these new conditions.

Tightly linked to the development of the state's role in the economy during the short twentieth century (1914–1991) was the dependent character of Chilean capitalism or the uneven way in which its economy inserted itself into the global market. Dependent capitalism, in fact, was a widely accepted way of describing the Chilean economy among important sectors of the national intellectual Left. The two modern cycles associated with mining extraction continue to define the national economy today within the well-known formula of a national economy characterized by having been an importer of manufactured goods and exporter of natural resources: nitratine from the middle of the nineteenth century until the end of the nineteen twenties and then copper from the nineteen tens to the present. Gross domestic product and state revenue has been directly associated with variations in tax policy for mining and extraction permits. The state's participation in copper extraction was not relevant until a cycle of new regulations initiated in the nineteen fifties was implemented, which included the nationalization decrees from the early seventies and the creation of a state copper company in 1976, paradoxically implemented by the military junta. The first nitratine cycle of mining extraction ended drastically thanks to the concurrent development of a cheaper, artificial substitute and the economic crisis of 1929. The crash further compounded the negative effects of the opening of the Panama Canal in 1914 and the displacement of Valparaiso as a key seaport in the Pacific.[8]

When considered from a historical perspective, the impact of the neoliberal reforms was a direct hit against the definition of class as class struggle. The transitional period ended a cycle of struggles that ran in parallel to the expansive role of the state during the short twentieth century by suppressing political dissent and redrawing legal system under the dictatorial state of exception. From this perspective, of class as a form of direct political struggle, class restructuring happened not in disregard of a legal framework but rather in order to implement a network of legal protections able to meet the requirements of a new form of accumulation. In this particular regard, and from the perspective of the emerging new capitalists, class continues to be a motor of history but without significant oppositional force. The fact that the transitional period, understood as the moment of emergence of a new dominant form of accumulation, was prompted in a context of dictatorial rule highlights the importance of periodization. Here, transition is not associated with democratization but rather with the reorganization of social classes and its inextricable connection with capitalist accumulation. As is usually the case in Latin America, this understanding of transition still associates state economic policy with changes in the economic infrastructure. As the Chilean case perfectly encapsulates, free trade agreements are the main example, not of democratization via capitalism, but of the violent preconditions of open markets.[9]

The transitional period effectively distributed classes in a different way. This was done not only negatively by the destruction or minimization of the prior form of accumulation, but mainly by the active creation of a new type of workforce without legal protections or collective rights and the constitution of a new capitalist class composed thanks to the consolidation and redistribution of property relations. Within this framework, the class composition of Chilean society was drastically altered in relation to the prior dominant regime of accumulation. The middle class, then, regained prevalence thanks to the combined effect of financialization and access to credit, urbanization and migration, unemployment programs, and the expansion of education via private provision. It was no surprise when analysis centered on the middle class, such as Martínez and Tironi's, began to emerge in order to give account of this new social composition.[10]

Since the closure of the transitional period, defined by the stabilization plan implemented as a correction to the first wave of economic reforms under Pinochet, the Chilean middle class has not only significantly expanded in size but also in the complex layering of its stratification thanks to the growth of the national economy as a whole. The social consensus that accompanied this process, often read in triumphalist terms, has been eroded over more than forty years of neoliberal accumulation. Of special note is the particular way in which, perhaps in a deeper way than in other Latin American countries, former entitlements such as pensions, education, health services, and housing turned into direct forms of accumulation. These most drastic forms of expropriation have given way, in recent years, to the massive waves of social protests signaling the limits of the political consensus that sustains the main pillars of the Chilean economy.[11]

Debates around the mode of production helped to frame the periodization of capitalism in the region. It is worth mentioning that Castells, Martínez and Tironi, and Ruiz Encina and Boccardo position themselves on this ticklish subject of the mode of production by basically rejecting its abstraction. They opt instead for a class characterization not of the transition from feudalism to capitalism but of the actual depiction of the dominant regime of accumulation and its internal tensions and transformations.[12]

These three studies share a characterization of accumulation with social histories focused on workers' movements and leftist politics, and the economic research that followed the double path of the theories of Underdevelopment and Dependency, both beginning in the 1960s. An orthodox, but not fully developed, line tended to name and describe the mode of production as feudal. However, this tendency was more a negative assumption than a research-based one. The characterization of the prevalent mode of production as feudal was based on the country and region lacking the main features and attributes assumed to be properly capitalist in the restricted sense of advanced industrialism since the middle and late-ninetieth century in Western Europe and the United States. Since this was not the case in any Latin American country, the most common line of research tried to explain both the form that feudalism acquired in the region and the mechanisms of transition out of it. Processes such as landed property regimes, protoindustrial developments, and changes in the composition of the peasantry, to name just a few of the most important ones, were sometimes forced into a mechanistic schema in which the overarching label of a feudal mode of production seemed to be too large and abstract to describe such heterogenous realities.[13]

Social historians conceived of their task as a response to traditional liberal and conservative historiographies inherited from the nineteenth century and aimed to account for and accompany the rise of the workers' movement and leftist party organization. Economic theorists reacted, respectively, to the theories of development and modernization advanced by the United Nations Economic Commission for Latin America and the Caribbean and by the emergent social sciences now institutionalized academically and professionally. However, from the perspective of the periodization of accumulation, social history and economic theory share assumptions regarding the expansive role of the state in terms of driving economic policy and creation of entitlements.[14]

An important contrast between these two fields of historic and economic inquiry has to do with their research methodologies or analytical approaches. The obvious, superficial contrast is that for social history, field research entailed the recollection of documentary newspaper and oral sources while the economic field was more concerned with the statistical record of economic performance. A more substantive difference, however, relates to the conception of what constitutes a transindividual class-subject. For such social historians, a working notion of class consciousness and its formation, forged in organized, collective entities such as unions and political parties, served as the crucial analytical unit. On the other hand, for the economists, class consciousness was not necessarily an object of research but more an effect of economic changes. In other words, at the most general level, these two fields of inquiry seemed concerned with both the forcing and the description of history at the subjective and material level. Whereas the historical development and structural position of class were sometimes conceived as analytically different, class formation and changes in class composition were not always emphasized thanks to a narrow adscription of class to urban industrialization.[15]

Since the 1970s, the relationship between class and accumulation has been a source of constant engagement in the field of social theory in Chile, such that changes in the operative definition of class in each of these three studies correspond to parallel shifts in the global pattern of accumulation. These transformations in the definition of class similarly reveal a tension among, on the one hand, class as a motor of history, as a form of direct political struggle, and as a social stratum; and, on the other hand, of moments or periods of accumulation from oligarchic dependency to developmental state policies to the current neoliberal regime. In each case, the nature of the relationship between the working definitions of class and accumulation purposely avoid their one-to-one correspondence. In other words, there is no strict alignment between a given subject-class definition and a preconceived notion of accumulation. In the cases surveyed here, one finds instead an effort to reveal changes in the dynamics of capitalist exploitation by observing significant changes in the symbiosis among organized labor, society, and class consciousness. In the 1980s, the influence of structuralist functionalism, and eventually, market research represented a drastic shift away from the Marxist perspectives that had shaped class analysis in Chile in the previous decades. My argument, in this respect, is twofold. First, I contend that a theory of social class should not depend on patterns of consumption based primarily on income and access to credit, but rather on a characterization of social structure in terms of both subjective and objective positioning. Second, I argue that an accurate depiction of the specificities of and shifts in capitalist accumulation requires that we relate such changes to the class structure of society. By signaling these key moments in the analysis of the Chilean social formation since the 1960s, my contribution ultimately aims to question the inheritance of 1980s market research in contemporary critiques of neoliberalism, showing instead how we can understand social class and capitalist accumulation as part of the same historical process.

To recapitulate, I have so far made three basic assertions. The first one concerns the solidification into orthodoxy of a weakening and displacement of class from important sections of social, cultural, and political analysis, beginning in the mid-seventies and early eighties. My second point is that throughout this period of more than forty years, class has, perhaps paradoxically, remained both a social fact and an important analytical element mainly in the form of the unprecise notion of middle classes. My last point is that the notion of class cannot be separated from accumulation. By this I mean that in order to characterize a social formation from the perspective of shifts in capitalist accumulation one also needs to pay attention to the ways in which classes are restructured in every case. Castells, Martínez and Tironi, and Ruiz Encina and Boccardo focused on class during a period in which the concept lost traction both inside and outside of Marxism. The key element that interests me with respect to this particular point is the sense in which they periodize the ebb and return of the notion of class without ever fully disavowing it.

Castells's book is representative of a moment of intense debate on class within Marxism in and beyond Latin America. Castells's Chilean period, which almost completely overlaps with the Popular Unity government, centered around the notion of class struggle. Somehow, this moment has been minimized or read as an interruption of his earlier and later focus on urbanization. The extent to which this interruption via class struggle defined for Castells a broader positioning within French Marxism (Lefebvre versus Althusser, for example) exceeds the framework of my contribution here but is indicative of deeper changes in some of Marxism's main theoretical orientations.[16]

Martínez and Tironi's study represents an almost complete reorientation from Castells's. Their work retains the notion of class but from the perspective of the "bourgeois" social sciences, and, specifically, sociological inquiry. There is no class struggle in Martínez and Tironi but class remains a central and useful category for them for describing social structure. For these authors, class does not represent a social antagonism but a category that contributes to social analysis from the point of view of income distribution. In turn, a given society is divided into classes because their income distribution is segmented by their acquisition power, which is determined by their level of professional specialization, among other things. Ultimately, Martínez and Tironi's modern view of society is one in which differentiation via specialization leads to improvements in living standards.[17]

For Ruiz Encina and Boccardo, a return to class as social conflict or antagonism is necessary in order to make sense of the economic reforms under Pinochet and their extension in the postdictatorial present. If Martínez and Tironi moved class outside of Marxism, Ruiz Encina and Boccardo wanted to bring class back as a category together with an expanded consideration of the place of social movements. Ruiz Encina and Boccardo's understanding of this intersection between class and social movements is one of the key features of their analysis but also their way of bypassing Marxism, even if the book is not necessarily framed in these terms.

The relation of these three studies to Marxism fluctuates between interiority and exteriority but also in the specific ways in which each describes the so-called middle class. In this case, the fluctuation moves from a perspective that privileges the social power of workers and peasants, and in which the emphasis on the middle class is not that prevalent, as in the case of Castells, to that of the two more recent studies, which make this social space a crucial one. Castells's apparent dismissal of the middle class in analytical terms is significant insofar as it allows us to grasp how the studies by Martínez and Tironi and Ruiz Encina and Boccardo, respectively, mobilize this category in order to insinuate the extent to which the economic reforms implemented under Pinochet's dictatorship responded to a shift in capitalist accumulation. For the Spanish sociologist, the middle class appeared as an element of the growing importance of state bureaucracy and the expansion of public goods such as education during the Chilean short twentieth century. Class mobility, or the crossing from one class stratum to another in terms of buying power, marked a departure from a more conventional Marxist approach privileging the relative position of a group within the productive structure of society in the definition and constitution of classes. In other words, the growing importance of the middle class somehow removed or displaced the core of class as a relation of expropriation of labor power. However, this same removal or displacement contributed to highlighting the role of stratification, or the detailed distribution of classes in and around the productive structure, as an unavoidable aspect of class analysis. In this regard, the middle class, as a construct, became the center of attention from different angles or perspectives.[18]

The middle class, with its multilayered composition, grew mainly via access to credit but this fact does not necessarily imply that its class position is related to buying power. This is the case when Ruiz Encina and Boccardo's study accepts the stratification model of Martínez and Tironi. Class analysis, such as Ruiz Encina and Boccardo's, would benefit from a more extensive and concrete exploration of the actual transformations of labor together with a permanent evaluation of the limits of the dominant and parallel forms of capitalist accumulation.[19] This orientation, already present in the last chapter of *Los chilenos bajo el neoliberalismo*, is a welcome return to an understanding of class as both political struggle and positioning related to expropriation of labor power. It serves as a reminder that there is no such a thing as accumulation without class.

These three studies consider or reconstruct different understandings of the relationship between class and accumulation even when they do not address this relationship explicitly in these terms. Despite this, the periodizations operative in all three analyses reveal shifts in capitalist accumulation or, more precisely, the transition from one dominant form of accumulation to another, and the extent to which these changes are linked to shifts in the configuration of social classes in Chile. In this sense, these studies share an understanding about the most distinctive elements of the pattern of capitalist accumulation shaping the Chilean social formation prior to neoliberalism. More broadly, these studies show us how a new configuration of class emerges as the inextricable result of shifts in accumulation. By highlighting these concatenated shifts between class and accumulation these studies help us to understand the Chilean case in historical perspective at the same time that they allow us an insight into similar processes throughout the region and beyond.

Notes

1. Compare the trajectories of Stuart Hall and Lawrence Grossberg. While the former articulated the classic formulations of cultural studies on class and race, the latter has tended to detach class from cultural analysis. See Hall, "A Sense of Classlessness" (1958) and Hall, "Race, Articulation, and Societies Structured in Dominance" (1980). See also Grossberg, "Strategies of Marxist Cultural Interpretation" (1984) and Grossberg, "The Indifference of Television, or, Mapping TV's Popular (Affective) Economy" (1987). For a recent return to Hall from a different perspective see Taylor's *Race for Profit*. For a good example on financialization and governmentality see Cocco and Cava, *New Neoliberalism and the Other*. On feminism in the influential Italian context see Casarino and Righi, *Another Mother*. For a different perspective within Italian feminism see, Fortunati, *The Arcane of Reproduction*.

2. The work of Ernesto Laclau and Chantal Mouffe is the most representative of this type of position. See *Hegemony and Socialist Strategy* and Laclau's earliest *Politics and Ideology in Marxist Theory*. Parallel to this trajectory, the work of Jean Cohen and Andrew Arato is also relevant and a complement to Laclau and Mouffe. See Cohen, *Class and Civil Society* and Arato, *From Neo-Marxism to Democratic Theory*.

3. André Gorz's *Farewell to the Working Class* and his posthumous *The Immaterial* are equally misleading. Herbert Marcuse was among the first Marxist scholars to coherently articulate a class analysis of the Soviet Union in his *Soviet Marxism*. For a succinct and informed account of capitalism and class in China, see Russo, "Class Struggle."

4. For a comprehensive account of this question see Franco, Hopenhayn, and León, *Las clases medias en América Latina*.

5. In this contribution I focus on Ruiz Encina and Baccardo's *Los chilenos bajo el neoliberalismo*. Both authors belong to the Santiago-based think tank Nodo XXI that has since produced a number of shorter studies on the labor force with the horizon of creating their own analytical categories detached from the inheritance of market research.

6. Martínez and Tironi's *Las clases sociales en Chile* forms part of a larger research project on class and stratification. See Martínez and Tironi, *Clase obrera y modelo económico*, and Martínez and León, *Clases y clasificaciones sociales*.

7. Castells, *La lucha de clases en Chile*, 126–30. Martínez and Tironi, *Las clases sociales en Chile*, 25–49. Ruiz Encina and Boccardo, *Los chilenos bajo el neoliberalismo*, 15–20.

8. See Cardoso and Faletto, *Dependency and Development in Latin America*; Gunder Frank, *Capitalism and Underdevelopment in Latin America*; and Gunder Frank, *Accumulation, Dependence, and Underdevelopment*.

9. For a detailed mapping of economic power since the neoliberal reforms see Dahse, *El mapa de la extrema riqueza*. Fazio, *Mapa actual de la extrema riqueza en Chile* and Fazio, *La crisis económica modifica el mapa de la extrema riqueza*.

10. Martínez and Tironi, *Las clases sociales en Chile*, 126–129.

11. The overemphasis on political transition, from dictatorship to democracy, presupposed an evaluation of the limitations of Allende's Popular Unity government. The turn away from political economy, and specifically class, was complemented by the rise of hegemony as one of the key terms to read politics without class. For an early study in this direction see Ottone Fernández, *Hegemonía y crisis en el Chile contemporáneo*.

12. Sempat Assadourian et al., *Modos de producción en América Latina*. See also Villalobos Ruminott and Starcenbaum in this collection.

13. See Cueva, *El desarrollo del capitalismo en América Latina*. Osorio, *Teoría marxista de la dependencia*.

14. Social history in Chile has a long and multifaceted set of authors. Two such studies include Vitale, *Interpretación marxista de la historia de Chile* and Salazar Vergara, *Labradores, peones y proletarios*. For two classic studies on Chilean economic development see Segall, *El desarrollo del capitalismo en Chile* and Riesco, *Desarrollo del capitalismo en Chile bajo Pinochet*.

15. For a critical assessment of this point see Zapata, *Clases sociales y acción obrera en Chile*.

16. Castells, *La lucha de clases en Chile*, 21–40. Castells participated in the famous seminar on class held in Mérida in 1971. See Benítez Zenteno, *Las clases sociales en América Latina*. *The Urban Question* was originally published in French in 1972. See also, *The City and the Grassroots*. A recent account on class struggle in the Latin American context can be found in Petras and Veltmeyer, *The Class Struggle in Latin America*.

17. Martínez and Tironi, *Las clases sociales en Chile*, 143–74.

18. Ibid., 215–18; Ruiz Encina and Boccardo, *Los chilenos bajo el neoliberalismo*, 111–15.

19. Martínez and Tironi, *Las clases sociales en Chile*, 87–129. Ruiz Encina and Boccardo, *Los chilenos bajo el neoliberalismo*, 41–46 and 148–73.

Works Cited

Arato, Andrew. *From Neo-Marxism to Democratic Theory: Essays on the Critical Theory of Soviet-type Societies.* Armonk, NY, and London: M. E. Sharpe, 1993.

Benítez Zenteno, Raúl, ed. *Las clases sociales en América Latina. Seminario Mérida, Yucatán 1971.* México: Siglo Veintiuno Editores, 1973.

Cardoso, Fernando Henrique, and Enzo Faletto. *Dependency and Development in Latin America.* Translated by Marjory Mattingly Urquidi. Berkeley: University of California Press, 1979.

Casarino, Cesare, and Andrea Righi, eds. *Another Mother: Diotima and the Symbolic Order of Italian Feminism.* Translated by Mark William Epstein. Minneapolis: University of Minnesota Press, 2019.

Castells, Manuel. *La lucha de clases en Chile.* México: Siglo Veintiuno Editores, 1974.

———. *The Urban Question: A Marxist Approach.* Translated by Alan Sheridan. Cambridge: MIT Press, 1979.

———. *The City and the Grassroots: A Cross-Cultural Theory of Urban Social Movements.* Berkeley: University of California Press, 1983.

Cocco, Giuseppe, and Bruno Cava. *New Neoliberalism and the Other. Bio-power, Anthropophagy, and Living Money.* Lexington: Lexington Books 2018.

Cohen, Jean L. *Class and Civil Society: The Limits of Marxian Critical Theory.* Amherst: University of Massachusetts Press, 1982.

Cueva, Agustín. *El desarrollo del capitalismo en América Latina: ensayo de interpretación histórica.* México: Siglo Veintiuno, 1983.

Dahse, Fernando. *El mapa de la extrema riqueza: los grupos económicos y el proceso de concentración de capitales.* Santiago: Editorial Aconcagua, 1979.

Fazio, Hugo. *Mapa actual de la extrema riqueza en Chile.* Santiago: Universidad ARCIS, LOM Ediciones, CENDA, 1997.

———. *La crisis económica modifica el mapa de la extrema riqueza.* Santiago: Centro de Estudios Nacionales de Desarrollo Alternativo, 2010.

Franco, Rolando, Martín Hopenhayn, and Arturo León, eds. *Las clases medias en América Latina: retrospectiva y nuevas tendencias.* México: Siglo XXI and CEPAL, 2010.

Fortunati, Leopoldina. *The Arcane of Reproduction: Housework, Prostitution, Labor, and Capital.* Translated by Hilary Creek. Edited by Jim Fleming. Brooklyn: Autonomedia, 1995.

Grossberg, Lawrence. "Strategies of Marxist Cultural Interpretation." In *Bringing It All Back Home: Essays on Cultural Studies,* 103–37. Durham: Duke University Press, 1997.

———. "The Indifference of Television, or, Mapping TV's Popular (Affective) Economy." In *Dancing in Spite of Myself: Essays on Popular Culture*, 125–44. Durham: Duke University Press, 1997.

Gorz, André. *The Immaterial: Knowledge, Value, and Capital*. Translated by Chris Turner. London and New York: Seagull Books, 2010.

———. *Farewell to the Working Class: An Essay on Post-Industrial Socialism*. Translated by Michael Sonenscher. London: Pluto Press, 1982.

Gunder Frank, Andre. *Capitalism and Underdevelopment in Latin America: Historical Studies of Chile and Brazil*. New York: Monthly Review Press, 1967.

———. *Accumulation, Dependence, and Underdevelopment*. New York: Monthly Review Press, 1978.

Hall, Stuart. "Race, Articulation, and Societies Structured in Dominance." In *Essential Essays, Volume 1, Foundations of Cultural Studies*, edited by David Morley, 172–211. Durham: Duke University Press, 2019.

———. "A Sense of Classlessness." In *Selected Political Writings: The Great Moving Right Show and Other Essays*, edited by Sally Davison, David Featherstone, Michael Rustin, and Bill Schwarz, 28–46. Durham: Duke University Press, 2017.

Laclau, Ernesto. *Politics and Ideology in Marxist Theory: Capitalism, Fascism, Populism*. London: NLB, 1977.

———, and Chantal Mouffe. *Hegemony and Socialist Strategy: Towards a Radical Democratic Politics*. London and New York: Verso, 2001.

Marcuse, Herbert. *Soviet Marxism: A Critical Analysis*. New York, Columbia University Press, 1958.

Martínez, Javier, and Eugenio Tironi. *Clase obrera y modelo económico: un estudio del peso y la estructura del proletariado en Chile, 1973–1980*. Santiago: Programa de Economía del Trabajo, Academia de Humanismo Cristiano, 1983.

———. *Las clases sociales en Chile: Cambio y estratificación, 1970–1980*. Santiago: Ediciones Sur, 1985.

Martínez, Javier, and Arturo León. *Clases y clasificaciones sociales: investigaciones sobre la estructura social chilena, 1970–1983*. Santiago: Centro de Estudios del Desarrollo Sur, 1987.

Osorio, Jaime. *Teoría marxista de la dependencia: Historia, fundamentos, debates y contribuciones*. México: Universidad Autónoma Metropolitana, Unidad Xochimilco, División de Ciencias Sociales y Humanidades, Itaca, 2016.

Ottone Fernández, Ernesto. *Hegemonía y crisis en el Chile contemporáneo*. Madrid: Lar, 1984.

Petras, James, and Henry Veltmeyer. *The Class Struggle in Latin America: Making History Today*. London and New York: Routledge, 2018.

Riesco, Manuel. *Desarrollo del capitalismo en Chile bajo Pinochet*. Santiago: Ediciones ICAL, 1989.

Ruiz Encina, Carlos, and Giorgio Boccardo. *Los chilenos bajo el neoliberalismo. Clases y conflicto social*. Santiago: Nodo XXI and El Desconcierto, 2014.

Russo, Alessandro. "Class Struggle." In *Afterlives of Chinese Communism: Political Concepts from Mao to Xi*, edited by Christian Sorace, Ivan Franceschini, Nicholas Loubere, 29–35. New York and Canberra: Verso and ANU Press, 2019.

Salazar Vergara, Gabriel. *Labradores, peones y proletarios: formación y crisis de la sociedad popular chilena del siglo XIX*. Santiago: Ediciones Sur, 1985.

Segall, Marcelo. *El desarrollo del capitalismo en Chile: cinco ensayos dialécticos*. Santiago: Editorial del pacífico, 1953.

Sempat Assadourian, Carlos, and Ernesto Laclau, Ciro Cardoso, Horacio Ciafardini, Juan Carlos Garavaglia. *Modos de producción en América Latina*. Buenos Aires and Córdoba: Siglo Veintiuno, 1973.

Taylor, Keeanga-Yamahtta. *Race for Profit: How Banks and the Real Estate Industry Undermined Black Homeownership*. Chapel Hill: University of North Carolina Press, 2019.

Vitale, Luis. *Interpretación marxista de la historia de Chile*. Santiago: Ediciones de Prensa Latinoamericana, 1967–1972.

Zapata, Francisco, ed. *Clases sociales y acción obrera en Chile*. México: Centro de Estudios Sociológicos y Colegio de México, 1986.

PART THREE

Sovereignty
and
Debt

CHAPTER EIGHT

The "Insurgent Subject" versus Accumulation by Dispossession in Álvaro García Linera and Jorge Sanjinés

IRINA ALEXANDRA FELDMAN

ÁLVARO GARCÍA LINERA, political theorist and current vice president of Bolivia, defined the popular multitudes engaged in the Water War (2000) as the new political subject of "plebeian power," and added that this subject would bring about the Proceso de Cambio (Process of Change) by broadening the sphere of the political beyond party politics and the mechanisms of representative democracy while opening it up to social movements. Since García Linera was sworn in as vice president in January 2006, his office has developed a robust pedagogical project of public education and outreach. Although this program emanates from the state, it is committed to widening the sphere of politics so that it can foster the formation of multiple subjectivities capable of countering the pressures of neoliberalism and neoextractivism that are characteristic of Bolivia's position on the periphery of global capital. This project of epistemic decolonization is underpinned by analytical tools originating in the Indianist and Marxist traditions of the twentieth century and is committed to the conceptual renewal of the class struggle for the twenty-first century, while simultaneously maintaining its claim to national sovereignty in the face of the encroachments of transnational capital.

Within this broad context, this essay examines how over the past decade García Linera, speaking not only as a theorist but also as a statesman, has argued for the necessity that two subjectivities, a nationalist and a decolonial one, take shape simultaneously. García Linera develops this argument through an unorthodox, albeit Marxist, use of the concept of accumulation—deploying at once references to the primitive accumulation of capital and of insurgent experience, which he views as a tool of resistance to the former. I examine this proposal as García Linera advances it in his 2012 essay *Las tensiones creativas del Proceso de Cambio* [Creative Tensions of the Process of Change]; and I read the film *Insurgentes* [Insurgents], from the same year, produced by Jorge Sanjinés and Grupo Ukamau, as the site where García Linera's theoretical proposals are performed. Experientially and theoretically, Sanjinés could be described as a product of the debates about political subjectivity and progressive politics that occurred during the second half of the twentieth century, specifically in the 1970s (the first Conference of Third World Cinema took place in 1975). García Linera, in turn, advocates for the importance of forging theoretical and ideological links with the generation of the leftist thinkers, artists, and activists that included Sanjinés. Both García Linera and Sanjinés often deploy the tools—theoretical, aesthetic, and didactic—developed during the 1970s. What do these tools look like in the twenty-first century and how do they work?

The Limitations and Achievements of MAS

As a country on the periphery of capital in the framework of what David Harvey terms "New Imperialism," Bolivia is subject to insatiable accumulation by dispossession, a process by which the commons is continuously transferred to the sphere of circulation of capital where use value is overridden by exchange value (Harvey 2003). In the case of Bolivia, the resources subject to this process have been mainly water and hydrocarbons. For a Marixst Indigenist theoretician and statesman such as García Linera, accumulation by dispossession is one of the main problems that confronts the Bolivian State. At the same time, eruptions of popular protest are triggered by those instances when the mechanism of accumulation by dispossession is laid bare, such as the 2000 Cochabamba Water War or the 2003 El Alto Gas War protests, which resisted the neoliberal project by agglutinating interclass and interethnic alliances.[1] In this sense, a different sort of accumulation emerges: through a dialectical reenactment of scenes of resistance, political subjectivities are produced that are capable of resisting the—also repeatedly enacted—scenes of dispossession and loss of the commons and natural resources.[2]

While facing this historical reality, the MAS (Movimiento al Socialismo/ Movement Toward Socialism) project known as the "Process of Change" is limited in its pursuit of economic sovereignty from the domination of global finance. Arguably, this is the reason why Jeffrey Webber has criticized the MAS government and García Linera for the insufficiencies and contradictions of their agenda, which has been, and continues to be, the basis of their electoral promise.[3] Two aspects of this agenda have proven especially problematic: the clashes, especially intense in 2010–11, between the State and the lowland indigenous groups over a stretch of road projected to run through the TIPNIS (Territorio Indígena y Parque Nacional Isiboro Sécure—Isiboro Sécure National Park and Indigenous Territory), and García Linera's book, *La geopolítica de la Amazonía* [The Geopolitics of the Amazon], which aimed to provide a theoretical backing for the government's decision to proceed with the road project. In her recent *Limits to Decolonization*, Penelope Anthias shows, in a similar vein, how the economic promise of "decolonization," understood as self-government and power over the country's hydrocarbon-based natural resources, has not become reality for the Guaraní communities of the Chaco, again singling out a limit to the decolonial rhetoric of the MAS.

While these critiques are justified by Bolivia's actual contradictions, both in the domestic and international arena, other studies show the achievements of the MAS government in bettering the lot of Indigenous urban populations. In her recent book, Nancy Postero relies on an ethnographic methodology to gauge Bolivians' perception of their country over the past ten years and to project their preferences for the next presidential elections. She interviews indigenous families newly settled in the cities of La Paz and Santa Cruz, trying to understand why people tend to say that they will vote for Evo again. Her findings, surprisingly, show that while the government's sway might appear most notable in the rhetoric of indigeneity and decoloniality, it is mostly in the realm of new economic opportunities where these respondents perceive MAS's potential effectiveness. Postero argues that demands for ethnic inclusion have given way to demands for economic stability and opportunity, as well as for government services such as medicine and schools. The desire and the demand that her interviewees express most frequently is that their children, unlike them, may go to school. This desire is becoming a reality in the neighborhoods of recent migrants to the city from the rural areas such as El Alto. Postero's recent book—not uncritical of MAS in other aspects—suggests that on the symbolic level, the demand for the epistemic decolonization or for the mitigation of endemic, neocolonial racism against Indigenous persons has been satisfied to some extent. It also suggests that, when Postero conducted these interviews (2015–17), the politics of vital needs superseded the demand for the ethnic equality.

How did this juncture come about in a country such as Bolivia, which is profoundly marked by deep class and ethnic inequalities and fissures as well as a great tradition of organization and protest? The visibility of the Indigenous person as the subject of the country's political arena is part of the new common sense in the Plurinational State of Bolivia. Though this visibility is not limited to the personal presence and performance of Evo Morales, it might be argued that it is an effect of the programmatic inclusion of, for instance, women wearing traditional Indigenous clothing in the various branches of the government. The government's extensive program of epistemic and institutional decolonization is multifaceted and inventive. It includes a broad array of varied initiatives in the fields of literature, science, ritual and institutional and intellectual public life.[4] Anti-imperialist education is at the core of this project aimed at the formation of subjects capable of resisting the ongoing processes of accumulation by dispossession in Bolivia. The vice presidency's educational project is the manifestation of a political will that aims to problematize a liberal understanding of freedom and democracy tied to the logic of the market. Arguably, we could conclude that MAS's main advances toward inclusion stem from this educational agenda, which comprehends both decolonial objectives and the promise of some degree of economic stability. The Sanjinés and Ukamau film *Insurgentes*, which was largely financed by the MAS government, but was not explicitly presented to the public as a government-funded cultural object, is an example of this multifaceted production of cultural objects aimed at decolonizing the Bolivian imaginary.

The vice presidency's multiform pedagogical project aims at producing subjectivities that stretch beyond the limits of the liberal subject, in accordance with the claims of the Plurinational State of Bolivia to have undertaken of a process of radical transformation.[5] Since the foundational moment of the Constituent Assembly of 2006, the MAS-led state has maintained a tense relation with the norms of electoral democracy. For example, many critics viewed as antidemocratic MAS's procedures aimed at guaranteeing that the new constitution would be approved by the Constituent Assembly.[6] On the other hand, MAS supporters took the drafting of a new constitution as an opportunity for a truly decolonial move, one that could not be contemplated within the limits of the liberal categories stemming from the Western "subject of universal rights" (a "universal" that has been historically limited to landowning white males). MAS's decolonial gesture thus arguably points to the limits of electoral democracy and requires the development of the subject supposed by what Nancy Postero, in her recent book, terms an "indigenous state,"[7] by which she refers to a state that strives to incorporate indigenous ways of governance, representation, and historical memory.[8]

García Linera on Primitive Accumulation and Subjectivity

In his conference titled "La construcción del Estado" (The Construction of the State), Álvaro García Linera refers specifically to the Water War of the year 2000 as the turning point in what he calls the revolutionary transformation of the Bolivian state from the perspective of the "políticas de las necesidades vitales [politics of vital needs]." The last drop that pushed the limit of the Bolivian people's tolerance, García Linera narrates, was the neoliberal state's move to privatize public resources, namely water, which enjoined the people to take political action in defense of their vital needs. This was the moment when local and contained protests ("protestas puntuales, casi irrelevantes") became effective in the struggle against the "sistema político neoliberal, estable, sólido [the neoliberal, stable, solid political system]." In an earlier publication, García Linera and other scholars showed how the popular resistance on the streets of Cochabamba illustrates the theoretical dimension of these events: "Los espacios de la política se han ampliado y extendido, a la vez que este movimiento deja un conjunto de instituciones políticas vacías, como el sistema de partidos. La política plebeya ha desbordado los espacios liberales, donde además el pueblo no está, sólo se dice que está representado [The spaces in which politics are practiced have multiplied and broadened, while this movement has emptied out a host of political institutions, for instance, political parties. Plebeian politics stretch beyond liberal spaces, from which the people are absent, and are only said to be represented]."[9]

These words were written by the militant García Linera, prior to the MAS's rise to state power. While García Linera's recent publications articulate a program from the same spaces that their author had pronounced dead in terms of political action—the party and the state—they also signal strong continuities with concepts expressed in his earlier writings. In his most recent texts, for example, García Linera reformulates the notion of what he calls a "politics of vital needs," which, opposed to the process of accumulation by dispossession, underscores tensions between industrialization and the "communitarian socialism of Vivir Bien" that balances human needs and the respect for natural resources.[10]

García Linera learns from these indigenous "communitarian forms of Living Well" and combines them with a Marxist critique of capitalism's logic of reducing nature and human labor to their exchange value. From this theoretical starting point, García Linera argues that the MAS government's take on industrialization differs from what might be termed "state capitalism," as practiced in Bolivia in the 1950s. He argues that by privileging the use value of the assets extracted from industrial processes over their exchange value, the government makes goods and services available to the general population and especially to the most needy, who previously did not have access to them.[11] As a result, "the State, through the surplus generated by industrialization, begins to gradually withdraw from the capitalist logic of private appropriation as an economic norm, and expansively introduces the logic of use value and of fulfillment of everyday needs, founded on communitarian and communist principles, as a guiding principle of economic activities."[12]

To the process of accumulation by dispossession by which the new imperialism controls, manages, and depletes peripheral economies, García Linera, theoretically, and Sanjinés, aesthetically, oppose the accumulation of the histories of indigenous, anticolonial, and anti-imperial subjects of action. In addition to the negative articulation of their anti-imperialist stance, their projects also depend on the positive articulation of a subject defined by its engagement in an intersubjective relation with nature. In these theorizations, the subject is born from political praxis. As evinced by Nancy Postero's account, García Linera and Sanjinés also trace a subject defined by its relationship to and demands on the state, as a residue or effect of MAS's traditional leftist focus on the control of state power in order to advance the distribution of wealth through economic planning and the nationalization of natural resources.

1781–2003: The Historical Depth of the Anticolonial and Anti-Imperialist Subject in *Insurgentes*

Because the Sanjinés and Ukamau film *Insurgentes* can be considered a "para-state"[13] production—and because it stages a dialogue in which two key Bolivian intellectuals discuss the meaning of social change, progressive politics, and political subjects—this paper examines it as the aesthetic realization of García Linera's theories about the formation of anti-imperialist subjectivities in the context of the "creative tensions" of the Bolivian Process of Change.[14] In *Insurgentes*, the representation of Indigenous subjects participates in the decolonial educational project at the heart of MAS's cultural agenda,[15] described above. This project of transforming the state through the formation of new political subjectivities places at its center the category of the indigenous.[16]

Through its very title, *Insurgentes* defines the subjects of history as "insurgents," meaning "rebels or revolutionaries."[17] The film revisits key moments of indigenous insurgency, narratively deployed in a jumbled, nonlinear timeline. These moments of insurgency can be understood as revolutionary moments, or in Walter Benjamin's terms, moments of danger that disorder history as teleology, and which we find reflected in the film's nonlinear narrative.[18] In a decolonial gesture,[19] the film proposes a counterhistory of indigenous rebellions, from colonial times until the presidency of Evo Morales, which it portrays as a revolutionary moment when a structural change is in effect achievable. It recuperates the figures of Tupaj Katari, Bartolina Sisa, and Zárate Willka, among others, in a series of stunning tableau-like scenes where the dialogue is kept to a minimum. The film connects, visually and narratively, the indigenous "insurgencies" occurring since 1781 with the Water War of 2000 and Gas War of 2003, events that led to the emergence of MAS as a political force. Through strong authoritative narrative devices of docu/fictional filmmaking, such as the use of historical photographs, a voiceover narrated by Sanjinés himself, and captions over the image that consolidate the interpretation by restricting the free play of signifiers possible in textless images (Barthes), the film functions as a didactic tool. Following the principles outlined in Sanjinés's 1979 essay "Teoría y práctica del cine junto al pueblo [Theory and Practice of Film Together with the People],"[20] Sanjinés and Ukamau use formal techniques that echo indigenous way of inhabiting the world, for example, by producing a collective subject instead of an individual hero, or incorporating landscape and nature as a part of the indigenous subject of history, through the device of "plano secuencia integral [integral long take]."[21] By adapting these principles, *Insurgentes* negotiates the necessity of addressing its audiences, particularly young people. The film accomplishes this through the aesthetization and heroic representation of the indigenous body, achieved by way of recognizable Hollywood techniques (close-up, low angle), which end up representing the indigenous heroes Katari and Sisa in a manner visually similar to the portrayal of heroes in a mainstream sci-fi or fantasy films. The aesthetization of indigenous bodies, the peculiar timeline of the film, and the tableau-like presentations of the characters aim to counter centuries of racist representation of indigenous bodies and subjects.

"Teoría y práctica de un cine junto al pueblo" (1979) advances a theory committed to exercising cinematic practice as a tool for bringing about social change and aimed at producing an indigenous subject capable of resisting systemic oppression. This framework defines its target audience as indigenous, working-class, and poor, and its distribution practices as strictly noncommercial.[22] Ukamau typically makes a film and then travels around Bolivia and the neighboring countries to screen it in indigenous communities and urban cinemas. The group elaborated the aesthetic, temporal sequencing, and montage of its films over the course of decades based on the principles of an indigenous worldview. The paradigmatic example is the early Sanjinés and Ukamau film *Yawar Mallku* [*Blood of the Condor*] (1969), which denounced the covert sterilization of rural Quechua women practiced by the Peace Corps during the 1960s. *Yawar Mallku*, filmed in Quechua with Spanish subtitles, and featuring nonprofessional indigenous actors, directly addressed its Quechua-speaking audience, and was made specifically to warn the indigenous rural populations about the state's ongoing sterilization practices. As Sanjinés recalls in several recent interviews,[23] *Yawar Mallku* was one of those rare cases when art actually succeeded at having an impact on social reality. Not only did the film warn indigenous people, it also helped bring about a trial against the Peace Corps, which culminated in 1971 under the progressive government led by General Torres, with the organization's expulsion from Bolivia.

In both its style and purpose *Insurgentes* follows the principles outlined in "Teoría y práctica" by privileging the communal protagonist over an individualized hero, thus reflecting, according to Sanjinés, the indigenous sensibility that the film aims to transmit. While it uses stunning visuals, it subordinates the aesthetic dimension to the film's message. According to the theory of committed cinema, the combined use of emotion elicited by dramatic narrative and striking visuals can serve the purpose of transmitting the message clearly and, thus, of effectively educating the viewers. Concretely, *Insurgentes* avoids sentimental proximity to the historical figures it depicts by representing them as larger-than-life characters whose very biography is the stuff of history. The film also avoids the graphic representations of the gruesome death and postmortem defilement of the corpses of indigenous insurgent leaders, such as the hanging of Bartolina Sisa or the execution by firing squad of Zárate Willka. The depiction of the physical demise of the heroes does not seek to elicit empathy from the audience, as it often does in a Hollywood war film. Instead, each atrocity is presented as the document of a historical instance of injustice, which moves the audience to become conscious of the repetition of these injustices and to analyze them. The Brechtian principle of estrangement is thus deployed in order to provoke a collective reflection about social reality, beyond an individual reaction of joy or sadness.

The *plano secuencia integral* is a signature cinematic device in Sanjinés and Ukamau's repertoire, which he describes as follows: "We were looking for a shot where the protagonist would be collective, a shot that would allow us *to integrate everyone* and to avoid the close-up, which is characteristic of European [filmic] language, of individualism, where individuality is augmented and exalted... this was decisive because this shot originates from indigenous peoples' way of telling stories."[24] This technique is a sort of inversion of Eisenstein's practice of montage as it refuses to use cutting and montage, and privileges the continuity of long pans and "organic" zooms. The *plano secuencia integral* thus constructs the collective subject of the film, and of history, which encompasses the landscape, the indigenous militant masses, and their leaders, who, notably, can be many and do not concentrate authority or symbolic intensity in one figure.

The key scene in *Insurgentes* uses the *plano secuencia integral* to visually connect the Gas War of 2003 and the (chronologically) first rebellion included in the film, that of Bartolina Sisa and Tupaj Katari in 1781.[25] This scene stages the working of the two opposing logics of accumulation mentioned earlier (accumulation by dispossession and accumulation of experience of resistance) and connects the subjectivity of the Gas War militants to that of the anticolonial leaders of the past. The voiceover narrates: "The dwellers of the city of El Alto, that neighbors La Paz, most of them Aymara Indians, *again* laid siege to the city of La Paz in October of 2003. They took this extreme measure, which was backed by the progressive middle class of the City of La Paz, to oppose a neoliberal government that intended to dispossess the Bolivian people of its hydrocarbon riches, obeying the demands of American empire."[26] This reflects exactly how the film, through the technical elements proper to Sanjines's filmmaking project, dialogues with MAS's political and educational agenda. The subject is Aymara, indigenous, and anti-imperialist. The citizens from El Alto are described as *again* laying siege to La Paz, where this "again" explicitly connects the 2003 siege with the 1781 siege and contributes to it historical depth and symbolic intensity. The film signals the operation of accumulation by dispossession ("dispossess the Bolivian people of its hydrocarbon riches") as their central grievance (as opposed to, say, ethnic strife).

After a cut, we see the insurgents at a council. A leader speaks, in Aymara, with Spanish subtitles: "Just as Tupac Katari has said, thousands and thousands would come, and here we are coming back."[27] Cut again, and we are watching tanks advancing from behind the first row of protesting women and men, with the Bolivian flag figuring prominently. A voice narrates in over, ensuring that audiences correctly understand the images: "This time, despite the spilled blood, a solid triumph, because the insurgents of October were able to make reality many of their demands. The popular triumph of October has done away with the neoliberal economic model and opened the political gates to the present revolutionary process that Bolivian society is currently experiencing."[28] This ideologically laden statement puts forward two main ideas: the Gas War has done away with neoliberal economic practices and opened up the sphere of political possibilities heralded by the MAS and the Process of Change. Similar to the reach and limitations of the MAS decade in Bolivia, the statement's first claim about the definitive exit from neoliberal logic is utopian in nature as it projects toward the future the vision of Bolivia's economic reality that the film's political project would like to see. On the other hand, the widening of the sphere of politics and the growing sense of having access to national resources is a fact attested to by the government's concrete policies and in the testimonies of Bolivian citizens.[29] This statement both recognizes MAS's achievements in the political sphere and further bolsters the project, defending the idea of sovereignty over the country's natural resources. Arguably, this declaration summarizes the film's political purpose.

The *plano secuencia integral* begins near the end of the voiceover. The camera pans, showing the streets of El Alto filled with debris and smoke, with many of the fighters visible against the background of the red brick and adobe architecture characteristic of El Alto. In the soundtrack, the vigorous music of indigenous instruments begins to overpower the shouts of the militants. In this manner, the very long pan shows a few side streets, and then arrives at one more side street where the audience sees, advancing from the distance, Bartolina Sisa and Tupaj Katari, coming toward the camera, which is located where the confrontation between the 2003 militants and the tanks is taking place. All the sounds cease and a long shot shows Sisa and Katari gallop to the sound of triumphant indigenous wind instruments, as if to join the fighters of the Gas War.

Tupaj Katari and Bartolina Sisa present a forceful political subject for the present, which emerges through the articulatory power of visual language: it is both rooted in centuries of coherent, accumulated resistance

Figure 8.1 Still from *Insurgentes*. Bartolina Sisa and Tupaj Katari on the streets of La Paz. Courtesy of Grupo UKAMAU and Jorge Sanjinés.

and simultaneously made hyper-contemporary through its association with recent revolts and representation through recognizable twenty-first-century filmic conventions. The continuity of the landscape of El Alto between 1781 and 2003 visually condenses and connects the moments of insurgency that occurred between these two key dates, as if merging the two disparate revolutionary events. This gives historical depth to the event closest to our present, legitimizing it by placing it in a continuum lasting more than two hundred years. The physically impossible, chronologically creative, and metaphysically laden return of Tupaj Katari and Bartolina Sisa—whose death we have already witnessed in the film by this moment—with Sisa riding a white horse in a representation that is conventionally recognizable as that of a national liberator (such as San Martín or Sucre), is underscored, visually, by the use of slow motion. Katari and Sisa gallop toward the camera, which is situated where the dwellers of El Alto fight at the barricades for the "nationalization of hydrocarbons," thus joining this most recent chronological instance of insurgence in the film. It is precisely through the enactment of historical memory that the film articulates insurgent subjectivities.

The captions that introduce *Insurgentes* deploy insurgent indigenous subjects as the site of resistance to the crude extractive logic of capitalist development: "Bolivian Indians, just as Indians from North America to Patagonia, understood that the role of man is to love and protect nature. Forming societies that put the 'we' before the 'I,' they established the basis for the only human society that is sustainable and not self-destructive. We dedicate this film to all the indigenous peoples of Bolivia."[30] This dedication dialogues neatly with one of the key reflections that García Linera puts forward in his 2012 text "Tensiones creativas del proceso de cambio." The tensions cited in the title emerge from the twofold understanding of nature expounded by the Bolivian State in a context attempting to accommodate the decolonial discourse on *vivir bien* and the push for development.[31] For García Linera, Bolivia must strive to attain both objectives—respectful interaction with nature and industrialization—if it is to step out of the depredatory logic of capitalism and cycles of accumulation by dispossession. García Linera argues that when industrialization is practiced in an exploitative manner, self-destructive capitalist forces are deployed; however, if a "contemplative attitude towards nature" is adopted, then the material poverty of Bolivian citizens is perpetuated.[32] García Linera considers that the responses to this tension—which will not be resolved, but needs to be lived and worked through—are to be found within the "communitarian forms" (communal forms), which "have deployed the tendency of another social form of development of the productive forces, one in which nature is conceived as an organic extension of human subjectivity, which must be protected for the sake of its creative continuity, since this also ensures the continuation of human existence for the next generations."[33]

Echoing García Linera's theorization, *Insurgentes* initiates the film with a mention of the indigenous "intersubjective relationship with nature" that reconfigures the unsustainable capitalist practices of continuous accumulation by dispossession.[34] The film concludes with a scene filmed on the recently constructed cable railway that connects the cities of La Paz and El Alto. This modernizing project, designed to benefit commuters between the two cities, exemplifies the MAS government's aim of shaping development projects in the function of an "alternative social form." The cable railway is an infrastructural project aimed at integrating the indigenous satellite city of El Alto with La Paz by using ecologically sustainable means. It serves both the La Paz city center, historically associated with the white and mestizo elites, and the city of El Alto from where, of course, the film's indigenous insurgents of the Gas War emerge. This recent innovation, inaugurated in September 2018, earned La Paz, a city geographically marked by its colonial history, the title of "smart city."[35]

In this scene, we see President Evo Morales exchange glances with Tupaj Katari, Bartolina Sisa, and Zárate Willka, the leaders and martyrs of the previous insurgencies, while riding the cableway. The final scene of the

Figure **8.2.** Still from *Insurgentes*. Evo Morales in the newly built La Paz-El Alto Cableway. Courtesy of Grupo UKAMAU and Jorge Sanjinés.

Figure **8.3.** Still from *Insurgentes*. Tupaj Katari and Bartolina Sisa ride the La Paz-El Alto Cableway. Courtesy of Grupo UKAMAU and Jorge Sanjinés.

film, like the scene of Katari and Sisa discussed above, is chronologically impossible. Precisely for this reason, it takes on an additional symbolic value, as it projects the future of Bolivia as both rooted in history and advancing, technologically, into the twenty-first century. It is precisely this scene that has earned the film pointed criticisms, for presenting Evo Morales as the culmination of a line of "insurgents." However, the cable railway moves, as we know, in a circular motion. The cable railway of history—as opposed to

Figure 8.4. Still from *Insurgentes*. Zárate Willka rides the La Paz–El Alto Cableway. Courtesy of Grupo UKAMAU and Jorge Sanjinés.

the Marxian locomotive—reorders the fractured timeline of the instances of insurgencies that we saw in the film, but in doing so, it also disavows teleological interpretations.

Conclusion: The Articulation of Theory and Aesthetics

In the texts jointly examined here, Alvaro García Linera and Jorge Sanjinés and Grupo Ukamau, refer to the changes that have been taking place in Bolivia over the last fifteen years as "revolutionary." García Linera refers to the "communist" horizon of the reforms. *Insurgentes* speaks of the "revolutionary process" that Bolivia is currently experiencing. Meanwhile, the changes that have been taking place in the present historical conjuncture can most accurately be described as progressive reforms that are successful in a number of ways, but that do not amount to a revolution that redraws social relations or steps out of the previous mode of production in order to inaugurate some other, postcapitalist social formation.[36]

In the face of this reality, García Linera's theoretical writings and *Insurgentes*' aesthetics shows that the assertion of radical change as if it were already a historical reality is necessary in order to articulate subjectivities committed to resisting practices of dispossession. At the same time, the very fact that a film such as *Insurgentes* could be made using state sponsorship suggests the possibility that the social and political processes of the last decade have indeed effected some change in the logic of political and aesthetic representation. On the other hand, in a utopian gesture, the film issues a demand for the economic sovereignty of Bolivia's future. By stating that through their mobilization of the symbolic and practical experiences of previous anticolonial struggles, the insurgents of the Gas War have *already* ousted the neoliberal logic of hydrocarbon economy, *Insurgentes* contributes to producing the subjects for whom this national sovereignty is a possible horizon for which to fight. Thus, by articulating a theoretical and aesthetic vocabulary of radical change, García Linera and *Insurgentes* sustain the accumulation of historical memory summoned to resist the onslaught of the new imperialism.

Notes

1. See García Linera, "La muerte de la condición obrera del siglo XX: la Marcha Minera por la Vida."
2. Accumulation, in this sense, for García Linera, is a historical memory and a vital force of indigenous resistance that comes largely from the spilled blood of the martyrs.
3. See Webber, *From Rebellion to Reform in Bolivia*; Webber, *Last Day of Oppression, and the First Day of the Same.*
4. To name just a few, the two hundred volumes published as part of the *Biblioteca Boliviana del Bicentenario;* the launch of the Tupaj Katari satellite (and the short film that celebrates it); the use of indigenous rituals in key political moments such as the presidential inauguration; the inauguration of the "Escuela Anti-Imperialista" for the Armed Forces; the public talks by world-renowned academics and intellectuals (Ernesto Laclau, Samir Amin, Slavoj Žižek, and David Harvey), organized by the vice presidency and held in La Paz; and the vice presidency's publications online, available free of charge, as well as García Linera's own theoretical writings. See Cuya Gavilano.
5. For instance, Evo Morales and García Linera consistently refer to the "ongoing cultural revolution" in public speeches.
6. Namely, moving the Constituent Assembly to Oruro in order to overcome an impasse in Sucre and thus approve the new constitution by the required two-thirds of the votes.
7. See Postero, *The Indigenous State.*
8. Historically, this tension in Bolivia has a long standing. In the historical moment following the 1952 Revolution, Indianista intellectual Fausto Reinaga wrote an essay denouncing the key Bolivian thinker about "national pedagogy" of Franz Tamayo. Reinaga attacked Tamayo for defending the

institution of the standing army in the context of the postrevolutionary moment. Their conceptual fight centered around the same issue: while Reinaga pushed for the decolonization of Bolivian society and for the full incorporation of the Indians, for Tamayo, the preservation of liberal democracy was a necessary priority in order to keep the communist threat and "chaos" at bay. While the nationalist horizon was key for both intellectuals, and both believed in the central role of education for producing the citizens of a new Bolivia, they disagreed on the definition of the political subject of post-1952 Bolivia. This latter disagreement was also reflected in their respective positions on institutions and on the Revolution itself.

9. García Linera, Gutiérrez, and Tapia, "La forma multitud de la política de las necesidades vitales," 192.

10. "El socialismo comunitario del vivir bien." García Linera, *Las tensiones*, 56.

11. "Por el contrario, los procesos de industrialización que están impulsando el Estado Plurinacional lo que hacen es, en primer lugar, generar un tipo de valor, en algunos casos bajo la forma de renta, que no se acumula privadamente ni se usufructúa de manera privada." García Linera, *Las tensiones*, 58–59.

12. "Entonces el Estado, a través del excedente generado en la industrialización, comienza a desprenderse gradualmente de la lógica capitalista de la apropiación privada como norma económica e introduce expansivamente la lógica del valor de uso de la satisfacción de necesidades, de *fundamento comunitario y comunista*, como principio rector de actividades económicas." García Linera, *Las tensiones*, 60.

13. See Cuya Gavilano. "Junto al pueblo."

14. An obligatory reference in the anthologies of the Third World Cinema, Revolutionary Cimena, and Nuevo Cine Latinoamericano of the 1970s, Sanjinés and Grupo Ukamau have been producing "militant cinema" since the 1960s, the most recent film being *Juana Azurduy, guerrillera de la Patria Grande* (2016). Sanjinés's corpus, according to both his admirers and detractors, presents a notable coherence. It narrates the histories of indigenous struggles against external and internal, systemic and epistemic domination. According to his own theories of Revolutionary Cinema, such an anti-imperialist agenda has always been at the very center of his project ("Teoría y práctica," 1979). Important technical innovations, which attempt to distance the Ukamau aesthetic from that of Hollywood and approach the political aesthetics of indigenous peoples, serve as formal support for Sanjinés's combative cinematic project. See Álvares Beskow, 22; Laguna, 12; Espinoza, 20.

15. Both intellectuals, García Linera and Sanjinés—one as a politician who arrived at the vice presidency after being imprisoned for active participation in the Aymara nationalist guerrillas under the command of Felipe Quispe, El

Mallku, the other as a foundational filmmaker for the New and Revolutionary Latin American Cinema in the 1970s—have, for decades, worked through the dilemma of widening the (liberal) sphere of politics by incorporating indigenous ways of inhabiting the world.

16. The debate on the place of indigenous subjects in liberal democracy is still ongoing, of course. Its roots can be traced to the long-standing question—since the *indigenismos* and *indianismos* of the early twentieth century—regarding the dialectic between the supposedly universal category of citizenship and the capacity of liberal democratic structures to adequately represent the ethnically heterogeneous realities of countries such as Bolivia—or any country, really. Additionally, thorny questions about the kind of alternately abstract or regionally specific indigenous subject invoked by such debates define these dialectics.

17. "A person who rises in forcible opposition to lawful authority, especially a person who engages in armed resistance to a government or to the execution of its laws; rebel" https://www.dictionary.com/browse/insurgent (Consulted 1/25/2020). The term carries the burden of the historical memory of "counterinsurgency" fighting methods, whose most famous success story was the ambush and assassination of Che Guevara in La Higuera.

18. Walter Benjamin, "On the Concept of History," 391.

19. In this sense decolonial theory is not postmodernist because it does not dispose of universalism, even if it talks of pluri-versalism. See Grosfoguel. "Decolonizing Western Uni-versalisms."

20. Sanjinés, *Teoría y práctica de un cine.*

21. A "normal" sequence shot is defined as a sequence shot in a long take that constitutes an entire scene. Such a shot may involve sophisticated camera movement. It is sometimes named by the French term *plan-sequence*. The use of the sequence shot allows for realistic or dramatically significant background and middle ground activity.

22. This is the reason why it is difficult to access Sanjinés and Ukamau films and often impossible to acquire them for a library collection.

23. Álvares Beskow, "Un cine de combate junto al pueblo," 25; Sanjinés, "Esa nación clandestina se ha vuelto insurgente," 86–91.

24. Álvares Beskow, "Un cine de combate junto al pueblo," 26. "Buscábamos un plano en el que el protagonista fuera colectivo, un plano que los pudiera integrar a todos y que prescindiera del close up, que es propio del lenguaje europeo, del individualismo, donde se incrementa y exalta la individualidad . . . eso fue determinante porque ese plano viene de la manera de contar las historias de los propios pueblos indígenas." I would like to point out the slippery nature of the terminology, in the original and even more so in translation. The confusion between "plano" and "toma" (and between "shot"

and "take") is very frequent. This is the reason I translate, uneasily, the *plano secuencia integral* as "integral long take" above, and then use the term in its original Spanish as Sanjinés uses it in his writings.

25. I discuss in detail these two key moments presented in the film—the 1781 and the 2003 rebellions—but *Insurgentes* also revisits other important historical episodes of indigenous insurgency: the rebellion of Zárate Willka, the Wars of Independence and the role of Juana Azurduy in its key battles, and the Chaco War. These events trace, nonlinearly, the accumulation of experience of insurgency that I discuss as opposing the logic of accumulation by dispossession.

26. "Los pobladores de la ciudad de El Alto, vecina a ciudad de La Paz, indios aymaras en su gran mayoría, *volvieron a cercar la ciudad de La Paz* en el octubre del año 2003. Tomaron esta extrema medida, que fue secundada por las clases medias progresistas de la propia Ciudad de La Paz, para oponerse al gobierno de corte neoliberal, que pretendía despojar al pueblo boliviano de su riqueza hidrocarburífera, obedeciendo las exigencias del imperio norteamericano." (My emphasis.)

27. "Como ha dicho Tupaj Katari, miles y miles van a venir, y estamos volviendo."

28. "Esta vez, a pesar de la sangre derramada, un triunfo rotundo, porque los sublevados de octubre lograron hacer realidad la gran parte de sus demandas. El triunfo popular de octubre acabó con el modelo neoliberal en la economía y abrió las compuertas políticas del actual proceso revolucionario que experimenta hoy la sociedad boliviana" (1.08.19).

29. See Postero, *The Indigenous State*.

30. "Los indios bolivianos, al igual que los indios de Norteamérica a la Patagonia, comprendieron que el papel del hombre es el de amar y proteger a la naturaleza. Al conformar las sociedades que anteponen un 'nosotros' al 'yo' sentaron el fundamento de la única sociedad humana perdurable y no autodestructiva. Dedicamos esta película a todos los pueblos indígenas de Bolivia."

31. The conflict surrounding the construction of the TIPNIS road through protected indigenous territory is emblematic of this tension.

32. García Linera, *Las tensiones*, 63.

33. Ibid., 61. "Han desplegado una tendencia de otra forma social del desarrollo de las fuerzas productivas en las *que la naturaleza es concebida como la prolongación orgánica de la subjetividad humana*, que se debe velar para su continuidad creadora pues de esa manera se garantiza también la continuidad de la vida humana para las siguientes generaciones."

34. Learning from these indigenous "communitarian forms" and combining them with the Marxist critique of capitalism's logic of reducing everything—nature and human labor—to its exchange value, García Linera argues that the MAS government's take on industrialization differs from what could

be termed "state capitalism" (as practiced in Bolivia in the 1950s). García Linera argues that by privileging the use value of the assets extracted from industrial processes, the government makes goods and services available to the general population and especially to the neediest, who were previously denied this access.

35. "Mi teleférico gana el premio."

36. This is a phenomenon similar to the one observed by Richard Westra with respect to Bernie Sanders's 2016 presidential campaign. While Sanders's platform was composed of demands and proposals that had once served as the solid basis of the democratic welfare state in Western Europe, and thus far from what could be called a socialist or communist agenda, Sanders nonetheless characterized his platform as a "socialist" one. See Westra, *Socialism in the XXIst Century*.

Works Cited

Álvares Beskow, Cristina, and Jorge Sanjinés. "Un cine de combate junto al pueblo. Entrevista con el cineasta boliviano Jorge Sanjinés." *Cinema Comparat/ive Cinema* IV, no. 9 (2016): 22–30.

Anthias, Penelope. *Limits to Decolonization: Indigeneity, Territory, and Hydrocarbon Politics in the Bolivian Chaco*. Ithaca: Cornell University Press, 2018.

Barthes, Roland. "The Rhetoric of the Image." In *Image, Music, Text: Essays*, translated by Stephen Heath, 32–51. New York: Hill and Wang, 2007.

Benjamin, Walter. "On the Concept of History." In *Walter Benjamin: Selected Writings*, edited by Howard Eiland, and Michael W. Jennings, 389-400. Vol. 4. Cambridge: Belknap Press of Harvard University Press.

Cuya Gavilano, Lorena. "Junto al pueblo y al estado: prácticas paraestatales del cine boliviano." Unpublished manuscript shared by the author. LASA 2018/Barcelona.

Espinoza, Santiago. "Sanjinés o el cine boliviano con y como teoría." In *Insurgencias. Acercamientos críticos a "Insurgentes" de Jorge Sanjinés*, edited by Gilmar Gonzáles, Mary Carmen Molina, and Sergio Zapata, 17–23. La Paz: Escuela Popular para la Comunicación, 2012.

García Linera, Álvaro. "La construcción del Estado." Facultad de Derecho de la Universidad de Buenos Aires. Buenos Aires, Argentina. 8 April 2010. Conference Talk. http://biblioteca.clacso.edu.ar/Argentina/iec-conadu/20171115043333/pdf_939.pdf.

——. "La muerte de la condición obrera del siglo XX: La Marcha Minera por la Vida." In *El retorno de la Bolivia plebeya*, 23–60. La Paz: Muela del diablo, 2000.

———. *Las tensiones creativas de la Revolución. La quinta fase del proceso de cambio*. La Paz: Ministerio de Trabajo, Empleo y Previsión Social, 2016.

———, Raquel Gutiérrez, and Luis Tapia. "La forma multitud de la política de las necesidades vitales." In *El retorno de la Bolivia plebeya*, 143–95. La Paz: La muela del diablo, 2000.

Grosfoguel, Ramón. "Decolonizing Western Uni-versalisms: Decolonial Pluri-versalism from Aimé Césaire to the Zapatistas." *Transmodernity: Journal of Peripheral Cultural Production of the Luso-Hispanic World* 1, no. 3 (2012): 88–104.

Harvey, David. *The New Imperialism*. London: Verso, 2008.

Laguna, Andrés. "Jorge Sanjinés y el renacer del pueblo." In *Insurgencias. Acercamientos críticos a "Insurgentes" de Jorge Sanjinés*, edited by Gilmar Gonzáles, Mary Carmen Molina, and Sergio Zapata, 11–15. La Paz: Escuela Popular para la Comunicación, 2012.

"Mi teleférico gana el premio Ciudad Inteligente para la Paz de América Latina." *Urgente.bo*, September 13, 2018, https://urgente.bo/noticia/mi-telef%C3%A9rico-gana-el-premio-ciudad-inteligente-para-la-paz-de-am%C3%A9rica-latina.

Postero, Nancy. *The Indigenous State: Race, Politics, and Performance in Plurinational Bolivia*. Oakland: University of California Press, 2017.

Sanjinés, Jorge. "Esa nación clandestina se ha vuelto insurgente." *La Migraña. La Revista de Análisis Político* no. 2 (2012): 86–95.

———, and Grupo Ukamau. *Teoría y práctica de un cine junto al pueblo*. México, [1979] 1980.

Webber, Jeffrey. *From Rebellion to Reform in Bolivia: Class Struggle, Indigenous Liberation, and the Politics of Evo Morales*. Chicago: Haymarket Books, 2011.

———. *Last Day of Oppression, and the First Day of the Same: The Politics and Economics of the New Latin American Left*. Chicago: Haymarket Books, 2017.

Westra, Richard. *Socialism in the 21st Century*. New York: Nova Publishers, 2017.

Filmography

Sanjinés, Jorge and Grupo Ukamau. *Yawar Mallku* (Sangre de Cóndor), Bolivia, 1969. Insurgentes (Jorge Sanjines, Bolivia, 2012).

Sanjinés, Jorge and Grupo Ukamau. *Insurgentes*. Bolivia, 2012.

CHAPTER NINE

Debt, Violence, and Subjectivity

ALESSANDRO FORNAZZARI

IF WE BEGIN WITH Karen Benezra's suggestive observation that one of the problems with Latin American social and political thought, at least since the 1959 Cuban Revolution, has been the separation of its focus into two seemingly autonomous spheres—the analysis of the mechanisms of capital's regimes of accumulation and the analysis of the subjective dimensions of political radicalization—then what the perspective of debt, since at least World War II on, does is take us in the opposite direction. Debt demands that we think about the way subjectivity and accumulation are collapsed into each other. I explore the problem of debt by engaging Maurizio Lazzarato's work on the subject, which builds on Nietzsche and Marx, and by contrasting it with Ricardo Piglia's essay on Witold Gombrowicz's time in Argentina (1939–1963) and with Pedro Lemebel's reflections on 1980s Chile. Piglia's observations on Gombrowicz and Lemebel's *crónica* provide windows onto two different moments of finance capitalism. World War II is briefly referenced at the beginning of Piglia's text as the event that produced Gombrowicz as a refugee, speaking a language, Spanish, that was not his own, and attempting to circulate in the Argentine cultural scene. Lazzarato's book offers a periodizing framework for understanding the twentieth-century development of debt and finance capital, and I explore two significant moments in this development through readings of the Piglia and Lemebel texts. The first period, which corresponds to the Piglia essay on Gombrowicz, is the post–World War II shift into the cycle of total war where the imbrication of military and civilian relations was heightened to a degree never before seen. Capitalist production became indistinguishable from the war economy. Science, technology, and social organization all needed to be thought of as products and instruments of this war economy. Lazzarato focuses on the central role that debt, credit, and financialization played in the functioning of this war economy. This integration of war, economy, and debt that began after World War II intensified in 1971 with the abandonment of the Bretton Woods Agreement, the dematerialization of money, and the gearing up of the cycle of accumulation that is now generally identified as neoliberalism. I explore this second period of financialization and debt through Lemebel's *crónica* on the popular market. Lazzarato's work moves away from a class-based understanding of debt and foregrounds subjectivation and noneconomic foundations of the market (most importantly, for Lazzarato, modern war, but historical processes such as colonialism and imperialism are relevant here). This thinking about debt focuses on the relationship between subjectivity and accumulation, and more specifically on the work of producing a subject that can make a promise. This debt subject is explored in Piglia's essay, revealing a debt society that obliterates time and rupture. Lemebel's *crónica* also foregrounds the relationship between debt and subjectivation—it interrogates the problems of identity, tradition, and historicism—but his notion of queer debt, as he articulates it in relation to the popular market, as a space of mutual socialization and potential democratization of capitalist consumption, brings us closer to Stephano Harney and Fred Moten's work on bad debt than to Lazzarato's indebted man.

Lazzarato's category of "indebted man" is not meant to name a new form of subjectivity; quite the opposite, it hearkens back to what he considers to be the most primordial of human relationships, the relationship between creditor and debtor. Rather, he makes the claim that in our current historical conjuncture, which is centered on the debt economy, the indebted man emerges with transformed characteristics and assumes a more dominant position in society. The two characteristics that interest Lazzarato about this figure are: first, how the debtor-creditor relationship collapses distinctions that have historically separated workers from the unemployed, consumers from producers, and retirees from welfare recipients, in other words, how debt in our time works as a totalizing category; and secondly, how the debt economy is a subjective economy, which means that debt brings together accumulation and subjectivity in a way that makes subjectivation productive for capital.[1] Lazzarato deems that indebted subjects have the power to mobilize because they overcome the differences that keep people disassociated: we are all debtors and capital is the universal creditor. I would add a third hypothesis that organizes Lazzarato's work on debt: his premise that "the paradigm of the social lies not in exchange . . . but in credit."[2] Lazzarato shifts the focus from what he perceives as a mistaken starting point—the equality of exchange—to the asymmetry of power that is fundamental to the debtor-creditor relationship. This move from the scene of exchange, which is based on a logic of equality, to debt, which exposes the asymmetry of power, goes hand in hand with a move from labor (based on the ideology of effort-reward) to debt, which works in terms of the morality of promise and and fault.

Lazzarato's concept of indebted man is informed by a combination of Nietzsche's second essay from *On the Genealogy of Morals* and Marx's "Comments on James Mill." Playing with the morphological similarities between the German words *Schuld* (guilt) and *Schulden* (debts), Nietzsche claims that guilt has its origin in debt. He posits that the most basic of human relationships is the contractual one between creditor and debtor. This setting of prices, determining values, and contriving equivalences is, for Nietzsche, the grounds for "thinking as such."[3] In this way the creditor-debtor relationship is the basis from which spring concepts such as justice, fairness, good-naturedness, and objectivity. One of the questions that Nietzsche addresses in this essay is the "tremendous process" of breeding an animal with the right to make promises. This is the labor of constructing a uniform, regular, calculable subject who is strong enough to complete a made promise in the face of obstacles, accidents, and other contingencies. This "tremendous process" of making a calculable subject is marked by blood and cruelty, specifically by the fixing of memories through pain and marks on the body. This is a Nietzschean version of primitive accumulation where regimes of discipline use techniques such as stoning, staking, quartering, and flaying in order to create subjects capable of participating in the promise of society. Nietzsche locates the origins of the state not in a contract, but in acts of violent conquest.

In Paris in 1844, Marx began what he called the "conscientious critical study of political economy."[4] The Paris Notebooks, and more specifically "Comments on James Mill," focus on developing a theory of alienated/estranged labor.[5] Familiar concepts associated with the later Marx, such as surplus value, concrete labor, and abstract labor are mostly absent from his thinking at this point, but the ground for this later project is being prepared by these early reflections on private property, money, credit, and debt. There is also a lot more thinking about unalienated labor, noncapitalist relations of exchange, human community, and use value in these pages than what you typically find in the later Marx.

Lazzarato connects the debtor-creditor relation to Marx's reflections on the transition from metal to paper money. For Marx, paper money is the "more perfect existence of money as money."[6] Paper is more an abstract and constructed material. It is less natural, less of this world: "Money [specifically paper money] appears as the product and yet as the non-product of man."[7] It is an alien material force (it seems to have none of the hidden or secret relationships that precious metals have to other commodities). Credit is the economic judgment on the morality of a man: "Instead of money, or paper, it is my own personal existence, my flesh and blood, my social virtue and importance, which constitutes the material, corporal form of the spirit of money. Credit no longer resolves the value of money into money but into human flesh and the human heart."[8] With the credit system, the antithesis between the capitalist and the worker becomes greater. It creates a new terrain for accumulation, the very existence and life of the poor is opened up to capital. To lack credit is equivalent to lacking trust and recognition. Those who are excluded from the credit system are marked as social pariahs.

What, in the Paris Notebooks, is the difference between an economy based on money exchange and an economy based on barter exchange? The two are linked in a progressive or developmentalist relation. Money represents a more "advanced" form of domination and estrangement than the barter relationship. And then both of these limits are surpassed in the credit relation. So barter is not an expression of unalienated exchange, it already implies a division of labor (the exchange of activity itself, not just the mutual exchange of products) and in this way creates an abstract being, a "spiritual and physical monster."[9] In the barter relation, labor is already, although only partly, a source of income. The product is produced as an equivalent, so it no longer has a direct relation to the producer.

Piglia, Gombrowicz, and the Debt Subject

For Ricardo Piglia, Witold Gombrowicz's 1947 literary pamphlet "Contra la poesía [Against Poetry]" is an example of an approach to literature that he calls "el escritor como lector [the writer-as-reader]." This approach isn't exclusively expressed in the content of Gombrowicz's text. It is also developed in the material context of its conveyance: an exiled Polish writer, living in poverty while trying to break into the literary scene, reads a polemical text, in broken Spanish, to a group of Argentinean intellectuals at Fray Mocho, a bookstore in Buenos Aires. Piglia reads Gombrowicz's provocation as a critique of the concept of "literariness," a reference to the Russian Formalists' idea that the poetic function of language can be distinguished from language's other functions (referential, emotive, conative, phatic, and metalingual). For Gombrowicz, objectivizing poetry as a specific form and identifiable function of language produces the worst kind of stereotyped, conventional, and "crystallized" verses. Literariness produces bad poetry. What he proposes instead is an approach to poetry as a *disposition* framed by the reader's expectations. This moves poetry away from debates about essences and the great works, and toward the struggle for understanding the conditions that generate expectations and define value. For Piglia, Gombrowicz's intervention in the Buenos Aires cultural scene, which was "explosive" and "scandalous" in 1947, has today become a dominant, commonplace, and habitual way of reading literature. Piglia identifies two key characteristics of the writer-as-reader approach: literary history is understood as a narrative that is always in dispute, always changing, and constantly being defined by the struggles of the present; and literary value is not internal or immanent to a text. There is no "literariness"; rather, value is generated in the intricate and changing modes of use.

Gombrowicz's decision to give the Fray Mocho talk in Spanish can be thought through from the perspective of the debtor-creditor relation. Throughout Piglia's essay on Gombrowicz, he emphasizes how the latter is a figure trying to break into circulation. As a poor, unknown refugee in a new territory, the question of how to make a name for yourself, how to enter into circulation so as to be read, takes on a renewed urgency.[10] Although living in poverty during his early period in Argentina, Gombrowicz passes himself off as a count, fabricating for himself a faux aristocratic subjectivity. This falsification or counterfeiting of the self is connected to the logic of the debtor-creditor relationship. Marx affirms that since, within a credit system, money only exists nominally, counterfeiting can only be undertaken in the material of the counterfeiter's own person. They have to make themselves into a counterfeit coin, obtain credit by stealth, by lying, by sleight of hand. Distrustful calculation is at the heart of credit and, as Marx states, distrust is the actual basis of economic trust.[11] If Gombrowicz is all about entering into circulation, why does he not give his talk in French? He was proficient in French, which, in Buenos Aires at that time, was a fashionable language for those participating in artistic soirées. Considering Gombrowicz's self-invention via the pseudo-identity of a count, French as a strategic linguistic choice seems to be the logical medium for breaking into circulation, achieving fame, and acquiring economic, social, and literary success. He could have charmed the audience with his fluidity, elegance, and sophistication. Instead, he chooses to give the talk in Spanish; a halting, indelicate, broken Spanish, a Spanish that Gombrowicz himself describes as childlike: "I am a totally unknown foreigner, I lack any authority and my Spanish is a small child who can barely speak. I can make neither powerful phrases, nor agile, nor distinguished, nor fine ones, but who knows if this obligatory diet won't end up being good for your health?"[12] To this perspective of speaking in a language that is not one's own (a key attribute of Deleuze and Guattari's minor literature), Piglia admixes and emphasizes the popular and motley origins of the Polish refugee's Spanish, understanding it as a language of *dispossession*, a language learned in the Retiro neighborhood, in the port bars among sailors and workers.[13] The point is that Gombrowicz's intervention is not simply about entering into the existing circuits of circulation, but about transforming them.

In attendance that evening at the "Contra la poesía" talk was the president of the Banco Polaco de Buenos Aires, who offered Gombrowicz a job at the bank. Starting in 1947, and lasting for a period of seven years, Gombrowicz worked at the Banco Polaco, but used much of his labor-time there surreptitiously writing his novel *Trans-Atlantic* during business hours. Here, Piglia's essay sets up a parallel between Gombrowicz robbing time from the bank for his writing—stealing time that does not belong to him—and finance capital as a time thief, possessing the future in advance by objectivizing it. For Lazzarato, finance capital is about subordinating all possibility of choice and decision that the future holds. Debt neutralizes time, it neutralizes the risk inherent to it, producing a society in stasis and foreclosing the creation of new possibilities.

Complaints from his coworkers eventually made this working/writing arrangement untenable, at which point Gombrowicz abandoned novel writing and found another literary form, the diary, with which he would be most associated.[14] I will return to the diary, but Gombrowicz's encounter with the banker is a pivotal moment in Piglia's essay because it marks a transition to an explicit reflection on the relationship between credit, money, and literature that will have the effect of resignifying the first part of the essay. The discussion about literariness had less to do with early-twentieth-century debates about literary criticism, and everything to do with thinking about the relationship between money and fiction.

The second part of Piglia's essay moves toward a more explicit reflection on the connection between poetry and money and between writers and bankers.[15] The crucial affirmation here is, "We could say that the bankers understand the poets; or in any case, that there is a relationship there that needs to be thought."[16] Piglia goes on to list the many illustrious poets and writers who have worked in banks and financial institutions, but as entertaining as this literary accounting is, it distracts from the issue at hand. The relationship that needs to be thought through, Piglia's assertion that "bankers understand poets," does not involve any professional overlapping, proximity, interactions, or familiarity as co-workers, but rather that the banker's concept of value reveals something of the secret of the poetic form. The banker reads the poet in a way that the pretentious admirers of excessively sophisticated poetry, which Gombrowicz so savagely disparaged in his Fray Mocho conference, can never hope to reproduce. Gombrowicz's argument was that there exists an agreed-upon convention in those literary spheres that stipulates that no one actually needs to read poetry at all, and to ask the kinds of questions that might reveal the operation of this convention (literariness) is considered to be in the poorest of taste.[17] Contrary to the Fray Mocho audience, who, according to Gombrowicz, is unable to read, the banker, who acts as a proxy of the credit system and thus someone capable of breaking the spell of money as an alien material force, is an exemplary reader. "The bank as a stage for the poets. Circulation, exchange, loans, credit, interest, the arbitrary nature of money, it is a convention, like poetry, Gombrowicz would say."[18] Piglia is, in the end, too timid in regard to how far he is willing to push the connection between poetry and money. Gombrowicz went farther. For starters, Piglia's understanding of money as a convention and an arbitrary sign scratches the surface of what Gombrowicz was doing. It was Aristotle who claimed that there is no common substance mediating between two products, and that instead there is a collectively agreed upon convention, money. Marx rejected this; he posits that there is a common substance that mediates between products and, simplifying, that that substance is abstract labor. And beyond this, the space of the bank, a space that Marx understood as the culmination and completion of the credit system, also moves us beyond conventional notions of money—money as convention—to a thinking of the credit system as one that exacerbates the antithesis between worker and capitalist. In the credit system, Marx explains, "the self-estrangement, the dehumanization, is all the more *infamous* and *extreme* because its element is no longer commodity, metal, paper, but man's moral existence, man's social existence, the *inmost depths* of this heart."[19]

In Volume 3 of *Capital*, Marx shows that the bank and bankers—as avatars of finance capital and stewards of the logic of self-valorizing money (what Arrighi identifies as capitalist accumulation's transitional moments of M-M')—provide coherence and strategies for industrial capitalists whose interests are deemed to be too diverse to represent the capitalist class as a unified front.[20] The conflict between the alternately creative and destructive work of finance capital in relation to older forms of capital accumulation comes to a head in the essay's final scene: Gombrowicz's interview with Jacobo Muchnik, a book editor at Fabril Editora. It is important to note how Piglia frames this interview. He is referring to the publication of Gombrowicz's diary into Spanish in 2005, after it has already circulated in a number of other languages. Piglia understands this translation as a debt that the Spanish language has with Gombrowicz's book: "It was complete in English, in French, and, of course, in Polish, but not in Spanish, until this year, and it seems to me that this is a debt that our language has had with this book"[21] The use of the imperfect tense in the Spanish maintains an ambiguity as to whether that debt was paid off with the publication of the translation, or whether it is even possible to pay off such a debt.

Three encounters structure Piglia's essay: Gombrowicz's encounter with a group of Argentine intellectuals at the Fray Mocho bookstore; Gombrowicz's encounter with the director of the Polish bank in Buenos Aires; and, finally, Gombrowicz's 1960 encounter with Jacobo Muchnik, the editor of Fabril Editora, a prestigious Argentinean literary press that published, according to Piglia, the most interesting European and North American literature of the time. In the latter encounter Muchnik generously offered to publish a new edition of Gombrowicz's 1947 novel *Ferdydurke* with a ten thousand–copy run and a money advance of equivalent to one-third of the rights.[22] Gombrowicz's response was, "That is what matters least to me" and his counteroffer was that in exchange for republishing his novel he wanted a contract for his *Diario argentino*, the book that he was currently writing.[23] Muchnik answered that he could not commit to publishing something that he had not read. Gombrowicz then produced two pages of his diary written in Spanish and insisted that they be read, then and there, while he waited. Muchnik was arrested by the writing, considered it extraordinary, but could not commit to publishing something that he had not read in its entirety. Muchnik concludes, "Gombrowicz did not reply and stood up. Reaching over the desk, he snatched his two sheets of paper out of my hands, while mumbling something that was either an insult or a farewell. Without further ado, he spun on his heels and left."[24]

There are a number of fiduciary elements that need to be teased out here. The two men are each functioning within two different temporalities. Muchnik's offer was premised on an investment in a known commodity from the past, the novel *Ferdydurke*, and resurrecting it for the present. Gombrowicz has no interest in doing that; he functions in terms of Nietzsche's debt time: the promise to pay in the future. From the perspective of debt, time is risk, it threatens to undermine the promise, so the debt subject must neutralize time. This is precisely what Muchnik cannot do. He says, repeatedly, that he cannot publish something that he has not read in its entirety. Neither the cautious editor nor the admirers of "pure" poetry function on the same level as Gombrowicz, they are not debt subjects, subjects formed to make promises. This is also why Gombrowicz needs an answer then and there. No one inquires about sending the completed manuscript at some future date; debt freezes time, neutralizes and empties it of new possibilities. According to Lazzarato, "living in a society without time, without possibility, without foreseeable rupture, is debt."[25] Gombrowicz, as the man who has the right to make promises, is physically represented in this last scene as a subject in movement—like capital in flight—the static obstacle that the encounter with Muchnik represents is but a blip; it only causes him to pivot, as he soars on to higher spheres of circulation. From Gombrowicz as a debt subject formed to make promises and freeze time, we turn our attention to the debt subject that Lemebel identified in his post-1973 *crónica* on the popular market.

Pedro Lemebel: The Consumption of Uneven Development and the "Arqueología del desecho"

Pedro Lemebel's 1995 *crónica* "Violeta persa, acrílica y pata mala [Persian Violet, Acrylic, and Bad Leg]" references diverse signifiers—"mercados ambulantes," "comercio cuneta," "mercado popular," and "mercados persas"— to explore the informal economy's creative use and recycling of commodities, the histories that have accumulated on the surface of these goods, and the relationship between popular subjectivity and neoliberalism.

Lemebel focuses on the disparate "uses" found for things in a space, the popular market, that privileges exchange. Class differences are translated into differences in use. For example, Lemebel focuses on the transformations of objects that circulated in elite/wealthy sectors of society and are used by the popular classes: "Noble fragments that ended up in auctions, biddings, and splendid tears because great grandmother's fan, the same one she used in her first *dancing* [dance] with the Count of Cañada, was taken by a *rota* [a pleb] to be used as a duster."[26] Lemebel's gaze also demystifies traditions by revealing how they were never actually patrician, but rather "pure tin, pure scrap, pure lies."[27] This circulation of falsifications is another kind of counterfeiting, different from the classic false coin, and different from the counterfeiting of the self that we discussed earlier in relation to Gombrowicz in Argentina, where, within a credit system, what is counterfeited is one's own person. Lemebel describes a counterfeiting that is of a different order; this is a collective, class-scale counterfeiting: "The haute bourgeoisie's worm-eaten scraps that the nouveau riche fight over in order to invent for themselves an aristocratic past."[28] Lemebel is clearly critical of these practices, but his *crónica* does not limit itself to critiquing a society based on relations of exchange. The popular market is presented as a space of passage and change, where popular subjectivities are made and remade, where people change jobs and transform themselves.

For Lemebel, the popular market's informal strategies include sleights of hand, plagiarism, *gato por liebre* (bait-and-switch), that is, all the different ways of sidestepping the police, the tax agent, and the political economist. These strategies correspond to what Verónica Gago dubs the strategies of popular baroque economies: "Anyone can consume anything. Products that are supposedly hierarchized by brand and cost become consumable by anyone."[29] Similarly for Lemebel, used clothing, flawed clothing, inverted logos (where, for example, Levi's becomes Veli's) all become "the clandestine access to the famous shopwindow through the worker's broken pocket."[30] And further on: "[A] certain form of social justice pervades low wage sectors that have access to a fancy computer for half-price, a little beat up, but intact."[31] The *crónica* begins to trace the idea of social justice that is being created in the alternative informal economies and sketches what a democratization of capitalist consumption might look like.

Lemebel begins the *crónica* tracing the movement of a Persian rug that crosses the "labyrinths of history" from Asia to Santiago to serve as a floor cover for a popular market.[32] This focus on transnational mobility and temporal discontinuity, the insertion of different temporalities, one into another, is the organizing principle through which Lemebel's narrative makes sense of the chaos, what he calls the *cambalache*, of the popular market. I call his strategy the consumption of uneven development. There is no better expression of this strategy than the following description: "The history of the popular market can be traced through the mixing of paleolithic fragments with the mass production of Tawainese commodities."[33] The strategy described here is to take the conventional notion of uneven development—Trotsky's amalgam of archaic and contemporary forms—and think about how difference is haggled over and alternately contained and controlled within the possibilities and limitations of the market. Lemebel gives us a list of the "cultural treasures" found in the popular market:

> From the gynecological stretcher that recalls the torture of open thighs, thousands of Editorial Quimantú books shedding their pages in the sun, dented pots and pans from before and after the military coup, black berets, boots, piles of military clothing with the terrifying olive green camoflage evaporating, red statues with their fists in their pockets, and many, many people in the mangy retrospective of the mirror that tarnishes all this end of the century garbage.[34]

The Benjaminian overtones regarding cultural treasures and barbarism echo loudly here, Lemebel's "arqueología del desecho" reads history through the commodities strewn across the stalls of the popular market. The list highlights the imbrication of torture and the health sciences, the changing political valences accumulated in the dents of the pots and pans (once associated with right wing protests against the *Unidad Popular*, now more politically ambiguous), army fatigues bleached by the sun and the fashions of the day, but that are still marked by the terror that they once inspired, and the kitsch value of plastic statuettes of revolutionary figures. The reference to Editorial Quimantú conjures memories of one of the *Unidad Popular*'s most ambitious cultural projects: a national publishing house committed to the democratization (through massive production and circulation) of knowledge in Chile. Lemebel's image of thousands of Quimantú popular editions falling apart and fading in the sun—books that escaped the military's bonfires after the coup, were forgotten for decades, and now reemerge as fetish objects for collectors—conjures a past written on the decaying materiality of those books.

Lemebel's reflections on the informal popular market produces a counternarrative to the narratives of the different transitions from credit exchange to money exchange. For example, in his book *Debt: The First 5,000 Years*, David Graeber asks who were the first people who looked at the world and calculated what they could get for all those things in the market: burglars, marauding soldiers, then perhaps debt collectors. Marauding soldiers—according to Graeber, the ideal subject for a money economy because you wouldn't want to exchange goods on credit with them—possessed gold and silver that they melted down from "some heirloom treasure, that like the Kashmiri gods, or Aztec breastplates, or Babylonian women's ankle bracelets, was both a work of art and a little compendium of history—could become simple, uniform bits of currency, with no history, valuable precisely for their lack of history, because they could be accepted anywhere, no questions asked."[35] Another way of framing this is Marx's idea that "money is a radical leveler," everything is reduced to the same metric; since everything has a price, all distinctions are extinguished.[36] Lemebel chronicles the diverse histories that the market logic attempts, in a way, to flatten, tapping into the kind of utopian flourishes sprinkled throughout the work of the younger Marx: "[Our] products would be so many mirrors in which we saw reflected our essential nature."[37] For example, a crucial moment in the *crónica* is the appearance of the miraculous glass that carries utopian echoes of the *Unidad Popular* and is found in the market: "Without being able to believe in the UNCTAD III glass that by some miracle was saved. As if this archaeology of the cast-off briefly refloats the utopian echoes in the valuation of its leftover impurities."[38] Again, the Benjaminian phrasing is striking: the past as a single catastrophe that keeps piling wreckage upon wreckage. The UNCTAD III refers to the building edified in 1972 during the period of the *Unidad Popular* with the intention of hosting the third in a series of rotating conferences called the United Nations Conference on Trade and Development (UNCTAD). The UNCTAD was the response of developing countries that opposed the World Trade Organization (at the time known as the GATT), the International Monetary Fund, and the World Bank. It was imagined, but never realized, as an alternative to these financial institutions, a place where developing countries could discuss the world market, multinational corporations, debt, aid, and technology. It is not coincidental then that the *crónica* points to the scattered debris of the UNCTAD III in order to conjure utopian echoes: one of its original functions was to defend against the tide of neoliberal financialization and, after the military coup, the building was one of the first places to be swept up by it.[39]

One of the ways Nietzsche's genealogical method interrupts historicist thinking is by separating the stubbornly fused coupling of origin and use. Origin and use may or may not maintain any direct relation over time (for Nietzsche, they are transformed by successive waves of regimes of will to power), but the residues of previous uses are also never entirely erased. If, for Nietzsche, the history of a thing is a continuous sign chain of new interpretations and adaptations—interpretations and adaptations constituted by unrelated causes and without a progression toward a goal—what Lemebel's *crónica* shows is the history of violence, resistance, and past utopian possibilities that are traced onto these leftover goods. However, as is often the case with Lemebel, his *crónica* does not allow us to linger for very long listening to the utopian echoes of the UNCTAD III emanating from the recovered vessel. A *lanza* (a pickpocket) being chased by the police abruptly disrupts the scene. The reflection is then obscured by the sounds of a "marimba azteca" that croons in a melodramatic and nostalgic register "Everyday I miss you more,"[40] which becomes a warning against engaging in a relationship with the siren song of the past.

For Lemebel, the space of the popular market allows him to see the impact of neoliberalism on the poor: "This contortionist poetics of contraband and bribery soften neoliberalism's impact on the poor."[41] What relationship is Lemebel establishing here between contraband, bribes, and neoliberalism? Are these popular practices a logic of neoliberalism? Or do they emerge in its shadow, as peripheral economic spaces, spaces of uneven neoliberal logics? There are moments in Lemebel when the popular market appears as a place of nonalienated community exchange, an alternative space to the highly developed credit system associated with the globalized and financialized space of the mall: "It is as if the variety of antique fantasies, imported and smuggled, inverts the super mall of private credit with the negative of the public auction."[42] But like the utopian echoes of the UNCTAD III, the logic of the market does not allow Lemebel to linger here for very long. As a subjectivity machine, the popular market envelops both the roots of subjectivity that Étienne Balibar describes: "subjectum" (person or thing) and "subjectus" (subordinate or submission). The popular market's concept of subjectivity is ensnared in both. Gago articulates this problematic through her use of the term *baroque economy* to describe the dynamic of informality as one that mixes logics and rationalities that are generally considered incompatible.[43] Lemebel understands this, the *crónica* ends with "la violeta persa," the forgotten remainder that stubbornly persists despite, at the end of the day, the attempts of the municipality's brooms to erase all traces of the popular market, "just a Persian violet forgotten in the rush, agonizing in its buccaneer law of traffic and *cambalache*."[44] *Cambalache* refers to both a world turned upside down and to barter. The latter refers not to the practices of a proto-communist Garden of Eden from which we have fallen by eating the forbidden fruit that is money. Rather, barter is caught up in the logic of alienated commodity exchange. Lemebel's work on the popular market performs a shift from a class-based point of view—in the sense of understanding cultural forms as expressions of a single class perspective (the bourgeois novel, for example)—and moves toward a more direct exploration of the role of culture, money, and exchange in 1980s Chile. In so doing, is Lemebel partaking in what Jameson has called an orthodox reading of the emergence of exchange value?[45] This reading, often associated with literary realism, refocuses on the physical properties of things (beyond their use value), the dynamic and lively relations developed by trade, and an interest in psychological and characterological traits. This is not what is going on in Lemebel's *crónica*. It is not the sensuous/physical properties of things that his gaze lingers on, but rather the malleable history of things, their reinterpretation, transformation, and adaptation, while at the same time registering the persistent historical traces of resistance, defense, and reaction to these changes. The examples that Lemebel presents are not examples of abstract forms that have been emptied of their content and that in and of themselves are uninteresting because, like money, their interest lies outside themselves. The things found in the popular market—the Persian rug, the UNCTAD III glass, the *violeta persa*—are interesting because they make possible a thinking of new combinations and articulations of history. The logic of finance capital—following Arrighi's cyclical historical narrative where capital abandons production and seeks to generate profit in nonproductive spaces (M-M')—is characterized, in part, by the falling away of context and territory; for Jameson's articulation of culture and finance capital, this is the space of the autonomous fragment of financialization that doesn't need the whole to be meaningful.[46] In revisiting these forms, Lemebel does not seek to return to them their lost content, context, territory, or use values; rather, his lens remakes them into materials for new combinations and articulations of history.

What does Lazzarato extract from Nietzsche and the young Marx for his thinking of debt? The key quotation that he repeats in his book is, "Credit does not solicit and exploit labor but rather ethical action and the work of self-constitution at both an individual and collective level."[47] The idea is that the creditor-debtor relationship functions in term of moral judgment and ethical action, and thus is thought in a different, but complementary, way than labor. Credit, moreso than labor, is an intensification of the alienation found in the labor process. Lazzarato's argument could be seen as both converging with and moving away from the Midnight Notes Collective's work on debt. They approach debt as a particular form of class struggle; class struggle between the working class and capital within the domain of debt. This is how they understand the post-1971 crisis of the Keynesian order and the shift from the space of the factories, streets, and rice paddies to the back rooms of central banks. Capitalist manipulation of debt, with an emphasis on heavy borrowing of the third world countries from international lenders, is understood as finance capital's strategy to regain control of the class struggle. Lazzarato's reading of neoliberalism differs from the Collective's interpretation because it displaces labor and the scene of equal exchange. For Lazzarato, debt and subjectivation are about making uniform, orderly, predictable subjects. In this way, Nietzsche's "calculating animal"—the origin of measure, evaluation, comparison, and accounting—has its origin in debt rather than in exchange or labor. Gombrowicz's journey is one of a subject that shifts from exchange (the logic of equality) to debt (the logic of the future and the promise). The asymmetry of debt relations is front and center. It doesn't ignore the noneconomic foundations of market exchange, the asymmetry of power, and the logic of ongoing primitive accumulation (the shadow of World War II saturates the essay). Lemebel's *crónica* builds on this shift, and his thinking about subjectivation opens up a space for political construction and experimentation. Lemebel refuses the outcome Lazzarato attributes to debt relations: "Living in a society without time, without possibility, without foreseeable rupture, is debt."[48] The distinction Lemebel establishes between the private credit of the mall—an asocial, privatized, and enclosed space—and the space of the popular market as a "public auction," a mutual space of socialization, echoes the work of Stefano Harney and Fred Moten on bad debt and the fugitive public: "It is not credit we seek nor even debt but bad debt which is to say real debt, the debt that cannot be repaid, the debt at a distance, the debt without creditor, the black debt, the queer debt, the criminal debt."[49] Lemebel's queer debt gestures toward a thinking beyond debt, or, more precisely a thinking beyond debt that is coupled to credit. This is the idea of bad debt, a debt that doesn't desire credit, a debt that accumulates beyond the creditor's ability to keep track, appraise, consolidate, or even forgive. Lemebel finds this bad debt in the unlikeliest of places: the market, the privileged site of commodity exchange. Within the space of the open-air market, even if it is only "for a moment," Lemebel focuses on a form of debt that escapes credit, on the sidelong glance that diverts the buyer's gaze from the commodity being appraised and toward the crotch of the seller, as Lemebel calls it, "The erotic lens that complicitously establishes a parallel deal."[50]

Notes

1. Lazzarato, *Indebted Man*, 8.
2. Ibid.
3. Nietzsche, *Genealogy of Morals*, 70.
4. Marx, *Collected Works*, 3:231.

5. The terms *alienated* and *estranged* are used synonymously throughout Marx's early text.

6. Marx, *Collected Works*, 3:214.

7. Ibid.

8. Ibid., 3:215.

9. Ibid., 3:220.

10. Circulation through literary translation is a theme that runs throughout the essay. What is interesting about Gombrowicz's circulation through translation is that it disorders the conventional directionality of literary translations from center to periphery: Gombrowicz's *Ferdydurke* was first translated from Polish into Spanish and then much later to French. By contrast, *Diary*, which is arguably his most important work, was not translated into Spanish until very late.

11. Marx, *Collected Works*, 3:214.

12. Gombrowicz, *Contra los poetas*, 11. "Soy un forastero totalmente desconocido, carezco de autoridad y mi castellano es un niño de pocos años que apenas sabe hablar. No puedo hacer frases potentes, ni ágiles, ni distinguidas, ni finas, pero ¿quién sabe si esta dieta obligatoria no resultará buena para la salud?" Unless otherwise indicated, all translations are my own.

13. Piglia, *Antología personal*, 85.

14. Rita Gombrowicz, *Diary*, 50.

15. This theme is repeated in many of Piglia's essays and fiction writing. Some of the major examples include "Roberto Arlt: La ficción del dinero," "Teoría del complot," and *Plata quemada*.

16. Piglia, *Antología personal*, 93. "Podríamos decir que los banqueros entienden a los poetas; en todo caso, hay una relación que habría que pensar."

17. Gombrowicz, *Contra los poetas*, 13.

18. Piglia, *Antología personal*, 93. "El banco, entonces, como escenario de los poetas. La circulación, el intercambio, los préstamos, el crédito, el interés, el carácter arbitrario del dinero, que es una convención, como la poesía, diría Gombrowicz."

19. Marx, *Collected Works*, 3:214.

20. Marx, *Capital*, 3:528.

21. Piglia, *Antología personal*, 97. "Estaba completo en inglés, en francés, en italiano y en polaco desde luego, pero no en español hasta este año, y me parece que es una deuda que tenía nuestra lengua con ese libro."

22. Ibid.

23. Ibid.

24. Ibid., 98. "Gombrowicz no me respondió, se puso de pie. Por encima del escritorio me quitó sus dos hojas, murmuró algo que no sé si fue un insulto o un saludo de despedida, y sin más giró sobre talones y se fue."

25. Lazzarato, *Indebted Man*, 47.

26. Lemebel, *Esquina*, 107. "Fragmentos nobles que terminaron en remates, licitaciones y lágrimas regias porque el abanico de la bisabuela, ese mismo que usó en su primer dancing con el Conde de la Cañada, se lo lleva una rota para usarlo de plumero."

27. Ibid. "pura lata, pura chatarra, puras mentiras."

28. Ibid., 106–107. "Restos carcomidos de la alta burgesía que los nuevos ricos se pelean para inventarse un pasado aristócrata."

29. Gago, *La razón neoliberal*, 83. "Cualquier persona puede, de pronto, consumir cualquier cosa. Productos que supuestamente están jerarquizados por costo y marca pasa a ser consumo para cualquiera."

30. "El acceso clandestino a la vitrina famosa por el bolsillo roto de los trabajadores." Lemebel, *Esquina*, 105.

31. Ibid., 108. "se permea cierta justicia social en los sectores de menos ingresos que acceden al súper computador a mitad de precio, un poco abullado pero intacto."

32. Cárcamo-Huechante's essay on this *crónica* discusses Lemebel's critical relationship to orientalism and, more specifically, how Lemebel reframes Alfredo Valenzuela Puelma's nineteenth-century orientalist image "La perla del mercader."

33. "El mercado popular traza su propia historia en la mezcla de retazos paleolíticos con la producción en serie de mercancías taiwanesas." Lemebel, *Esquina*, 106.

34. Ibid., 108. "Desde la camilla ginecológica que recuerda la tortura de los muslos abiertos, miles de libros de la Editorial Quimantú deshojándose al sol, cacerolas abolladas de antes y después del golpe, boinas negras, bototos, rumbas de ropa milica evaporando el camuflaje verde oliva del terror, estatuas rojas con el puño en el bolsillo, y mucho, mucho pueblo mirándose en la retrospectiva roñosa del espejo que empaña esta basura de fin de siglo."

35. Graeber, *Debt*, 386. For Graeber, and anthropologists in general since at least Marcel Mauss, the standard accounts of monetary history have generally periodized this history incorrectly: "We did not begin with barter, discover money, and then eventually develop credit systems. It happened precisely the other way around" (897).

36. Marx, *Capital*, 1:229.

37. Marx, *Collected Works*, 3:17.

38. Lemebel, *Esquina*, 109. "Sin poder creer en el vaso de la UNCTAD III que se salvó de milagro. Como si esta arqueología del desecho reflotara por un momento los ecos de la utopía en el avalúo de sus escorias."

39. The UNCTAD III building has been subject to several different uses since its origin in 1972. Its was transferred to the Ministry of Education after the conclusion of the United Nations conference and it was renamed the Centro Cultural Metropolitano Gabriela Mistral. After the 1973 military coup,

it was renamed Edificio Diego Portales and became the headquarters for the military junta after the bombing of the presidential palace, La Moneda. The building then became a conference center, which burned down in 2006. Coming full circle, upon its reconstruction, it was rebaptized as the Centro Cultural Gabriela Mistral in 2010.

40. Lemebel, *Esquina*, 109. "Te extraño cada día más."

41. Ibid., 108. "Bajo esta poética contorsionista del contrabando y la coima, se atenúa el impacto neoliberal en los pobres."

42. Ibid., 105. "Como si en la variedad de fantasías anticuarias, importadas y matuteras, se invirtiera el súper mall de crédito privado por un negativo de remate público."

43. Gago, *Razón neoliberal*, 18.

44. Lemebel, *Esquina*, 109. "Solamente alguna violeta persa olvidada en el apuroagoniza en su ley bucanera de tráfico y cambalache."

45. Jameson, "Culture and Finance Capital," 146. "Herein lies the unorthodox kernel of these orthodox explanations: for it is tacitly assumed that with the emergence of exchange value a new interest in the physical properties of objects comes into being."

46. Ibid., 250.

47. Lazzarato, *Indebted Man*, 55.

48. Ibid., 47.

49. Harney and Moten, *Undercommons*, 61.

50. Lemebel, *Esquina*, 106. "La lupa erótica que complicita un negocio paralelo."

Works Cited

Balibar, Étienne. "Citizen Subject." In *Who Comes After the Subject?* edited by Eduardo Cadava, Peter Connor, and Jean-Luc Nancy, 33–57. New York: Routledge, 1991.

Cárcamo-Huechante. Luis. "Las perlas de los 'mercados persas': estética y economía de la crónica urbana en Pedro Lemebel." In *Desdén al infortunio: sujeto, comunicación y público en la narrativa de Pedro Lemebel*, edited by Fernando A. Blanco and Juan Poblete, 157-79. Santiago: Editorial Cuarto Propio, 2010.

Gago, Verónica. *La razón neoliberal: economías barrocas y pragmática popular.* Buenos Aires: Tinta Limón, 2014.

Gombrowicz, Rita. Prologue to *Diary*, by Witold Gombrowicz. Evanston, IL: Northwestern University Press, 1988.

Gombrowicz, Witold. *Contra los poetas*. Buenos Aires: Mate, 2005.

Graeber, David. *Debt: The First 5,000 Years*. Brooklyn: Melville House, 2011.

Harney, Stefano, and Fred Moten. *The Undercommons: Fugitive Planning and Black Study*. Wivenhoe: Minor Compositions, 2013.

Jameson, Fredric. "Culture and Finance Capital." In *The Cultural Turn: Selected Writings on the Postmodern, 1983–1998*, 136–61. London; New York: Verso, 1998.

Lazzarato, Maurizio. *The Making of the Indebted Man: An Essay on the Neoliberal Condition*. Translated by Joshua David Jordan. Los Angeles: Semiotexte, 2012.

Lemebel, Pedro. *La esquina es mi corazón: crónica urbana*. Santiago: Editorial Cuarto Propio, 1997.

Marx, Karl. *Capital: A Critique of Political Economy*. Vol. 1. Translated by Ben Fowkes. New York: Penguin Classics, 1990.

———. *Capital: A Critique of Political Economy*. Vol. 3. Translated by David Fernbach. New York: Penguin Classics, 1993.

———, and Friedrich Engels. *Collected Works of Karl Marx and Friedrich Engels, 1843–44*. Vol. 3. New York: Lawrence and Wishart, 2010.

Midnight Notes Collective. Introduction to the New Enclosures. No 10. 1990 http://www.midnightnotes.org/newenclos.html.

Nietzsche, Friedrich Wilhelm. *On the Genealogy of Morals*. New York: Vintage Books, 1967.

Piglia, Ricardo. *Antología personal*. Barcelona: Editorial Anagrama, 2015.

CHAPTER TEN

Psychotic Violence: Crime and Consumption in the Apocalyptic Phase of Capitalism

HORACIO LEGRÁS

No one pays attention to these killings, but the secret of the world is hidden in them.—ROBERTO BOLAÑO, *2666*

IN *THE FEMICIDE MACHINE*, Sergio González Rodríguez offers a somber image of Ciudad Juárez. Between 2009 and 2011, the city was ranked as the most violent nonwar zone in the world for three consecutive years. At that time, "images poured out of the desert . . . with visions of beheadings, carjackings, child assassins, abandoned houses, extortion . . . the bodies of raped and murdered women dumped in public spaces."[1] The violence hounded working women with particular tenacity. The victims "were abducted from the streets . . . taken by force into safe houses . . . raped, tortured, and murdered at stag parties or orgies."[2] Marcela Lagarde y de los Ríos notes that the modality of the victims' death speaks of their subtraction from any form of social bond, even that of hatred: "They were killed in cold blood and their bodies were left in the street, in the desert, or in open spaces."[3]

Aberrant, pathological, and unprosecuted, the violence against women put into circulation a new word in the Spanish vocabulary: *feminicidio*—a crime committed not against a person but against a category. Rosa-Linda Fregoso and Cynthia Bejarano notice that deaths of men are numerically higher in Ciudad Juárez than those of women; however, unlike women, "men are not killed *because* they are men."

In any discussion of violence, Walter Benjamin's "Critique of Violence" often comes readily to mind. The teratology of death that surrounds narco-violence in Mexico—especially regarding the femicides—exceeds all the oppositions that Benjamin deploys in his text for thinking violence, be it that of natural versus historical violence or that of law-preserving versus law-making violence. Benjamin himself provides the clue for such incommensurability when, in the opening paragraph of the essay, he spells out the parameters of his investigation as "that of expounding [the] relation [of violence] to law and justice."[4] Even when the most pervasive answer to the femicides is an attempt to reintegrate their meaning into the juridical sphere, the violence of Juárez relates to that order only negatively. It is not an ordinary type of violence, but a psychotic violence.

The expression "psychotic violence" is not meant to offer a psychological profile. It says nothing about the perpetrators of this violence. Psychotics are rarely violent.[5] What is at stake is a characterization of the violence itself and its links to some salient aspects of the contemporary world. As I will suggest below through a reading of Rita Laura Segato's *La guerra contra las mujeres*, some fundamental traits of this violence reappear in the extreme individualism and anomie proper of consumer capitalism and its forms of governmentality.

In its uttermost generality, psychotic violence is a violence without other: an act performed *as if* the other didn't exist—actually performed in the utter indistinction between reality and the *as if*. By "other," I mean simultaneously those others who are present before me on an everyday basis (my fellow humans) as well as the binding system of habits, cultural and political beliefs that allows the construction of a common world. In the mid-1950s Jacques Lacan famously tied psychosis to the rejection of the law and the consequent inability to build a stable notion of reality.[6] For the psychotic, it is the inability to submit to the binding nature of words that paves the way for the dissolution of reality and the social bond. When the avenues to the Other are blocked, so are the paths of empathy. Psychotic violence is the violence of the breakdown of the human bond.

It may seem that by dubbing this violence psychotic, I preempt the interpretation of the events that I try to clarify. But this is not the case. As a matter of fact, the word *psychotic* was suggested to me by the forms of activism that have surrounded, as a web of meaning, the almost intractable anomie of the crimes. These forms of redress rest on an implicit diagnosis of the crimes as betraying an aberrant abandonment of social and communal ties. For González Rodríguez "The criminals ... act so openly that their actions can only be read as a generalized attack on the social order and the rules of coexistence."[7] In response to the anomie created by the crimes "[a] particular culture ... emerged ... constituted by literary and poetic, pictorial, sculptural, musical, photographic, theatrical, filmic, and other artistic creations."[8] Kathleen Staudt notices that "[a]t the border, anti-femicide activists have communicated, silently and loudly, with the use of symbols. ... They painted names and colors in crosses, dresses, and public signs. ... Victims' mothers and activists repeated stories, showed pictures, and gave personal testimonies at rallies, creating vivid memories with personal names and faces attached to them."[9] In the absence of juridical redress the quest for justice becomes an obsessive quest for meaning. Counterintuitively, bodies that have been stripped of any signification, tossed outside the networks of state, family, and community, are perceived as containing a message or hiding a meaning. For Julia Estela Monárrez Fragoso, "It is possible to read the mutilated bodies as 'signs' that circulate socially."[10] For Rita Laura Segato, "The femicides are messages sent by a subject/author who can be identified, located, and profiled only by rigorously 'listening' to these crimes as communicative acts."[11]

Against the anomie of the crimes, their lack of expression, and their anchoring in an evil without passion, activists and analysts undertake a restitution of the absent socius and set out to strengthen the binding character that the law seems to have lost in confronting a reality that only recognizes as its limit the dissolution of every limit. However, the problem of a reality is never that of its limits; but rather that of the legality that authorizes it.

Crisis in the Real

A perverse uncertainty pervades discussions regarding the number and pathologies of the crimes. Are they (relatively) few, as reported by the State of Chihuahua, or are they more than what is usually believed, as several NGOs and private investigations claim? Even acknowledging different ranges in dates, how can the counts be so disparate? And why are there so many different attempts to count?[12] The imprecise nature of these calculations extends to other areas of Juárez's "reality." A striking element throughout the bibliography and cultural production surrounding the femicides is the impossibility of actually establishing which sets of data are mobilized by the crimes. This crisis reached such proportions that in 2009 the Inter-American Commission on Human Rights rejected the data presented by the Mexican authorities on the femicides on the grounds that it was unreliable.[13] The existence of contradictory versions; the inability to solve even one case of the forced disappearances of women and children; the grotesque involvement of police forces in the illegal trafficking of drugs and human beings; and finally the impotence of efforts to construct a conceptual framework capable of accounting for the femicides bespeaks a profound crisis in the function of the state as a guarantor of truth in a country where the relationship between the state and truth is a particularly strong one, insofar as the drive to count the uncounted and to represent the unrepresented constituted the pillar of the social order built after the Mexican revolution (1910–1920).

Julián Cardona, one of the first photographers to document the femicides, notices that Mexican institutions are "connected less and less to reality," in a situation in which not only does the state look, but reality itself appears to be unapproachable.[14] For Cardona, Juárez attests to a generalized collapse of authorizing narratives whose most notorious effect is that "appearances and perceptions have displaced mechanisms of the past that once offered meaning within a collective coexistence."[15] Since Fredric Jameson published his landmark analysis of John Portman's Bonaventure Hotel in Los Angeles, there has been an increasing awareness in the humanities that forms of collective coexistence depend on the infrastructural materialities that we are invited to inhabit.[16] For centuries, the city had contributed to the elaboration of a political experience of life. When González Rodríguez writes that in Juárez "wild, unregulated economic speculation led to the creation of irrational, unplanned, and overlapping urban grids," exposing traditional communities to rapid disintegration, he does so against the background of a long history of the Latin American city as a space for transversal sociability. In *The Lettered City*, Angel Rama makes the point that it is impossible to separate the recognizable Latin American urban grid from the colonialist impetus behind its design. However, as a sphere of relatedness, the planned city exceeds the narrow limits of its original governmental impulse. The city does not only discipline and exclude but, by distributing the spaces of law and obedience, also creates venues for transgression and desire. A political biography of any central plaza in Latin America will confirm these points. The activists of Juárez rely on this century-old architectonic when they display the notes looking for missing girls in the old radial center of the city.

The *maquila* lies at the center of the disintegration of traditional urban sociabilities in northern Mexico. Juárez was strategically engineered to take advantage of the proximity of the United States and its colossal and dynamic economy. The city withstood badly the storm of capital that came down from the north and completely transformed its way of life. Waves of foreign "investment" transformed Juárez into an early instance of the neoliberal enclave economy by subjecting it to a radical spatial splintering that tore apart any semblance of a social fabric.[17] The splintered city, like the splintered society, breaks down the integrative model of high modernism and puts an end to the centuries-old association of the city with a space of elaboration of conflicting systems of symbolic belonging and political adjudication.

The logic of splintering is patent in the abyss that divides *maquila* and city space. The *maquiladora* machine is planned, self-regulated, serviced, and well connected to the world by the rules of post-Fordist global exchange. The city machine is defunded, orphaned, and anomic. A female worker in a *maquila* travels from the most advanced facilities the world can offer today to the poorest and worst serviced urban environments in the time that it takes for the buses (owned and operated by *maquila* companies) to deposit her in the outskirts of Ciudad Juárez. The disconnection between *maquila* and city, the production of wealth and multiplication of poverty, created a recognizable neoliberal stillness in which it becomes increasingly difficult to imagine political action and even basic social agency. Isabell Lorey has suggested that this material breaking down of urban spaces and the services associated with it is the precondition for the full implementation of precarization as the governmental ethics of the neoliberal redrawing of contemporary life.[18]

Women, Sovereignty, and the Second State

Initial research and commentary on the crimes of Juárez focused on the patriarchal underpinnings of Mexican culture as an explanatory principle for the crimes. Marcela Lagarde y de los Ríos sees "the patriarchal, hierarchical, and social organization of gender" as a major determination of violence against women.[19] Historical, regional, and sociological reasons are also often adduced in the analysis of the feminicides. Particularly salient for my argument is Julia Monárrez Fragoso's mention of a widespread reification of women and the pressure of neoliberal globalization on the production of consumable identities, both of which she views as fundamental to the renewed forms of gender subjection and its aberrant consequences.[20] However, it is in the work of Rita Laura Segato that we find a decisive attempt to connect the history of patriarchal domination, the strictures of the capitalist form of production, and the emergence of a new (pathological) form of subjectivity as keys to the crimes

In *La guerra contra las mujeres* [The War Against Women] (2016), Segato argues that the crimes testify to a collusion of ancient patriarchal prejudices with the neoliberal ideal of a total depoliticization of the public space. The constant designation of femicides as "crimes of passion" obscures their true social and historical articulations. So "even as the contemporary femicides are carried out in the midst of the clamor, spectacle, and score-settling of para-state wars, they never manage to emerge from their private capture in the imaginary of judges, attorneys, media editors, and public opinion in general."[21] The juridical prejudice that allocates women to the sphere of the domestic runs against the well-documented fact that the female body has always entertained a fundamental relationship to sovereign punishment. If this is so, the crimes of Juárez can perhaps be understood in terms of an epochal mutation in the notion of sovereign power itself and, more specifically, in terms of the disengagement of sovereignty from the figure of the state in favor of its inscription on the obscene side of capitalist accumulation. From under the shadow of a weakening state emerges what Segato calls "a second state" and subsequently renames it as "a second reality."[22] Like the first (legal) state, the second state, too, relies on sovereign punishment for its operation—although this punishment is no longer an attribute of the law.

The hypothesis of a second state grows from the increasing power of spheres of deregulated and often illegal forms of capitalist accumulation that predominate in the world today. Large portions of the production of wealth in the world originate in "an endless chain of illicit businesses" that "produce massive sums of undeclared capital."[23] This chain also includes, but is not limited to, drugs and human trafficking, various forms of labor exploitation facilitated by the unrestricted deregulation of the labor market (from office cleaning to private security, the latter reaching in some cases the scale of a small army), the black market in electronics, clothing, cell phones, and alcohol, in addition to that of (often adulterated) medicines, gambling (which, even when legal, is often combined with other illegal activities), internet networks devoted to scams, child pornography, and the production of malware and ransomware. Included in this category are also "goods that flow from the periphery to the metropolis, such as gems, lumber, or even exotic animals."[24]

The second state latches onto the first at the threshold of financialization. If we consider that the role of the state lies in the protection of property rather than in the protection of life, then, Segato continues, we can recognize in the gangs and violence that spread in several regions of the world, the paramilitary forces of an alternate state. Though such extreme forms of violence seem gratuitous, they are, in fact, a signature. What the signature says is that such violence is committed by people wielding the "capacity for cruelty and the power over death that high-risk enterprises require."[25]

For Segato this individual is simultaneously pathogenic and exemplary. The profile of the criminals of Juárez replicates the modal subjectivity of our times:

Today the psychopathic personality would seem to be the personality structure best equipped to operate functionally in the order instituted by the apocalyptic phase of capitalism. The psychopathic profile, with its ineptitude for transforming hormonal excess into affect and emotion; its need to constantly intensify stimuli to achieve their effect; its definitively non-binding structure; its indifference toward its own pain and—consequently, and even more so—that of others; its alienation, its encapsulation, and its unrootedness from both its own landscapes and collective ties; its instrumental and objectified relation to others . . . seem indispensable for operating in an economy organized to the extreme by dehumanization and the absence of limits.[26]

Good Father, Bad Father

In his genealogy of the governmentalization of the state—which marks the transition from the sovereign to the modern state—Michel Foucault resorts to the image of the father in order to shed light upon the process by which a set of biopolitical norms become immanent to society. Governmentality addresses the question of how to introduce an "economy, in other words, the manner of adequately managing individuals, goods, and wealth, as can be done within a family, like a good father who knows how to direct his wife, his children, and his servants."[27] Foucault's mention of the "good father" brings to mind Freud's example of the bad father in *Totem and Taboo*: the tyrannical father who enjoyed unrestricted access to all women and whose death inaugurates the realm of culture proper.[28] The murder of the Urvater creates a society of brothers and inaugurates the possibility of symbolic inheritance. The condition for the emergence of culture is thus tied to the cancellation of unrestricted enjoyment whose tamed forces can be redirected toward social aims. The good father of the Foucaltian example pays homage to the management of expectations of pleasure and the administration of enjoyment which, according to Max Weber, produces capitalism in the Protestant world. This genealogy provides a context for Todd McGowan's assertion that what we are witnessing today is the shift from a form of capitalist subject anchored in restraint to a new one grounded in expenditure and the possibility of unlimited enjoyment. [29] While the system of legalities that Freud saw exemplified in (rather than originating in) the reconstruction offered in *Totem and Taboo* is in principle consistent with the reproduction of the social delineated in Weber's *The Protestant Ethic and the Spirit of Capitalism*, the system of legalities upon which Segato's psychopatic personality is rooted represents an unprecedented challenge to a form of constitution of the social that Freud believed to be so stable that he traced it back to primeval times. What does this mean? That the ground is once again stirring under our feet. In the 1980s, American feminists decried a Lacanian symbolic that they perceived as contingent and yet unchangeable. Yet, there is by now a considerable bibliography that maps a structural change in the shape of the symbolic at the hands of the neoliberal injunction to enjoy without limits.

Arguments about the dysfunctional shape of the social link on the horizon of capitalism are not new.[30] Already in 1979, in *The Culture of Narcissim*, Christopher Lasch noted the role of consumerism in introducing new social pathologies. In the introduction to the Slovakian translation of Lasch's book,[31] Slavoj Žižek underlines the compulsory nature of consumer enjoyment, which now constitutes a new ethic. In this ethics, enjoyment becomes a duty, one by which, as Žižek puts it, "individuals feel guilty not for violating moral inhibitions by way of engaging in illicit pleasures, but for not being able to enjoy."[32] Contemporary capitalism feeds off of a perverse relationship to the law, a law that we are constantly invited to disavow but without actually experiencing it. All transgression becomes a simulacrum of transgression. All freedom vanishes when there is an occlusion of the limit against which that freedom can be measured. The legality that Freud once imagined as quasi-eternal was premised on three principles: the centrality of prohibition (incest and killing a totemic animal or member of the totem); the necessity of enduring delays before real or imaginary urges (exogamy); and the historicizing function of symbolic mediation (a trade learned from parent to children). Consumer society fosters an illusion of unlimited satisfaction; it imposes a sense of urgency and immediacy that weakens our ability to tolerate delays and increases our impatience with everything belonging to spheres that demands maturation and patient elaboration (such as work in the humanities); it diminishes the singularity of the subject marking its history as increasingly irrelevant in a culture characterized by the ceaseless, and no less superficial, renewal of its codes of production. This society rejects the unconscious as a relic and—perhaps as a consequence of this—shows fewer and fewer signs of tolerating frustration, division, or the fatal admixture of good and evil present in all registers of life. In a conceptual sense, however, the market presupposes the barred subject of lack, since it is to this lack that it directs its pledge. But it does so by disavowing the structural nature of this lack—by assuming that no desire can emerge outside the purview of its means. Žižek dubs this procedure "answers without questions." The flood of new consumer items "masks the 'empty place' from which desire emerges and creates a saturated field where the 'impossible' desire "can no longer be articulated."[33]

Unsurprisingly, attempts at bringing about social redress in Juárez regularly invoke a vindication of the political value of taboo. In *More or Less Dead*, Alice Driver criticizes Charles Bowden's *Juárez: the Laboratory of Our Future* for publishing actual photos of murdered men and women.[34] Bowden's book—which was published in English in 1998 and includes texts by Noam Chomsky and Eduardo Galeano—was never translated into Spanish due in part to the graphic nature of its material. This form of implicit censorship looks like a displaced and delayed attempt to instantiate a prohibition. If Bowden's book can be said to be taboo that would imply the existence of a law to be transgressed, which, according to the logic of the market, no longer exists, as the crimes of Juárez confirm with pathological zeal. Something similar can be said of Sergio González Rodríguez's decision to print white pages in those sections of *The Femicide Machine*s where photographs of murdered women were to be shown. Instead, the reader is confronted with captions of absent photos. While we can hardly object to this decision, it is still possible to read in it a compensatory gesture pointing to the instantiation of a taboo as another strategy that seeks, as have so many others in Juárez, to reconstitute the absent socius and the law as the binding manifestation of the symbolic pact.

Ordinary Psychoses

Segato's "psychopathic personality" is not intended as a clinical description, nor is it intended as a metaphor. It is, rather, a border concept that invites us to take notice of a historical intimacy with the pathological. Such mutation cannot have gone unnoticed by therapists or practitioners of psychoanalysis. Of special interest here is a notion introduced very cautiously by

Jacques-Alain Miller: ordinary psychoses. The basic idea, born from clinical evidence, is that we are confronted with a subjectivity that, without being psychotic, is characterized by an increasing inability to refer its conduct to the regulative function of the law. This short circuit forces partial disconnections of the subject from the symbolic chain. The resulting gaps are covered up with substitutes (*suppléance*) of the law.[35] Since no substitute is equal to the law, this system of substitutions is therefore very dynamic: it is comprised of the sum total of identifications that allows the narcissistic pathological subject of modernity to go on with his/her life. Now, these substitutes are not free-floating symbolic elements accessible to all. They and their performance are socially disaggregated in such a way that one's access to increased economic means guarantees greater access to better functioning substitutions. As for those without means, they are the target of selective medicalization, which represents "a form of diffused governance that substitutes everyday common-sense categories and practices for rational and technical ones so as to vitiate the moral and political meaning of subjective complaints and protests."[36]

The rise of ordinary psychoses does not turn psychosis into a generalized style of the social link. Psychosis is still characterized by the foreclosure of the name of the father—by the disavowal of castration and the law. However, the facility with which capitalist discourse blocks the imaginary of castration (by proclaiming that there must be, in principle, satisfaction of all needs) speaks of a generalized predisposition of the human subject for that type of capture. The delirious metaphor that was once the province of the psychotic is generalized as a fundamental mechanism of contemporary society. Even more poignantly, the most widespread symptoms of late capitalism, which always imply a deficit of symbolization in favor of a more or less direct inscription of discomfort ("excesses, harassment, cuts, accidents, substance abuse, intoxications, bizarre tattoos, anorexia, self-mutilations, random aggression, self-aggression, and even suicide"),[37] seem to have more in common with the psychotic structural maladjustment between the subject and its body than with the old tolerable neuroses in which we have all been more or less educated.

In the Order of Praxis

The question emerges, almost naturally: What is to be done? What injunction does this configuration make upon those of us who are, in Segato's apt expression, "professionals of the word"? What is to be done is to make an appeal for politics, for imagining the future that appears to have been foreclosed by capitalist discourse. This is urgent. But what is urgent is not necessarily what we should do first. Urgency itself, insofar as it is a trademark of consumerism's inability to sustain delays and the time of maturation, may well be one of our enemies. What is to be done is to introduce a pause, a split second of reflection, and slow down the urge to act (an act without consequences) that characterizes our present.

Why is it that something needs to be done? Something is constantly "being done"! It so happens that, sensing this problem, society—and especially so in its first world instantiations that are subsequently disseminated as "solutions" to the rest of the world—has embarked on a mad proliferation of substitute foundations, that is, supplements, and substitutions for the law, in Miller's sense, which aim to reinforce the subjective configuration of the present at the site where that subjectivity seems to be giving way. If one of the most salient aspects of public mourning in Juárez passes through the cultural instantiation of an absent symbolic, in first world locations the withering of symbolic law is registered in the proliferation of norms that have become more a matter of etiquette than a question of self-examination. All times have known norms. But not all times have lived in the shadow of their constant debasement in the form of ready-mades whose most disquieting power is to divest the subject of even a semblance of freedom. As a rule, the norms commanded by these supplements are as rigid and inflexible as meaning is for the psychotic personality.

This risk is not new. Rey Chow quotes Thomas Elsaesser's observation that certain postcolonial contexts are impregnated by an attitude that "turns the machine of surveillance . . . into an occasion for self-display."[38] We cannot defeat the discourse of the master using its own categories, because domination itself has become a categorical affair, something well exemplified by the fact that all criticism of domination can be retrofitted into the system as an occasion for profit. The danger here is a total subsumption of the discourse of emancipation under an imaginary dimension of emancipation itself, and thus the cancellation of its symbolic efficacy. Chow prefaces her discussion of the traps of identity with an epigraph by Roland Barthes, in which the French thinker characterizes fascism not as an interdiction on language, but rather as an incitement to say "the correct thing" in the eyes of the fascist. It is in the light of this interpretation that we should read the somber tonality of Chow's criticism of the objectification of the colonial other "for a good cause":

The machines of surveillance here are not war airplanes but the media— the networks of communication, which, in the academic world, include the classroom, conferences, publications, funding agencies and even letters of recommendation. With the large number of students (rightly) devoted to the constructions of difference, and of publishers (rightly) seeking to publish new, unexplored materials, fascism had reasserted itself in our era.[39]

Chow's observation is not empowering—but does it weaken our position or our resolve? There is an abyss between the crimes of Juárez and the discourses that address them. It is this abyss that fosters our suspicion of language in all its registers. Have we not reached the end of language and its uses? It is not just that language falls short of its task, but that in addressing what it cannot address language becomes a mockery of itself, a waste, a redoubling of the impotence before injustice that is one of the trademarks of our times. What do we expect to accomplish by talking about investigations, papers, documents, testimonies, and, even worse, sometimes, about novels? On the other hand, the activism around Juárez presents itself—unmistakably—as a fight for language. Conversely, this pessimism about the possibilities of language, this powerlessness of discourse which is difficult to endure, is in itself an essential aspect of the system that has produced the crimes of Ciudad Juárez.

I don't think it is too much of a stretch to venture that Roberto Bolaño felt the same trepidation before he embarked on writing "The Part About the Crimes" in 2666: the impossibility of talking responsibly about the crimes and the unavoidable responsibility of talking. It is to this dilemma that "the part" owes the dry style that has frustrated so many readers. Gabriel Giorgi has noticed that Bolaño mimics in his text the biopolitical gaze of the state.[40] Insofar as Bolaño positions himself in this biopolitical perspective he does not relate to the victims of Juárez by envisioning any form of redress. As a matter of fact, redress is a logical impossibility in this case, because the body of the victim is isolated from any social signification by the forensic gaze.[41] As a matter of principle, the forensic rejects the partition between life and death. It deals only with corpses. In Being and Time, Heidegger—whose aversion to a merely biological treatment of the human is well known—makes a distinction between the perished and the deceased and points out that only the latter reflect the dignity of Dasein. Biological or empirical death and the cessation of life in an individual can never coincide, since every Dasein—whose being is made of existential possibilities—is necessarily more than itself. Those who visited the Museo de la Tolerancia (Museum of Tolerance) in Mexico City in recent years may remember as one of the most impacting images of the exhibits the "to-do lists" prepared by the departed girls, often sketching out plans to complete high school, undertake vocational studies, paint a room, or change the curtains. These to-do lists, in their reliance on patience, waiting time, and maturation, are the exact reverse of the dominant relationship of the narcissistic pathological personality to time. The plans speak of goals that can in no case be accomplished in solitude, outside mediation, a mediation that was cut short by the thirst of the instantaneous. In 2666, where a forensic-like style delivers the bodies to statistical insignificance, the projective dimension of existence disappears. The capture of the dead body in a scientific, medical network evacuates a priori any vestige of meaning or expressivity. But it also represents, according to a variety of registers or necessities (juridical, biological, professional), just a transitory status of the body. The forensic body is the body in abeyance—not only temporarily separated from its possibilities existentially but also severed from the networks of meaning that seek to welcome it into a human form of death. Sometimes Bolaño annotates that no one reclaimed the body. In these cases, the body in abeyance is released without having transitioned to a human death. As I have previously shown, political activism has taken this abandonment and stillness as both the target and the symptom of the type of world on which the crimes feed. By reintroducing an absent symbolic mediation, the activists of Juárez diagnose the social deficit of the present as a political deficit and offer a roadmap for treating this deficit. Symbolic redress targets, knowingly or not, the biopolitical suspension of the symbolic pact. This is its efficacy. Symbolic redress cannot content itself with building a memory for the victims, as several commentators have put it. There is no private memory of atrocious deeds, because the atrocious itself depends on the consideration of others in order to attain the all-too-unbearable dignity of its concept. It is the social in its totality—and not just the forgetting of the victims—that is implicated in the forms of remediation practiced around Juárez. However, the limits of their remedial power are also the limits of discourse and praxis to reconstitute the space of the commons as the space of political efficacy. How this is to be done is a question that installs itself with ever-increasing force as the first decades of the new century pass.

In a perspicacious reading of 2666, José Ramón Ruisánchez Serra shows that the justice that is unavailable in the perspective of forensic language emerges insidiously, indirectly, and without much fanfare, in other parts of the novel. Ruisánchez Serra reads the stories that surround "The Part About the Crimes," "the most risky of the parts in 2666," as existing in an economic relation with other stories of justice and struggle. There is in Bolaño, Ruisánchez Serra says, "a banality of evil but also a banality of the good, a good that has nothing exceptional about it, a good that just happens in the randomness of human affects: for 'The Part About the Crimes,' would be completely illegible without the apparently subsidiary stories of those who struggle, fall in love and fail in Santa Teresa."[42]

The banality of the good does not constitute an instance that is heroic or utopian in any way. While I sympathize with Ruisánchez Serra's idea of reading Bolaño beyond prophecy and utopia, I wonder if that random good that makes the world consist (and that makes "The Part About the Crimes" readable) does not constitute a utopian form in its own right. In the novel, language is the utopia of Juárez. This utopia operates under incredible and increasing constraints. Is this not what Bolaño himself intimates when he uses a forensic, divested language to narrate the crimes? But why should language and stories incarnate a utopian function? The answer that Derrida furnished more than twenty-five years ago seems to me to retain its validity today: because language adumbrates both the need and the structural insufficiency of the law.[43] The insufficiency of the law lies at the origin of the subject's response—a subject that is nothing but that response. Conversely, what concerns us throughout this essay is the inflexibility of a command that pretends to empty out all traces of freedom and contradiction.

The discourse of the university (the discourse of these pages) itself is structurally traversed, as Slavoj Žižek says, by a tension between "constant self-revolutionizing," on the one hand, and "bureaucratic totalitarianism conceptualized in different guises as the rule of technology, of instrumental reason, of biopolitics," on the other.[44] Such rarefaction concerns literature deeply in its status as a discourse that, in principle, "can say everything."[45] It is in this authorization to say everything that I read a sort of empty prophecy in 2666. In these times of "the overcoming of any symbolic activity by actions" and "the proliferation of pathologies of the act";[46] in these times of symbolic deficit and anemic metaphoric mediations, literature—a practice that is more and more domesticated, put in place—still encapsulates that dimension of the word that has yet to be fully expropriated by the forces of a neoliberal causation. Such expropriation is a constant possibility. It is one of the things that is being done. Its goal is not to silence us and render us mute, but rather to deliver us into the fold of an inconsequential word.

Notes

1. Driver, *More or Less Dead*, xii.
2. González Rodríguez, *Femicide Machine*, 72–73.

3. Lagarde y de los Ríos, "Preface," x.

4. Benjamin, "Critique of Violence," 277.

5. Fink, *A Clinical Introduction to Lacanian Psychoanalysis*, 77. On the other hand, the word *psychosis* has emerged constantly in reports that profile sexually aggravated feminicides. See, for instance, Lagarde y de los Ríos, "Introduction," xiii.

6. Lacan, *Seminar. Book III. The Psychoses.*

7. González Rodríguez, *Femicide Machine*, 12.

8. Lagarde y de los Ríos, "Preface," xii.

9. Staudt, *Violence and Activism*, 19.

10. Monárrez Fragoso, "Victims," 60.

11. Segato, "Territory," 80. Segato's book on the femicides is *La guerra contra las mujeres*.

12. Faced with this situation Julia Estela Monárrez Fragoso establishes and provides her own count in *Juárez, trama de una injusticia*, 93.

13. González Rodríguez, *Femicide Machine*, 77.

14. Ibid., 86–87.

15. Ibid., 87.

16. Jameson, *Postmodernism*, 39–44.

17. On splintering see Graham and Marvin, *Splintering Urbanism*; Graham and McFarlane, *Infrastructural Lives.*

18. Lorey, *State of Insecurity*, 1–5.

19. Lagarde y de Los Ríos, "Preface," xix and xi.

20. Monárrez Fragoso, "Victims," 61.

21. Segato, *Guerra*, 23. Since Segato wrote these lines, women's movements across Latin America have focused the attention of entire societies upon the political nature of violence against women.

22. Ibid., 75.

23. Ibid., 73.

24. Ibid.

25. Ibid., 43.

26. Ibid., 101–102.

27. Foucault. *Security, Territory, Population*, 133.

28. Freud, *Totem and Taboo.*

29. McGowan, *Real Gaze*, 51.

30. See for instance, Sennet, *Culture of New Capitalism* and Verhaeghe, *What About Me?*

31. Lasch, *Culture of Narcissism.*

32. Žižek, *How to Read Lacan*, 204.

33. Žižek, "'Pathological Narcissus,'" n.p.

34. Driver, *More or Less Dead*, 6.

35. Miller first references "ordinary psychosis" in the context of psychoanalytic conferences imparted in the 1980s. Closely related to this is the notion

of generalized foreclosure that Miller discusses in his 1986–87 seminar *"Ce qui fait insigne."* *L'orientation lacanienne: le cours de Jacques-Alain Miller.* Miller summarizes his position in "Ordinary Psychosis Revisited."

36. Biehl, Good, and Kleinmann. "Introduction: Rethinking Subjectivity." 3.

37. Malamud, "Una imagen NO vale," 36.

38. Chow, *Ethics after Idealism*, 30.

39. Ibid., 30.

40. Giorgi, *Formas comunes*, 63.

41. Waizman, *Forensic Architecture*, 4.

42. Ruisánchez, *La reconciliación*, np.

43. Derrida, "Force of Law."

44. Žižek, "Objet a in Social Links," 108.

45. Derrida, "This Strange Institution Called Literature," 37.

46. Malamud, "Una imagen NO vale," 129.

Works Cited

Benjamin, Walter. "Critique of Violence." In *Reflections: Essays, Aphorisms, Autobiographical Writing*, translated by Edmund Jephcott, 277–300. New York: Schocken Books, 2007.

Biehl, João, Byron Good, and Arthur Kleinmann. "Introduction: Rethinking Subjectivity." In *Subjectivity: Ethnographic Investigations*, edited by João Biehl, Byron Good, and Arthur Kleinmann, 1–33. Berkeley: University of California Press 2007.

Bolaño, Roberto. *2666*. Translated by Natasha Wimmer. New York: Farrar, Straus, and Giroux, 2008.

Chow, Rey. *Ethics after Idealism: Theory–Culture–Ethnicity–Reading*. Bloomington: Indiana University Press, 1998.

Comaroff, Jean, and John Comaroff, eds. *Millenial Capitalism and the Culture of Neoliberalism*. Durham: Duke University Press, 2001.

Derrida, Jacques. "Force of Law: 'The Metaphysical Foundation of Authority.'" In *Deconstruction and the Possibility of Justice*, edited by Drucilla Cornell, Michel Rosenfeld, and David Carlson, 3–67. New York: Routledge, 1992.

———. "This Strange Institution Called Literature: An Interview with Jacques Derrida." In *Acts of Literature*, edited by Derek Attridge, 33–75. New York: Routledge, 1992.

Driver, Alice. *More or Less Dead: Feminicide, Haunting, and the Ethics of Representation in Mexico*. Tucson: University of Arizona Press, 2015.

Fink, Eugene. *A Clinical Introduction to Lacanian Psychoanalysis: Theory and Technique*. Cambridge: Harvard University Press, 1999.

Foucault, Michel. *Security, Territory, Population.* Translated by Graham Burchel. New York: Palgrave Macmillan, 2009.

Fregoso, Rosa-Linda, and Cynthia Bejarano. "Introduction: A Cartography of Feminicide in the Americas." In *Terrorizing Women: Feminicide in the Américas,* edited by Rosa-Linda Fregoso and Cynthia Bejarano, 1–44. Durham: Duke University Press, 2010.

———, eds. *Terrorizing Women: Femicide in the Américas.* Durham: Duke University Press, 2010.

Freud, Sigmund. *Totem and Taboo.* Translated and edited by James Strachey. In *The Standard Edition of the Complete Psychological Works of Sigmund Freud.* Volume 13. 1–255. London: W. W. Norton, 1990.

Giorgi, Gabriel. *Formas comunes: Animalidad, cultura, biopolítica.* Buenos Aires: Eterna Cadencia, 2014.

González Rodríguez, Sergio. *The Femicide Machine.* Translated by Michael Parker-Stainback. Los Angeles: Semiotext(e), 2012.

Graham, Stephen, and Colin McFarlane, eds. *Infrastructural Lives: Urban Infrastructure in Context.* New York: Routledge, 2015.

Graham, Steve, and Simon Marvin. *Splintering Urbanism: Networked Infrastructures, Technological Mobilities, and the Urban Condition.* New York: Routledge, 2001.

Hardt, Michael, and Antonio Negri. *Empire.* Cambridge: Harvard University Press, 2001.

Kristeva, Julia. *New Maladies of the Soul.* Translated by Ross Guberman. New York: Columbia University Press, 1995.

Lacan, Jacques. *The Seminar. Book III. The Psychoses, 1955–56.* Translated by Russell Grigg. London: Routledge, 1993.

Lagarde y de los Ríos, Marcela. "Preface: Feminist Keys for Understanding Feminicide: Theoretical, Political, and Legal Construction." In *Terrorizing Women: Feminicide in the Américas,* edited by Rosa-Linda Fregoso and Cynthia Bejarano, xi–xxvi. Durham: Duke University Press, 2010.

Lasch, Christopher. *The Culture of Narcissism: American Life in an Age of Diminishing Expectations.* New York: W. W. Norton, [1979] 1991.

Lorey, Isabell. *State of Insecurity: Government of the Precarious.* Translated by Aileen Derieg. Brooklyn: Verso, 2015.

Malamud, Diana. "Una imagen NO vale más que mil palabras." In *Psicoanálisis y cultura,* edited by Ricardo Mauro, 127–32. Buenos Aires: Lugar Editorial, 2017.

McGowan, Todd. *The Real Gaze: Film Theory after Lacan.* Albany: State University of New York Press, 2008.

Miller, Jacques-Alain. "Ce qui fait insigne." *L'orientation lacanienne: le cours de Jacques-Alain Miller.* 1986–87 seminar. http://jonathanleroy.be/wp-content/uploads/2016/01/1986-1987-Ce-qui-fait-insigne-JA-Miller.pdf.

———. "Ordinary Psychosis Revisited." *Psychoanalytical Notebooks*, no. 26 (2013): 34–35.

Monárrez Fragoso, Julia Estela. "The Victims of the Ciudad Juárez Feminicide." In *Terrorizing Women: Feminicide in the Américas*, edited by Rosa-Linda Fregoso and Cynthia Bejarano, 59–69. Durham: Duke University Press, 2010.

———. *Juárez, Trama de una injusticia: Feminicidio sexual sistemático en Ciudad Juárez*. Ciudad Juárez, Mexico: Colegio de la Frontera Norte.

Ruisánchez Serra, José Ramón. *La reconciliación. Bolaño y la literatura de la amistad en América Latina*. Unpublished manuscript.

Segato, Rita Laura. "Territory, Sovereignty, and Crimes of the Second State: The Writing on the Body of Murdered Women." In *Terrorizing Women: Feminicide in the Américas*, edited by Rosa-Linda Fregoso and Cynthia Bejarano, 79–92. Durham: Duke University Press, 2010.

———. *La guerra contra las mujeres*. Madrid: Traficantes de Sueños, 2016.

Sennet, Richard. *The Culture of New Capitalism*. New Haven: Yale University Press, 2006.

Staudt, Kathleen. *Violence and Activism at the Border: Gender, Fear, and Everyday Life in Ciudad Juárez*. Austin: University of Texas Press, 2008.

Verhaeghe, Paul. *What about Me? The Struggle for Identity in a Market-Based Society*. Translated by Jane Hedley-Prôle. Brunswick, Australia: Scribe, 2014.

Waizman, Eyal. *Forensic Architecture: Violence at the Threshold of Detectability*. New York: Zone Books, 2017.

Washington Valdez, Diana. *Harvest of Women: Safari in Mexico; the Truth about Mexico's Bloody Border Legacy*. Burbank, CA: Peace at the Border, 2006.

Žižek, Slavoj. *How to Read Lacan*. London: Granta Books, 2006.

———. "Objet a in Social Links." In *Jacques Lacan and the Other Side of Psychoanalysis: Reflections on Seminar XVII*, edited by Justin Clemens and Russell Grigg, 107–28. Durham: Duke University Press: 2006.

———. "'Pathological Narcissus'" as a Socially Mandatory form of Subjectivity." 1986. https://m3.manifesta.org/catalogue5.htm.

CHAPTER ELEVEN

Postmigrancy: Borders, Primitive Accumulation, and Labor at the U.S./Mexico Border

ABRAHAM ACOSTA

ON SUNDAY, NOVEMBER 25, 2018, just three days after the nation's Thanksgiving holiday, the world witnessed the United States government suddenly shut down the busiest port of entry along the U.S./Mexico border at Tijuana, Mexico.[1] News reports indicate that on that day, U.S. Border Patrol forces fired tear gas into Mexican territory at members of a migrant caravan congregated just along the Mexican edge of the border. The Central American migrants, including many women and children, had been holding peaceful demonstrations along the Mexican side of the border protesting apparent delays by U.S. Customs and Border Protection (CBP) to open up applications processing for asylum seekers. The caravan migrants argued that they were not simply being turned away by U.S. immigration authorities, they were actively being prevented from even reaching the U.S. border port of entry to frustrate their ability to formally request asylum. Reports suggest that what incited the skirmish were dozens of migrants suddenly breaking from the march and storming through a Mexican police blockade in an attempt to reach the United States. The plan, no doubt, was that once on U.S. soil and approached by CBP officials, these migrants would immediately surrender and formally declare their plea for asylum. More than two dozen canisters of tear gas were used against the migrants to deter their reaching the United States. The Port of Entry was closed for several hours and opened later that day after the migrants and other witnesses to the event were dispersed.

By all accounts it was a very tense moment, with political and historical implications. That day one saw U.S. CBP officials intentionally discharge weaponry into the sovereign territory of its southern neighbor in an attempt to thwart migrants--themselves from an entirely other region--from gaining unlawful entry into the United States. At the same time, this was neither a unique nor an unprecedented event; border skirmishes like this have and continue to occur throughout the world, and comparisons were drawn almost immediately between scenes such as those seen in Tijuana that day and those taking place between Palestinians and the State of Israel on a regular basis.

There is, of course, something I find of specific critical significance in this border encounter. For years now, the San Ysidro Port of Entry has ceased to be a "hot" crossing point for migrants seeking to enter the United States unlawfully. In *The Beast: Riding the Rails and Dodging Narcos on the Migrant Trail*, author Óscar Martínez reveals to those seeking to understand contemporary Central American migration to the United States, that San Diego as a crossing zone has been effectively locked down for more than twenty years now.[2] Martínez reminds us that in the not-too-distant past, the U.S./Mexico border was marked only by short six-foot fences to "slow, not stop the crossing the migrants," and that images from that era show migrants being received by Border Patrol agents in Santa Claus outfits handing out gifts to the children.[3] Things, however, changed dramatically in the post-NAFTA era. "What was a wire fence in 1980 was a metal wall in 1994," he tells us, and by 1997, with the enactment of Operation Gatekeeper and Operation Hold the Line, the modern, militarized, wall that we know today "was born."[4] Contrary to widely disseminated narratives currently being promoted by our very own government, unlawful migration through San Diego is "futile . . . practically a voluntary surrender to the Border Patrol."[5]

In fact, as Martínez documents, Tijuana is now, rather, a "city of deportees," by which he means that there are now more deported migrants from the United States currently inhabiting Tijuana than there are Mexican and Central American migrants seeking entry to the U.S. through it.[6] This fact does not imply of course, that the number of apprehended migrants from any given sector has any correlation with the estimated number of unlawful entrants presumed to have entered through the same region. Martínez informs us that the Department of Homeland Security practices what is called "lateral deportation," which means deporting detained unlawful migrants at ports of entry far removed from their original point of arrest.[7] Given the degree of extensive militarization and surveillance at both the Tijuana/San Diego and Ciudad Juárez/El Paso border that make it that much more difficult to get back in, migrants are more often deported through these high-level checkpoints than at any other. In short, one simply does not go through the Tijuana/San Diego area to enter the United States unlawfully. Most certainly, a caravan encompassing scores if not hundreds of migrants would not steer itself toward the San Ysidro Port of Entry if the migrants' goal was unlawful entry.

In this confrontation between caravan migrants and CPB agents on November 25, the specific target of the police blockades and the tear gas were not the conventional migrant-figures of the "illegal immigration" debate in the United States, that is, Mexican nationals seeking unlawful entry into the U.S. to "steal" jobs, "smuggle drugs," so on. Rather, the specific targets of this force were a caravan of hundreds of refugees from Central American countries migrating openly, transparently, and collectively through Mexico toward the United States border with the sole purpose of surrendering to authorities and actuating a verbal plea for asylum. In other words, despite the near constant conflation in the public sphere between asylum seekers and unlawful entrants, the use of force inflicted upon the former that day was disproportionate and difficult to overlook in reflecting upon the question of migration today.

Of course, this is not to suggest that other migrant groups warrant being tear-gassed either. Nor am I unaware of key distinctions in asylum law between economic and political refugees. (Such stipulations imply that economic conditions alone do not qualify as grounds for political asylum.) In her book *Asylum Speakers*, April Shemak provides a contemporary cultural and juridical history of asylum-seeking migrants from the Caribbean.[8] She notes that since its inception under international law, the "refugee" as a juridical figure was always already inscribed in global economic terms. That is, the term *refugee*, which on the one hand intended to signify simply "one who had left one's state of origin owing to political events," could not at the same time include colonial rule into its definition of a "political event" since this would open the door for all those seeking asylum from colonialism itself.[9] This is something European powers wanted to prevent at all costs. This is why the designation of "well-founded fear" ("accompanied by persecution and or the threat of persecution") became a necessary addendum to the documentation process and why economic reasons alone never served as sufficient grounds for requesting asylum.[10]

The intersection between capital and global migration is hardly accidental. In fact, and not unlike poverty, this social predicament doesn't exist naturally but must be produced, with manufactured conditions. Ironically, these conditions are usually produced through moments of upheaval from a previous social order. The conventional history of capitalist modernity grounds itself as the narrative of peasant liberation from feudal society. In the present, this narrative of expropriation leading to mass waves of migration undoubtedly follows any international incident involving the sudden destabilization of a country's or region's economy (via sanctions, currency devaluations, coups, so on). And yet, while Marx's account in *Capital* does not deny this fundamental characteristic of capitalism, his critique springs from those new beginnings. The name Marx gives to the violent and irruptive transition from feudal to capitalistic society is, as we know, primitive accumulation.

Charting a critical path, Marx employs a figure in his work that effectively demonstrates the contradictions at work in primitive accumulation. In chapter 28, Vol. 1 of *Capital*, entitled "Bloody Legislation Against the Expropriated Since the End of the Fifteenth Century," Marx writes: "The proletariat created by the breaking-up of the bands of feudal retainers and by the forcible expropriation of the people from the soil, this free and rightless proletariat could not possibly be absorbed by the nascent manufacturers as fast as it thrown upon the world."[11] Translator Ben Fowkes appends the following note to his use of the word *rightless* in the passage, adding: "Here, as elsewhere in this context, Marx uses the word '*vogelfrei*', literally 'as free as a bird', i.e. free but outside the human community and therefore entirely unprotected and without legal rights."[12] In this context, and at the most decisive historico-political conjuncture signaling the emergence and the virtual prostration of the newly created wage-laborer, the very condition of rightlessness under primitive accumulation is figured through the word *vogelfrei* as a most radical form of freedom. That is, primitive accumulation, wage labor, and ultimately even migration, taken to their foundational dimensions, obtained from conditions of rightlessness conceived of as freedom; that is, a form of freedom issuing from a sheer rightlessness to belong or pertain.

> The proletariat . . . could not possibly be absorbed by the nascent manufacturers as fast as it was thrown upon the world. . . . These men, suddenly dragged from their accustomed mode of life, could not immediately adapt themselves to the discipline of their new condition. They were turned

in massive quantities into beggars, robbers and vagabonds, partly from inclination, in most cases under the force of circumstances.[13]

If primitive accumulation is the process wherein the peasant is violently divorced from their means of production, released from all the guarantees and protections provided by the previous social order, and left with only their own labor power to sell, then primitive accumulation represents not some bygone foundational historical event within capitalist development, but rather an ongoing and continuous process of capitalism's seemingly interminable subsumption of peoples and natural resources. Consequently, it is possible that what we are currently witnessing today is the continuation of a hemisphere-wide process of primitive accumulation. I name the present historical conjuncture, signaled here between the migrant/laborer's "freedom" and "rightlessness," a postmigrant one. What this may mean regarding questions on borders and juridical implications related to the reproduction of capital is the subject of the present discussion.

Let us return briefly to Marx's account of primitive accumulation. Marx observes that "the starting-point of the development that gave rise both to the wage-laborer and to the capitalist was the enslavement of the worker."[14] He then goes on to conceive of this "enslavement" as "the history of primitive accumulation," in which "the expropriation of the agricultural producer, of the peasant, from the soil is the basis of the whole process."[15] However, and in virtually the same breath, he suggests that primitive accumulation, which serves as the name for the prehistory of capital (as well as the mechanism that reproduces it), also marks the peasant's "emancipation" from the previous order.

> The immediate producer, the worker, could dispose of his own person only after he had ceased to be bound to the soil, and ceased to be the slave or serf of another person. To become a free seller of labour-power, who carries his commodity wherever he can find a market for it. . . . Hence the historical movement which changes the producers into wage-labourers appears, on the one hand, as their emancipation from serfdom and from the fetters of the guilds, and it is this aspect of the movement which alone exists for our bourgeois historians. But, on the other hand, these newly freed men became sellers of themselves only after they had been robbed of all their own means of production, and all the guarantees of existence afforded by the old feudal arrangements. . . . The advance made consisted in a change in the form of this servitude, in the transformation of feudal exploitation into capitalist exploitation.[16]

Of course, this emancipation cuts both ways. Emancipation in this passage is enlisted as the figure through which to understand the condition of a peasantry that has been expropriated from the soil and hurled into urban centers and factories. And yet, Marx emphasizes that it would be a mistake to diminish or disallow the magnitude of this transition, which amounts to no less than a critical alteration in the terms and stakes of the prevailing political order. That is, for Marx, the transition from feudalism to capitalism, despite being understood as a mere shift in the form of the peasant's servitude and exploitation, is still a narrative of liberation. The operative phrase in this passage, no doubt, is "a change in the form of this servitude." While each order represents a servile and exploitative environment, this formal similarity nevertheless does not make them equal; rather, the irreducible difference between the two is precisely what is needed to understand both primitive accumulation and the freedom that conditions it, in much the same way in which migration is also produced and conditioned by primitive accumulation. This freedom, this "change in the form of this servitude" is precisely what allows labor flows to take place, and therefore, similarly, what also conditions transnational migration in and of itself. In formally equivalent ways the migrant is also inscribed into a narrative that rationalizes their need to flee their home countries as an escape from poverty and to search for work abroad. If in the past primitive accumulation was understood as the historical process that, in the English case, had the effect of alienating peasants from the land and channeling them to urban centers, we now quite clearly see the way in which primitive accumulation serves as the mechanism that also creates the condition of contemporary transnational migrancy toward the United States and its major cities.

Given this backdrop, our scene at the Port of Entry in San Ysidro takes on a more critical and urgent consistency. What the world saw that morning was an amassment of heterogeneous--"rightless" and "free"--migrant groups with different objectives at the U.S./Mexico border: one group that aimed to cross the U.S./Mexico border silently and without detection, the other which aimed to reach the border, secure audience with CPB officials at the U.S. Port of Entry and perform the speech-act that will initiate the years-long asylum process. Yet from the "outside" these groups are indistinguishable; they are all poor and nonwhite. From the "outside" they all look like the potential unlawful entrants imagined of the former group, "criminals" "doing it the wrong way." Juridically (and economically), however, we know there is a difference, a minimal gap, even if they, as groups of poor nonwhites, appear to phase in and out from one another as an indistinct whole. We know there is a difference even if that difference neither preexists nor conditions their migrant itinerary. That is, we know there is a difference even if that difference only ever emerges when positioned alongside other "free and rightless" migrant groups at the border itself.

This differential in the perception and treatment of asylum seekers from otherwise "purely economic" migrants highlighted that day at the San Ysidro Port of Entry is not lost on all parties; U.S. border officials see and recognize this differential value as well. They too, it seems, recognize the fundamental difference underwriting the asylum seeker. This difference, moreover, is being framed by immigration and security policy experts as being a larger threat to national security (or whatever the claim may be) than the simple unlawful entrant looking for work. This degree of divergence with migrants from Central America also has historical salience. Shemak goes on to document the extent to which Central American migrants were also differentially treated in the asylum process during the 1980s. She notes (quoting at length):

> The U.S. policy toward Central American refugees (Honduras, Guatemala, and El Salvador) during the Reagan Administration in the 1980s was much less accommodating than its policy toward Vietnamese and Cubans under the previous Carter administration. The United States took the approach of sending development "aid" into the region in an attempt to stabilize the economies in the region and keep people from migrating north. It also encouraged refugees to resettle in other countries such as Mexico. The majority of Central American refugees did not meet the asylum criteria in the 1980 Refugee Act, despite the fact that the United Nations generally viewed them as refugees. . . . [T]he U.S. requirements placed more stringent parameters on individual applicants to prove their well-founded fear. The United States responded to the migration of hundreds of thousands of Central Americans with increased border patrols and detentions. Thus, most Central Americans who entered the United States were illegal. White Nicaraguans had a bit more success than Salvadorans and Guatemalans seeking asylum, the U.S. policy was overwhelmingly against granting asylum to Central Americans.[17]

Several things are of interest in this passage from Shemak. The first of these is the establishment of a historical precedent by the United States in its differential treatment of Central Americans seeking asylum. And this, even as U.S. intelligence agencies themselves were revealed at the time to be responsible for the military counterinsurgence and genocidal violence (what Shemak refers to as "aid") that generated the refugee crisis in the first place. Not only did the United States refuse to view Central Americans as refugees, they simultaneously heightened the requirements they needed in order to qualify for asylum. Furthermore, Shemak reveals the ways in which certain policy objectives during the 1980s, such as coercing Central Americans to resettle in Mexico, are the same as those pursued by the United States today. Lastly, and this is the perhaps the most impactful revelation, is the proposition that the closure and heavy militarization of major U.S. ports of entry in the 1990s may ultimately have had more to do with preventing asylum seekers from reaching the United States than with disincentivizing "economic" migrants seeking unlawful entry. While the general public received mixed, often factually incorrect, messages about the intent of caravan migrants reaching U.S. borders, government actions confirm recognition by the U.S. that not all migrants are the same, that they do not obtain with the same juridical and economic value. If, since at least the 1970s, U.S. Border Protection officials have proven themselves willing to go to even greater lengths to prevent asylum seekers from getting close enough to utter the phrase "I request asylum," then one can conclude that for the U.S. government, migrants seeking asylum are even more undesirable (i.e., obtain with less value) than the unlawful entrants simply seeking work.

This confrontation between asylum seekers and U.S. border security forces one to reflect critically on the relation between migration in the context of neoliberalism and posthegemony in the Americas. Indeed, this scenario may be revealing of something deeper about contemporary neoliberalism as it unfolds throughout the hemisphere, particularly as it regards the increasingly juridical nature of capitalist development or of the increasingly economic expedience of one's juridical status. One way or the other, it seems clear that what we are witnessing are the effects of certain radical transformations in capital's relationship to state sovereignty and citizen-labor populations, oftentimes in the form of the economic overdetermination of the administration of juridical categories relevant to migration. In recent years, much work has been produced under the proposition that new political formations are emerging in the contemporary Americas which no longer conform to established theories of territorial sovereignty and governance. Termed "posthegemony" by critics in the field, this concept is a provocation aimed at coming to terms with the increasing discordance between contemporary theories of state power and the intensified historical contradictions brought about by the neoliberal restructuration of the nation-state.[18] Critics, such as Gareth Williams, highlight the urgency and need to chart another critical path toward the political, when he states,

> If we understand globalization as an epochal resituating and redesigning of everything related to the word "we," along with all the conceptual and political legacies and forms of social arrangement that have accompanied that word throughout modernity, then words such as "nation," "territory," "power," "control," "freedom," "war," "life," etc. no longer mean what they used to and are therefore in need of reevaluation.[19]

The terms of political modernity "no longer mean what they used to and are therefore in need of reevaluation." This shift in the contemporary grounds of modern political organization does not necessarily suggest of course, that the nation-state no longer exists or has become obsolete, because it hasn't; it appears to still serve a function vital to global capital. Nor should arguments critical of this shift convince us into thinking that the nation-state represented some kind of ideal form of social organization that was ultimately betrayed and corrupted by global capitalism, for there was never a time in the history of the nation-state where it was not profusely and intricately entwined in conflicts with communities over land, labor, and wages. Rather, what is at stake in this idea of the posthegemonic is not only a concern over a historical era bearing witness to acute, cumulative, economic, and juridical effects resulting from successfully undermining Latin American countries' ability to curb U.S. imperialism in the hemisphere, but also of the need to fundamentally reevaluate our assumptions about political order and the political present in the history of capital.

Given how much of Marx's account of primitive accumulation dovetails with questions over global migration, as both the foundational source of wage labor and increasingly as a market through which migrants are trafficked, the present discussion reflects on what I am calling a "postmigrational" social dynamic. With this I understand a new form (and subject of) migration emerging from a juridical-historical conjuncture. This dynamic comprehends an unprecedented compounding and intensification of legal, juridical, and economic codes within and between states under contemporary global capitalism. I understand the migrant under this postmigrational watershed the way Marx perceived the production of flax before and after primitive accumulation. Of the flax itself, he notes, "The flax looks exactly as it did before. Not a fiber of it is changed, but a new social soul has entered into its body. It now forms part of the constant capital of the master manufacturer."[20] Which is to say, while the migrant "looks exactly as it did before," a new social soul has entered the migrant's body, constituting a newly transformed "part of the constant capital of the master manufacturer".

With the term *postmigration* I attempt to account for the formally induced heterogeneity generated by the reproduction of capital itself, which is often misconceived as the production of sameness, interchangeability, seriality, or homogeneity. I find Silvia Federici's understanding of this difference under primitive accumulation itself quite compelling and worth keeping in mind. She asserts:

> Primitive accumulation, then, was not simply an accumulation and con-centration of exploitable workers and capital. It was also *an accumulation of differences and divisions within the working class*, whereby hierarchies built upon gender, as well as "race" and age, became constitutive of class rule and the formation of the modern proletariat.[21]

Here, Federici acknowledges the ways in which accumulation is as much about the reproduction of difference as it is about concentration of capital. This is not only to reiterate, of course, that differentiation and concentration are not only active and inextricable dynamics under primitive accumula-tion, but also that, given the present discussion, these processes are equally constitutive of any modern border region, including the San Ysidro Port of Entry. To this proposition therefore we need simply substitute "migrants" for "working class" and situate this dynamic at, and along, the very borders one traditionally presumed were meant to keep this kind of heterogeneity at bay.

Other scholars have also addressed this question. For instance, in *Border as Method: Or, the Multiplication of Labor*, authors Sandro Mezzadra and Brett Neilson outline emergent economic and political dynamics across and within national borders under conditions of contemporary globalization, wherein, "[B]orders, far from serving simply to block or obstruct global flows, have become essential devices for their articulation ... finely tuned instruments for managing, calibrating, and governing global passages of people, money, and things."[22] They go on to argue that, contrary to assumptions about their simple and violent function as mechanisms of exclusion, borders also func-tion as "devices of inclusion that select and filter people and different forms of circulation in ways no less violent than those deployed in exclusionary measures."[23] Seen in this way, borders begin to appear as generalized dynamics of accumulation rather than simple national and geopolitical boundaries.

With equal force, Massimilano Tomba also attempts to account critically for the conjuncture of all these juridical/economic processes at the modern state border. He argues:

> Borders, clearly in today's world, express their economic-political significance by directing flows of labor-force, creating new ethnic divisions of labor, and defining wage areas that can only be reproduced by blocking a massive movement of migrants. Borders do not define only the perimeter of a state, but there are internal and external boundaries that define different zones of valorization. These differences are due to the relationship between two dimensions: cost of the labor force, and therefore control over the mobility of migrant workers; and dissemination of machines and technology.[24]

Here, Tomba suggests that borders do not simply direct labor flows, they also "create new ethnic divisions of labor" and "define different zones of valorization," which is to say that borders not only create highly diverse labor groups, but, more importantly, they also create differential and unequal relations *between* labor groups. It is this dynamic of differentialization that generates value upon which circulation and exchange depend.

But how, specifically, does this happen? Exactly how does differentiation under accumulation take place? Tomba reminds us that primitive accumulation is part of a still even larger and more generalized labor-incorporating process within the capitalist framework. Citing Marx, Tomba designates formal subsumption as a process wherein the "capitalist mode of production encounters and subsumes existing forms without creating a homogenous world."[25] The phrase "without creating a homogenous world" is particularly crucial here as Tomba seeks to remind us that capitalism requires divergence as much as it does uniformity. He argues that "the expansion of capital and its constant attempt to subsume different forms of production into the global market generates a multiplicity of temporal frictions, asynchronies, and anachronisms that . . . capital uses on its own advantage."[26] What this means, of course, is that capitalism merely inherits and reconfigures pre-existing social and labor forms into what he refers to as the "plasticity" of the capitalist mores of production.[27] As he indicates, these other forms of exploitation meeting up against capitalism "change their own shape, even if they apparently maintain similarities with their pre-existing semblance."[28] Capital, then, handles, negotiates, and interlaces all other existing labor forms into (and within) one central modality.

Tomba may be of assistance in providing an explanatory model even if in a tangential, indirect way, as there's a longer arc here I want to track. The formal mechanism that mediates and integrates these heterogeneous forms of labor is what Marx calls socially necessary labor time (SNLT). Tomba, following Marx, suggests that it is only in relation to SNLT that these other forms of labor reveal their true value. One the one hand, it is only through SNLT that commodities express their value, but also, it is only via SNLT that surplus value can be obtained. He argues, "The value of a commodity depends on the amount of socially necessary labor-time objectified in the commodity is not the labor-time that is spent for its production. Socially necessary labor-time can be either greater or smaller than the individual time spent for the production of a use-object."[29] And it is here, following Tomba's insights on borders and technology that the question of migration reveals a fuller dimension.

> The difference between capitalists who exploit work of diverse productivities is therefore necessary in order to extract relative surplus value from the benefits of technological innovation.... The introduction of a new machine increases extra-relative surplus value only if the productivity of the necessary social labor remains lower. This becomes possible through the prevention of the general spread of new technological innovations and machines. In other words, automated production remains profitable until there are low-tech areas of production where the innovation has not been employed, and in which a proportional increase in the extraction of absolute surplus value occurs in order to compete within the capitalist market.[30]

If the value of a commodity does not depend on the amount of labor time actually expended on it, but rather on what the accepted SNLT algorithm dictates, then any nominal increase in the rate of production of the individual commodity will yield a higher rate of surplus value. Surplus value, then, is available for a producer if there are other producers of the same commodity using less efficient production methods and/or paying their labor a higher wage relative to the former. While technology is almost always invoked as the means by which production rates can be increased, this is not the only condition that enables the generation of surplus value. For surplus value to obtain at all, there must be both producers who currently employ technology and those who do not, and surplus value is only gleaned from the margin between the two rates of production. In short, technology is only economically meaningful if it is also restricted. If generalized as part of the production of a certain commodity, all economic advantage from that technology evaporates.

What this tells us is that these artificial restrictions on technology, to the extent that they create differentiation and competition between commodity producers, operate in much the same way as geopolitical borders. That is, any economically meaningful impact derived from either technology or migrant labor derives principally from their selective and artificial restriction. If restricting the implementation of technology (and/or more efficient modes of production more broadly) is just as important as the technology itself, then one can assert with equal force that the restriction of migrant labor at border zones is just as important as the migrant him/herself. Formally, any economic advantage derived from migrant labor is equivalent to the economic advantage derived from the implementation of technology, and as such, both participate in the same underlying logic of accumulation. One may even go farther to suggest that under a postmigrational reading, borders like the San Ysidro Port of Entry not only restrict and regulate flows of labor, but in so doing also serve as tools of capital by producing migrant groups with highly differentiated juridical statuses.

As with the feudal peasant under primitive accumulation, "a change in the form of this servitude" means, in Tomba's words, formal subsumption's "orientation of production towards the valorization of value and, therefore, towards the world market."[31] At the same time, the "orientation" of which Tomba speaks with regard to formal subsumption is grounded on yet another process: a fundamental, irremediable, "miscount" in governmental accounts of contemporary migrancy to the United States. As R. Andrés Guzmán illustrates, government figures of unauthorized migrants are only ever estimates, and these estimates are only ever arrived at via negative determination.

If one looks at the Department of Homeland Security's population estimates, however, one can see that it attains its estimate of the undocumented population by subtracting the "legally resident population" from "the total foreign-born population living in the United States." The total foreign-born population and the legally resident population are established through a combination of census figures and data maintained by other government institutions. Evident in this example is that the size of the undocumented population is determined negatively. As a subset that is in the country without authorization, and thus has eluded the count of the state in this regard, it is precisely counted by the state as that part of the population that is "uncounted." The minimal degree of state recognition that this subset obtains through the state's estimate of its size does not so much entail its positive representation, but rather signals the state's estimation of its own miscount.[32]

Guzmán does not simply suggest that the inability to arrive at accurate figures of undocumented migrants in the United States is what prevents effective U.S. border management policy. Instead, he suggests that ultimately this "miscount" is neither accidental, that is, the result of bad data, nor even a juridical or economic problem at all, but rather a necessary and integral component of the neoliberal mechanics of accumulation. Guzmán continues:

> It demonstrates the way in which the interpretation of sectors of capital and the state can lead to the state aiding the miscount for capital's benefit. This is at bottom a neoliberal logic through which the state itself adopts a certain antistatism (i.e., it limits its own power of the court) in order to create room through which capital can operate more profitably by more ruthlessly exploiting workers situated at the margins of legality.[33]

Guzmán highlights the deep operational mandate assumed by the posthegemonic wager: the state limits its own power in order to facilitate capitalist accumulation. Thus, the "orientation . . . towards the world market" of which Tomba speaks obtains consistency via a fundamental "miscounting" by the State of the total undocumented labor force within its sphere. In this model, the border both serves as the site of "orientation . . . towards the world market" as well as the source of the "miscount" itself. The San Ysidro Port of Entry on November 25, 2018, is but one of many instances that uncovered the "miscount" that subtends this "orientation . . . towards the world market."

Postmigration is the name I use to account for these multiple, contradictory, and compounded processes. How does this postmigrant dynamic make itself visible within cultural production? As Sergio Villalobos-Ruminott reminds us, the contemporary Latin American social text suffers from a deep and far-reaching neoliberal restructuring of national and international economic models and systems of governance.[34] Not only has this sudden and violent shift provoked a profound crisis in the notion of modern state sovereignty itself, but it has simultaneously conditioned an entirely illiterate aesthetic conjuncture marked by literature's inability to adequately represent the brutal and precarious aspects of life under neoliberalism. He argues, "It is not that literature fails to dutifully represent the suffering of subalterns; it is that language fails to account for the brutal condition of a history without redemption."[35] This breakdown or rift in the relation between what he calls "the literary corpus" and "the juridical corpus" amounts to a foundational reconfiguration of the social contract, one now premised on neoliberal biopolitics and the mere management of life in an age beyond any teleological foundation, whether theological or historical. Villalobos-Ruminott's observations lead him to engage with contemporary literary production by foregrounding such themes as narcotrafficking, violence, and immigration:

> To consider literature as a biopolitical representation of life implies the transformation of the historical function of the literary as one defined by disarticulation of the so-called lettered city from the national state. This means that it is possible to interrogate certain regional narratives in terms of "a new social contract," that is, according to a new configuration of life.... Perhaps this is the kind of interrogation that the present imposes upon us: the possibility of reading biopolitical processes through the literary imagination of the present as a ciphered critique of contemporary political economy, a political economy that renders life precarious by trying to control and productivize its savage proliferation.[36]

No doubt, the question of migration in the Americas today is no less confused and compounded, precisely because primitive accumulation has proven to be an unending and unyielding force of expropriation and deterritorialization. And for Villalobos-Ruminott, in this current disintegrated social ordering, literature cannot but be derelict in its historical conscription to define and promote the nation-state—its territories (both urban and rural), its increasingly trait-specific population, its increasingly wage-labor economy, etc.—and has now been recast into a material and textual site with which to explore neoliberal political economy's very relation to life itself; that is, as a means to reflect upon the sheer, and deeply embedded, biopolitical calculations and processes at play within contemporary literary imagination.

If, today, given the ongoing if uneven process of primitive accumulation and subsumption in the neoliberal era, rightlessness and "disorientation" continue to be produced and staged as freedom and through differential migrant status, however tragic in form, how then to read narratives of itinerant migration by Central Americans crossing Mexico to reach the United States, as in Óscar Martínez's *The Beast*? Should we understand Martínez's observation that "there are those who don't migrate, they flee" as an instance of freedom or constraint?[37] How can one possibly grasp the element of freedom implicit, even if retroactively, in the anecdote shared among train travelers. In his book, Martínez addresses the story of one migrant in particular who got his leg chopped off by the wheel of the train he was trying to board, and who, upon seeing the injury and realizing its implications, "put his head under the next wheel."[38] Or alternatively, how can one comprehend the radical freedom inscribed within the lone law of the train that all travelers are forced to accept as a condition of their transport, "This is the law of the Beast. . . . There are only three options, give up, kill, or die."[39]

If, according to Tomba, "orientation towards the world market" appears as the critical aspect defining formal subsumption, for Martínez, we see that, for migrants, "orientation" is also an important operation at stake in their crossing. And it is no longer necessarily limited to the "orientation" needed to cross into the United States, but rather the orientation needed to survive deportation that forms part of the formal subsumption process. Martínez describes the migrants he sees emerging after deportation back to Mexico: "They emerge disoriented with a plastic bag in their hands that contains the official notice verifying their forced return home."[40] Martínez calls these recently arrived migrantes "recién llegados que quieren orientación," or recent arrivals looking for advice.[41] He goes on to note that the only ones lucky enough to find a particular migrant shelter for Central Americans are those who lost their way: "Those few Central Americans who are lucky enough find a clean place to stay are the disoriented ones."[42]

What can we make of this relationship between "orientation towards the world market," differential migrant statuses, and the "disorientation" that results from deportation? How can we begin to understand not only competing, differential migrant statuses, but also differential deportation practices as part and parcel of capitalist accumulation? This is precisely what is at stake in what I am calling postmigration.

Notes

1. https://www.nytimes.com/2018/11/25/world/americas/tijuana-mexic o-border.html.

2. Óscar Martínez, *The Beast*. Originally published in Spanish as *Los migrantes que no importan*.

3. Ibid., 146; 144 [164; 162]. Citations include page numbers from the Spanish edition in brackets.

4. Ibid., 147; 146 [165; 164].

5. Ibid., 151 [168].

6. Ibid., 149 [166].

7. Ibid.

8. Shemak, *Asylum Speakers*.

9. Ibid., 6.

10. Ibid.

11. Marx, *Capital*, 876.

12. Ibid.

13. Ibid.

14. Ibid., 875.

15. Ibid., 876.

16. Ibid., 875.

17. Shemak, 51.

18. See Acosta, "Crisis and Migration in Posthegemonic Times"; Acosta, "The Posthegemonic Turn"; Beverley, *Subalternity and Representation*; Williams, *The Other Side of the Popular*; Williams, *The Mexican Exception*; Levinson, *Market and Thought*; Beasley-Murray, *Posthegemony*. These discussions, emanating from the field of Latin American cultural studies, mark provocative and ever-relevant attempts at coming to terms with the increasing discordance between contemporary theories of state power and the intensified historical contradictions brought about by the neoliberal restructuring of the nation-state.

19. Williams, "On Global War and the End of the Katechon," 3.

20. Marx, 909.

21. Federici, *Caliban and the Witch*, 63–64; emphasis in original.

22. Mezzadra and Neilson. *Border as Method*, 3.

23. Ibid., 7.

24. Tomba, "On the Capitalist and Emancipatory Use of Asynchronies," np.

25. Ibid.

26. Ibid.

27. Ibid.

28. Ibid.

29. Ibid.

30. Ibid.

31. Ibid.

32. Guzmán, *Universal Citizenship*, 110.

33. Ibid., 110–11.

34. Villalobos-Ruminott, *Heterografías de la violencia*.

35. Ibid., 52. "No es que la literatura no represente debidamente el sufrimiento de los subalternos, es que el lenguaje ya no alcanza para dar cuenta de la condición brutal de una historia sin redención." All translations from Spanish are mine unless otherwise noted.

36. Ibid., 61–62. "considerar la literatura como representación biopolítica de la vida inmediatamente nos lleva a comprender el cambio en la función histórica de lo literario como una desarticulación entre la llamada ciudad letrada y el Estado nacional. Esto significa que es posible interrogar cierta narrativa regional según un "nuevo contrato social", es decir según una nueva configuración de la vida.... Quizás en esto consista la interrogación que se

nos impone en la actualidad, en la posibilidad de leer los procesos biopolíticos a través de la imaginación literaria contemporánea como una cifrada... una crítica de la economía política contemporánea, aquella que precariza la vida intentando controlar y productivizar su proliferación salvaje."

37. Martínez, 1 [14].

38. Ibid., 52 [66].

39. Ibid., 60 [73].

40. Ibid.,, 238 [261] "Salen desorientados con una bolsa de plástico en sus manos, donde llevan el acta en la que consta su forzado regreso a casa."

41. Ibid., 240 [262].

42. Ibid., 249 [271]. "Los pocos centroamericanos que tienen la suerte de encontrar este impoluto albergue son los desorientados."

Works Cited

Acosta, Abraham. *Thresholds of Illiteracy: Theory, Latin America, and the Crisis of Resistance*. New York: Fordham University Press, 2014.

———. "Crisis and Migration in Posthegemonic Times: Primitive Accumulation and Labor in La Bestia." In *Dialectical Imaginaries: Materialist Approaches to U.S. Latino/a Literature in the Age of Neoliberalism*, edited by Marcial Gonzalez and Carlos Gallego, 241–62. Ann Arbor: University of Michigan Press, 2018.

———. "The Posthegemonic Turn." In *New Approaches to Latin American Studies: Culture and Power*, edited by Juan Poblete, 255–71. New York: Routledge, 2018.

Beasley-Murray, Jon. *Posthegemony: Political Theory and Latin America*. Minneapolis: University of Minnesota Press, 2010.

Beverley, John. *Subalternity and Representation: Arguments in Cultural Theory*. Durham: Duke University Press, 1999.

Federici, Silvia. *Caliban and the Witch: Women, the Body, and Primitive Accumulation*. Brooklyn: Autonomedia, 2004.

Guzmán, R. Andrés. *Universal Citizenship: Latina/o Studies at the Limits of Identity*. Austin: University of Texas Press, 2019.

Levinson, Brett. *Market and Thought: Meditations on the Political and Biopolitical*. New York: Fordham University Press, 2004.

Martínez, Óscar. *Los migrantes que no importan: En el camino con los centroamericanos indocumentados en México*. Barcelona: Icaria Editorial, 2010.

———. *The Beast: Riding the Rails and Dodging Narcos on the Migrant Trail*. Translated by Daniela Maria Ugaz and John Washington. New York: Verso, 2014.

Marx, Karl. *Capital: A Critique of Political Economy*. Translated by Ben Fowkes. New York: Vintage Books, 1977.

Mezzadra, Sandro, and Brett Neilson. *Border as Method, or, the Multiplication of Labor*. Durham: Duke University Press, 2013.

Shemak, April Ann. *Asylum Speakers: Caribbean Refugees and Testimonial Discourse*. New York: Fordham University Press, 2011.

Tomba, Massimiliano. "On the Capitalist and Emancipatory Use of Asynchronies." Unpublished Manuscript.

Villalobos-Ruminott, Sergio. *Heterografías de la violencia: Historia nihilismo destrucción*. Buenos Aires: Ediciones La Cebra, 2016.

Williams, Gareth. *The Mexican Exception: Sovereignty, Police, and Democracy*. New York: Palgrave Macmillan, 2011.

———. *The Other Side of the Popular: Neoliberalism and Subalternity in Latin America*. Durham: Duke University Press, 2002.

———. "On Global War and the End of the Katechon: Four Theses on Posthegemony." Unpublished Manuscript.

PART FOUR

The Subject
and
Nature

CHAPTER TWELVE

Marx's Theory of the Subject

BRUNO BOSTEELS

A theory of the subject should take into account the full ambivalence of the conditions of its operation.—JUDITH BUTLER, *The Psychic Life of Power: Theories in Subjection*

If the economic take-off of the West began with the techniques that made possible the accumulation of capital, it might perhaps be said that the methods for administering the accumulation of men made possible a political take-off in relation to the traditional, ritual, costly, violent forms of power, which soon fell into disuse and were superseded by a subtle, calculated technology of subjection.—MICHEL FOUCAULT, *Discipline and Punish: The Birth of the Prison*

We (the undivided divinity operating within us) have dreamt the world. We have dreamt it as firm, mysterious, visible, ubiquitous in space and durable in time; but in its architecture we have allowed tenuous and eternal interstices of unreason, which tell us it is false.—JORGE LUIS BORGES, "Avatars of the Tortoise"

Positing the Presuppositions:
The Hegelian Dialectic as the Logic of Capitalism

How does the logic of capitalism begin? Even if only from hearsay, we are all supposed to know how in the section on primitive so-called accumulation in the *Grundrisse* Karl Marx uses the Hegelian logic of the positing of the presuppositions to describe the violent origin of capitalism. For this new mode of production to emerge, an aleatory encounter must have taken place between at least two factors, which constitute its actual conditions or effective presuppositions: on the one hand, free labor delinked from its old communal bonds, and, on the other, money accumulated in the form of capital. Capitalism itself does not produce these presuppositions but finds them already there, placed or posited before it. However, the most powerful ideological effect of capitalism as a historical mode of production—the fundamental fantasy that tends to hide precisely its historical character so as to turn capitalism into the only mode of production that is thinkable either in classical political economy or in the spontaneous ideology of everyday life—consists in producing the semblance that the conditions of its becoming are in reality the effects and attributes of its own being: as if, instead of finding them already in existence before it, capitalism indeed posited the effective presuppositions of its own existence. As Marx explains, "While, therefore, the presuppositions for the transformation of money into capital appear as the given, external *presuppositions* for the emergence of capital; as soon as capital has become capital, it creates its own presuppositions, namely the possession of the real conditions for the creation of new values *without exchange*—by means of its own production process."[1] In this sense, at the level of ideological semblance, we might speak of capitalism's Munchausen effect: the new social order seems to pull itself up by its own hair, as if it depended on nothing else but its own autonomous action. Much of Marx's effort is devoted to undoing the pernicious effects of this semblance by laying bare the violent and contingent historical beginnings of capitalism in the hope of seeing foreshadowed in this critique the no less violent and contingent ends of capitalism.

Now it is also well known that in his mature or scientific works, especially after 1845, when together with Friedrich Engels he would have finished settling accounts with his erstwhile philosophical consciousness, Marx is supposed to have completely abandoned the influence of Hegel. For the canonical Louis Althusser and his student-collaborators, the task consists in understanding when, why, and how there occurs a radical break with the whole Hegelian legacy and what this means for the Marxist philosophy of dialectical materialism, or the materialist dialectic. And yet, the central question involved in Marx's rupture with his idealist philosophical past could also be formulated in another way. Not: What were the nefarious ideological effects of Hegel's influence on Marx's analysis? But: Why is the scheme of the Hegelian speculative dialectic so well suited to describe the historical becoming of capitalism? In other words, in what way could we say that capitalism itself, in both its historical genesis and its internal functioning, obeys the laws of Hegel's dialectical logic—even, or especially, in its idealist guise? As Marx announced in one of his earliest, supposedly still humanist and ideological texts, "Critique of the Hegelian Dialectic and Philosophy as a Whole": "Let us provisionally say just this much in advance: Hegel's standpoint is that of modern political economy."[2] In what way can we say that this provisional statement has been confirmed even later on as key to all of Marx's work?

This last question is not exactly the same as the one that Slavoj Žižek has been asking for many years now. In fact, the evaluation of Hegel and Marx is repeatedly turned upside down again in Žižek's writing. If, for the author of *Less Than Nothing: Hegel and the Shadow of Dialectical Materialism*, Marx still falls into the trap of believing in the promise of communism as a liberation of the absolute movement of development of the economy, freed of its capitalist fetters, Hegel in Žižek's reading by contrast indicates that this limit is constitutive of the logic of development as such. In other words, the shortcoming is not Hegel's, for remaining at the level of the movement of absolute thought, but Marx's, for believing in the potential for the absolute movement of history to become liberated from its fetters. The answer to this mistake, therefore, cannot consist simply in removing the obstacles but instead requires that we recognize in them a point of the real inherent in the system itself. Marx, by imagining communism as a kind of superior stage of capitalism liberated from its inherent obstacles and contradictions, would have remained blind to the perverse materialist kernel common to both Christianity and the Hegelian dialectic. He would not have been able to understand that antagonism in some way traverses the very definition of the subject in its radical finitude, recognized according to Žižek only by Hegel and, after him, by Lacan. "In response, one can argue that neither Marx nor Freud is really able to think antagonism: ultimately, they both reduce it to a feature of (social or psychic) reality, unable to articulate it as constitutive of reality itself, as the impossibility around which reality is constructed—the only thought able to do this comes later, originating in the differential logic of 'structuralism.'"[3] This is why Žižek can continue to read Hegel for all eternity through the structuralist lens of Lacan's logic of the signifier, with the good conscience of being at the same time hypercritical of late capitalism—more critical, in any case, than Marx himself.

Instead of seeking a Lacano-Hegelian critique of Marx, however, the task becomes wholly different when we ask ourselves another question: What exactly in Hegel's logic corresponds so well to the coming into being of capitalism that its influence seems to have been inescapable for Marx? And a possible answer can be found precisely in the scheme of the positing of the presuppositions, whose logic continues to define Marx's theory of the subject well after his supposed rupture with Hegel. The notebooks that make up the *Grundrisse*, after all, were written more than a decade after their author, according to the Althusserian thesis of the break, was supposed once and for all to have settled his accounts not just with the Hegelian dialectic but also with the uncritical criticism of Hegel among the Young Hegelians. But the fact is that the movement of the positing of the presuppositions continues for a long time after the alleged break to leave its mark on Marx's thought in his critique of capitalism. In this sense, it is crucial to understand both his methodology and his own theory of the subject. It is, moreover, a logic whose steps can also be found in new and unexpected guises in the work of a wide range of contemporary thinkers—some but not all of them being ex-students of Althusser, who in this way completely run counter to their old teacher's most famous argument, according to which the subject is only ever a purely ideological category.

Let us recall how the logic of the positing of the presuppositions allows Marx to articulate his unique perspective on the history of the becoming of capitalism. He describes this history from a materialist standpoint, based on the real or effective preconditions of capitalism, instead of deriving his account of political economy from the purely notional movement of the concept. "This manner of approach is not devoid of premises. It starts out from the real premises and does not abandon them for a moment," Marx and Engels had anticipated in *The German Ideology*. "The premises from which we begin are not arbitrary ones, not dogmas, but real premises from which abstraction can only be made in the imagination. They are the real individuals, their activity and the material conditions of their life, both those which they find already existing and those produced by their activity."[4] More importantly, this principle of starting out from the effective historical presuppositions applies not only to the method of analysis but also to its object. This is one explanation for why, assuming that Hegel's standpoint is indeed that of modern political economy, the critique of the former likewise coincides with the critique of the latter. Just as the abstractions of speculative thought are not self-generated "thought-entities," so too neither "free" labor nor money accumulated as capital is the product of capitalism itself. Rather, they constitute the latter's real or effective historical presuppositions. Once these factors come into being, however, the ideological effect is such that, peculiarly, a kind of circular loop capitalism posits the conditions of its becoming as if they were the results of its proper being: "These presuppositions, which originally appeared as prerequisites of its becoming—and therefore could not arise from its action *as capital*—now appear as results of its own realisation, reality, as *posited* by it—*not as conditions of its emergence, but as results of its being*. It no longer sets out from presuppositions in order to become, but is itself presupposed, and, setting out from itself, it itself creates the presuppositions for its maintenance and growth."[5] Finally, it is only under the spell of this semblance, which obliterates the violent process of its coming into being through the process of primitive so-called accumulation (only so-called, because it would be better to describe it as a process of primitive expropriation), that the authors of classical political economy can present the capitalist form as universal, eternal, and conform to an equally universal and eternal essence of human nature.

We thus begin to understand the enormous critical function of the section on primitive or originary accumulation for Marx, not only in the *Grundrisse* but also, though with less flirting with the Hegelian language, in the better-known chapters at the end of Volume One of *Capital*. This is because, without the introduction of a critical perspective on the violent process of its becoming, through the movement of the enclosures, the legislation against vagrancy, the colonialist expansion, and so on, capitalism effectively appears as a historical mode of production whose singularity consists in the constitutive forgetting of its own bloody historicity. By contrast, it is only if and when we can show that this circle cannot be closed, if we have at our disposal "signs" or "indications" as vestiges of such a violent past in the present, that we can also see "foreshadowings," as Marx says—using the English term in his notebooks—of an alternative, postcapitalist future:

> These indications, together with the correct grasp of the present, then also offer the key to the understanding of the past—a work in its own right, which we hope to be able to undertake as well. This correct approach, moreover, leads to points which indicate the transcendence of the present form of production relations, the movement coming into being, thus foreshadowing the future. If, on the one hand, the pre-bourgeois phases appear as *merely historical*, i.e. transcended premisses, so [on the other hand] the present conditions of production appear as conditions which *transcend themselves* and thus posit themselves as *historical premisses* for a new state of society.[6]

In sum, critical analysis must insert itself in these gaps that keep the maddening loop of capital from coming full circle. Instead of pretending to lift ourselves up by our own bootstraps, we must find a foothold in the holes that show that capitalism is not an undivided regime, firm in time and ubiquitous in space, without seeing that it also contains tenuous interstices of unreason, which show us the path to know that it is false. In fact, continuing on along the same path, Marx proposes that it is possible not only critically to know the falsity of the present social whole, based on its inherent contradictions, but also actively to produce the conditions of its future overcoming:

> The barrier to *capital* is the fact that this entire development proceeds in a contradictory way, and that the elaboration of the productive forces, of general wealth, etc., knowledge, etc., takes place in such a way that the working individual *alienates* himself; that he relates to the conditions brought out of him by his labour, not as to the conditions of *his own*, but of *alien wealth*, and of his own poverty. But this contradictory form is itself vanishing and produces the real conditions for its own transcendence.[7]

At this point of the discussion, however, the fundamental question arises as to how we should conceive of the subject of this transcendence. Who is, finally, the subject of the process not just of primitive or originary accumulation as the great secret of capitalism but also of its negation or overcoming in what would be tantamount to communism for Marx?

Here, I am not trying to regurgitate the argument for the proletariat as the identical subject-object of history, both target of exploitation (as working class) and agent of revolution (as universal non-class). Rather, the questions I want to raise concern the categories of the theory of the subject implied in this argument. Bluntly put: Why does the same Hegelian logic serve Marx in describing both the coming into being and the possible overcoming of capitalism? Or the other way around, why does the figure of the positing of the presuppositions in both cases appear to us in the guise of a subject? Why do we not seem able to think of the subject without relying on some version or other of the logic of the positing of the presuppositions?

Not Only as (Incomplete) Substance but also as (Divided) Subject: The Post-Hegelian Consensus

Especially if we take into account the indications about the comings and goings of "substance" and "self-consciousness" in post-Hegelian philosophy as reconstructed in *The Holy Family* and *The German Ideology*, with one lineage or tendency of thought favoring the sensuous/material presuppositions that are always already given and the other the transcendental-ideal act or deed of positing, we can ask ourselves if Marx's own theory of the subject does not remain stuck in the framework of this logic for the positing of the presuppositions, which more broadly speaking would mean that we stay trapped in yet another version of German idealism. If this logic serves to describe both the origins of capitalism and the process of its end, we would continue to think as essentially capitalist subjects even or especially in the desire or drive to overcome the violent history of capital's becoming, hidden behind the semblance of an autonomous self-constitution based on its own results.

Here, as Žižek also indicates in *Less Than Nothing*, we find ourselves before a fundamental ambiguity in Marx's theory of the subject, intimately related to that other ambiguity which is his conflicted relation to Hegel: "This is perhaps also the reason why Marx's reference to Hegel's dialectic in his 'critique of political economy' is ambiguous, oscillating between taking it as a mystified expression of the logic of capital and taking it as a model for the revolutionary process of emancipation."[8] To define the fundamental premises of his materialist vision of history, Marx, in *The German Ideology* but also later in his so-called mature or scientific works, appears to maintain the scheme of an articulation typical of much post-Hegelian philosophizing in general. On the one hand, he defines history on the basis of its real conditions or historical presuppositions, instead of considering the labor of the spirit or consciousness to be a wholly self-generated activity devoid of all premises, as was the case, according to all the Young Hegelians, with the speculative dialectical philosophy of their old master in Berlin. But, on the other hand, Marx also posits that human activity or praxis can in some way reboot itself while at the same time changing its circumstances: "History is nothing but the succession of the separate generations, each of which uses the materials, the capital funds, the productive forces handed down to it by all preceding generations, and thus, on the one hand, continues the traditional activity in completely changed circumstances and, on the other, modifies the old circumstances with a completely changed activity."[9]

The key to Marx's new materialism, as opposed to what he considers to be the old or superannuated materialism in the style of Feuerbach, consists precisely in maintaining a dialectical relation between the pole of materiality (up to that moment contemplated only in its character of sensuous objectivity, but not as practical activity, in the materialism of Feuerbach's type) and the pole of activity (up to that moment recognized only in philosophical idealism of Fichte's type). In addition to the first thesis, this can be gleaned most clearly and succinctly from the sixth of Marx's "Theses on Feuerbach," according to which there exists no essential human nature, but "man" instead is defined by a set of historically determinate social relations. And yet, this ensemble of relations can in turn be subjected to a process of revolutionary transformation. In other words, everything would appear to indicate that a kind of circular turning back upon itself defines not only the becoming of capitalism but also the social history of humanity as a whole, including in its revolutionary phase. In the third of the "Theses on Feuerbach," this is precisely how Marx defines his concept of radical practice or praxis: "The coincidence of the changing of circumstances and of human activity or self-change can be conceived and rationally understood only as *revolutionary practice*."[10]

If we ask ourselves what remains of Marx today, I would say it is precisely this theory of the subject in all its ambiguity, based on the Hegelian model of the positing of the presuppositions. Marx offers us a peculiar theory of the subject, one that is dialectical, materialist, but above all historical. He shows that, contrary to what Alain Badiou once suggested in his own *Theory of the Subject*, there is not a single and undivided theory of the subject shared between Marx and Freud, or between Lenin and Lacan ("The truth is that there is only one theory of the subject," Badiou wrote. And, as if to anticipate Žižek's fundamental argument: "Lacan is ahead of the current state of Marxism and we must take advantage of this advance so as to improve our Marxist affairs.")[11] Rather, I would argue that this unified theory of the subject is itself the product of a long and protracted history and that to see this we do well to consider first that there exist various theories of the subject in the plural, but without for this reason having to fall in the trap of either eclecticism or relativism:

1 *structural* or *transcendental* theories, according to which the structure of the subject is one and always the same;
2 *evental* or *contingent* theories, according to which the emergence of the subject is a rare and always aleatory event;
3 *historical* or *genealogical* theories, according to which the subject did not always exist in its present form but emerges as such only in determinate material and historical conditions.

Various combinations of these different types are certainly possible. Thus, for example, Adrian Johnston in much of his work can be said to have pursued an articulation of a theory of the subject that would be both transcendental and evental and can claim to operate simultaneously on the ontogenetic and the phylogenetic levels: accounting not only for the way all human beings are individuated from within the split materiality of nature as something more than natural, along the lines of an argument traced back to Hegel's philosophy of nature, but also for the way individuals may sometimes, on the occasion of a rare event, be jolted into becoming political or amorous subjects in Badiou's sense. Given what we know about the legacy of Kant and Hegel as discussed among others in *The Holy Family* and *The German Ideology*, it is therefore not surprising that Johnston should present his philosophy explicitly as a new form of German idealism, which he labels "transcendental materialism" or, more recently, "critical-dialectical naturalism," and which would include an account of the genesis of transcendental subjectivity itself in dialogue with the work of Gilbert Simondon and Catherine Malabou. "For transcendental materialism as critical-dialectical naturalism, if the thinking subject is transcendental in the sense of instantiating conditions of possibility for knowing, then pre/non-thinking material nature is meta-transcendental in the sense of constituting in turn the conditions of possibility for the very existence of such a transcendental subject as emergent (and not, as per subjective idealism, always-already given)," Johnston explains. "One might characterize this as a meta-transcendentalism of anthropogenesis, of the becoming-transcendental-subject of the human animal (an account even Kant himself felt compelled to flirt with in his *Anthropology from a Pragmatic Point of View*)."[12]

Another combination, for which we can find elements in Michel Foucault's final lecture courses at the Collège de France, might be able to articulate the structural with the historical orientations by providing us with a genealogical account of the thresholds for the coming into being, the bifurcating, and, alternatively, the discrediting and falling into oblivion of particular "practices of reflexivity of the self" as constitutive of the modern subject, for example, around the shift in dominance between "knowledge of the self" and "care of the self," a shift that we could mark with the name of René Descartes, even though Foucault also insists that such a decisive "event" cannot be reduced to just one person or date: "It seems to me that the 'Cartesian moment,' again within a lot of inverted commas, functioned in two ways. It came into play in two ways: by philosophically requalifying the *gnothi seauton* (know yourself), and by discrediting the *epimeleia heautou* (care of the self)."[13] By focusing on such thresholds or moments of bifurcation, the late Foucault is capable of writing what he also calls a history of practices of subjectivity.

Finally, going still a step farther, we might ask whether certain events such as the gradual consolidation of the three monotheistic religions of

Judaism, Christianity, and Islam; or the rise of capitalism, colonialism, and anticolonial wars of liberation, for example, did not in turn profoundly alter the structure of what can be understood by subject, whether as community, nation, individuality, selfhood, personality, and so on: notions that surely no self-proclaimed materialist can afford to conflate under a single heading. Not only would the subject always respond to the structure of an event, as in the evental theories that otherwise might still remain transcendental, but certain historical events also would be capable of reacting back on and transforming the structures of subjectivity themselves, which are to be defined in the fuller theory.

This last hypothesis clearly undergirds the analysis in the *Grundrisse*, for example, with regard to the historical formation of what Marx calls "the isolated individual," the hero of the "Robinsonades" typical of classical political economy. "The individual and isolated hunter and fisherman, who serves Adam Smith and Ricardo as a starting point, is one of the unimaginative fantasies of the 18th century. Robinsonades which, contrary to the fancies of the historians of civilisation, by no means signify simply a reaction against over-refinement and a reversion to a misconceived natural life," Marx explains in the *Grundrisse*. He continues: "They saw this individual not as an historical result, but as the starting point of history; not as something evolving in the course of history, but posited by nature, because for them this individual was the natural individual, according to their idea of human nature. This delusion has been characteristic of every new epoch hitherto."[14] But Marx's work, in my opinion, also offers us the possibility of reorganizing the different orientations mentioned above in a supplementary articulation, a kind of meta-historicization or historicization to the second degree, which would allow us to examine the history of the becoming-ahistorical and transcendental of one particular and historical theory of the subject, namely, the one reflected in and inherited from Kant and Hegel. To understand this, however, would require that we look at these philosophical figures and the theories or -*isms* for which they stand as the precipitates of wider social, economical, and political processes, struggles, and transformations.

Today, admittedly, the discussion rarely if ever reaches this last level. Rather, going back to the Hegelian parlance, we might say that there exists a vague but also sweeping consensus in contemporary thought, which holds that there is something like a subject only when and because the substance is incomplete, fissured, or traversed by the less than nothing of an internal gap. This was something observed early on by Ernesto Laclau in his preface to one of Žižek's first major works, *The Sublime Object of Ideology*: "There is subject because the substance—objectivity—does not manage to constitute itself fully: the location of the subject is that of a fissure at the very centre of the structure."[15] But this same insight, which I have elsewhere connected to Badiou's work, is something we can also find repeated in almost identical form among philosophers and theorists as varied as Judith Butler, Jason Read, or Sandro Mezzadra, more attuned to Jacques Derrida, Michel Foucault, and Toni Negri than to Althusser or Lacan.

The subject, then, would always be defined structurally by an excess or excrescence over and above its substantial determination. In other words, there is agency or the possibility of subjectivation only because the determination of the power of objectivity is not complete. "Agency exceeds the power by which it is enabled," Butler posits in *The Psychic Life of Power: Theories in Subjection*, as though this postulate were always and everywhere an irrevocable and transcendental law of subjectivity as such. "As a subject *of* power (where 'of' connotes both 'belonging to' and 'wielding'), the subject eclipses the conditions of its own emergence; it eclipses power with power. The conditions not only make possible the subject but enter into the subject's formation. They are made present in the acts of that formation and in the acts of the subject that follow."[16] Or, to use an even more succinct formulation from *Excitable Speech: A Politics of the Performative*: "Whereas some critics mistake the critique of sovereignty for the demolition of agency, I propose that agency begins where sovereignty wanes."[17]

Now, when they do not limit themselves to registering the structural possibility of the subject due to the necessary lack and/or the excess of the substance, these descriptions tend to come closer to the process of actual subjectivization and approach the level of something that might be called an act or event, by typically following a circular logic of the subject's turning back upon itself, which once again could be seen as being analogous to the Hegelian logic of the positing of the presuppositions. The most remarkable aspect of this description, though, concerns a process for the appropriation or assumption of the conditions of possibility of a subject's formation that at the same time, in a circular loop, would be a turning back upon itself so as to exceed and transform these conditions. "A power *exerted on* a subject is nevertheless a power *assumed by* the subject, an assumption that constitutes the instrument of that subject's becoming," Butler explains. "As a condition, power precedes the subject. Power loses its appearance of priority, however, when it is wielded by the subject, a situation that gives rise to the reverse perspective that power is the effect of the subject, and that power is what subjects effect."[18] This also means that the set of conditions or presuppositions that precede the subject, as the result of the latter's assumption of power, come to be seen as the effects of the subject's own self-positing.

In fact, before Butler and others would come up with original formulations of their own, nobody had contributed more to the new consensus regarding the positing of the presuppositions at the heart of the theory of the subject than Žižek, beginning in the concluding chapter of *The Sublime Object of Ideology*, which not coincidentally receives the title, like so many chapters and subsections throughout all of his work, of a quote from Hegel's *Phenomenology of Spirit*, "Not only as *Substance*, but also as *Subject*": "The 'act before the act' by means of which the subject posits the very presuppositions of his activity is of a strictly formal nature; it is a purely formal 'conversion' transforming reality into something perceived, assumed as a result of our activity."[19] For Žižek, however, this act of formal conversion cannot ever be complete. The subject cannot appropriate everything that is presupposed as objectively given, as if it were purely the result of its own positing. Impeding what would have been a process akin to a Feuerbachian inversion of theology back into anthropology, the act of positing the presuppositions also has its constitutive limit, due to the excess or leftover that stubbornly resists being sublated by the self-positing subject. Traversing the fantasy means precisely accepting and identifying with the symptomatic piece of the real that is the leftover of the process of symbolization itself. This is why Žižek, drawing once again the parallelism with Lacan, concludes in *The Sublime Object of Ideology* that in addition to positing the presuppositions, the subject's positing, in its turn, must be presupposed as emerging from the split introduced—in the subject as much as in the substance—by this stubborn remainder. "*This is the way 'substance becomes subject'*: when, by means of an empty gesture, the subject takes upon himself the leftover which eludes his active intervention. This 'empty gesture' receives from Lacan its proper name: the signifier; in it resides the elementary, constitutive act of symbolization."[20]

Do we then continue to think along the lines of a modern-day Munchausen? Have we still not left the circle traced by the positing of the presuppositions, only now extended into the presupposing of the act of positing as derived from a fundamental negativity or deadlock? If the logic of this process constitutes the fundamental fantasy of capitalism, would we continue to be fundamentally capitalist subjects even in our drive to overcome it in the direction of a postcapitalist, if not communist future? Would this be Marx's legacy for contemporary thought today in its impossible settling of accounts with Hegel's speculative dialectic? Or one day will we be able to write a history and theory of the subject that might be capable of giving an account of the violent process of its own becoming, without falling into the trap of a circular repetition of the same violence that brought it into being?

Beyond the Self-Made Subject:
A Metahistory of the Transcendental Turn

The self-made man: in the deliberately ambiguous sense of a man who makes himself and a self made into a man, a man's man (both alpha male and omega male, so to speak), is this not the fundamental illusion of the subject sustaining capitalist ideology? This illusion, in turn, supposes two further hypotheses. The first is that capitalism is inseparable from the production of a new notion of subjectivity, if not the only notion that as a result of this development we have come to associate with the modern subject, for which philosophy teachers typically credit Descartes—with or without the consideration of Augustine as a dark precursor. At the level of the history of humankind, in other words, that schoolbook example of philosophical prestidigitation known as the modern Cartesian subject, a redundancy if there ever was one, must in turn be understood historically and materially in terms of how a thinking thing can set itself up with absolute and unshakable certainty over and above the extended thingness of the surrounding world. What is more, and this would be the second hypothesis involved in the semblance of the self-made subject, the turn whereby capitalism recursively posits the presuppositions of its own becoming would be homologous to the turn whereby any subject thereafter comes to conceive of itself in relation to the structures—be they linguistic, symbolic, political, economical, and so on—that determine it.

With regard to the first of these hypotheses, already Foucault in *Discipline and Punish* suggested that the takeoff of capitalist accumulation in the West was inseparable from the takeoff of a whole new set of technologies for administering the accumulation of men: "In fact, the two processes—the accumulation of men and the accumulation of capital—cannot be separated; it would not have been possible to solve the problem of the accumulation of men without the growth of an apparatus of production capable of both sustaining them and using them; conversely, the techniques that made the cumulative multiplicity of men useful accelerated the accumulation of capital."[21] Just as capitalism, for Marx, rises up only in the violent process of so-called primitive accumulation, so too the modern subject, for Foucault, is only the result of the violent processes of so-called modern biopolitical accumulation and discipline. Both discursively and at the level of new technologies of power, in any case, the subject would no longer be just the invention of some lonely philosopher in his hut working his way through six *Meditations on First Philosophy* as if to reproduce the Godlike process of his own genesis and rest on the seventh day. Instead, we should be able to provide a historical and materialist reframing of the modern philosophical theory of the subject, which otherwise remains strictly speaking idealist, from Descartes all the way to Kant, Fichte, and Hegel as well as their latter-day criticisms and reincarnations.

Let us reconsider, for example, the way in which this philosophical tradition in its final stages finds a synthetic expression in Butler's attempt in *The Psychic Life of Power* to reconcile a theory of subjection with the findings of poststructuralist theory. One of the most striking aspects of this account, as I mentioned before, is the way in which the quanta of force or drive that are not yet subject are said to turn back upon themselves so as to assume the power structures to which the resulting subject otherwise remains tethered. Once this vengeful process of turning back upon itself crosses a certain threshold, however, the constitutive dependency of the subject on those power structures to which it is so passionately attached seems to fall into oblivion. "The 'I' emerges upon the condition that it deny its formation in dependency, the conditions of its own possibility," Butler also suggests. She continues: "This apparent contradiction makes sense when we understand that no subject comes into being without power, but that its coming into being involves the dissimulation of power, a metaleptic reversal in which the subject produced by power becomes heralded as the subject who *founds* power. This foundationalism of the subject is the effect of a working of power, an effect achieved by reversal and concealment of that prior working."[22] Now, after what was said before about the relation of co-dependency between the capitalist mode of production and the modern mode of subjection, could we not also say that this metaleptic reversal is strictly homologous with the Munchausen effect of capitalism? And, both at the ontogenetic level of the child entering into adulthood and at the phylogenetic level of the history of human subjectivity entering the age of so-called Cartesian modernity, does the notion of a self-positing "I" not depend on the erasure of the traces of the violent process whereby the subject of capitalism posits the presuppositions of its own historical becoming so as to affirm the inalienable rights and duties of its sovereign being?

Butler's greatest contribution to the theory of the modern subject consists in pinpointing the inescapable ambivalence inherent in the process of positing the presuppositions. "What does it mean for the agency of a subject to *presuppose* its own subordination? Is the act of *presupposing* the same as the act of *reinstating*, or is there a discontinuity between the power presupposed and the power reinstated?" she asks rhetorically, the intended answer obviously being negative: "Power considered as a condition of the subject is necessarily not the same as power considered as what the subject is said to wield. The power that initiates the subject fails to remain continuous with the power that is the subject's agency."[23] All kinds of obscure psychic scenarios come in to fill the gap of this discontinuity. But at no point is there any doubt in this account that subject and substance are indeed articulated through a relation of either failure or excess. "If the subject is *neither* fully determined by power *nor* fully determining of power (but significantly and partially both), the subject exceeds the logic of contradiction, is an excrescence of logic, as it were," Butler adds, echoing but never quite quoting some of Marx's most famous statements. "To claim that the subject exceeds either/ or is not to claim that it lives in some free zone of its own making. Exceeding is not escaping, and the subject exceeds precisely that to which it is bound."[24] In fact, this logic of excess, whereby there is a subject or agency whenever substance or sovereignty fails to constitute itself, is constantly affirmed as if it were always and everywhere the case, making *The Psychic Life of Power* as weirdly and uncannily ahistorical as Badiou's *Theory of the Subject* or Žižek's work from *The Ticklish Subject* to *Less Than Nothing*. The closest we come to a note of historicity in Butler's account is when she suggests that hers might be a theory of agency in "postliberatory" times, presumably meaning that we can no longer believe in a theory of liberation based on the hypothesis of a "free" subject, which would be the liberal self lying outside of the oppressive power structures but possibly also alluding to the fact that we live in an age in which liberation struggles are definitely over and done with. Yet everywhere else, as in her careful readings of the classics from Hegel to Nietzsche and from Freud to Althusser, this theory of "the" subject seems to be floating timelessly in thin air.

Here, to conclude, I can only outline how Marx—who is notably absent from *The Psychic Life of Power*—might help us re-historicize the becoming ahistorical of the dominant theory of the subject that in my view we have come to associate all too narrowly with the legacies of German idealism. In fact, two or three brief indications will have to suffice as foreshadowing a history and theory of the subject that is yet to come. The first indication concerns the reasons why the process of positing the presuppositions cannot be closed into a circular loop. For Marx, this is due neither to the ambivalence of language nor to the negativity of the death drive, which he would have failed to recognize, but to the fact that capitalism cannot produce either labor power or the earth's natural resources on which it depends for the production of value. This is why, unlike Hegel's system whose logic and terminology he otherwise adopts, Marx's view of capital is that of an open system: "Marx demonstrates that capitalism is an open system with respect to the past, because its conditions of existence were posited in a pre-capitalist period," Hiroshi Uchida comments in his study of Marx's Grundrisse and Hegel's Logic. "For that reason Marx critically suggests that Hegel's Logic, in which an ideal subject or 'idea' appears to posit itself and all other objects, is similar to political economy, in which value and capital do likewise."[25] Furthermore, the impossibility of closing the circle whereby the ideal of the modern subject violently turns back upon the circumstances of its own becoming and in vain tries to establish a cut between itself and that which precedes it, reproduces itself at a number of different levels and scales. Of these, the ones that interest me in particular are not only the individual or ontogenetic level of the child's passage into adulthood and the evolutionary or phylogenetic level of the passage from the inorganic to the organic and from the animal to the human animal. Rather, my focus is on the material, social, economic, and political history whereby the "free" individual rises up as the essential standard bearer of the subject as such, but only as the result of the violent ripping apart of those communities who in retrospect will come to be labeled primitive, premodern, or archaic. This alone is what allows the modern, liberal, and enlightened subject theorized in European philosophy to set itself up as a new stage, an exit from the self-incurred immaturity or non-age also described less euphemistically as premodern barbarism or dependency. Even the very notion of a "pure," a priori or transcendental approach to the question "What is man?" as the fourth underlying question beneath the three critical questions "What can I know?" "What must I do?" and "What may I be allowed to hope for?" depends in the last instance on material processes such as the division of labor. "Where labor is not so differentiated and distributed like that, where everyone is a jack-of-all-trades, professions still remain in a most barbarous state," Kant himself points out in the Preface to the Groundwork of the Metaphysics of Morals. He continues:

> It would by itself be an object not unworthy of consideration to ask whether pure philosophy in all its parts does not require its own specialist,

and whether the learned profession as a whole might not be better off if those who, conforming to the taste of their public, are in the habit of peddling the empirical mixed with the rational in all sorts of proportions unknown to themselves—who call themselves independent thinkers, but others, who prepare the merely rational part, ponderers—were warned not to pursue two occupations at once that are very dissimilar in the way they are to be carried out, for each of which a special talent is perhaps required, and which united in one person produce only bunglers.[26]

To this, Marx might have replied not only that abstraction is real, meaning that only the real processes of capitalist accumulation, modernization, and exploitation produce the practical truth of categories such as labor or production "in general," but also that communism is meant to undo the division of labor that even in the eyes of Kant undergirds the modern age of critique in its break from dependency or barbarism.

Finally, the point of a Marxist-inspired theory of the subject is not just to historicize and contextualize the different figures of the individual, the group, the community, the people, or the nation-state and their internal divisions in terms of race, gender, class, language, profession, sexual orientation, ethnicity, and so on. Nor is it to highlight the presence of an underlying anthropological constant or transcendental invariant, based on the violent turn and dissimulation of the subject's metaleptic reversal in the production and reproduction of its material life. Rather, if this process has indeed been able to produce the effect of a unified theory of the subject after all and not just an eclectic banquet offering of multiple subject positions and theories in the plural, this is because the history of capitalism through bloody conquest and colonial expansion over the last five centuries has in fact managed to become unified all across the surface of the Earth.

Notes

1. Marx, *Grundrisse*, 388. For the renewed interest in Marx's theory of primitive accumulation, see in particular Federici, *Caliban and the Witch*; Walker, "Primitive Accumulation and the Formation of Difference"; and Morris, "*Ursprüngliche Akkumulation*." My thanks to Orlando Bentancor, Adrian Johnston, and Gavin Walker for ongoing conversations reflected in the following pages.

2. Marx, "Critique of the Hegelian Dialectic and Philosophy as a Whole," 333.

3. Žižek, *Less Than Nothing*, 250. See also Žižek, *The Fragile Absolute*, 17–18; and *The Parallax View*, 266–67. For an excellent discussion of the relation between Marx and Žižek, see Walker, "Žižek with Marx."

4. Marx and Engels, *The German Ideology*, 31 and 37.

5. Ibid., 387–88.

6. Marx, *Grundrisse*, 389.

7. Ibid., 465.

8. Žižek, *Less Than Nothing*, 250.

9. Marx and Engels, *The German Ideology*, MECW 5: 50. For my interpretation of these passages and the legacy of the Young Hegelians as split between the positing and the presupposing, I owe a debt to Pierre Dardot and Christian Laval, *Marx, prénom Karl*.

10. Marx, "Theses on Feuerbach," 4.

11. Badiou, *Theory of the Subject*, 115.

12. Johnston, "Meta-Transcendentalism and Error-First Ontology." See also Johnston, *A New German Idealism*; and, for the earliest formulations of his transcendental materialism, see Johnston, *Žižek's Ontology*.

13. Foucault, *The Hermeneutics of the Subject*, 14.

14. Marx, *Grundrisse*, 17–18.

15. Laclau, "Preface," xv.

16. Butler, *The Psychic Life of Power*, 14–15.

17. Butler, *Excitable Speech*, 15–16.

18. Ibid., 11 and 13.

19. Žižek, *The Sublime Object of Ideology*, 218.

20. Ibid., 220–21.

21. Foucault, *Discipline and Power*, 221. Foucault uses the expression "mode of subjection" earlier in the same text, see ibid., 24.

22. Ibid., 9–10 and 15–16.

23. Ibid., 12.

24. Ibid., 17.

25. Uchida, *Marx's* Grundrisse *and Hegel's* Logic, 121 and 138.

26. Kant, *Groundwork of the Metaphysics of Morals*, 4.

Works Cited

Badiou, Alain. *Theory of the Subject*. Translated and introduced by Bruno Bosteels. London: Continuum, 2009.

Borges, Jorge Luis. "Avatars of the Tortoise." In *Labyrinths Selected Stories and Other Writings*, edited by Donald A. Yates and James E. Irby, 178–84. New York: New Directions, 1964.

Butler, Judith. *The Psychic Life of Power: Theories in Subjection*. Stanford: Stanford University Press, 1997.

——. *Excitable Speech: A Politics of the Performative*. New York: Routledge, 1997.

Dardot, Pierre, and Christian Laval. *Marx, prénom Karl*. Paris: Gallimard, 2012.

Foucault, Michel. *The Hermeneutics of the Subject: Lectures at the Collège de France, 1981–1982*. Edited by Frédéric Cros and translated by Graham Burchell. New York: Palgrave Macmillan, 2005.

——. *Discipline and Punish: The Birth of the Prison*. Translated by Alan Sheridan. New York: Vintage, 1977.

Federici, Silvia. *Caliban and the Witch: Women, the Body, and Primitive Accumulation*. New York: Autonomedia, 2004.

Kant, Immanuel. *Groundwork of the Metaphysics of Morals*. Edited by Mary Gregor and Jens Timmerman and Introduction by Christine M. Korsgaard. Cambridge: Cambridge University Press, 2012.

Johnston, Adrian. "Meta-Transcendentalism and Error-First Ontology: The Cases of Gilbert Simondon and Catherine Malabou." In *New Realism and Contemporary Philosophy*, edited by Gregor Kroupa and Jure Simoniti. London: Bloomsbury, forthcoming.

——. *A New German Idealism: Hegel, Žižek, and Dialectical Materialism*. New York: Columbia University Press, 2018.

——. *Žižek's Ontology: A Transcendental Materialist Theory of Subjectivity*. Evanston: Northwestern University Press, 2008.

Laclau, Ernesto. "Preface." In Žižek, *Sublime Object of Ideology*, ix–xv. London and New York: Verso, 1989.

Marx, Karl. "Critique of the Hegelian Dialectic and Philosophy as a Whole." In *Economic and Philosophic Manuscripts of 1844*. Volume 3 of Karl Marx and Friedrich Engels, *Collected Works*, 326–46. London: Lawrence and Wishart, 2010.

——. "Theses on Feuerbach." In Karl Marx and Friedrich Engels, *Collected Works*. Vol. 5, 3–5. London: Lawrence and Wishart, 2010.

——. *Grundrisse*. In Karl Marx and Friedrich Engels, *Collected Works*. Vol. 28. London: Lawrence and Wishart, 2010.

——, and Friedrich Engels. *The German Ideology*. In Karl Marx and Friedrich Engels, *Collected Works*. Vol. 5, 19–661. London: Lawrence and Wishart, 2010.

Morris, Rosalind C. "*Ursprüngliche Akkumulation*: The Secret of an Originary Mistranslation." *boundary 2* 43, no. 3 (2016): 29–77

Uchida, Hiroshi. *Marx's* Grundrisse *and Hegel's* Logic. Edited by Terrell Carver. London and New York: Routledge, 1988.

Walker, Gavin. "Primitive Accumulation and the Formation of Difference: On Marx and Schmitt." *Rethinking Marxism* 23, no. 3 (2011): 384–404.

——. "Žižek with Marx: Outside in the Critique of Political Economy." In *Repeating Žižek*, edited by Agon Hamza, 195–212. Durham: Duke University Press, 2015.

Žižek, Slavoj. *Less Than Nothing: Hegel and the Shadow of Dialectical Materialism*. London and New York: Verso, 2012.

——. *The Fragile Absolute—or, Why is the Christian Legacy Worth Fighting For?* London and New York: Verso, 2000.

——. *The Parallax View*. Cambridge: The MIT Press, 2006.

——. *The Sublime Object of Ideology*. London and New York: Verso, 1989.

CHAPTER THIRTEEN

The Impasses of Environmentalism: Subjectivity and Accumulation in the World-Ecology Project

ORLANDO BENTANCOR

THE PRESENT ESSAY QUESTIONS the place of subjectivity in the revolutionary critical dismantling of the opposition between nature and society that is unfolding in the so-called world-ecology project, a multidisciplinary approach led by Jason Moore, author of *Capitalism in the Web of Life: Ecology and the Accumulation of Capital*.[1] For Moore, neither eco-Marxism, the fashionable theories of the Anthropocene, or even official environmental history can entirely account for the current environmental crisis for the simple reason that these approaches ignore the deep historical "conditions and causes" of the present predicament. The ultimate condition and cause of the environmental crisis is the separation between humanity and nature, which Moore conceptualizes as a foundational act of violence that is intrinsically connected to the emergence of colonial/racial capitalism in the sixteenth century. To bring forth the historical and material "conditions and causes" of the crisis is to unsettle "the idea of Nature and Humanity in the upper case: ecologies without humans, and human relations without ecologies."[2] By compartmentalizing nature and humanity, "Anthropocene stories do something unintentional—but deeply violent. For the history of humanity and nature conceals a dirty secret of modern world history."[3]

Taking Moore's materialist critique of the separation of humans and nature seriously has led me to question of the role of the subject in the world-ecology project. My aim in fleshing out Moore's concepts, which are based on the centrality of the notion of humans as environment-making beings, is to highlight the need to combine a critique of the separation of nature with an account of the ontological genesis of this separation. To this end, Slavoj Žižek's synthesis of psychoanalysis and German Idealism helps to account for the place that the subject and the capitalist drive occupy in capitalist ecology as an environment-making process. In this essay, I argue that the subject is the product of a material nature that denaturalizes itself in an operation of division in which the web of life radically transforms itself through a web of material beings. This immanent ontogenesis is consistent with Moore's historical materialist critique of the human/nature division: the virtual insubstantial subject is irreducible to yet inseparable from the material web of life because it is nothing but the self-sundering of this material web of life itself. Far from reinforcing the notion of humans without nature or nature without humans, the notion of the subject as the self-sundering of material substance is not only useful but also indispensable for completing the critique of the Anthropocene narrative.

The separation between nature and society presupposed by the Anthropocene narrative subsumed larger portions of humanity under the rubric of "nature," an ideological operation that was instrumental for putting both the biosphere and colonial subjects to work, mobilizing "the unpaid work and energy of humans—especially women, especially the enslaved—in service to transforming the landscapes with a singular purpose: the endless accumulation of capital."[4] In one and the same move, global capitalism put both extrahuman nature and non-European people to work in the service of the accumulation of profit. According to Moore:

> [S]ome people became Humans, who were members of something called Civilization, or Society, or both as in Adam Smith's "civilized society". From the beginning of capitalism, however, most humans were either excluded from Humanity—indigenous Americans, for example or were designated as only partly Human, as were virtually all European women. As with property, the symbolic boundaries between who was—and who was not—part of Nature (or Society) tended to shift and vary; they were often blurry; and they were flexible. But a boundary there was, and much of the early history of modern race and gender turns on struggles over that line. (Is it so different today?)[5]

Ultimately, sixteenth-century colonial/racial capitalism transformed what was a web of life into something out there called "Nature," understood as environments without humans, while vast portions of humanity were also considered as part of this Nature, understood as "natives" or "*naturales*."

Moreover, for Moore the "Anthropocene's historical perspective" is complicit with the Cartesian division between nature and humanity. Moore employs the term *Cartesian dualism* as a shorthand for referring to the ontological presuppositions that undergird the separation of nature and humanity. The subordination of body to mind served as an ontological foundation to make humans "masters and possessors of nature."[6] Cartesian dualism, according to Moore, "was a key organizing principle for an emergent capitalist civilization."[7] The Human/Nature separation was practically inseparable from a simultaneously ontological and epistemological way of organizing the world that underpinned the international division of labor between civilized humans and less-than-human "natural" beings between the fifteenth and eighteenth centuries.[8] As Moore posits, Cartesian dualism finds its expression in three axioms behind the emergence of the colonial/capitalist world system: (1) the imposition of an "ontological status upon entities (substances) as opposed to the relationships (that is to say energy, matter, people, ideas, and so on became things)"; (2) the centrality of a "logic of either/or (rather than both/and)"; and (3) the "idea of a purposive control over nature through applied science."[9]

The alliance between the Anthropocene narrative and Cartesian dualism eclipses the actually existing colonial and material relations through which women and men "make history within the web of life."[10] Instead of using the term *Anthropocene*, which is contaminated by Cartesian dualism and directly complicit with colonial/racial capitalism, Moore proposes the term *Capitalocene* which sees Capitalism not only as an economic and social formation but also as something "more profound," a way of "organizing nature and therefore a new way of organizing the relations between work, reproduction, and the conditions of life."[11] Capitalism does not *have* an environment-making process, it directly *is* an environment-making process.

Capitalism as a way of organizing nature entails three historical processes. The first one is what Marx called primitive accumulation, the acts of violence that were the historical condition of possibility for making humans dependent on the mediation of money to survive. The second one is the advent of new forms of territorial power after the long feudal crisis (ca. 1315–1453) that accompanied the transition from land to labor productivity.[12] The third process, directly associated to the separation of humanity and nature, was the emergence of new symbolic systems as ways of knowing and controlling the world. The transformation of labor power and land into property was materially dependent on "a symbolic-knowledge regime premised on separation—or alienation."[13] Moore equates this new knowledge regime with a series of "scientific revolutions" that made possible the emergence of a process that "threatens us all today: putting the whole of nature to work for capital."[14]

Above all, Moore denounces this "separation from nature" as illusory since it is impossible to escape the material dependence on the web of life, in spite of the complex processes that "bundled the symbolic and the material in a world-praxis remaking the world in the image of capital."[15] Moore sees the protean and metamorphosing power of a deterritorialization of capital that expands "commodity frontiers" as being based on "dualism, separation, mathematization, the aggregation of units."[16] As a result of this transformation of the world into exchangeable units, "the web of life could be reduced to a series of external objects—mapped, explored, surveyed, calculated for what Nature could do for the accumulation of capital."[17] Human labor productivity became the substance of value—"measured without regard for its cultural biophysical and cooperative dimensions."[18] This was human work as "abstracted, averaged, deprived of all the meaning but for one: value as the average labor-time making the average commodity."[19] The process of naturalization of certain humans and the creation of Nature as external was crucial for the transformation of all reality into "value." Moore explains:

> To turn work into labor-power and land into private property was to transform nature into Nature. In equal measure, this transformation produced Society as something outside of Nature, the better that Society could turn Nature into a set of discrete units, into a repertoire of calculable objects and factors of production. Marx tells us, famously, that the relations of capital and labor "drip with blood and dirt". Does not also the dualism of Society and Nature? [20]

As mentioned above, the conquest of the Americas is a crucial moment in the history of the separation of the worker from the products of her labor. Colonization produced a shift in value and productivity where land productivity under feudal conditions mutated into labor productivity under the hegemony of the modern world market. This shift in the process of valorization is central to the twenty-first-century environmental crisis because the emergence of land and labor productivity was inseparable from an "entirely novel" reconfiguration of the "relation between human activity and the web of life."[21] For the first time in history, forces of nature, now transformed into work/energy, were deployed to advance the productivity of human work as subordinated to exchange value. At this point, Moore introduces what I consider a central contribution to Marxist theories of value:

> All other activity was devalued and appropriated in the service to advancing labor productivity in a narrow zone of commodification. Thus: the birth of Nature which implied and necessitated the birth of Society, both dripping with blood and dirt, was the necessary ontological counterpoint to the separation of producers from the means of production.[22]

The separation between nature and humanity parallels the separation of the producers from the means of production because it is an ontological real abstraction, an act of foundational violence, that is inseparable from the alienation and expropriation of both paid and unpaid labor. Valorization depends on an asymmetrical configuration of paid labor productivity (surplus value created by valorization and exploitation) and unpaid work (surplus value created by appropriation and extraction). Moore, drawing on Maria Mies's *Patriarchy and Accumulation on a World Scale*, argues that the amount of work commodified under the rubric of socially necessary labor depends on a *disproportionally* greater volume of work outside the cash nexus "but within the reach of capitalist power."[23] Hence, the appropriation of the unpaid labor of "women, nature, and colonies" is the fundamental material condition of the exploitation of labor power in the commodity system.[24] This disproportionality between "paid work," reproduced through the cash nexus, and the "unpaid work," reproduced outside the circuit of capital, is the motor of the endless process of accumulation. In essence, "value does not work unless most work is not valued."[25] Moore extends the notion of primitive accumulation to include the work/energy of nature: "Every act of producing surplus value, then depends on a greater act of appropriating the unpaid work of human and extra-human natures."[26] Moore introduces the concept of cheap nature as a "free gift" or "externality" that contributes to the creation of value within the commodity exchange process. Moreover, the concept of "externality" occupies the same structural position in capitalist ecology as the gendered, colonial, and racialized forms of labor. In sum, the devaluation of nature and the unpaid labor of women, slaves, and colonial subjects are the material conditions of the self-valorization of capital. It is of vital importance to emphasize the asymmetrical character of this dialectics of value and devaluation, where the violence of devaluation precedes not only chronologically but also ontologically the production of exchange value. In his pioneering examination of the role of the Nature/Humanity dualism,

Moore advances a sophisticated dialectics of devaluation where that which has no value is the source of the self-valorization of capital.

Double Internality and Metabolic Exchange

Since Moore is especially interested in the different historical ways in which capitalism "incorporates work/energy into its re/production of wealth, life, and power," he proposes a dialectical method called "double internality," which is an attempt to overcome the dualism of Nature/Humanity by focusing on "the flows of power and capital in nature, flows of nature in capital and power."[27] Double internality sees humans and extrahuman beings as mutually constituted in a process of co-production where humans are both producers and products of nonhuman forces. It is a dialectical method derived from Karl Marx's materialist conception of the interactions between humans and nature. Moore's double internality parallels Amy E. Wendling's argument that Marx's epistemological-technological break deconstructed the opposition between man and nature by seeing human and technological forces as part of a single universal energy. It also finds strong resonances with the work of Anson Rabinbach, who contends that Marx erased the difference between human (society) and nonhuman (the inorganic productive forces in nature and technology) by conceiving the human body as an energy-producing machine. Finally, there is also a conceptual link between Moore's double internality and Deleuze and Guattari's assertion of the ultimate unity of the producer and the product, which blurs the distinction between industry and nature.[28]

In chapter 7 of the first volume of *Capital*, Marx develops his notion of labor, describing it as a metabolic relationship between humans and nature. Humans not only actualize their essence or spirit by artificially transforming the natural world: by changing nature, humans change themselves because there is no preexisting fixed human "essence" before its actualization. Marx reconceptualizes the relation between nature and humanity by emphasizing the centrality of external objects (both natural and artificial sources of use value) in the constitution of humans as living species. This process is a metabolic exchange where humanity projects itself in the inorganic environment by incorporating the environment into itself:

> Labour is, first of all, a process between man and nature, a process by which man, through his own actions, mediates, regulates and controls the metabolism between himself and nature. He confronts the materials

of nature as a force of nature. He sets in motion the natural forces which belong to his own body, his arms, legs, head and hands, in order to appropriate the materials of nature in a form adapted to his own needs. Through this movements he acts upon external nature and changes it, and in this way he simultaneously changes his own nature.[29]

This paragraph provides an understanding of labor as a membrane of negotiations between human and nonhuman nature. Moore's ontological and historical critique of the separation of humans and nature is a corollary of Marx's assertion that humans confront nature as "a force of nature." When Moore argues that labor is part of nature and that capitalism is an environment-making process, he is developing the potentialities of Marx's notion of metabolism as a mutually constitutive exchange of forces between the organism and the environment.

Moore conceives the double internality of "nature-in-humans" and "humans-in-nature" in terms of a dialectics of "extroversion" that overcomes the boundaries between interior and exterior:

All species "build" environments—they are "ecosystem engineers." But some engineers are more powerful than others. Humans have been especially powerful. This is not simply because of thought and language—which are of course central—but also because hominid evolution favored distinctive extroversions: a smaller digestive system and the use of fire as an external stomach; a narrower birth canal and community as external womb; less hair and the production of clothing and shelter as external fur. That list could be extended. The point is to highlight the ways in which evolutionary processes were powerfully co-produced: humanity is a species-environment relation.[30]

It is instructive to associate Moore's double internality to Leroi-Gourhan's theory of exteriorization, according to which human actualization takes place through artificial transformation of nonhuman nature in a process that retroactively constitutes human essence. Leroi-Gourhan narrates a story according to which the history of humanity's self-liberation from environmental constraints is also one of "exteriorization" that goes from the fabrication of the flint axe to the digital revolution. In Leroi-Gourhan's words: "The whole of our evolution has been oriented towards placing outside ourselves what in the rest of the animal world is achieved inside by species adaptation."[31] Far from falling into a sort of vulgar reductionism that naturalizes humans, double internality is a dialectical process where humans put themselves out of themselves in an external environment, retroactively creating their own interiority. In sum, the "humanity" of "humanity-in-nature" is not simply separated from "nature" but dependent on its material conditions of possibility, while the "nature" of "nature-in-humanity" is, to borrow Jacques Lacan's expression, "extimate," that is, not only external but internal to humanity.

In short, Moore provides an elegant and powerful synthesis of feminism, postcolonial theory, eco-criticism, and Marxism by associating the Human/Nature dualism with the emergence of colonial/racial capitalism that fuels the modern world system. Moore's synthesis is based on a profound insight: the perception of the problem of the environmental crisis, that is, the illusion of the separation of nature and humanity, is part of the problem itself. In other words, the advocates of the Anthropocene presuppose a rigid separation between nature and humanity, which is the ideological distortion that caused the environmental crisis. Another important contribution by Moore is his suggestion that this separation is linked to a dialectics of value and devaluation that, in turn, links the material conditions of capitalism to a disproportionately greater act of appropriation. To understand humans as environment-making beings is to dismantle the dualistic ontology that made possible the emergence of capitalism in the sixteenth century and replace it with a more complex dialectics between "nature-in-humans" and "humans-in-nature." Moore asserts that instead of asking, "How did humanity become separated from nature? And how do humans disrupt nature, causing environmental degradation? (And eventually, crisis?)," it is necessary to ask: "First, how is humanity *unified* with the rest of nature within the web of life? Second, how is human history a *co-produced* history, through which humans have put nature to work—including other humans—in accumulating wealth and power?"[32] Moore argues in favor of a dialectical holism where humans are part of nature and are, therefore, producers and products of the environment. This dialectical holism brings forth the following crucial question: "How do humans *fit* into the web of life, understood as a totality of distinctive and interpenetrating evolutionary trajectories?"[33] The task of the historian, then, is to examine how humans are unified with nature and how civilizations "fit" within nature."[34] Let us take notice of how Moore wants to replace the question about the genesis of the separation with a question about how humans fit into the web of life within a broader process of co-production. Does this replacement mean that his historical account of the link between this separation and the history of colonial/racial capitalist expropriation is an ideological illusion of the superstructure devoid of any ontological impact on reality? If social formations simply *fit* the web of life, why does the illusion emerge in the first place?

Once we agree with the need to consider humans with respect to their material conditions in order to avoid the fetishization of nature as a separate entity, another problem arises: How is the illusion of a historically situated, disembodied subject (the pure form of interiority of the Cartesian subject) inscribed back into the ontological process of production if we need to account for the agency of this violent abstraction? This question opens the door for a productive exchange between world-ecology and a robust theorization of subjectivity: If humans transform themselves by transforming the environment, what is the ontological status of the subject once we consider humans as a product of the metabolic exchange of human and extrahuman material forces? Is there a place at all for the subject in the world-ecology project? Is there a third link that mediates between the mutual interaction between "nature-in-humanity" and "humanity-in-nature"?

After bringing the question of the subject in the world-ecology project, I aim to think through double internality to its ultimate consequences: the more humans are part of the web of life, the more we presuppose an insubstantial subject. The more we deconstruct the opposition between nature and humanity, the more humans are included in an exterior network of tools and material forces. The more humans are part of the network of material forces, the more the subject emerges as an illusion. And yet, the more the subject emerges as a distorting illusion, the more we need to include this illusion *back* into the material world. Placing this illusion back into the material world is the only way to account for its power, which is both performative and ideological. If the violence of separation has some effect in material reality, the dialectical unity of human and extrahuman relations is also a *negative* unity, one that presupposes the subject as the empty void of the self-negating agency. After all, when describing the metabolic exchange between humans and nature, Marx asserts that humans *confront* nature as another material force within nature, suggesting that this confrontation, far from being pacific and balanced, is antagonistic and violent. In sum, the wager of this text is that if we are to respect the centrality of the critique of the violence of devaluation of nature, it is necessary to shift perspectives and start asking a different question: Instead of asking how humans fit into the web of life, it is necessary to ask, Why do humans behave like "misfits" that need to transform the Eenvironment? To answer this question, it would be necessary to explore the link between a philosophical-metapsychological ontogenesis of the human/nature separation and how it is inscribed back into nature, allowing certain social formations such as capitalism to put nature to work in the service of accumulation. To pursue this line of reasoning it would be useful to bring the complete opposite perspective of ecological Marxism to the conversation. I am referring to Slavoj Žižek's Hegelian-Lacanian notion of the subject, which is, at least apparently, at odds with the world-ecology project. In the following section I will engage in the task of unpacking Žižek's concept of the subject as a "misfit." He defines a subject-out-of-joint as one that is inseparable from an endless drive that subtracts humans from their environment, allowing them to *put nature to work* while also introducing rifts, crises, and disruptions within the biosphere.

The Subject-out-of-joint and the Metabolic Loop

In *Less than Nothing*, Žižek accuses ecology of being a misanthropic ideology that is guided by the wish to return to a complete harmonic union with a preexisting and balanced nature. Žižek associates this kind of ecology to a "totalitarian" experience akin to Stalinism or religious fundamentalism. In his view, ecology runs the risk of becoming a hegemonic ideology, a new "opium for the masses," as soon as it starts to limit human agency for the sake of preserving nature.[35] Žižek does not hesitate to accuse this kind of ideology of being fixated on the critique of the Cartesian subject in the name of a notion of human finitude "embedded in a bio-sphere."[36] For him, in ecological ideology, the Earth becomes something sacred "that should not be unveiled totally, that should and will forever remain a Mystery, a power we should learn to trust, not dominate."[37]

Žižek emphasizes the negative consequences of the way ecological ideology blames humanity for disturbing natural homeostasis. In his view, humanity becomes the excremental waste that needs to be exterminated in order to reestablish balance. Popular narratives of the catastrophic revenge of Mother Earth repeat the cliché that humans become the source of unbalance when they are guided by their hubristic will to power. Žižek argues that this proves the ideological character of deep ecology: "What this means is that there is nothing more distant from a truly radical ecology than the image of a pure idyllic nature cleansed of all human dirt."[38] Humanity becomes an "unnatural excess," a foreign body that cannot be integrated into the ecological account of Nature. At the root of the exclusion of the subject from a supposedly sacred and balanced nature, Žižek locates a conceptual distribution between the natural and the human that basically separates nature and humanity.

Let us clarify that none of these critiques apply to Moore, who is a fierce critic of the ideology behind catastrophism: "The Cartesian narrative unfolds like this. Capitalism—or if one prefers, modernity or industrial civilization—emerged *out of* Nature. It drew wealth *from* Nature. It disrupted, degraded, or defiled *Nature*. And now, or sometime very soon, Nature will exact its revenge. Catastrophe is coming. Collapse is on the horizon."[39] Moreover, Moore argues that Cartesian dualism and colonial/racial capitalism are the silent presupposition behind the fantasy that nature is balanced. Precisely, the call for seeing humans as both producers and products of the web of life is Moore's way of avoiding the misanthropic consequences of deep ecology. Nevertheless, while I wholeheartedly endorse Moore's dialectics of double internality, I also agree with Žižek's diagnosis of the subject as the impossible extimate kernel around which the symbolic field of ecology is structured. At some point the critique of the human/nature dualism produces an impasse in ecological thinking: on the one hand the independent Cartesian subject is the source of capitalist ecological crisis, and on the other hand, the independent subject is also the traumatic kernel around which ecological discourse circulates.

Another paradoxical point of convergence between Moore and Žižek can be found in their completely opposite ways of placing humans back into nature. Žižek's line of argument begins by explaining how, in ecological thinking, humanity is an "anti-nature" that disturbs or controls nature artificially, and then moves to affirm that, humans are still "part of nature" precisely because "there is no nature."[40] When Žižek claims that "there is no nature," he is implying that nature is not a preexisting positive substantial or noumenal realm independent of humans, but an incomplete, inconsistent, and dynamic struggle between competing forces. Once again, we are in the presence of an impasse produced by the simultaneous convergence and divergence between both thinkers. While Moore thinks that it is necessary to bridge the gap created by the Cartesian subject by treating humans as a peculiar kind of environment-making natural species, Žižek thinks that humanity is closest to nature "when it brutally establishes its division from nature, imposes on it its own temporary, limited order, creating its own 'sphere' within the natural multiplicity."[41] Žižek does not hesitate to embrace this paradox: if humanity is part of nature, then artificial negation of nature is also part of nature. While Moore emphasizes the need to bring forth a dialectical unity of humans and nonhumans, Žižek introduces dialectical negativity there, where humans are part of nature because nature is already denaturalized from within. While Moore criticizes the violence of abstraction, Žižek celebrates it as the infinite right of subjectivity to tear apart the inconsistent realm of natural phenomena. Instead of taking sides in these divergent interpretations of the meaning of humans' belonging to nature, I propose to treat Žižek and Moore's apparently incompatible perspectives as part of the same impasse: external humanity or antinature is internal to nature, part of nature, precisely because there is no Nature as external substantial or noumenal entity outside its environment-making relation with humans. Although I agree with Žižek's insight into the need to account for the role of the negative subject in the process of violent abstraction, I side with Moore's critique of this abstraction as directly linked to primitive accumulation and colonial/racial capitalism.

Subject and Drive

This section presents an account of the ontogenetic genesis of the subject as an empty void that never fully fits the environment in Žižek's psychoanalytically informed philosophy. Adrian Johnston provides an explanation of the ontogenetic path of Žižek's negative subject as a misfit that does not fit the environment in terms of a transition from a "subject-in-itself" to a "subject-for-itself" by means of the mediation of a third "subject-out-of-joint." Let us briefly define each of these terms. First, Johnston identifies the "subject-in-itself" with an acephalous conflict between drives within the plane of an incomplete, open, antagonistic, and unbalanced combination of material forces. In my own interpretation of double internality, I associate this plane of nature with "nature-in-humanity," an unruly and antagonistic corporeal reality. Second, the "subject-for-itself" is the subject as an empty void that is the byproduct of the failure to represent the "subject-in-itself" after the emergence of imaginary/symbolic realm of experience. This empty X relates to nature by relating to itself, and I associate it with "humanity-in-nature," the cogito-like subjectivity that tames the corporeal nature it proceeds from. Between these two subjects there is the "subject as out-of-joint" that is the main focus of this section, as the vanishing mediator between nature and culture, that emerges out of a "stubborn attachment" to operators of subjectification. This subject is the effect of "an endless drive towards nothing," and "an obstinate repetitive fixation on a contingent object that subtracts the subject from its direct immersion in reality."[42]

In the absence of any preexisting transcendent master that would guarantee a preordained chain of means and ends, the violent and impermanent material plane of bodies and fluxes contracts itself into certain objects that work as operators of subjectification (images, signs, or tools) within a multiplicity of contingent virtual possibilities. This unbalancing overinvestment in privileged operators of subjectification aims to tame and stabilize the fluctuating and disharmonious cacophony of material reality. The attempt to overcome material nature as a violent flux of existence gives birth to the "subject-out-of-joint," producing "a maladaptive inertia" that deviates "from patterns of self-preservative adaptation in relation to its enveloping environs."[43] What was once a useful and adaptive contraction in an object risks becoming a useless behavior once the environmental conditions change. In sum, the "stubborn attachment" to an object engenders a misfit "subject-out-of-joint" that does not fit the environment because is not smoothly integrated into the vital flow of material change.

As Johnston elaborates, this maladapted character alludes to "the mysterious inertia testified to by the odd persistence of non-advantageous or disadvantageous patterns in human life."[44] For instance, certain symbolic and imaginary structures recur "despite no longer possessing any utility in terms of the natural/rational self-interests of the organism."[45] The "object" of this stubborn attachment stands out against the environment as a "coagulated blockage, a point of resistance to the mundane material flow of alteration over time."[46] Bringing Moore's "extroversions" to this discussion, it is possible to interpret the exterior "tools" as so many operators of subjectification meant to stabilize the violent flow of "nature-in-humanity." The persistence of this maladapted "stubborn attachment" is nothing but what psychoanalysis calls the "death drive," the compulsive power of repetition inseparable from a malfunction in human nature, a dysfunctional disruption that results from the stubborn attachment to specific operators of subjectification. There is a dysfunctional maladaptation because material nature, or, in world-ecology parlance, "nature-in-humanity," is not a preordained cohesive, harmonious, and integrated organic unity, but a violent and chaotic plane of flows and contradictions between competing drives. This subject-out-of-joint refuses to surrender to "environmental pressures to alter adaptively so as to fit into a temporarily given milieu."[47] Moreover, the fact there is a gap between the subject and the environmental background, "the fact that a subject never fully fits its environment, it is never fully embedded in it, *defines* subjectivity."[48]

The subject-out-of-joint is "a transcendental condition of culture: a kind of malfunction which acts as a necessary vanishing mediator between nature and culture."[49] Žižek remarks that the passage from nature to culture is not direct: "[O]ne cannot account for it within a continuous evolutionary narrative: something has to intervene between the two, a kind of 'vanishing mediator,' which is neither Nature nor Culture—this In-between is silently presupposed in all evolutionary narratives."[50] In sum, neither evolutionism nor functional survivalism can explain the emergence of the subject-out-of-joint as the vanishing mediator between "nature-in-humanity" and "humanity-in-nature," because this mediation results from an excessive investment that produces its resistance to environmental adaptation, a dysfunctional fixation that prompts the subordination of the environment to certain historically contingent operators of subjectification. This dysfunctional fixation is directly related to capitalist expansion, as will become evident in the next section.

By bringing the "subject-out-of-joint" into the picture, it is possible to avoid the risk of presupposing a harmonious and balanced totality, a conflict-free divine nature. The "subject-out-of-joint" with the environment can account for its relative or illusory separation from nature while providing a mediation between an inconsistent and fragmentary "nature-in-humanity." The latter, in turn, accounts for the ideological performativity of certain "extroversions," which take the form of attachments to environmental strategies and that also function as operators of subjectification. Even if the Cartesian subject is a virtual illusion, it is an illusion that organizes actual material reality, namely, an illusion that actually steers capitalism, and has real effects on the material network of life. In sum, it is possible to think double internality in the following terms: "nature-in-humans" is an open, antagonistic, heterogeneous field of forces that prompts the emergence of excessive contractions on certain "extimate" tools or operators of subjectification, producing a virtual and insubstantial subject-out-of-joint, a subject that then exerts some causal performative power ("humans-in-nature") that in turn generates new networks or configurations. Reintroducing the notion of a virtual and insubstantial subject into double internality makes visible a sort of "metabolic loop" that takes place when the subject that results from a dysfunctional attachment relates to itself by relating to the environment. The transition from "nature-in-humanity" (the place of the subject-in-itself) into a "subject-out-of-joint" (as a mediator between "nature-in-humanity" and "humanity-in-nature") produces a third element, a "subject-for-itself," a faceless, anonymous, and virtual insubstantial X that, while being the product of extrahuman nature, proceeds to "posit its presuppositions," subordinating the environment to itself by differentiating the internal from the external world. Once the subject emerges through the interaction between the human body and the environment, the web of life becomes "mediated" by the activity of the "subject-for-itself."

This is Žižek's well-rehearsed topic of "positing the presuppositions," the retroactive loop, according to which the subject generates the very material conditions that engender and sustain it, causing a self-relating negativity that perverts/inverts the "natural" order, thus introducing a radical pathological imbalance. An unnatural X emerges out of the contradictions and tensions inherent to the web of life, via the stubborn attachment to out-of-joint objects. However, once this subject emerges, it retroactively changes its own material conditions. It is important to note that, in spite of gaining some relative autonomy or power over its material conditions, this subject is not one substance separate from another material substance, but the material substance "staring back at itself." An inherent part of Žižek's Hegelian dialectics is that the intervention of the subject is not an "external reflection" separated from the network of corporeal causes but a "reflexive determination" of this network, directly inscribed into the material Real itself. The subject is not just the separate substance, or, in dialectical parlance, an "external determination" completely separate from another substance called nature. The subject is the product of material nature that denaturalizes itself in a division where the web of life sees itself through one of its material beings. This "reflexive determination" opens up a whole new perspective on Moore's reflection on how humans are part of nature: the virtual insubstantial subject is irreducible to, yet inseparable from the material web of life because it is nothing but the web of life staring back at itself. We have, therefore, constructed a sequence that goes from nature-in-humanity (subject-in-itself) to humanity-in-nature (subject-for-itself) by means of the vanishing mediation of a virtual and insubstantial misfit (the subject-out-of-joint).

Johnston's ontogenetic perspective can help us to shed some light on Moore's double internality on the condition that we read the moment of "separation" not only as an obstacle but also as a condition of possibility that puts the subject back into the material substance: the flows of nature in humanity are the incomplete and inconsistent antagonistic field of forces that invite an excessive contraction within material reality, making possible the emergence of flows of humanity in nature, and prompting the emergence of social formations and modes of subjection/subjectification that *intervene* in nature by transforming it from within. Paradoxically, to avoid the threat of a philosophical monism that would result from the complete expulsion of an unnatural subject in its attempt to avoid dualism, it is necessary to "redouble" double internality by placing the flows of humanity-in-nature back into the flows of nature-in-humanity. The gap between nature and humanity is internal to material nature itself; the subject is the denaturalized product that is inseparable from the dysfunctional incompleteness of nature. If there is a mutual co-production of nature and humanity, it is because nature is not a balanced preexisting unity, a well-functioning complete teleological machine, but a violent fluctuation of flows that invites the emergence of a subject that is not the external reflection of material substance but its immanent distortion. The subject is not a positively given substance but the relational and transient antagonistic exchange between the human and the extrahuman that keeps the totality of capitalist ecology together.

Drive and Capitalism

The problem of the subject-out-of-joint is intertwined with Žižek's conceptualization of capitalism as drive. The stubborn attachment to a surplus value coupled with the notion of compulsive repetition allows Žižek to explain capitalism as the "Real" of "drive," that is, as the endless expanded self-reproduction of capital. Žižek interprets the formula of capital (M-C-M') in terms of a Lacanian drive where the aim is not to achieve a goal (satisfy needs) but to reproduce itself. A psychoanalytic reading of Marx's formula of capital allows Žižek to view the critique of political economy as a way of traversing the fantasy of a natural, self-engendering process by shifting from the "goal-oriented stance of consumption" (C-M-C) to the endless self-reproduction of the process (M-C-M). The ultimate aim of the process is not the satisfaction of needs, as the defenders of capitalism claim, but to reproduce itself at the expense of everything else. Žižek remarks: "Drive inheres to capitalism at a more fundamental, *systemic*, level: drive is that which propels the whole capitalist machinery, *it is the impersonal compulsion to engage in the endless circular movement of expanded self-reproduction*."[51] (The circulation of capital has no limits precisely because the goal of capital is not to satisfy human needs but the "endless" production of surplus value. The capitalist "drive belongs to no definite individual—rather, it is that those individuals who act as direct "agents" of capital (capitalists themselves, top managers) have to display it."[52] Although it could be argued that this idea of capitalist drive is nothing but a metaphor, technically, Žižek understands this drive in terms of a "'Real' that will somehow survive even under conditions of a global ecological catastrophe."[53] As a result, the "real" of capitalist reproduction works independently of the demands of reality or the environment. It is real in the sense of determining the structure of material social processes themselves, because "the fate of whole swathes of the population and sometimes of whole countries can be decided by the 'solipsistic' speculative dance of Capital that is follows its process of self-valorization with 'blessed indifference' to how its movement disrupts the environment."[54]

What is then the connection between this notion of capitalist drive and the world-ecology project? We can argue that the dysfunctional stubborn attachment to surplus value is also the motor force of capitalist ecology as an environment-making process. This drive *is* the capitalist subject-out-of-joint with the environment, whose aim is not to satisfy needs more efficiently but the endless reproduction of the process. In other words, the capitalist drive is the stubborn attachment to a surplus object-out-of-joint. It functions as a promise of value to come, parasitizing the self-reproduction of the web of life, and remains completely indifferent to the environmental consequences of this attachment. Capitalist drive is the dysfunctional short circuit in the web of life, a misfit subject-out-of-joint that results from the excessive attachment to surplus value, while creating the illusion that it posits/produces nature as something completely external and subordinated to itself, in other words, that nature is just a presupposition entirely posited by capital.

If we follow this line of reasoning, we can reformulate the conflict between the object of capital as accumulation and the subject as labor in terms that account for the ecological crisis. On a more fundamental level, the concept of ecological crisis thus shares an elemental notion not only with Žižek's notion of capitalist drive as linked to self-valorization, but also with Moore's separation as devaluation; namely, the notion that the stance of the denatu-ralization of nature, arising from the experience of a historically dated social formation, is inseparable from a violent act of devaluation that is the con-dition of capitalism as an environment-making process. In spite of making an important contribution to the understanding of the endless expansion of the self-valorization of capital in terms of a compulsory drive, Žižek has "less than nothing" to say about how both nature and workers *produce* value while being devaluated. In other words, Žižek tends to see material nature as a presupposition that is completely posited by the subject, an "imbecilic inertia of material reality," or a "flat stupid reality that is just there" that needs to be tamed by humans in a process of violent abstraction that, according to him, has to be not only celebrated but radicalized.[55] Žižek's Hegelian flights of thought make him forget the ontogenesis of the subject in favor of a pre-existing abyssal void, which sometimes works as a fetish. This explains why Žižek's attacks on ecology and his defense of the infinite right of subject's negativity to tear apart reality through abstraction are far from being mere provocations. While Moore sees the web of life as a producer and product of social formations, Žižek's conflation of static and ontogenetic analysis often sees nature purely as a product posited by capitalism.[56] Žižek's Eurocentric indifference to the way extractivist colonial/racial capitalism contributes to the creation of value must be corrected by Moore's emphasis on how every act of self-valorization of capital depends on a disproportionately larger act of material appropriation and devaluation of the unpaid labor of "women, nature and colonies." The reinscription of the subject into the world-ecology project produces the following impasse: the retroactive self-valorization of capital determines material reality, and yet, every act of creation of value proactively depends on a disproportionately greater act of capture/devaluation of the environment, not only historically but also ontologically. The object of the ecological crisis is nothing but the conflict between these two positions: the fundamental feature of today's ecological crisis is the inherent antagonism between nature as an active material condition that produces value and nature as a mere product posited by capital that erases its condition of possibility, the long history of colonial and material devaluation.

Notes

1. Moore is also the prolific author of a myriad of articles and of Patel and Moore, *History of the World*. See also Moore, *Anthropocene or Capitalocene?*
2. Moore, *Anthropocene or Capitalocene?*, 78.
3. Ibid. In this text I do not examine the polemics between Moore and the proponents of the Anhtropocene within Marxism because my aim is to examine the possible role of subjectivity in the world-ecology project. For the development of the polemics see Foster and Clark, "Marxism"; Moore, ed., *Anthropocene or Capitalocene?*; Malm, *Progress*; Cunha, "Anthropocene as Fetishism."
4. Moore, *Anthropocene or Capitalocene?* 79.
5. Ibid., 87.
6. Descartes, *Discourse on the Method*, 51.
7. Moore, *Anthropocene or Capitalocene?* 84.
8. Ibid.
9. Ibid., 88.
10. Ibid., 83.
11. Ibid., 85.
12. Ibid.
13. Ibid., 86.
14. Ibid.
15. Ibid.
16. Ibid., 87.

17. Ibid.
18. Ibid.
19. Ibid.
20. Ibid., 88.
21. Ibid., 89.
22. Ibid., 98–99.
23. Ibid., 91.
24. Ibid., 92.
25. Moore, *Capitalism*, 54.
26. Moore, *Anthropocene or Capitalocene?* 92.
27. Ibid., 90.
28. See Deleuze and Guattari, *Anti-Oedipus*; Rabinbach, *Human Motor*; Wendling, *Karl Marx*.
29. Marx, *Capital*, 1:284
30. Moore, *Capitalism*, 11.
31. Leroi-Gourhan, *Gesture and Speech*, 42.
32. Moore, *Capitalism*, 9.
33. Ibid., 12.
34. Ibid.
35. Žižek, *Less than Nothing*, 979.
36. Ibid.
37. Ibid.
38. Ibid., 373.
39. Moore, *Capitalism*, 5.
40. Žižek, *Less than Nothing*, 373.
41. Ibid.
42. Ibid., 496.
43. Johnston, *Žižek's Ontology*, 196.
44. Ibid., 183.
45. Ibid.
46. Ibid.
47. Ibid., 190.
48. Žižek, *Parallax View*, 45.
49. Žižek and Daly, *Conversations*, 80.
50. Žižek, *Ticklish Subject*, 36.
51. Žižek, *Parallax View*, 61; emphasis added.
52. Ibid.
53. Žižek, *Mapping Ideology*, 1.
54. Žižek, *Less than Nothing*, 244.
55. Ibid., 499, 643.
56. For a critique of Žižek's theme of "positing the presuppositions," see Bosteels, "Twenty Theses."

Works Cited

Bosteels, Bruno. "Twenty Theses on Politics and Subjectivity." *ZINBUN*, no. 46 (2016): 21–39.

Cunha, Daniel. "The Anthropocene as Fetishism." *Mediations* 28, no. 2 (2015): 65–77.

Deleuze, Gilles, and Félix Guattari. *Anti-Oedipus: Capitalism and Schizophrenia*. Minneapolis: University of Minnesota Press, 1983.

Descartes, René, and Ian Maclean. *A Discourse on the Method of Correctly Conducting One's Reason and Seeking Truth in the Sciences*. Oxford: Oxford University Press, 2006.

Foster, John Bellamy, and Brett Clark. "Marxism and the Dialectics of Ecology." *Monthly Review* 68, no. 5 (2016): 1–17.

Johnston, Adrian. *Žižek's Ontology: A Transcendental Materialist Theory of Subjectivity*. Evanston: Northwestern University Press, 2008.

Leroi-Gourhan, André. *Gesture and Speech*. Cambridge: MIT Press, 1993.

Malm, Andreas. *The Progress of this Storm. On Society and Nature in a Warming World*. London: Verso Books, 2017.

Marx, Karl. *Capital: A Critique of Political Economy*. Vol 1. Translated by Ben Fowkes. New York: Penguin Books, 1976.

Mies, Maria. *Patriarchy and Accumulation on a World Scale: Women in the International Division of Labour*. London: Zed Books, 2014.

Moore, Jason W. *Capitalism in the Web of Life: Ecology and the Accumulation of Capital*. London: Verso, 2015.

——, ed. *Anthropocene or Capitalocene? Nature, History, and the Crisis of Capitalism*. Oakland: PM Press, 2016.

Patel, Raj, and Jason W. Moore. *A History of the World in Seven Cheap Things: A Guide to Capitalism, Nature, and the Future of the Planet*. Berkeley: University of California Press, 2018

Rabinbach, Anson. *The Human Motor: Energy, Fatigue, and the Origins of Modernity*. Berkeley: University of California Press, 2016.

Wendling, Amy E. *Karl Marx on Technology and Alienation*. New York: Palgrave Macmillan, 2011.

Žižek, Slavoj. *Mapping Ideology*. London: Verso, 1995.

——. *The Parallax View*. Cambridge: MIT Press, 2006.

——. *The Ticklish Subject: An Essay in Political Ontology*. London: Verso, 1999.

——. *Less than Nothing: Hegel and the Shadow of Dialectical Materialism*. London: Verso, 2012.

——, and Glyn Daly. *Conversations with Žižek*. Cambridge: Polity, 2010.

CHAPTER FOURTEEN

"Non-Capital" and the Torsion of the Subject

GAVIN WALKER

The essence of the vanishing term is to disappear, but it is at the
same time that which exists the most—as Whole, as cause of itself.
Only that which is missing from a Whole can give it consistency.[1]
—ALAIN BADIOU, *Theory of the Subject*

IN HIS 1982 *Theory of the Subject*, as well as his 1985 *Peut-on penser la
politique?* Alain Badiou's dominant point, central to his reading of Hegel,
concerns the logic of "scission," a logic in which everything must be divided
between itself and its definition or representation derived from the place
it occupies, its "placement." Badiou attempts, by adding to the traditional
Marxist vocabulary of *antagonism* and *contradiction* the concept of *torsion*,
to develop a formal investigation of the capacity of the subject (or rather,
what Badiou specifies with the phrase "the subject, if such an effect exists")
not to be bound by its placement, without which everything would be purely
submitted to the law, a formal presentation to be sure, but one devoted not
solely to the formal *logic* of this torsion, but to its emergence in struggle.
This torsion of the subject on itself, an attempt to imbricate force and place
(we might *translate* "force and place" as "politics and structure"), rather than
simply the naive opposition of individual and system, is concerned above all
with how structure "works on itself," but also how this "relapse" (*Rückfalle*)

of structure is from the outset intertwined with the subjective moment of intervention. In order to ground the starting point, or moment of departure of a *political* intervention in relation to a given structure, Badiou invents the concepts of "outplace" (*horlieu*) and "splace" (*esplace*), recalling the very specific "torsion" of referral in Marx between the "interior" and "exterior" of systematicity implied in capital by the externality of the labor power commodity to the production process that paradoxically requires it *in the interior*.

This marks a crucial intervention into the logic of the impasse or aporia that nevertheless holds the structure of capital together by emphasizing that the work of the subject back on itself must *begin from* this very impasse. In Marx, although this impasse is structural or "given" by capital, nevertheless there is always an excess of subjectivation "passing through" it—as the relations of production shift in a movement over the landscape of the development of the forces of production, the innovative capacity of labor becomes more and more central to capital (to "place" in Badiou's terms), paradoxically opening up more and more the self-disclosure of the subject's capacity to intervene. This logic in Marx is fundamentally one of "supposition" and "presupposition" (*Setzung; Voraussetzung*), and it is this logic that Badiou can be seen to develop or extend into a general theory of *politics*.

In contemporary theoretical work, particularly its radical political inflection, there is a tendency to emphasize two divergent conceptions of the subject: on the one hand, following post-Heideggerian antihumanism, to emphasize the instability, inaccesibility, and even impossibility of the subject; on the other hand, following a certain humanist orientation, to uphold the militant subject as a presence, a plenitude, and the bearer of politics. However, the Marxian critique of political economy provides for a divergent mode of understanding the relation between the subject and its "placement," the capitalist accumulation process, particularly in *historical* terms. Utilizing this logic of torsion as a means to grasp another mode of entry into this fraught relation, we will pay initial attention to the peculiar category of "non-capital" (*Nichts-Kapital*) in Marx, its relation to the theory of the transition, and the theoretical effects this mode of inquiry can exert on the theory of the subject today.

"Non-Capital"

> The constraint drives the repetition. Perversion's repetition is executed through the fantasy of a vital function, which, being unintelligible, acts as a constraint; it is unintelligible because it is isolated from the organically intelligible whole.[2]—KLOSSOWSKI, *La monnaie vivante*

In her most famous work, written at the historical moment of the full-blown operation of the classical colonial system and its particular characteristic combination of imperial expropriation joined to the global export of finance capital, Rosa Luxemburg wrote, "Capital cannot accumulate without the aid of non-capitalist organizations, nor, on the other hand, can it tolerate their continued existence side-by-side with itself."[3] This formulation has often been theorized as a means to understand the specific theoretical question of *primitive* or *originary* accumulation—the peculiar and excessive violence of the initial historical moment of capital accumulation, based on social and historical forces exterior or prior to those of the establishment of exchange relations, or the sphere of circulation, as the central form of the reproduction of the social world—but we ought to note carefully that Luxemburg is in fact talking about *accumulation in general*. In other words, this tense peculiarity, whereby capital both needs and abhors *non-capital* is not solely a feature of the problem of the origin, the violent and excessive commencement at the first dawning of the thereafter-cyclical logic of the capitalist circuit; it is a problem of capital's quotidian interiority as well.

But what, in our world, can even be considered "non-capital"? After all, capital is not a thing, but a social relation, the relation of self-expanding value. As a social relation, capital is a derivation of the social order, composed by ourselves. That is, contrary to the common wisdom, which sees capital as an "alien force" and some substantial image of the human being as "originary," it is not the case. "Non-capital" does not mean some prior substance that would be usurped or perverted by the advent of capital: after all, "we" are not "non-capital," but what Marx called the "self-conscious instruments of production" (*selbstbewußten Produktionsinstrumente*), a terrifying phrase. In other words, we are a part of capital, the individual microlaboratories in which we nurture the labor power that will become, in the labor market, the inputs of variable capital for the production process. The human being is a part of capital, perhaps not wholly, but a component part of its total makeup. "Non-capital" as a term, as a concept, is barely addressed by Marx, except in one long excursus, one that is literally "at the margins" of Marx's work, even marginal within his previously *unpublished* work, and only there by negative illumination, so to speak.

In a little-remarked section of the texts on "pre-capitalist economic formations" in the *Grundrisse* manuscripts, Marx writes: "The original formation of capital does not, as is often supposed, proceed by the accumulation of food, tools, raw materials or in short, of the objective conditions of labour detached from the soil and already fused with human labour." Immediately after this seemingly innocuous point, Marx notes here, in parentheses, the following:

> Nothing is more obviously and superficially circular than the reasoning which argues (a) that the *workers* who must be employed by capital if capital is to exist as such, must first be *created* and called into life by *its* accumulation (waiting, as it were, on its "Let there be labour"); while (b) capital could not accumulate without alien labour, except perhaps its own labour. I.e., that capital might itself exist in the form of *non-capital* and *non-money*, for prior to the existence of capital, labour can only realize its value in the form of handicraft work, of petty agriculture, etc.; in short, of forms, all of which permit little or *no accumulation*, allow for only a small surplus produce, and *consume* the greater part of that. We shall have to return to the concept of "accumulation" later.[4]

What Marx points out is that the original or primitive accumulation, seen from the vantage point of classical political economy, rests on a completely circular form of reasoning according to which capital was an *inevitable*, quasi-natural development of the social landscape. In this optic, capital would be an ever-present undercurrent, constantly straining against the fetters of the social bond to emerge, and in a period of what Marx called "manufactures in the strict sense" (i.e., handicraft work with an expanded division of labor rather than artisanal precapitalist production), capital would begin to function even before its own advent, so to speak. What Marx instead points out is that without the *historical process* of separation, according to which the laborer is divorced from the previous social arrangement, capital cannot *accumulate*, and without accumulating, capital is more or less absent as a social relation. In other words, he points out that it is accumulation that releases into the world the echo of the originary separation that enables (perhaps paradoxically) a certain subjective destitution of the individual, which in turn *convokes them as a subject of capital*. In other words:

> [Capital's] *original formation* occurs simply because the historic process of the dissolution of an old mode of production, allows value, existing

in the form of *monetary wealth* to *buy* the objective conditions of labour on one hand, to exchange the *living* labour of the now free workers for money, on the other. All these elements are already in existence (*Alle diese Momente sind vorhanden*); their separation itself is a historical process (*ihre Scheidung selbst ist ein historischer Prozeß*).[5]

Capital's formation, in this sense, is not the accumulation of wealth in the commonsensical understanding, but the accumulation of the worker him- or herself. That is, we see immediately that there is no possibility to separate out the question of one's subjectivity from the broader social arrangement called "capital." Above all, we cannot say in any coherent way that capital is solely an alien force, while "the subject," (whatever that might be in the end) is a type of "non-capital." Certain tendencies in Marxist theoretical analysis imagine that we are merely passive monads dominated by the "automatic Subject" that is capital. But to say this merely restates from the other side of the equation exactly the confusion inherent to classical political economy, according to Marx. Capital is not "inhuman," but a social relation based on the accumulation *of* subjectivity:

> Capital unites the masses of hands and instruments which are already there. *This and only this is what characterizes it. It brings them together under its sway* (Es agglomeriert sie unter seiner Botmäßigkeit). This is its real accumulation; the accumulation of labourers plus their instruments at given points. We shall have to go into this more deeply when we come to the so-called accumulation of capital.[6]

Marx would eventually go much more deeply into the accumulation of capital in Volume 2 of his greatest work, when he takes up the reproduction schemes, the point on which Rosa Luxemburg began her own expansion of the theory of the accumulation process. But what is its conclusion, in short? It is that "[capital] is evidently *a relation and can only be a relation of production*."[7]

Yet, Marx also emphasizes that capital is not simply called into existence the very first time the capitalist accumulation cycle takes place, as if we could even historically encounter and isolate such a moment. Rather, capital is in gestation already *inside* social forms that are not themselves capital, but that require this catalyst of the accumulation of subjectivities to function. That is already a quite strange concept, but it is one that is crucial to an understanding of Marx's work as a critical theoretical analysis of the becoming of capitalism, the emergence of this social form as the dominant focal point of society. It concerns, above all, the transition, a question that is not raised to the level of a concept in Marx. And the fact of this peculiar nonbirth or stillbirth of the capitalist mode of production means not just that the prior forms are weirdly conditioned by capital, by their own future, but the reverse as well, that capital never quite succeeds in erasing its *peripeteia*, the twists and turns, the hazards and chances, the winding and unlikely road that led to its own emergence. In other words, the traces of the feudal order, the traces of all sorts of prior formal determinations, remain within capitalist society. They are, however, not "remnants" in the strict sense, in that they are not "out of time," but rather *displacements* or slippages. The past quite literally cannot exist in the present, so when we talk in historiographical terms about the force exerted by the past on the present, what we are talking about is a relation of force within the present accumulated by means of apparatuses that *conduct* the past into present forms. Perhaps the best way to explain this peculiar relation is by a short detour into an odd medical phenomenon. Take, for example, the situation of a woman pregnant with twins. Occasionally, after the initial diagnosis identifying not one, but two foetuses in the mother's womb, one twin's foetus essentially "disappears," becoming absorbed into the other, such that there are no longer two separate beings but now only one. And yet, in such a situation, it has sometimes happened that years later, once the individual is grown, a peculiar pain in the shoulder, for example, turns out on close analysis to be due to a secondary pair of teeth—a *remnant* of the absorbed absent twin—displaced and embedded in a divergent part of the human body. We see here something close to the understanding of "transition" that is implied in Marx.

Later, in the *Theories of Surplus Value*, he writes enigmatically that "accumulation itself merely presents as a *continuous process* what in *primitive accumulation* appears as a distinct historical process, as the process of the emergence of capital and as a transition from one mode of production to another." And this echoes his famous injunction that "[s]o-called primitive accumulation, therefore, is nothing else than *the historical process* of divorcing the producer from the means of production." In other words, it is a historical process; not a logical one. It *appears* as that which is originary, because it expresses what must come before or prior to the *historicity* of capital, insofar as this itself is expressed by that which "has happened" or that which has been inscribed into the circulation-surface. As Deleuze and Guattari once wrote, "This whole logic of preaccomplishment is concretized in the following formulation: 'In order to give a positive meaning to the idea of a 'presentiment' of what does not yet exist, it is necessary to demonstrate that what does not yet exist is already in action, in a different form than that of its existence.'"[8] Capital's historicity consists in the fact that this "memory" of enclosure is etched or inscribed into capital as the social surface, or the sphere of circulation—it is always partial due to the necessity of incessantly revisiting its origins, conjuring them up only to erase them as prior. That is, the surface resists being thrown back onto its past, and in this way constitutes the excessive force of history always surging up in the present, every time labor power is commodified.

On the one hand, for Marx, the subject must be the concentrated expression of the explosive energy of the masses, wholly contingent on the "evental" nature of politics (in the sense of "all hitherto existing history is the history of class struggle"), and on the other hand the subject must somehow simultaneously be the distillation or concentrated product of the transition from the antagonism (*Gegenstand*) between labor and capital to the contradiction (*Widerspruch*) between the development of the productive forces and their corresponding relations of production and, in this latter sense, must therefore be merely the expression or result of this inevitable historical contradiction, just a sign of the metahistorical process itself. This ruptural space, in which the rare or abyssal space of the subject flickers in and out of presence, between the "iron necessity" of capital's logic and the "random order of computation" in which capital encounters a preexisting semiotic and territorial field, always exists in a paradoxical or nonverifiable relation to the "reified" human being as political expression of the impossibility of the commodification of labor power. Yet, fundamentally, labor power does not exist in typical sense. Labor power is called into being when its use value, labor, is employed in the process of production. At that point, labor power is retrospectively made to have existed; in other words, its basic temporality is exactly the future anterior ("It will have been"). When capital needs to expand, it presumes the existence of a supply of labor power, but it conceals to itself the hazard of securing this supply. It posits for itself a semblance that fills the void and allows the circular logic of its cycle to smoothly continue.

Capital reveals a situation in which its structuring truth—labor power (and land)—is tendentially absent from it and must be forced back into it in order to "carry through" the politicality of this outsidedness. Capital's outside, what is past the line traced around the theoretical object called capital, is something that can never be separated from the object. In other words, capital cannot *be* itself without this outside called labor power. Yet labor power is not an "absolute" outside: in truth, it does not exist as such; it is produced or emerges as a "semblance" so that capital can bridge its irredeemable gap with the body of the worker or the flux of life. The "truth" of the situation called "capital" is precisely the semblance of labor power that is differentially "included" into capital's body as a foreign element. In order for capital to be whole, to be complete, capital must, paradoxically, acknowledge its own incompleteness, or testify to its parasitism. Hence, in order to incorporate the "indirect" or subcontracted production of labor power, capital must disclose this weakness. But this fact alone does not furnish a politics. All it does is acknowledge the pseudo-completeness of capital, the "banal" or "mediocre" fact that capitalism is an oscillating space of differentiation in homogeneity that "coquets" as a pure circle. Politics, however, is precisely what is excluded by the "always-already counted," by the "numerical reduction" according to which "what is there" is the guarantee or legitimation of the situation's own attempt to naturalize itself.

With the help of perhaps not the most obvious "fellow traveler"—Alain Badiou[9]—let us return and try to make sense of *another* conception of the political subject capable of incorporating into it this perverse torsion of the production of the presupposed subjectivity we share under capital.

The Torsion of the Subject

We are always inside—the margins are a myth. The language of the outside is a dream that one never stops renewing.[10]—FOUCAULT, "L'extension sociale de la norme"

Where the dream is at its most exalted, the commodity is closest to hand.[11]—ADORNO, *In Search of Wagner*

In a short text devoted to a general explication of his former teacher's thought, Quentin Meillassoux argues that Alain Badiou "represents without a doubt one of the possible becomings of Marxism, divided since its beginning between critical thought and revolutionary eschatology." He continues: "Badiou's uniqueness seems . . . to consist in the fact that he isolates from Marxism its eschatological part, separates it from its pretensions—which he judges to be illusory, based on economic science—and delivers it, ardently, to subjects distributed among all kinds of struggles, political as well as amo-rous."[12] This statement in effect expresses a general consensus among Marxists that Badiou's thought is both internal to Marxism in a broad genealogical sense, but simultaneously external to its typical trends and tendencies. This above all concerns the place of *the economic* in his thought, a question we have partially dealt with elsewhere (although much work in this direction remains to be done),[13] which in turn folds back into other questions that concern the very foundations and basic concepts of Marx's work. To state from the outset something that ought to belong to the conclusion, Badiou's thought may contain, however, paradoxical or even surprising dimensions of the Marxian critique of political economy, dimensions that might allow this work to find new avenues of development and spaces of intervention.

The status of Marxism itself holds a complex position in Badiou's work. Rather than a logical-historical system formed around a "process without a subject," as it was for his own teacher Althusser, for Badiou the problem is the precise inverse: "The object of Marxism, is none other than its subject: the political subject."[14] There is here an attempt to build a sort of formal taxonomy of Marxism itself, schematized in terms of the object of Marxist analysis—this is what Badiou refers to as "the real of Marxism." What does this "real" consist in? It is precisely the concept of "revolution." If the "real" of Marxism—in Lacanian terms, the unrepresentable, foundational element of Marxism, whose coherence is lost through its inevitable symbolization in language—is nothing other than "the revolution," the question, crucial to the difference between the Marxist orientation and all other political forms of revolutionary politics, is the relation between the situation in which such a revolution would arise—capitalist society—and the forms of subjectivity that would furnish the basis for such a break or split from its operative logic.[15]

For Badiou, this emerges around a specific relation at the center of Marxist theory, but a relation that is not immediately clear. "The bourgeoisie/proletariat antagonism designates the relation of classes as *impossible*, whereby it *delimits the real of Marxism*."[16] We have now added a new concept to this taxonomy, the "impossible" relation of class as a delimitation, a marking of the boundaries of the "real" of Marxism, that is, the revolution. This class antagonism, the crucial relation at the core of the critical analysis of capital, is here treated not as a *relation as such*, but as a sign or mark that designates this relation itself as *impossible*, a theoretical operation that is then taken from the interior of Marxist theory to its meta-exterior, and utilized as an impossibility that signifies the boundaries of this "real" of Marxism. But if the revolution is Marxism's "real," delimited by this "impossible" class relation, how and in what ways does Marxism's "object," that is, the political subject, relate to and intertwine with this conception of revolution as a project, as a goal? Here, Badiou lays out the formal contours of the problem: "The real is what the subject encounters, as its chance, its cause, and its consistency. I will come back to this triplet: chance, cause, consistency (*hasard, cause, consistance*)."[17]

This revolutionary "real" of the object of Marxism for Badiou is located in this "triplet" of chance, cause, and consistency, a sequence of terms that we should understand by means of a second "triplet" in Badiou's work:

> Marxism's field of operation has three analogical properties: it is infinite, it has torsion, and it is finite-generated. Why? First, because the event-element, which is the raw material of mass politics, is infinite. It is infinite at every moment because its theoretically-countable nature, from a political point of view, is simply fictional. Second, because repetition is interrupted by the event in order to produce in the All a different coherence of the torsion point. And finally, because the presentation elements of all politics—classes—are definitely a finite number.[18]

In order to think a certain "formal" presentation of Badiou's work on this point, we ought to overlap or superimpose these two triplets: chance, cause, consistency on the one hand, and infinity, torsion, and finite-generation on the other. What ties these two triplets together is the peculiar status of the subject for the Marxian critique of political economy, and its relation to the peculiar position of the labor power commodity within the overall logic of capital's functioning. Here, we begin from the notion that there is a scission from the outset, a division into two, the formation of a pairing. Badiou writes, "In a topology from which we might think the pair exterior/interior, what is the site of these two terms, 'bourgeosie' and 'proletariat'? Economism, which is fond of distinctions, posits the exteriority: bourgeois is whoever owns the means of production. Proletarian, whoever is separated from them and has at his disposal only his *labour power* [*force de travail*], which he sells. Now there is something that is certainly not wrong! We know what follows. This topological exteriority changes over into a functional interiority. This is the revenge of the place [*la revanche du lieu*]."[19] Badiou continues, "Torsion functions as the border limit of algebra. Torsion is perverse: subject." The algebra of the class relation is "perverted" by the rare possibility of the subject. Capital demands a structure through which the continuity of a *seeming* subject is always presumed or presupposed; anticapital/ism must begin from the standpoint of the *rarity* of the subject, precisely because the subject that is presumed by capital is always a sort of simulacrum or facsimile of the subject, that is, it presumes the subject as if it were a continuity, rather than a rupture.

The concept of "scission"—we should keep in mind the proximity of "scission" to Marx's understanding of "separation," which we touched on earlier—plays a crucial role in Badiou's conception of the subject, not only as a conceptual innovation in the domain of politics, but as a central element in his intervention into the Hegelian dialectic. He writes, "At the heart of the Hegelian dialectic we must disentangle two processes, two concepts of movement, and not just one proper view of becoming that would have been corrupted by a subjective system of knowing. Thus: a) a dialectical matrix covered by the term alienation; the idea of a simple term which unfolds itself in its becoming-other, in order to come back to itself as an achieved concept. b) a dialectical matrix whose operator is the scission, and whose theme is that there is no unity that is not split [*il n'y a d'unité que scindé*]. There is not the least bit of return into itself, nor any connection between the final and the inaugural."[20] Already here we have an important rejoinder to the theory of alienation, the foundational concept on which the naive humanist concept of the subject—so remote from that theorized in Marx's understanding of the accumulation process—is grounded. But if we are not to conceive of the subject's inaccessible grasp of itself as simply alienated from it by means of some structural, external feature, which, once overturned, would rejoin its harmonious essence, how are we to think about the political subject, so radically absent in our conjuncture?

Badiou makes a wager that only a formalist presentation of this question can enter into its essence, and develops this point at some length, even within a sort of quasi-mathematical logic (quite unlike that which we will see deployed particularly in *Being and Event*). Let A stand for "something"— this "something" must be located within its own proper identification or surrounding structure, to which Badiou will give the term P. Ap therefore, expresses the location of something within its index of identification, or its "place." This term P, which expresses the totality of the forms of identification or predication of a given something or A, provides us with a glimpse of the "space of placement" obtaining for A, what Badiou names with the neologism "splace" (*esplace*; "espace de placement"). This split of self and self as determined is represented as follows: A = A Ap. In other words, A is never wholly unto itself, but always accompanied by an inner scission, A Ap. A thus works back on itself, or Ap = A Ap with Ap recurring onto its own "place" within this formal presentation. We might call this the capacity of the subject to not be *completely* bound by its "placement," without which everything would be purely submitted to the law—but this is a formal presentation, and nothing ever emerges in this formal manner, but in struggle.

Badiou takes from this formalist presentation not only a way of talking about the relationship of subject and structure—or politics and the social background—he also derives from it a formal presentation of typological political orientations within the Marxist paradigm. Thus, "rightwing deviation" (associated with the proper name of Liu Shaoqi) consists in an excessive obsession with structure P, or what we would otherwise call an "economism," the naive belief that simply by altering certain structural features of the economy—but ignoring cultural education and political development at the ideological level—the political subject of the future order will simply emerge as a secondary effect. On the other hand, the "leftwing deviation" (associated in classical Cultural Revolution *dramatis personae* with the name of Lin Biao—and who could forget the author of that most hyper-subjectivist of global '68 pamphlets *Let the Peoples of Africa, Asia, and Latin America Drop the Spiritual Atom Bomb of People's War*) would instead be an excessive obsession with subject's givenness and freedom, with the all-powerful possibility of political consciousness as the sole determining factor of historical development (that is, "A" with no predicates).

Yet, Badiou is careful not to imagine that it is something easy or simple to chart a pathway between the Scylla of "A" and the Charybdis of "P." He instead draws particular attention to a form of "relapse" in the Hegelian sense that he calls the "revenge of place"—the "topological exteriority changes over into a functional interiority"—which is no less than a formal, generic mode of posing the problem of labor power within the Marxian register, a problem whereby one must locate the political potential of the overturning of the scenario in the same site wherein the apparent "subject" is nothing more than a side effect of its own full placement within the structure. After all, in capitalist society, labor power ends up as nothing more than the form of variable capital, which it takes when its use-value, labor, is utilized as an input in the production process. The structure vengefully rears its head exactly at the moment the proletariat thinks it is free.[21]

In some sense, this is a concept of the "empty case," that which is "punched out" of a hole in the systematic presence of the structure, which itself is held together by something lacking. For Badiou—and clearly for Marx—it is not that there is some simple lack at the center of the social structure, it is rather that the structure consistently misidentifies and even *misses* its own center. But in broad theoretical terms, such modes of analysis share with a variety of philosophical genealogies the notion of the logic of an impasse or aporia that paradoxically holds the structure together—where Marx (and later Badiou in this theory of torsion) provides for us a point of departure from the existing binary structure of the theoretical humanities is the intuition that the work of the subject back on itself must begin from this impasse, that the subject's forced absence or ontological destitution is precisely the precursor or condition of possibility that then forms the surrounding atmosphere for the possibility of politics.

In Marx, this logic is complex but central to the entire enterprise—insofar as the social impasse is structural, nevertheless there is always an excess "passing through" of this moment of structural rupture. As the relations of production shift, the innovative capacity of labor becomes more and more central to capital (P, or "place"), rendering more and more rare the subject's explosive capacity, but producing more and more instances wherein its instability is traversed. It is impossible to say that this is still an overestimation of P, as in the economism associated with the name of Liu Shaoqi, because capital is nothing less than the hard kernel of A, wherein P must paradoxically be knitted together by something belonging to A, the labor power commodity whose use-value is precisely the labor employed as variable capital in the production cycle. Therefore, A and P are always implied as the overall schema A Ap and cannot be disaggregated. And yet by the intensification of this schema's density, the possibility of A comes more and more to the forefront—"The existence in action of the contradiction between splace and outplace, whatever they are, is the scission of the outplace. Scission is that by which the term is included in the place as out-of-place."[22] What is included in place (structure) as out-of-place is nothing less than the subjective dimension of labor power, which must be interior to P in order to hold it together, but whose repetition cannot be guaranteed except by an appeal to an entire series of suppositions and presuppositions that function only internal to A, to its individuality and singularity. Such a theoretical structure provides a very different understanding of the relation of the subject and its placement than that of the simple opposition of humanism and antihumanism.

In contemporary theoretical work, it is frequently Foucault who is appealed to when we seek to think the implosion of the plenitude of the humanist subject, while those who uphold some imagination of the political subject as a necessary form are often vilified for this "traditional" or "metaphysical" stance. But what does Foucault even propose vis-à-vis the genealogy of thought in which he would situate himself?

> Bataille in a way, Blanchot in his own manner, Klossowski too also shattered, in my view, this founding self-evidence of the subject and created forms of experience in which the shattering and annihiliation of the subject, the reaching of its limits, its spillage beyond its limits plainly showed that it did not have the original self-sufficient form philosophy classically attributed to it.[23]

It is impossible to disagree with Foucault here, unless one adhered to the most naive and credulous conception of the social. But did we not see exactly how Marx already bridged these two conceptions? The "founding self-evidence of the subject" has been in doubt since Hegel, if not before. What Marx emphasized for us is not that the proletarian subject is some harbinger of the good society, simply and obviously synonymous with the empirical worker, but that such a proletarian subject is strictly *absent* within the accumulation of subjectivity that is interior to capital. Because Marx treats the empirical worker not as a subject, but as the "guardians" (*Hütern*) or "bearers" (*Träger*) of labor power, the peculiar dynamic of inclusion and exclusion that brings capital and the subject into relation is precisely this type of torsion that Badiou so carefully theorized.

While we can say with no uncertainty that it is today nearly impossible to imagine some founding plenitude and originary substantiality of the subject, the political limits of this insight remain significant. What shall we do with this liminal, self-undermining, fragmented, and indeed *illusory* conception of subjectivity? How can such an understanding of the unstable realm of the subject assist in practical interventions wherein *there is a subject to be found*? In practical terms, subjects of political processes do in fact emerge. We can of course admit that they are retroactively convoked *as* subjects, in Badiou's terms, but nevertheless their emergence and function is neither impossible nor void: it functions in spite of this inherent slippage, which, for example, the theory of translation sees in its misidentification of the schema of substance, which the critique of political economy sees in the peculiar retroactive determination of the labor power commodity, or which psychoanalysis sees in the subject as an effect, not the origin, of the drive. But in all these circumstances, linked to the force of intervention around the advances of theoretical antihumanism, what possibility remains for politics, which is, at base, another term for the subjective intervention into or against the circumstances that gave rise to it? So we face in some sense a paradox, one in which we are torn between the negative identification of the subject as an *effect* that masquerades as an originary substance, and a positive identification of the subject as a necessary part of a process that *had to have happened,* and therefore must have been there from the start, always in this "future anterior" tense. It is not merely a confrontation between "humanism" and "antihumanism"—the theoretical naivety of the humanist conception of the subject has long since been established in thought. But it is perhaps a question of forcing into existence another conception of the political con-sequences of antihumanism than simply its immediate applicability to the immediate scenario. What we lack is a theory of *levels of analysis* that allows us to understand the logical, historical, and politically practical dimensions of the subject, this concept that seems to haunt us, returning with the force of necessity at exactly the conceptual point at which it appeared to have been exhausted.

In other words, are we cursed to wander the theoretical landscape of today, torn between the "impossible" plenitude of the subject, and the naive humanist belief that we ourselves are immediately accessible subjects of history? What Marx shows us in the peculiarity of the accumulation process—with its commencement in the contortions of the so-called primitive accumulation—is that there is, in some strong sense, an entirely separate mode of understanding the torsion of the subject and its surrounding structure, derived from the very dynamics of capitalist society, yet not reducible to them. Capital provides us with a structure that itself acts as if it contains no exteriorities whatsoever, while openly relying precisely on labor power and land, which it cannot internally produce. Such a structure, in which we might even say that *misrecognition* is the only self-consciousness available—or more rigorously that misrecognition is not its disabling Achilles' Heel, but the very motor-force of the structure itself—we cannot say that all subjective intervention is foreclosed. Rather, it is a structure that *imagines itself* as closed, but which, through precisely the recurrent accumulation process, discloses the possibility of the emergence of a subject of politics.

Badiou's work emphasizes that there is here a torsion through which the "real of revolution" discloses itself precisely *through* the impossibility of the class relation, but it is also this structure of "relapse" that provides an image of how the subject, and therefore political organization both must persist and yet undermine itself. Here we might recall the strange formulation of Mao: "The Communist Party and the democratic parties are all products of history. What emerges in history disappears in history. Therefore, the Communist Party will disappear one day, and so will the democratic parties. Is this disappearance so unpleasant? In my opinion, it will be very pleasant. I think it is just fine that one day we will be able to do away with the Communist Party and the dictatorship of the proletariat. Our task is precisely to hasten their extinction."[24]

To cut a long theoretical story short, the subject that appears in history as the subject of the exchange process, will disappear in history too. Badiou reminds us that the critique of political economy is not the mere analysis of capitalism's functioning, its perverse character in which all instabilities are smoothed over in the form of exchange, but also a theoretical tool for the possibility of a proletarian politics. Here, Badiou produces a specific homology—just as a proletarian politics hinges on the paradoxical elimination of "every place wherein something like a proletariat could be composed," so too the question of political organization depends on building an apparatus in order to "hasten the extinction" of the apparatus itself. This is Badiou's innovation in the concept of the subject's rarity—a concept through which he reminds us that the critique of political economy is not a set of insights into capital's logical motion, but a blueprint that shows us capital's ontological "weak link" in the form of labor power or variable capital. In this sense, Badiou's basic perspective, building on the Marxian schematics of the place of the subject within the critique of political economy, echoes the following extremely clear, powerful, and politically important statement of one of the most supposedly "theoreticist," "abstract," and "apolitical" figures in the history of Marxist political economy, Uno Kozo:

> The pure theory of capitalism must represent the capitalist commodity economy as if it were a self-perpetuating entity in order to divulge the laws of its motion. It therefore seems to me completely impossible for economic theory to demonstrate at the same time a transformation that involves the denial of those laws. I certainly do not mean that economic theory, for this reason, should assert the permanence of capitalist society.... But neither the pure theory of capitalism nor empirical studies of an actual capitalist economy, nor for that matter the stage-theoretical analysis of capitalist development, offer *an economic explanation* of the process of the transition from capitalism to socialism. *This is the role of the subject in the organizational practice of the socialist movement*—the practice of this subject is not a process of mere clarification of economic necessity but rather is the utilization of the social sciences, the basis of which is political economy, to the greatest extent possible within the movement.... In any case, whether or not the victory of socialism is necessary depends on the practice of the socialist movement itself, and not directly on the economic laws of motion of capitalist society. But with the economic laws of motion, the class-character [*kaikyūsei*] of capitalist society is laid bare, and this throws light on the general economic foundation of the class-character of previous societies, and thus at the same time clarifies the historicity [*rekishisei*] of capitalist society. It is on the basis of this knowledge that socialist movements can scientifically assert the necessity of the transformation of capitalist society.[25]

We should remind ourselves here of Lenin's great line, "Politics is the concentrated expression of economics," but not to simply imbricate these dimensions: the displacement of the economic sphere for an overemphasis on politics leads to a blind subjectivism; but equally the reduction of politics to a mere outcome of the economic process is simply an economism, imagining social change in secular Calvinist terms, as fully preordained by the cosmic order. The question of the subject—the political subject—is not a search for an eternal substance that we could fantastically discover ourselves as, but rather the search for this *rare, nearly-impossible* position that would provide us a point of entry into the necessity of a politics of *struggle,* precisely because capitalism will never collapse on its own. What better expression of the essential problem of the rare but precious political subject, situated in the volatile flow of the accumulation process, could we find, than another famous dictum of Mao? "If you don't hit it, it won't fall."

Notes

1. Badiou, *Theory of the Subject*, 64.
2. Klossowski, *La monnaie vivante* (unpaginated).
3. Luxemburg, *The Accumulation of Capital*, 345.
4. Marx, *Marx-Engels Werke*, Bd. 42, 413–14.
5. Ibid., 414.
6. Ibid., 415.
7. Ibid., 421.
8. Deleuze and Guattari, *A Thousand Plateaus*.
9. The reason is simply that the relation between the thought of Badiou and the political-economic work of the Marxist tradition is tense and unresolved. No one has done more work to think the stakes of Marxism for Badiou's thought than Bruno Bosteels. See his crucial *Badiou and Politics*, along with numerous other writings.
10. Foucault, "L'extension sociale de la norme," 77.
11. Adorno, *In Search of Wagner*, 91.
12. Meillassoux, "History and Event in Alain Badiou."
13. Walker, "On Marxism's Field of Operation."
14. Badiou, *Théorie du sujet*, 145; *Theory of the Subject*, 127.
15. I would take another opportunity to develop further these formulations of Badiou as an attempt to make a formal, internal logic of Marxism as a political doctrine.
16. Badiou, *Theory of the Subject*, 127; *Théorie du sujet*, 145.
17. Ibid.

18. Badiou, *Théorie du sujet*, 170.

19. Badiou, *Theory of the Subject*, 154.

20. Badiou, *Theory of the Subject*, 3–4; *Théorie du sujet*, 21–22.

21. It would be instructive to think the relation between Badiou's "revenge of place" as the reappearance of the dominant structure at precisely the moment of apparent subjective freedom in contrast to Karatani's thesis that it is exactly the position of selling labor power when the capitalist is dependent on these potential inputs of variable capital, that the proletariat is in a position of power. See Karatani, *Architecture as Metaphor*.

22. Badiou, *Theory of the Subject*, 15; *Théorie du sujet*, 33.

23. Foucault, "La scène de la philosophie," 590.

24. Mao Zedong, "On the Ten Major Relationships," 1956. See for a development of this point Walker, "The Body of Politics" and "Limits and Openings of the Party."

25. Uno Kozo, *UKc*, vol. 2, 163–64.

Works Cited

Adorno, Theodor W. *In Search of Wagner*. Translated by Rodney Livingstone. London: New Left Books, 1981.

Badiou, Alain. *Théorie du sujet*. Paris: Seuil, 1982.

———. *Peut-on penser la politique?* Paris: Seuil, 1985.

———. *Theory of the Subject*. Translated by Bruno Bosteels. London: Bloomsbury, 2013.

Bosteels, Bruno. *Badiou and Politics*. Durham and London: Duke University Press, 2009.

Deleuze, Gilles, and Félix Guattari. *Mille plateaux*. Paris: Minuit, 1980.

———. *A Thousand Plateaus*. Translated by Brian Massum. Minneapolis: University of Minnesota Press: 1987.

Foucault, Michel. "La scène de la philosophie." In *Dits et écrits II, 1976–1988*, edited by Daniel Defert and François Ewald, 571–94. Paris: Gallimard, 2001.

———. "L'extension sociale de la norme." In *Dits et écrits II, 1976–1988*, edited by Daniel Defert and François Ewald, 74-78. Paris: Gallimard, 2001.

Karatani Kōjin. *Architecture as Metaphor: Language, Number, Money*. Translated by Sabu Kohso. Cambridge: MIT Press, 1995.

Klossowski, Pierre. *La monnaie vivante*. Paris: Éric Losfeld, 1970.

Luxemburg, Rosa. *The Accumulation of Capital*. London: Routledge, 2003.

Mao Zedong. *Selected Works*, 5 volumes. Beijing: Foreign Languages Press, 1975.

———. *Miscellany of Mao Tse-Tung Thought (1949–1968)*. Springfield: Joint Publications Research Service, 1974.

Marx, Karl, and Frederick Engels. *Collected Works*, 50 vols. Moscow, London, and New York: Progress Publishers, Lawrence and Wishart, and International Publishers, 1975–2009.

Marx, Karl, and Friedrich Engels. *Werke*, 40 vols. Berlin: Dietz Verlag, 1962.

Meillassoux, Quentin. "History and Event in Alain Badiou." *Parrhesia: A Journal of Critical Philosophy*, no. 12 (2011): 1–11.

Uno Kozo. *Uno Kozo chosakushū*, 11 vols. Tokyo: Iwanami Shoten, 1973.

——. *Principles of Political Economy*. Translated by Thomas Sekine. New Jersey: Harvester Press, 1980.

Walker, Gavin. "The Body of Politics: On the Concept of the Party." *Theory and Event* 16, no.4 (2013): np.

——. "The Dignity of Communism: Badiou's Communist Hypothesis." *Socialism and Democracy* 25, no. 3 (2011): 130–39.

——. "Limits and Openings of the Party: A Reply to Jason E. Smith." *Theory and Event* 16, no. 4 (2013): np.

——. "On Marxism's Field of Operation: Badiou and the Critique of Political Economy" *Historical Materialism* vol. 20, no. 2, (2012): 39-74.

——. "The Regime of Translation and the Figure of Politics" *Translation: A Transdisciplinary Journal*, no. 4, (2014): 30–52.

Contributors

ABRAHAM ACOSTA is associate professor of Spanish and Portuguese at the University of Arizona. He is author of *Thresholds of Illiteracy: Theory, Latin America, and the Crisis of Resistance* (Fordham University Press, 2014).

KAREN BENEZRA is junior professor of Art, Theory, and Critique at the Leuphana University of Lüneburg. She is author of *Dematerialization: Art and Design in Latin America* (University of California Press, 2020) and an editor of *ARTMargins* (MIT Press).

ORLANDO BENTANCOR is associate professor of Spanish and Latin American Studies at Barnard College. He is author of *The Matter of Empire: Metaphysics and Mining in Colonial Peru* (University of Pittsburgh Press, 2017).

BRUNO BOSTEELS is professor of Latin American and Iberian Cultures and of the Institute for Comparative Literature and Society at Columbia University. He is author of *Marx and Freud in Latin America: Politics, Psychoanalysis, and Religion in Times of Terror* (Verso Books, 2012), *Badiou and Politics* (Duke University Press, 2011) and *The Actuality of Communism* (Verso Books, 2011).

IRINA ALEXANDRA FELDMAN is associate professor of Spanish at Middlebury College. She is author of *Rethinking Community from Peru. The Political Philosophy of Jose María Arguedas* (Pittsburgh University Press, 2014).

ALESSANDRO FORNAZZARI is associate professor of Hispanic Studies at the University of California—Riverside. He is author of *Speculative Fictions: Chilean Culture, Economics, and the Neoliberal Transition* (University of Pittsburgh Press, 2013).

DAVID KAZANJIAN is professor of English and Comparative Literature at the University of Pennsylvania. He is author of *The Colonizing Trick: National*

Culture and Imperial Citizenship in Early America (University of Minnesota Press, 2003) and *The Brink of Freedom: Improvising Life in the Nineteenth-Century Atlantic World* (Duke University Press, 2016).

HORACIO LEGRÁS is professor of Spanish and Portuguese at the University of California—Irvine. He is author of *Literature and Subjection: The Economy of Writing and Marginality in Latin America* (University of Pittsburgh Press, 2008), and *Culture and Revolution. Violence, Memory, and the Making of Modern Mexico* (University of Texas Press 2017).

JAIME ORTEGA REYNA is a researcher at Universidad Autónoma Metropolitana—Xochimilco (Mexico). He is author of *Leer* El Capital, *teorizar la política: Contrapunteo de la obra de Enrique Dussel y Bolívar Echeverría en tres momentos* (Universidad Nacional Autónoma de México, 2018) and *La incorregible imaginación: La recepción de Althusser en América Latina* (Doble Ciencia, 2019).

PABLO PÉREZ WILSON is an independent researcher based in New York City. He is the editor of two journal special issues dedicated to the work of Marilena Chauí and León Rozitchner, respectively.

MARCELO STARCENBAUM is a researcher at Universidad Nacional de La Plata (Argentina). He is editor of Mauricio Malamud's *Escritos, 1969–1987* (Editorial Doble Ciencia, 2017) and co-editor of *Lecturas de Althusser en América Latina* (Editorial Doble Ciencia, 2017).

MASSIMILIANO TOMBA is professor of History of Consciousness at the University of California—Santa Cruz. His latest books are *Marx's Temporalities* (Brill, 2012), *Attraverso la piccolo porta. Quattro studi su Walter Benjamin* (Mimesis, 2017) and *Insurgent Universality: An Alternative Legacy of Modernity* (Oxford, 2019).

SERGIO VILLALOBOS-RUMINOTT is professor of Spanish at the University of Michigan–Ann Arbor. He is author of *Soberanías en suspenso. Imaginación y violencia en América Latina* (La Cebra, 2013), *Heterografías de la violencia. Historia, nihilismo, destrucción* (La Cebra, 2016) and *La desarticulación. Epocalidad, hegemonía e historicidad* (Ediciones Macul, 2019).

GAVIN WALKER is associate professor of History and Classical Studies at McGill University. He is author of *The Sublime Perversion of Capital: Marxist Theory and the Politics of History in Modern Japan* (Duke University Press, 2016) and editor of *The Japanese '68. Theory, Politics, Aesthetics* (Verso Books, 2020).

Index

abigarramiento (becoming motley), 18, 21, 77, 138, 146–47, 150
acculturation, 95, 107n1. *See also* transculturation
accumulation, and subject/subjectivity, 1–2, 13–14, 22n2. *See also* class; historical development, and accumulation; postmigrancy; total conversion; transculturation
accumulation by dispossession: overview of, 46, 85–86n19; critique, 176–77, 178, 179–80, 183, 186, 192n25. *See also* dispossession
Acosta, Abraham, 18–19, 233–51
activism, and femicide in Ciudad Juárez, 217, 218, 226–27, 229n21
Adelman, Irma, 83–84n6
Adorno, Theodor W., 302
aesthetic representation, and films, 180, 182, 188–89, 190n14
agency, 58, 59, 265, 268–69, 283, 284
Alemán, Jorge, 7
Althusser, Louis: class struggle, 165; conjuncture, 15; finite theory, 138, 151n3; forces of production, 138, 140, 144, 151n3; Marxism and, 256, 258, 303; mode of production debates, 79, 80, 86n22, 87n25; socioeconomic formation in 1960s and 1970s, 126–27, 128, 129, 130–31; theory of the subject, 265, 269

Americas: antidispossessive politics, 60–61; dispossession, 50, 51–57; posthegemony and, 240–41, 249n18; primitive/originary accumulation, 45, 58, 60; Yucatán dispossession case, 46, 52–58, 60. *See also* Andean region; indigenous (Indian) communities; Latin America; *and specific communities, and countries*
Andean region: capitalism's philosophy of history, 70, 71; hybrid subsumption and, 97–98, 109n18; mode of production debates, 78, 85n14; transculturation and, 91, 92, 93, 94–95, 100–104, 107n1; utopianism, 92, 97, 100. *See also* Peru
Anderson, Kevin, 125–26
Anthias, Penelope, 177
anthropology, 10, 93–94, 105–7, 108n5, 108n7. *See also* total conversion
antidispossessive politics, 45, 46, 49, 57–58, 60–61. *See also* dispossession
anti-imperialism, 73–74, 178, 180–81, 183, 189, 190n14. *See also* imperialism
Argentina: cultural scene, 195, 198–99, 200, 201, 202, 204; neoliberalism, 4, 8, 11–12, 13; social democracy, 3, 4; socioeconomic formation in 1960s and 1970s, 3, 4, 5, 22n2, 118, 119. *See also* Cuadernos de Pasado y Presente; *and specific social theorists*

class: overview of, 167nn5–6; accumulation and, 155, 162, 163, 168n11;
capitalism and, 3, 4–5, 10–11; class
composition, 11–12, 158, 161, 163;
class struggle, 156, 159, 161, 165, 166;
cultural studies, 158–59, 166, 167n6;
displacement of class, 155–56, 167n1,
167n3; historical-political context,
10–12, 156–57, 162–63, 164, 167; middle
class, 156, 161–62, 165–66; neoliberalism critique, 155, 158, 159–60, 163–64;
peasants, 76, 162–63, 165; politics/
political theory and, 1, 4, 6–7, 8–9;
proletarian and, 72, 81, 99, 106. *See
also* peasants; working class
class and totality in Marxism: overview
of, 17–18; totality, 14, 117–18, 126, 128,
129, 131, 138. *See also* Aricó, José; capitalism; class; Cuadernos de Pasado y
Presente; socioeconomic formation
class composition, 11–12, 158, 161, 163.
See also class; class and totality in
Marxism
Clastres, Pierre, 85n17
La cola del diablo (Aricó), 4, 22n5
collective subject/subjectivity, 13, 20, 100,
104, 181, 183
"Comments on James Mill" (Marx), 197,
209n5
commons, 38–40, 47, 49, 50–51, 62n22
communitarianism, 70, 77–78, 179–80,
186, 192n34
consumer capitalism, 216, 222–23, 225
"Contra la poesía" (Gombrowicz), 198,
200
*A Contribution to the Critique of Political
Economy* (Marx), 78, 120, 122, 130, 143
Cortés, Martín, 6, 13–14, 120, 122, 130
Coulthard, Glen Sean, 50
credit: creditor-debtor relationship, 196,
197, 198, 208, 209; financialization,
161–62; Marxism, 201; money and,
198, 199. *See also* debt
Crespo, Horacio, 120
crisis of Marxism, 17, 18, 138, 140, 141,
150

"Critique of the Hegelian Dialectic and
Philosophy as a Whole" (Marx), 257
Cuadernos de Pasado y Presente (Past
and Present Notebooks, 1968–83):
Aricó as director/editor, 22n2, 83n4,
118, 119; *A Contribution to the Critique of Political Economy* (Marx),
120–21, 122; *El porvenir de la comuna
rural rusa* (Marx and Engels), 124;
Pre-Capitalist Economic Formations
(Marx), 120, 121, 122; *Revelaciones
sobre la historia secreta del siglo
XVIII* (Cuaderno 1), 120, 124; Russia,
122, 131; socioeconomic formation
and, 120–21, 122. *See also* socioeconomic formation in 1960s and 1970s,
and Cuadernos de Pasado y
Presente
Cueva, Agustín, 137, 138

Danielson, Nikolai, 124–25
debt: overview of, 19, 196–97; circulation
and, 199–200, 201, 203, 204, 210n10;
creditor-debtor relationship, 196,
197, 198, 208, 209; exchange value,
207, 212n45; finance capital and,
19, 195–96; language and, 200, 202,
210n10; money and, 196, 198, 199;
queer debt, 196, 209; subject/subjec-
tivity and, 195, 196–97, 208, 209; time
and, 196, 200, 202–3; violence and,
197, 206, 208. *See also* credit
decolonial theory, 84n13, 177, 178–79, 181,
186, 191n19
del Barco, Óscar, 81, 83n4
Deleuze, Gilles, 7, 82n2, 200, 280,
300–301
dependency theory, 74–76, 83n6,
84nn11–12, 84n13, 138, 151n2
deportation of migrants, 234, 235, 248.
See also Central American migrants/
migration, and United States;
migrants/migration
Derrida, Jacques, 228, 265
Descartes, René, and Cartesian dualism:
theory of the subject, 263, 267, 268;

world-ecology project, 276–77, 283, 284, 285, 288

development theory, 71–73, 83n6

Diary (Gombrowicz), 200, 202, 210n10

differentiations, and subsumption, 28, 31–32, 35–36

displacement of class, and accumulation, 155–56, 167n1, 167n3

dispossession: overview of, 16, 17, 19, 45–46; agency and, 58, 59; Americas, 50, 51–57; antidispossessive politics, 45, 46, 49, 57–58, 60–61; asylum law in U.S. and, 59–60; commons, 49, 50–51, 62n22; indigenous/Indian communities, 46, 52–57, 58, 60; not-yet-present/present and, 46, 57–58, 60–61; primitive/originary accumulation and, 46–48, 54–55, 58–59; prior possession and, 45, 49, 50, 51, 54, 61n7; property theft, 48–49, 50–52, 54; slave labor and, 52–57; social stratification and, 91, 106; the state and, 39, 53–54; subject/subjectivity and, 49–51, 55–56; Yucatán dispossession case, 46, 52–58, 60. *See also* accumulation by dispossession

double internality, and world-ecology project, 280–84, 285, 286, 288, 289

Driver, Alice, 223

DuBois, W. E. B., 46

Dussel, Enrique, 83n4, 144

Echeverría, Bolívar, 82n2, 83nn3–4, 85n18, 142

economy, and economic migrants to U.S., 239, 240, 245. *See also* political economy; political economy critique

El concepto de formación económico-social (Cuaderno 39), 126, 130

El porvenir de la comuna rural rusa (Engels), 124

El porvenir de la comuna rural rusa (Marx), 124

emancipation: asynchronisms and, 35–40; capitalism and, 261; dispossession and, 49; peasants and, 236, 237–38; working class and, 123–24. *See also* freedom and rightlessness

Engels, Friedrich, 122–23, 124–25, 258, 260–61, 263

England, 27, 36–37, 97, 106, 123, 238

enslaved Africans, and dispossession case, 46, 52–57, 58, 60. *See also* slave labor

environmental crisis, 275, 278–79, 282. *See also* world-ecology project

Escritos sobre Rusia (Marx and Engels), 124

eventalized theories, 262–63, 264

exchange value, 176, 180, 192n34, 207, 212n45

exploitation: overview of, 2, 10, 33–35, 70, 75; capitalism, 31, 32, 37, 237–38, 243; feudalism, 37, 237–38; formal subsumption, 28, 76, 96; hybrid subsumption and, 33, 97, 108–9n16, 109n18; "non-capital"/noncapitalist communities and, 97, 110n25; wage labor, 10, 12, 74, 75, 98

Faletto, Enzo, 74, 83n6

Fanon, Franz, 70

Favilli, Paolo, 128

Federici, Silvia, 242

Feldman, Irina Alexandra, 19–20, 175–94

femicide in Ciudad Juárez, Mexico: overview of, 14, 19, 215; activism and, 217, 218, 226–27, 229n21; consumer capitalism and, 216, 222–23, 225; data, 217–18, 229n12; discourse and, 224–26, 227–28; *feminicidio* defined, 215–16; financialization, 220–21; governmentality, 216, 218, 219, 221–22; juridical sphere, 216, 217, 220, 223, 225; justice/injustice, 216, 217, 220, 226, 227; neoliberalism, 219, 220; ordinary psychoses and, 223–24, 229n35; patriarchy and, 219–20, 221–22; psychotic violence, 216–17, 221, 222, 229n5; state violence and, 220, 223, 228, 229n21

Ferdydurke (Gombrowicz), 202, 203,
210n10
Fernández Diaz, Osvaldo, 80
feudalism: capitalism and, 71–73, 83n6,
140, 152n7; mode of production debates
and, 162–63; transition in mode of
production and, 36–39, 71, 72–73, 76,
77–78, 237–38. *See also* peasants
Feuerbach, Ludwig Andreas von, 261–62,
266
films, and politics/political theory: overview of, 14, 15, 19–20, 178, 189n5; aesthetic representation, 180, 182, 188–89,
190n14; anti-imperialism, 180–81, 183,
189, 190n14; collective subject/sub-
jectivity, 181, 183; indigenous/Indian
communities' representations, 181–83,
184, 185–86, 190nn14–15, 191n21,
191n24; *Juana Azurduy, guerrillera de
la Patria Grande* [prod. Sanjinés and
Ukamau, 2016] (film), 190n14; *plano
secuencia integral* (integral long take),
181, 183, 184, 191n21, 191n24; political
subject, 184–85; *Yawar Mallku* [prod.
Sanjinés and Ukamau, 1969] (film),
182. See also *Insurgentes* [prod. Sanjinés and Ukamau, 2012] (film); *and
specific film producers*
finance capital, 12–13, 19, 146, 195–96,
202, 208
financialization, 161–62, 196, 208, 220–21
finite theory, 138, 151n3
Flores Galindo, Alberto, 100
forces of production: capitalism and,
141–46, 149, 150, 152nn14–15, 153n18;
Marxism and, 79, 141–43, 144, 145,
152n14, 152nn14–15; socioeconomic
formation and, 120–21, 125, 146. *See
also* labor/labor power
Formaciones económicas precapitalistas
(Marx), 78
formal subsumption: capitalism and,
243; English working class and, 27,
36–37; exploitation and, 28, 76, 96;
global migration and, 243, 245, 248;
historical-political context, 27–28, 77,
78; Marxism and, 27, 32, 33, 76, 96, 243;
subsumption and, 27–28, 32, 33, 40
Fornazzari, Alessandro, 19, 195–213
Foucault, Michel: governmentality and
the father, 221–22; history of the present, 57–58; social formation/relation,
302, 307–8; theory of the subject, 255,
263, 265, 267–68, 272n21
Fowkes, Ben, 236
freedom and rightlessness, 236–37, 238–
39, 247–48. *See also* emancipation
Fregoso, Rosa-Linda, 216
French structuralism, and Cuaderno,
119, 126, 129, 132
Freud, Sigmund, 12, 80, 221, 222, 257,
262, 269
Furtado, Celso, 84n12

Gago, Verónica, 8, 11–13, 204, 207
Garavaglia, Juan Carlos, 84n8, 129–30
García Linera, Álvaro: accumulation
by dispossession critique, 176–77,
179–80; anti-imperialist subjectivities, 180–81; communitarianism,
179–80, 186, 192n34; decolonial
theory, 186; exchange value, 180,
192n34; films and politics/political
theory, 19–20, 176, 178, 189n5; indige-
nous/Indian communities' representations, 190n15; *La geopolítica de la
Amazonía*, 177; *Las tensiones creativas
del Proceso de Cambio*, 19, 176, 186;
Plebian Power, 5–6; *Popular Identities
in Bolivia*, 5–6; primitive/originary
accumulation, 85n17, 176; revolutionary transformation of Bolivia,
179, 188; vice presidency, 175, 190n15;
Water War of 2000, 175, 176, 179
Gas War of 2003, 176, 181, 183, 184, 186,
189, 192n25
The German Ideology (Marx and Engels),
258, 260–61, 263
Gil, Mauricio, 151n1
Giorgi, Gabriel, 226
global migration, 236, 241, 242, 243,
245, 248. *See also* Central American

nature-in-humanity, 282, 283, 286, 287, 288, 289

Negri, Antonio, 6, 8, 10–11, 12, 93, 144, 265

Neilson, Brett, 242

neoliberalism: overview of, 7–8; Americas and, 240–41, 249n18; Argentina, 4, 8, 11–12, 13; from below, 11–13; Bolivia, 175, 176–77, 179, 183, 184, 189; Chile, 158, 159–60, 162, 163–64; critique, 155, 158, 159–60, 163–64; femicide in Ciudad Juárez and, 219, 220; finance capital and, 12–13; financialization and, 155, 196, 206; posthegemony and, 240–41, 249n18; postmigration and, 245–46; subject/subjectivity and, 203, 207, 208

Nietzsche, Friedrich Wilhelm, 195, 197, 203, 206, 208, 209, 269

"non-capital"/noncapitalist communities: overview of, 297–98; labor/labor power and, 5, 37–38, 40, 94–95, 97–98, 297, 301–2; property and, 98, 99–100, 101–2, 109n24, 110n25–26; subsumption and, 5, 37–38, 40, 97–98; theory of the subject and, 296, 299; transculturation and, 94–95, 97–98, 101–4. See also capitalism

non-waged/unpaid labor, 32, 35, 97–98, 276, 279, 291, 292. See also labor/labor power; slave labor; wage labor

not-yet-present/present, 46, 57–58, 60–61. See also dispossession

Nueve lecciones sobre economía y política en el marxismo (Aricó), 130–31

Obama, Barack, 59

ordinary psychoses, 223–24, 229n35. See also femicide in Ciudad Juárez, Mexico; psychotic violence

orientalism, 85n14, 125–26, 211n32

Ortega Reyna, Jaime, 18, 20–21, 137–54

Ortiz, Fernando, 91, 107n1

outplace, 296, 307

Paris Notebooks (Marx), 197, 198

Parsons, Talcott, 83n6

Pasado y Presente (1963–65, 1973), 118

patriarchy, 219–20, 221–22

Patricio, Juan, and dispossession case, 46, 52–58, 60

peasants: accumulation and, 76, 162–63, 165; Andean region, 97, 98, 99, 102; capitalism, 72–73; emancipation and, 236, 237–38; England and, 97, 106, 238; primitive/originary accumulation, 97, 105, 106, 237–38, 245. See also feudalism

Pech, Fabiana, and dispossession case, 46, 52–54, 56–57, 58, 60

Pérez Wilson, Pablo, 17, 20–21, 155–71

Peru: Hispanic Catholicism and, 91, 102–3; indigenous/Indian communities, 70–71; modernization and, 92–93, 94, 95–96, 98, 101, 102–3, 106, 110n26; property and, 98, 99–100, 101–2, 109n24, 110n25–26. See also Andean region

Piglia, Ricardo, 19, 195–96, 199, 200, 201

Pinto, Aníbal, 84n12

"placement", 295, 305, 306

plano secuencia integral (integral long take), 181, 183, 184, 191n21, 191n24

Plebian Power (García Linera), 5–6

Polanyi, Karl, 84n12

Polar, Cornejo, 85n17

political economy: overview of, 2, 3, 5, 7–8; class and accumulation, 155, 168n11; classical political economy, 46–47, 256, 259, 264, 298, 299; communitarianism, 70, 77–78, 179–80, 186, 192n34; Marxism, 15, 80–81, 141; theory of the subject and, 257, 258, 261, 308, 310

political economy critique: overview of, 1–2, 81, 150; Marxism, 296, 303, 304; proletarian and, 309–10; theory of the subject and, 257, 258, 261, 308

political subject, 175, 184–85, 189–90n8, 302, 303, 306, 311

politics and political theory: overview of, 1, 2–3, 7–8; antidispossessive politics, 45, 46, 49, 57–58, 60–61; class and,